Praise for *Fallen Tigers*

"This work is the new standard for analyzing the role of Chinese partisans in the rescue and repatriation of downed American flyers, and it will remain so in perpetuity. The author's ability to work in Chinese as well as English is of enormous benefit, as is his careful combing of the downed aircraft records to build a complete database of all the aircraft losses. *Fallen Tigers* is a huge contribution."

—Paul J. Springer, author of *America's Captives: Treatment of POWs from the Revolutionary War to the War on Terror*

"Using extensive primary materials, Jackson chronicles the fate of the Flying Tigers in China and offers wonderful personal narratives from the flyers in wartime. The author's apparent Chinese language skills make this an important addition to the field."

—S. Mike Pavelec, author of *Airpower Over Gallipoli, 1915–1916*

"In *Fallen Tigers*, author Daniel Jackson has taken an innovative approach to telling the history of the air war in China during World War II by folding it into the stories of Allied aircrewmen shot down behind Japanese lines and led to safety by local Chinese, who often risked their own lives in the process. Ample charts, graphs, maps, and photos complete this compelling work."

—Carl Molesworth, author of *Flying Tiger Ace: The Story of Bill Reed, China's Shining Mark*

"Even historians specializing in World War II may be surprised by the large number of US pilots shot down over China, the scene of one of the great forgotten air campaigns of that global conflict. Jackson is uniquely qualified to tell this fascinating story in all its complexity as a military aviator, as a scholar with a deep understanding of the period he describes, and as a writer of the highest order. His real-life experience as a pilot shows. He has the ability to really bring the reader into the cockpit."

—Peter Harmsen, author of *Japan Runs Wild, 1942–1943*

"An outstanding book that should be read by every American."
—Ted Spitzmiller, author of *The History of Human Space Flight*

"An interesting collection of remarkable adventures—adventures not always survived—undertaken by Americans who fell from the sky to a strange and dangerous land in a time of war."

—Stone & Stone Second World War Books

"Moving and brilliant. From the very first page, this account of American airmen fighting in the skies of World War II China grips readers and never lets them go. This book is both an outstanding work of military history, explaining the immense strategic importance of American air support in defense of wartime China against the Japanese, and a human story, telling an unknown story of courageous Americans saved by ordinary Chinese citizens. Even those who think they know World War II will need to read this book."

—Rana Mitter, author of *China's Good War: How World War II Is Shaping a New Nationalism*

"*Fallen Tigers* remains a very human story at heart."

—*World War II* magazine

Fallen Tigers

Fallen Tigers

The Fate of America's Missing Airmen in China during World War II

Daniel Jackson

UNIVERSITY PRESS OF KENTUCKY

Copyright © 2021 by The University Press of Kentucky
Paperback edition 2025

Scholarly publisher for the Commonwealth, serving Bellarmine University, Berea College, Centre College of Kentucky, Eastern Kentucky University, The Filson Historical Society, Georgetown College, Kentucky Historical Society, Kentucky State University, Morehead State University, Murray State University, Northern Kentucky University, Spalding University, Transylvania University, University of Kentucky, University of Louisville, University of Pikeville, and Western Kentucky University.
All rights reserved.

Editorial and Sales Offices: The University Press of Kentucky
663 South Limestone Street, Lexington, Kentucky 40508-4008
www.kentuckypress.com

Library of Congress Cataloging-in-Publication Data

Names: Jackson, Daniel, 1987- author.
Title: Fallen tigers : the fate of America's missing airmen in China during World War II / Daniel Jackson.
Other titles: Fate of America's missing airmen in China during World War II
Description: Lexington, Kentucky : The University Press of Kentucky, [2021] | Series: Aviation & air power | Includes bibliographical references and index.
Identifiers: LCCN 2020053361 | ISBN 9780813180809 (hardcover) | ISBN 9780813180823 (pdf) | ISBN 9780813180816 (epub)
Subjects: LCSH: United States. Army Air Forces. Air Force, 14th—History. | China. Kong jun. American Volunteer Group—History. | United States. Army Air Forces. China Air Task Force—History. | World War, 1939-1945—Search and rescue operations—China. | World War, 1939-1945—Missing in action. | Sino-Japanese War, 1937-1945—Aerial operations, American. | World War, 1939-1945—Campaigns—China. | Sino-Japanese War, 1937-1945—Participation, American. | Military assistance, American—China—History—20th century. | United States. Army Air Forces—Biography.
Classification: LCC D790.22 14th .J33 2021 | DDC 940.54/8—dc23

ISBN 978-1-9859-0231-2 (pbk. : alk. paper)

Member of the Association
of University Presses

Contents

Author's Note   vii
Prologue: Missing in Action   xi

1. Aerial Oppression   1
2. Hope for China   12
3. Doolittle's Raid   23
4. Enemy Occupation   36
5. China Air Task Force   52
6. Hong Kong   62
7. Aerial Offensive   77
8. Shipping Is the Key   89
9. Thanksgiving Day   99
10. Ambush at Jiujiang   109
11. Operation Ichi-Go   120
12. Collateral Damage   132
13. With the Communists   145
14. The Secret Airfield   155
15. Thai Fighters   172
16. The Final Offensive   187
Epilogue: Memory   202

Acknowledgments   207
Appendix A: Timeline   209
Appendix B: Chinese Transliteration   221
Notes   223
Bibliography   249
Index   257

Photographs follow page 144

Author's Note

The story of America's missing airmen in China during World War II lies buried in thousands of government reports; it involves a cast of thousands and spans the length and breadth of East Asia. The purpose of this book is to determine the true military and social dimensions of the war through the experiences of these airmen. For this, I relied predominantly on archived primary sources, scouring official records and every available missing aircrew report (MACR) and evasion report filed by the American Volunteer Group (AVG), China Air Task Force (CATF), and the Fourteenth and Twentieth Army Air Forces. The result is a database of 680 aircraft and 1,832 airmen reported missing on missions over China, Indochina, and Thailand. The database is available online at forgottensquadron.com.

For the many colorful narratives and anecdotes that enliven the text, I depended on extensive interviews and correspondence with veterans and their relatives, their memoirs, and on contemporaneous diaries, reports, and letters home. The events I have reconstructed are thus based on rigorous research, rather than creative license.

This book does not encompass the entirety of the US Army's China-Burma-India (CBI) Theater. While the Tenth Army Air Force fought in India and Burma, airmen who bailed out or crash-landed there faced very different circumstances and completely different social and political dynamics than existed in China. Their stories, though fascinating and no less dramatic, are not featured here. Additionally, the roughly six hundred transports lost flying the airlift between India and China encountered a different set of challenges than combat air forces in China and have previously been the subject of serious historical research. Their incredible experiences are also not recounted

viii   Author's Note

here.

Major General Claire Lee Chennault, commander of the AVG, CATF, and Fourteenth Army Air Force, had a reputation as a poor administrator, leaving much to be desired from his reports and paperwork. Fortunately, most MACRs and evasion reports originated at the squadron level. The Air-Ground Aid Section, a unit dedicated solely to the safe return of missing airmen, collected, processed, and preserved these reports. Where MACRs did not exist, squadron or group mission reports provided the relevant information. Far from a mere representative sample, the resulting dataset is a near-complete record of every airman who crashed or bailed out more than a day's journey from a friendly airbase.

Aggregating and analyzing these reports provides a view of China's war across its geographic breadth free from political, ideological, or mythologizing lenses. The Army Air Forces used MACRs as a repository for all information pertaining to those crews who failed to return from missions. This information served to account for, find, and aid missing airmen. Air-Ground Aid Section representatives or squadron intelligence officers debriefed airmen who returned and compiled their experiences into evasion reports. These reports, meant to help subsequent evaders and kept secret for decades after the war, remained free of self-glorification and Cold War politics. They are a rare honest and unfiltered witness to China at war.

They are also more typical of the American experience than existing popular literature. Memoirs of fighter aces, even when historically accurate, are hardly representative.[1] Only seventy-six American pilots received credit for shooting down five or more enemy airplanes in the CBI Theater. By contrast, in May 1944 alone, the Army Air Forces counted 1,643 aircrews on hand in CBI, including fighter pilots, reconnaissance pilots, and bomber and transport crews of anywhere from two to fifteen men each. Most of these men (officers and enlisted)—including pilots, navigators, bombardiers, gunners, crew chiefs, and radio operators—did not routinely tangle with Japanese fighters in swirling dogfights. In fact, one of the interesting statistics that emerged from aggregating these reports is that Japan's ground forces, rather than its air force, presented the greatest threat to American aircraft in the theater.[2]

A further utility of these reports is the ability to map political influence throughout wartime China. The experiences of fallen airmen scattered across the entire country provide a sampling of the influence, predominance,

Author's Note   ix

and effectiveness of the Imperial Japanese Army and various Nationalist, Communist, warlord, and collaborationist groups. Among American and Chinese leaders, Gen Joseph W. Stilwell, the American theater commander, claimed the Nationalists did not or would not fight; General Chennault claimed they did and would effectively with the support of his planes; Mao Zedong claimed the Communists fought ferociously against the Japanese while the Nationalists focused on wiping out the Communists; and Generalissimo Chiang Kai-shek claimed his Nationalist troops held the Japanese at bay even as the Communists resisted him and undermined his leadership.[3] These competing and contradictory claims make for choppy historical waters to navigate. The reports filed by airmen and intelligence officers provide a ground-truth perspective divorced from these partisan narratives.

Ultimately, the story that emerges is one of cooperation and fraternity between ordinary Americans and Chinese. In the modern era of escalating rivalry and confrontation between the United States and the People's Republic of China, this story of wartime friendship can serve as a touchstone for cooperation instead of conflict in the twenty-first century. Furthermore, America's efforts in China depended on local forces enabled by American advisors, equipment, and air support. This dynamic—much different from the United States' efforts in other theaters of the war—more closely mirrors its present military conflicts. Understanding the successes and failures of US policy in China during World War II can inform efforts today. Most importantly, the brave Chinese and Americans who joined together to fight a common enemy deserve to be remembered—especially the more than four hundred airmen still listed as missing in action.

Most American sources on this topic use the Wade-Giles romanization of people and place names. I used a large number of Chinese sources, however, and in an effort to continue fusing Chinese and American research, I decided to use the modern Pinyin romanization for people and place names in mainland China, and Wade-Giles for place names on the island of Taiwan. This should make it easier for researchers to find these locations on modern maps. Wade-Giles spellings often vary anyhow—Pinyin provides an easy method of standardization. For the reader's benefit, I provide the characters and Wade-Giles transliterations for some of the Chinese words used throughout the text in Appendix B.

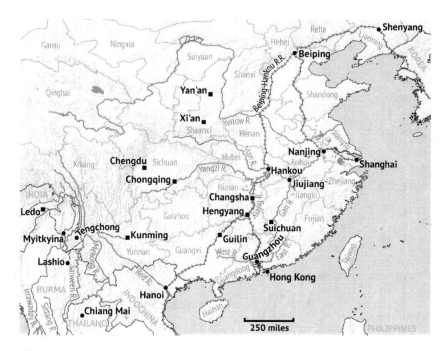

China Theater—World War II

Prologue

Missing in Action

May 6, 1944
120 miles southwest of Hankou, China

First Lieutenant Lee Gregg looked across the expanse of sky to the fighters holding station several hundred feet to his left and right. They appeared motionless, suspended in the heavy haze. Only the bobbing needle of his airspeed indicator and feedback of the air through his control yoke betrayed the formation's forward progress. He led the four P-38 Lightnings of Black Able Flight as they cruised at twenty thousand feet—high above the swampy, lake-strewn Chinese countryside. Behind him, Fred Scudday led Black Baker Flight with four more Lightnings, while just above he could see the leading element of seven Blue Squadron P-51 Mustangs. Through the clouds and mist, he could barely make out the fourteen B-25 Mitchells flying five thousand feet below the top cover. More than two dozen "Sharks"—Fourteenth Air Force slang for P-40 Warhawks, with their trademark predatory grins—packed in tight around the bombers as close escort. Still over a hundred miles from the target, Gregg allowed the steady thrum of his fighter's twin engines to lull him into a comfortable complacency.[1]

This disparate collection of fifty-four planes represented the largest aerial armada yet assembled by the American air forces in China. It seemed laughably puny by the standards of any other theater. Massive fleets of hundreds—if not thousands—of warplanes pummeled targets daily in Europe and the Mediterranean. For the Allies, China had always existed near the bottom of a long list of priorities and at the end of a perilously long supply line. Yet now,

xii   Prologue

in May 1944, the Chinese fought desperately against the most massive Japanese ground offensive of World War II. Half a million troops of the Imperial Japanese Army surged into central China, threatening to break the back of Chiang Kai-shek's Nationalist regime. The "Flying Tigers" of the Fourteenth Air Force, the US Army's smallest numbered air force, threw themselves into the breach to help their embattled allies. Colonel Clinton D. "Casey" Vincent, commander of the Fourteenth's most forward-deployed wing, scraped together every airplane he could find to hit enemy supplies stockpiled at Hankou, a vital port city dominating the confluence of the Han and Yangzi Rivers. Lee Gregg knew the colonel counted on his P-38s and Blue Squadron's P-51s to get the bombers through to the target.

"Zeros!"[2]

Blue Leader's tense voice broke through the radio static, jolting Gregg from his reverie. His pulse quickened as he scanned for enemy fighters.

"Two o'clock high!"

There: he saw them high and to his right. Radioing for his flight to drop their tanks and follow him, he pushed the throttles forward. His fighter surged with nearly three thousand horsepower. The big P-38, a new "J" model with hydraulic-boosted ailerons, felt nimble in his hands as he quickly banked and hauled the yoke back into his lap. Black Able Flight stayed with him—Lieutenants Jones, Longueil, and Opsvig all maintained formation. They brought their gunsights to bear on the Japanese, together unleashing a torrent of .50-caliber machine-gun and 20-millimeter cannon fire. Suddenly, dozens of enemy fighters swarmed from every direction out of the mist. Gregg felt the impact of machine-gun rounds hit his plane and a searing pain shoot through his left ankle.

"Bailing out!" he heard Jones frantically yell through the radio. Then Gregg's fighter lurched forward. His head struck the instrument panel. His world went black.[3]

Leading the last element in the last flight of P-51s, 1st Lt Glen Beneda witnessed the initial contact; three P-38s fell from the dogfight in flames, trails of smoke diffusing into the haze. A fourth Lightning dove away on one engine. Amid the carnage, a solitary parachute blossomed, slowly bearing its human cargo toward the ground. Beneda quickly readied his Mustang for combat. Reaching down with his left hand, he pulled the release for his underwing fuel tanks. The right tank dropped away, but the left remained attached. His fighter skidded sideways from the sudden asymmetry. Instinctively, he stomped on the right rudder pedal to counter the drag. Then he saw the mottled green fighter in front of him; its wings, sweeping forward to meet a straight leading edge, bore the distinctive red "meatballs" of the rising sun. He pressed in to attack. Hardly had he closed with it when a hail of bullets caught him from behind. He craned his neck to look back.

"Blue Baker Four, three Zeros above us!" he radioed his wingman. "Follow me down!" As Beneda rolled to dive away, his Mustang snapped into an accelerated stall, pulled by the drag from the drop tank still clinging stubbornly to his left wing. Another volley of bullets riddled his plane and it plummeted downward. Beneda struggled to regain control as the dial on his altimeter spun through feet in the thousands; he finally managed to pull out at eight thousand feet. He looked around to get his bearings. Apparently, he had left the enemy far behind. A sense of relief washed over him. His wingman, he noted, had also disappeared. Then, with startling abruptness, his engine quit. The full-throated roar of the 12-cylinder Merlin gave way to an eerie, empty whistling of wind. In that moment, deep over enemy territory, Glen Beneda knew he had to bail out.[4]

Meanwhile, when Lee Gregg came to, he found himself hurtling toward the ground. The control yoke shook in his hands as the tail bucked violently, resisting his every effort to recover. The nose pitched over, steepening the dive, the airspeed approaching the critical Mach number for the fighter's thick wings. Gregg's P-38 had entered a high-speed compressibility stall. He quickly disconnected his oxygen tube and radio equipment and released his seat restraints. Straining forward, he grabbed hold of the emergency hatch release on top of the control panel. He pulled it back and the canopy tore away. The suction instantly ripped him from the cockpit. Still dazed from the attack and foggy in his tenuous consciousness, Gregg had no idea of his speed or altitude. He frantically pulled at his ripcord. With the opening shock, a new wave of intense pain shot through his back, catapulting him once more into unconsciousness.[5]

For the briefest of moments after Beneda jumped, he seemed to hang in the air above his crippled fighter. Then, as it pulled away, the horizontal stabilizer collided violently with his right leg. Reeling from the hit, he grabbed at his ripcord and pulled hard. A white silk parachute unfurled above his head. Slowly, he drifted down toward the vibrant green landscape below. The landing brought with it a sharp jolt of agony. He stood painfully in what he found to be a waterlogged and excrement-reeking rice paddy. A group of

xiv   Prologue

farmers stood some distance away, eyeing him warily. He pulled a cloth flag from his back pocket, unfolded it, and held it over his head.

"Meiguo! Meiguo!" he yelled, identifying himself as an American. But the men—frightened or otherwise reticent—would not approach him. Finally, one of them pointed in the direction of a pair of huts uphill from the paddy. Beneda trudged that way through the mud. His leg throbbed. A man stepped out from one of the huts as he drew near. The fallen airman took a small booklet from his jacket pocket and opened it to a page of key phrases written side by side in English and Chinese. He pointed to the line asking to be taken to friendly guerrillas. The man seemed to understand and motioned for him to follow.

The farmer led him to a nearby village and ushered him inside a squat, gray mudbrick building with a low tile roof. He offered him a bowl of rice and a pair of chopsticks. Beneda fumbled with the chopsticks for a few minutes and then pantomimed a request for a spoon. The house overflowed with the excited activity of the farmer's parents, siblings, and children; the sudden arrival of this strange foreigner shocked them all. The hubbub only heightened the American's uneasiness and he found it difficult to eat much. His leg, meanwhile, had begun to bruise black and blue where it had hit the fighter's tail, and the pain began to bother him. The farmer gathered some provisions and a few hours later they departed, walking by the shallow lake where Beneda's plane had crashed. It lay upside down now, completely submerged. A crowd of villagers combed the water, picking up twisted bits of metal. The pilot watched for a moment, dimly aware of a gnawing sense of shame he felt for losing the fighter. Then he and his escort continued onward. At eight o'clock that evening they finally arrived at a guerrilla outpost. The soldiers there wore tattered cotton uniforms without insignia. Beneda eyed them nervously. They looked back, equally uneasy. One of them approached him.

"Sidalin. Mao Zedong. Balujun. Xinsijun."[6]

The airman stared uncomprehendingly.

"What is your name?" the soldier asked in broken English.

"Beneda."

"Ben Ni Da," the soldier slowly repeated. The pilot wrote his name and rank on a piece of scrap paper and handed it to him; it was the soldier's turn to stare uncomprehendingly. He left and returned a short while later, leading the airman to a makeshift bed. Beneda passed an uneasy night, still in anxious ignorance as to the identity of his hosts.

The next morning the soldier escorted him to a local command post and presented him to the officer in charge.

"I am Tong Shiguang," the officer introduced himself in passable English. "I am leader of this prefecture. You are under the protection of the communist New Fourth Army."[7]

Dueling feelings of anxiety and relief welled within Beneda; Chiang Kai-shek had outlawed the New Fourth Army, claiming it had refused to follow orders and engaged in armed rebellion against the government. Rumors circulated of a rogue collection of cutthroats and thieves. Though grateful to not be in the hands of collaborators or the Japanese, Beneda did not know what to expect. His survival still seemed to hang in the balance.

Meanwhile, when Lee Gregg finally regained consciousness, he found himself lying on the ground, still in his parachute harness. He attempted to stand, but the pain from a cracked vertebra and the shrapnel wound to his ankle overwhelmed him; again he passed out. The next time he awoke, he saw two farmers standing a short distance away.

"Meiguo!" he called weakly. But the two seemed reluctant to approach. Drifting in and out of consciousness, Gregg soon found himself surrounded by eight men. They stared at him. Six quickly departed, but the remaining two took everything from his pockets, his parachute, his insignia, and his jungle kit with its medicine and knife—everything but his clothes. Then they too disappeared. Gregg drifted out again and awoke to find eight men around him once more, this time with a wooden door, a rope, and a pole. They improvised a stretcher and carried him to a nearby sampan. The next four days blurred together in painful semiconsciousness—sometimes he would wake to find himself rushing through the night on a stretcher; other times he would find himself in a house or on a boat. Eventually, the men delivered him to the New Fourth Army, and a young medic began looking after his injuries.[8]

Both Lee Gregg and Glen Beneda thus began a nearly fifty-day odyssey back to American control through war-torn China. Injured and alone, they found themselves completely dependent on the Chinese civilians and Communist guerrillas who chose to rescue them. Remarkably, their experience typified that of many American airmen. During World War II, the US Army Air Forces reported at least 680 aircraft and 1,832 airmen as missing on combat missions in the China Theater. The Japanese captured less than 5 percent of these fallen Tigers, while 31 percent died, and 22 percent remain listed as

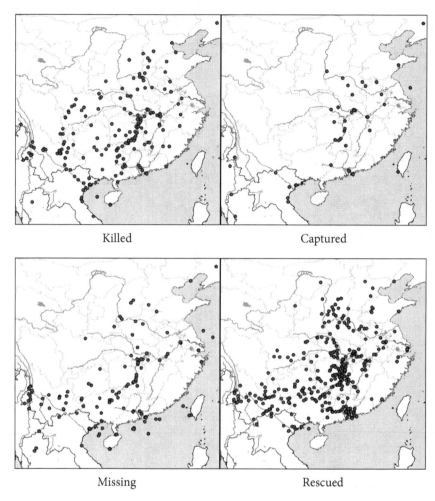

The Fate of America's Missing Airmen

missing in action. Approximately 42 percent returned safely to American airbases.

The percentage of dead and missing (all now presumed dead) corresponds closely to the statistics of Allied aircraft operating over occupied Europe. Astonishingly, however, while underground organizations delivered less than 25 percent of airmen in Europe back to Allied control, more than 90 percent of those who survived in China returned to friendly territory. Like Gregg and Beneda, each of the more than seven hundred rescued airmen

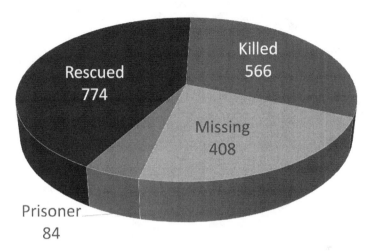

Fate of America's Missing Airmen

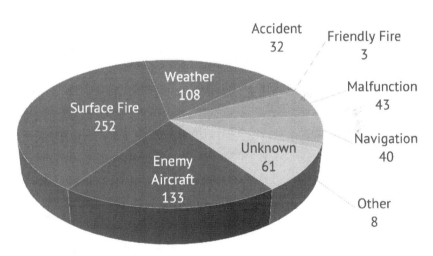

Missing Aircraft in China by Cause

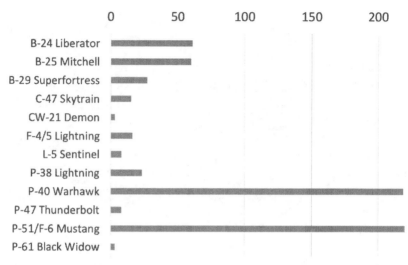

Missing Aircraft in China by Type

depended entirely on the selfless heroism of Chinese soldiers and civilians. Incredibly, these extraordinary feats remain largely unknown in the United States.[9]

For the young pilots, navigators, bombardiers, radio operators, flight engineers, and gunners who survived their crash or bailout, a perilous journey through an embattled, alien land became a seminal experience in their lives. Even before they arrived in China, the romance of the Far East and mystique of the Orient filled their imaginations. Their service in the remotest corner of World War II meant the adventure of a lifetime. Few of them chose to serve in China; apart from the one hundred aviators who suspended their military commissions to join the American Volunteer Group (AVG), most underwent the same selection and training—and had the same lack of choice as to the location of their overseas assignment—as did their peers fighting in Europe and the Pacific.

Legendary fighter pilot and grizzled veteran of the war against Japan, Claire Lee Chennault inculcated new arrivals in the hard-won wisdom of his aerial guerrilla tactics. Chennault commanded the AVG, China Air Task Force (CATF), and Fourteenth Army Air Force—all of which became known colloquially in China and abroad as the "Flying Tigers." He strove to embed experienced leaders in his groups and squadrons to further mentor and motivate his airmen. Several AVG veterans, including David Lee "Tex" Hill and George B. "Mac" McMillan, returned on subsequent tours to command squadrons and groups. Their practice of leading from the front added immeasurably to the combat effectiveness of Chennault's command and infused the can-do spirit of the AVG into the Army Air Force organizations that followed it.

Despite the confidence vested in Chennault's tactics and in the experience of their commanders, young airmen still faced combat with some trepidation. They fought a savage guerrilla air war in a remote and dangerous land; the prospect of having to crash-land or bail out loomed ominously over each of them. They had ample cause to worry—less than half of those reported missing survived. This was due both to the perils of war and to the state of aviation technology in the 1940s. Aviation, after all, was still relatively new, with narrow safety margins often exacerbated by inadequate training. Of course, the majority of missing airmen fell to enemy fire, and chances for survival drop precipitously when someone is trying to kill you. For those who managed to cross that violent threshold to become evaders, their world shrank dramatically from the grand sweep of hundreds of miles, horizon to horizon, to the granular view of a single rice paddy. The challenges they faced on the ground included injury, disease, malnutrition, pursuit or capture by the enemy, and language and cultural barriers between them and their rescuers. None succeeded without the help of Chinese soldiers and civilians.

The ordeal of evasion, often spanning weeks or months and sometimes covering hundreds of miles, gave the Americans a keen appreciation for their Chinese allies. These young men arrived in China filled with racialized preconceptions and stereotypes. Close contact during evasion transformed racism into respect and replaced a vacuum of knowledge with close coordination. Upon return to American control, these airmen brought a new understanding back to their units, giving their comrades new hope and confidence should they find themselves in similar circumstances.

Chinese rescuers often underwent their own transformative journey. Many of them had never seen a white man before. Few had traveled beyond their home district. A significant number could not read or write. The Imperial Japanese Army practiced swift revenge against anyone suspected of aiding American airmen. Rescuers helped not only at their own peril but at the peril of their families, their neighbors, and their villages. In a brutal war that began four and a half years before the United States became involved, the

xx   Prologue

Chinese knew the risks they undertook by defying the occupiers. Yet defy them they did.

To understand why, one must appreciate the powerful symbolism of American warplanes in China. Unlike in Europe, North Africa, the Pacific, and even Burma, American airpower comprised the Western Allies' only combat forces in the country. Anglo-American strategy prioritized defeat of the Nazis. Rather than committing ground troops to China, President Franklin Roosevelt decreed American support would consist of an airlift from India to supply a small number of military advisors and a combat air force. Aerial supply and aerial warfare, therefore, assumed a critical importance to the survival of China and defeat of Japan on the Asian mainland.[10] While the ground war between Chinese and Japanese troops remained a stalemate from 1939 to 1944, American warplanes ranged across the entire country. American airmen bailed out or crash-landed in twenty-nine of modern China's thirty-four province-level divisions. American warplanes and evading airmen thus became the most visible signs of resistance against the Japanese. They became a new hope for war-weary China.

Soldiers and civilians from all walks of life and political persuasions helped these airmen, including Nationalists, Communists, warlords, and even alleged collaborators. Despite deep divisions throughout wartime China, helping American evaders transcended politics. These grassroots interactions between individual Americans and Chinese, often without influence or oversight from their respective military commands or governments, formed the basis of deep, lasting relationships that far surpassed the effects of any official cooperation—or postwar enmity—between the United States and China. The fate of America's missing airmen therefore reveals not only the unexpected nature of World War II in its remotest theater but also a touching story of Chinese-American cooperation that overcame racial, social, and political boundaries to echo through history to this day.

1

Aerial Oppression

September 13, 1940
Chongqing, China

The plaintive moan of air raid sirens rose above the crowded clamor of the city's narrow streets. Two red, ball-shaped paper lanterns swung from the top of a towering flagpole erected on the high ground. Spotters had detected dozens of enemy warplanes winging their way up the Yangzi River toward Chongqing. Soldiers, civilians, and government officials calmly filed into air raid shelters dug into the city's steep cliffs to wait out the bombardment. By the summer of 1940, Japanese bombing had become as much an inevitable feature of the Chongqing landscape as the seasonal shifts in weather.

Deep in the interior, Nationalist China's wartime capital lay secreted behind the seemingly impenetrable mountain borders of Sichuan Province. The Yangzi and one of its tributaries, the Jialing, bounded the promontory on which the city perched. The rivers joined northeast of the remote metropolis before thundering through perilous gorges to the fertile plains of central China. The chill of winter wrapped the city in fog and mist—a protective shroud that fell away in the sweltering heat and humidity of summer. Every May through September, hundreds of Imperial Japanese Army and Navy bombers swarmed from out of their bases near Hankou to fix their bombsights on this city on a hill. Their expert marksmanship focused lethal explosive payloads on the key center of gravity for the entire Asian war—the will of the Chinese people. Yet the panic that had accompanied the start of this aerial onslaught subsided within a matter of weeks. Somehow, without much of an air force and with few anti-aircraft guns to speak of, the people carried on with grim determination.[1]

2   FALLEN TIGERS

Twenty-seven bombers droned overhead the city that day, maintaining flawless formation in rigid Vs. A few flak bursts exploded harmlessly well below their altitude. The Chinese Air Force launched thirty-four Soviet-built fighters to challenge the raiders, including nineteen Polikarpov I-15 biplanes from the 4th Fighter Group. Sub Lieutenant Xu Hua-jiang flew one of the open-cockpit, fixed-gear fighters in the formation. They failed to intercept the Japanese bombers, but as they headed back toward the airfield at Baishiyi, enemy fighters "bounced" them in an ambush from above. "I had never seen this type of aircraft before," recalled Xu, "and did not expect that this new Japanese aircraft would be so fast, powerful, and effective."

It was unlike anything the Chinese pilots had yet encountered: a blunt radial engine, long, tapered fuselage, an enclosed cockpit, and a powerful combined armament of guns and cannon. The Japanese had unleashed their new Mitsubishi A6M Type Zero Carrier Fighter. It could fly faster and higher than anything the Chinese had to throw at it, and it could even dogfight with their nimble biplanes. "I surveyed the whole combat space as we engaged the enemy," recounted Xu. "I saw our planes being chased away and some of our pilots bailing out. I was also hit many times." With black smoke billowing from his exhaust pipe and his engine hemorrhaging oil, Xu managed to crash-land in a rice paddy, suffering only minor injuries.[2] Most of his comrades did not fare as well. In the thirty-minute battle, thirteen Zeros downed thirteen Chinese fighters and seriously damaged eleven more, killing ten pilots and injuring eight without taking any losses.[3]

The new Mitsubishi would eventually gain such notoriety—in China and in the early days of the Pacific War—that American pilots came to refer to all Japanese fighters informally as "Zeros." Even in official reports, they often referenced the same aircraft interchangeably by this generic term and by their specific type. During Lee Gregg and Glen Beneda's dogfight southwest of Hankou on May 6, 1944, for example, the pilots referred to their ambushers as Zeros but in their reports identified them specifically as Ki-43 Army Type 1 "Hayabusa" (Peregrine Falcon) Fighters, known by their Allied codename "Oscar."[4]

Alternating between field glasses and a movie camera, a retired US Army Air Corps captain by the name of Claire Lee Chennault often watched these air battles from the ground. "Like hawks in a chicken yard," he remarked of the new fighters.[5] Superior to anything the Chinese could field, the "Zero" had achieved complete air dominance. China's Aeronautical Affairs Commission[6] immediately ordered the remnants of its air force withdrawn from combat to preserve a corps of experienced pilots.[7]

Chennault had arrived in China on May 31, 1937, forced to leave the service because of his failing health and radical views on fighter aviation. His ideas had formed crossways to those of the Air Corps; the brass thought of fighters as outmoded and bombers invulnerable. They did not want to hear his thoughts on fighter tactics. Already self-conscious of his humble upbringing in rural Louisiana, Chennault took criticism of his ideas personally. Though his subordinates found him warm and charismatic, his superiors thought him exasperating, impatient, and combative. They gladly hastened his departure from active duty. Upon his retirement, Song Meiling (also known as Madame Chiang), the wife of Generalissimo Chiang Kai-shek, hired him to make a comprehensive evaluation of the Chinese Air Force. The Chiangs believed a modern air arm essential to their project of uniting China under the Guomindang, or Nationalist Party, while also keeping it from disintegrating in the face of Japanese imperialism. The job paid $12,000 a year—far more than Chennault's Air Corps salary and enough to take care of his wife and eight children back in Louisiana. War broke out just five weeks after his arrival.[8]

China could only field a hodgepodge fleet of obsolete airplanes against the state-of-the-art Japanese air force. Its pilots, though brave, lacked skill and experience. Many had graduated from the Italian-run flying school at Luoyang, which boasted a dubious 100 percent completion rate. Chennault found these flyers "a menace to navigation." He immediately offered his services to Chiang in whatever capacity the generalissimo saw fit. He knew the war would give him an opportunity to test his ideas in combat.

Ever since his time as an instructor at the Air Corps Tactical School in the early 1930s, Chennault had realized he must solve the problem of intelligence before he could mount an effective aerial defense. "Without a continuous stream of accurate information keeping the fighters posted on exactly where the . . . bombers were, attempts at interception were like hunting needles in a limitless haystack," he wrote. Defending fighters could only intercept attacking bombers before they reached their targets, "if furnished timely information." This became the basis of an air-raid warning system he helped establish around the Nationalist capital at Nanjing at the end of July 1937. With the guidance of this network, Chinese fighters managed a number of successful intercepts, claiming fifty-four bombers shot down in just three

4 FALLEN TIGERS

days in mid-August. Then the Japanese began sending ample fighter escort, inflicting crippling losses on the defenders.

Chennault often stood atop Nanjing's Metropolitan Hotel during these raids, smoking a Camel cigarette, watching the Japanese, and studying their tactics. But the consummate fighter pilot would not content himself to remain on the ground. He convinced Madame Chiang to buy him a Curtiss Hawk 75 Special, the blunt-nosed, fixed-gear predecessor of the P-40. He soon found himself maneuvering through enemy flak and fighters over the Yangzi valley.[9] He never claimed to have been more than an observer on these flights, but many of his men later alleged that he actively engaged the Japanese in combat. Some estimated he shot down as many as fifty-five enemy planes. "There can be no question. Dad flew combat against the Japs," his son Max later asserted. The Chinese apparently paid him a $500 bounty for every plane he downed—the same terms they later applied to the American Volunteer Group. According to Max, "That's the money he used to put me though college."[10] Chennault himself always remained mum on the issue, happy to leave his combat experience ambiguous—and happy to insinuate. "Many times I went aloft in the Hawk to umpire air battles over Nanjing, Nanchang, and Hankou and found that umpire-baiting was as popular in China as it is in Brooklyn," he would tell his men. "The baiters paid a price."

In light of the rapid disintegration of the Chinese Air Force, Chiang secured the support of the Soviet Union. The Soviets sent four "volunteer" squadrons of fighters and two of bombers to join the fight in China. Their arrival in November 1937 signaled a wane in Chennault's influence. Chiang pulled him from combat and sent him to Kunming, the capital of Yunnan Province in the far southwest of the country. There he trained Chinese pilots to fly thirty new Hawk 75s.[11] Soviet support had an expiration date, however. Tension between the USSR and Japan erupted into full-scale battle along the border between Japanese-occupied Manchuria and Soviet-allied Mongolia in the summer of 1939. Despite winning an overwhelming victory, the Soviets began pulling their "volunteer" air force out of China following a cease-fire agreement in September. The last Soviet airmen withdrew from combat by early 1940.[12]

Meanwhile, in May 1939 the Japanese began conducting relentless terror-bombing attacks against Chongqing, Kunming, and the other population centers of Free China. To the Imperial Japanese Army, the bombing of Free China seemed the next logical evolution in its brutal subjugation of East Asia. In

1937 its mechanized forces had overrun Beiping and swept across the north China plains. Its troops defeated Chiang's best divisions in savage urban fighting around Shanghai and continued to Nanjing, where they ruthlessly punished the people for their resistance. Japanese forces drove all the way up the Yangzi to Jiujiang and finally Hankou. The deaths of untold thousands of Chinese soldiers and civilians attended each of these conquests: 187,000 soldiers at Shanghai and at least 260,000 soldiers and civilians at Nanjing.[13] By the summer of 1940, Japan controlled China's skies, along with 95 percent of its industry, one-fourth its area, and half its population.[14] But its land offensive had ground to a halt—at Zhengzhou in the north, where Chiang ordered his generals to breach the Yellow River dams; at Changsha in the center, following General Xue Yue's remarkable defense of that city; and at Kunlun Pass in the south, the result of a determined counterattack by two armored divisions of China's Fifth Army. Inevitably, the population of Free China swelled with refugees. Displaced by war, they found themselves with nowhere to go, trapped by crippling poverty and hyperinflation—pinned to the bullseye of Japanese bombers. Unable to progress on the ground and in complete control of the air, Japan determined to bomb the Chinese into submission.[15]

As in much the rest of Free China, the people of Zhijiang, in western Hunan Province, lived under the constant threat of aerial attack. Even in the outlying villages, people refrained from wearing light-colored hats or clothing for fear of coming under the guns of marauding Japanese planes. Gong Kaibing lived in a small village three miles outside of town. He had served with the Nationalist police force in the city before the war, but his father's ailing health compelled him to return home to work the family farm. Sometimes he watched as upward of two dozen bombers droned overhead on their way to pummel Zhijiang, defenseless save for a pitiful battery of four antique Russian guns. The people had no recourse except to shelter in caves or trenches; they could do little more than absorb the punishment and carry on.[16]

At the center of the storm stood Generalissimo Chiang Kai-shek, resolute and unbending. "We will fight for a hundred years, if necessary," he declared in an address to the Chinese people. "We are losing battles, but we need only to win the final battle. China will never yield!"[17] Ironically, he had been reluctant to fight the Japanese at first, thinking such action would interfere with his project of uniting fractured China under the Guomindang. Though his suppression of the Communists and campaigns against the warlords had done much toward that end, Nationalist China remained fragile

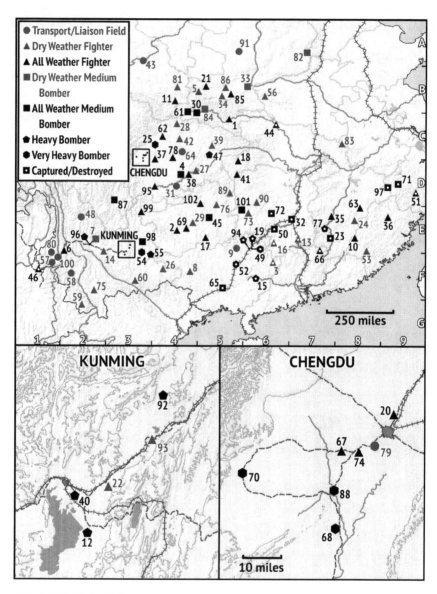

Allied Airfields in China

1. Ankang—C5
2. Anshun—E4
3. Babu (Patpo)—F6
4. Baishiyi (Peishiyi)—D4
5. Baoji (Paoki)—B5
6. Baoshan (Paoshan)—E2
7. Beitun (Peiting)—E2
8. Bose (Pai-Se)—F4
9. Chang'anzhen (Changanchen)—E5
10. Changting—E8
11. Cheng Xian (Chenghsien)—B4
12. Chenggong (Chengkung)—Left Inset
13. Chenzhou (Chenhsien)—E7
14. Chuxiong (Tsuyung)—F2
15. Danzhu (Tanchuk)—F6
16. Daoxian (Taohsien)—E6
17. Dushan (Tushan)—E5
18. Enshi—D5
19. Ertang (Erh Tong)—E6
20. Fenghuangshan—Right Inset
21. Fengxiang (Feng-Hsiang)—B5
22. Ganhaizi (Kan Hai Tze)—Left Inset
23. Ganzhou (Kanchow)—E7
24. Guangchang (Kwang Chang)—E8
25. Guanghan (Kwanghan)—C4
26. Guangnan (Kwangnan)—F4
27. Guangyangba (Kuang-Yang-Pa)—D4
28. Guangyuan (Kuang-Yuan)—C4
29. Guiyang (Kweiyang)—E4
30. Hanzhong (Hanchung)—C4
31. Hejiang (Ho-Chiang)—D4
32. Hengyang—E7
33. Huayin—B6
34. Huxian (Hu-Hsien)—B5
35. Ji'an (Kian)—E7
36. Jian'ou (Kienow)—D9
37. Jianyang (Kienyang)—D4
38. Jiulongpo (Chiu-Lung-P'u)—D4
39. Kaijiang (K'ai-Chiang)—C5
40. Kunming (Wujiaba Field)—Left Inset
41. Laifeng—D5
42. Langzhong (Lang-Chung)—C4
43. Lanzhou (Lanchow)—A3
44. Laohekou (Laohokow)—C6
45. Laohuangping (Laohwangping)—E5
46. Leiyun (Loi-Wing)—F1
47. Liangshan—C5
48. Lijiang (Li-Chiang)—E2
49. Lijiazhen (Li Chia Chen)—E6
50. Lingling—E6
51. Lishui—D9
52. Liuzhou (Luchow)—F5
53. Longyan (Lungyen)—E8
54. Luliang—F3
55. Luoping (Lo-P'ing)—F3
56. Lushi—B6
57. Mangshi—F1
58. Mengsa—F2
59. Mengxi (Meng-Hsi)—G2
60. Mengzi (Mengtze)—F3
61. Mianxian (Mien-Hsien)—B4
62. Mianyang—C4
63. Nancheng—E8
64. Nanchong (Nan-Ch'ung)—C4
65. Nanning—F5
66. Nanxiong (Namyung)—E7
67. Pengjiachang (P'eng-Chia-Ch'ang)—Right Inset
68. Pengshan—Right Inset
69. Qingzhen (Tsing Chen)—E4
70. Qionglai (Kiunglai)—Right Inset
71. Quzhou (Chuchow)—D9
72. Shaoyang (Paoching)—E6
73. Shawan—E6
74. Shuangliu (Shwangliu)—Right Inset
75. Simao (Szemao)—F2
76. Sinan (Szenan)—E5
77. Suichuan (Suichwan)—E7
78. Suining—C4
79. Taipingsi (Taipensu)—Right Inset
80. Tengchong (Tengchung)—F1
81. Tianshui—B4
82. Varoff Field—A7
83. Wujiadian (Valley Field)—C8
84. Wuqusi (Wuchusze)—B5
85. Xi'an (Hsian)—B5
86. Xianyang (Hsien-Yang)—B5
87. Xichang (Hsi-Ch'ang)—D3
88. Xinjin (Hsinching)—Right Inset
89. Xiushan (Siushan)—D5
90. Xupu (Hsupuhsien)—D6
91. Yan'an (Yen-an)—A5
92. Yangjie (Yangkai)—Left Inset
93. Yanglin—Left Inset
94. Yangtang (Yang Tong)—E6
95. Yibin (Ipin)—D4
96. Yunnanyi (Yun-Nan-I)—E2
97. Yushan—D9
98. Zhanyi (Chan-I)—E3
99. Zhaotong (Chaotung)—E3
100. Zhennancun (Chenanso)—F1
101. Zhijiang (Chihkiang)—E5
102. Zunyi (Tsun-I)—D5

8   FALLEN TIGERS

and unfinished. But despite Chiang's reticence, the people made it clear they would no longer tolerate inaction in the face of brazen displays of Japanese aggression.[18] Sequestered in the remote wilderness of Shaanxi Province, the Chinese Communist Party, the generalissimo's professed mortal enemies, insisted on a United Front. Warlords and disparate political groups pledged their support to the greater cause of resisting the invader. Even Long Yun, the one-eyed warlord of Yunnan, and Yan Xishan, the so-called model governor of Shaanxi, rallied to his banner. Though none of them could agree on politics, they agreed China must remain Chinese. Thus although China did not then exist as a unified political entity, without a doubt it existed as a cultural one—a fractured state but a cohesive nation. And even those who thought Chiang a corrupt fascist could not help but admit his stoic defiance made him a powerful symbol of resistance. He never became the undisputed leader of a united China, but for a time, he managed to helm a fragile coalition against a common enemy.[19]

At Chiang's direction, China embarked on a construction project akin in scale and consequence to the Great Wall; a people without an air force built more than one hundred airfields. Gravel runways dotted the land, from Yunnan and Sichuan Provinces in the southwest, to Shaanxi in the north, Hunan and Guangxi in the center, and Jiangxi, Guangdong, and even Fujian in the east—an area spanning more than four hundred thousand square miles. They built these airfields by hand, thousands of men, women, and children rising like human ant heaps, their worksites looking like medieval battlefields, with banners waving and dust clouds billowing from tens of thousands of conscripts working and singing. To build airfields capable of handling the weight of four-engine heavy bombers, they had to dig as much as five feet into the ground and lay a stone foundation. They quarried the rock by hand, carried it in baskets on their backs, crushed it, and laid it in the ground—all without modern machinery. They smashed more of it to fine gravel for the top layer and sealed it with mud, packing down each layer and leveling it smooth with enormous concrete rollers pulled by up to two hundred people. This enterprise harnessed China's richest resource—its people—to build what they hoped would one day become the springboard from which they would push back the invader.[20]

The airfields seemed a vain hope, but what else did they have? The disciplined, professional army of the nascent Nationalist state largely perished in its fighting withdrawal up the Yangzi from 1937 to 1939. Chiang had no

Aerial Oppression 9

choice but to depend on the warlords and semi-autonomous provinces to assemble a disparate coalition of conscripts and refugees in its place.

Only thirteen years old when the war began, Liu Zhenghua grew up in a wealthy peasant family in Hubei Province. His uncle, an educated man who went to school in Japan, ensured Liu attended a prominent primary school in Hankou. When the Japanese captured the city in 1938, Liu and his classmates escaped to Changsha, under the guns of enemy warplanes the entire way.

Despite his family's wealth, Liu decided he wanted to serve in the army. He journeyed to Hengyang in 1941 to take the entrance exams for the Central Military Academy.[21] After passing, he found himself assigned to the branch in Kunming.[22] It took him and his fellow cadets three long months to walk more than six hundred miles to Yunnan Province. Several starved to death while traveling through the impoverished countryside along the way. The survivors arrived to find a Dante-esque sign hanging over the entrance to the academy grounds: "Enter not this gate, you who are afraid of death." The ominous message promised further trials for young men who had already escaped the advance of Japan's army, fled under the guns of its air force, and survived a perilous journey across the devastated countryside. The sign, however, reflected the reality of an army hemorrhaging company-grade officers in years of combat against a better-equipped foe. The academy compressed its curriculum into an intense course of study, but even then, Liu received his commission as an infantry officer early, departing for the front lines in April 1944.[23]

While Liu volunteered to become an officer, the conscripts that made up the enlisted ranks came from the poorest strata of the peasantry, the *lao baixing,* or "old hundred names," common people who could not bribe their way out of servitude. Once rounded up by local magistrates, they found themselves marched away in chains to their assigned regiments, oftentimes never to see their loved ones again. "They were a sorry lot," an American intelligence officer wrote of conscripts in Sichuan Province. "Bare-legged, they sat at the roadside, straw-sandaled. Most of the bare, browned legs and many of the faces were spotted with putrid, running sores. Scaly skin diseases had dried in their hair and, as they sat there stolid and stupid, flies crawled along the tracks of old but still livid scars."[24]

The sorry state of the Nationalist Army was symptomatic of much deeper issues. As the war dragged on, a cloud of graft, corruption, and misery settled across the land with weary ubiquity. Chiang promised he would institute reforms—but only after he finished consolidating the nation under his Nationalist regime. Consolidation and reform had a complex interplay, though. The government depended on tenuous agreements with capricious warlords and landed gentry for military power and economic solvency. Efforts to reform thus met with fierce resistance. On the other hand, delaying reforms antagonized liberals, disenfranchised the poor, and fueled Communist propaganda. Chiang could decide between either his government collapsing without the support of the powerful or sowing the seeds of future revolution; there seemed to be little middle ground.[25]

Americans who witnessed the corruption of conscription and the "squeeze" of crooked bureaucrats did not always understand the limited reach of the Guomindang. They assumed the central government presided over a cohesive state. Nationalist propaganda reinforced this perception. In the resulting mire, most did not see a people who resisted bravely for eight long years. Instead they saw poverty, superstition, corruption, inflation, black marketeering, and political division. These iniquities seemed so ingrained in everything they witnessed, they believed them to be the result of some crucial weakness in the government, the culture—maybe even the people themselves. They did not recognize them as symptoms of a prolonged and brutal war; they mistook effect for cause.[26]

Nationalist China's progressively tenuous circumstances made military victory an increasingly remote possibility. Though the ground war had bogged down in an intractable stalemate since 1939, the introduction of the new Zero fighter changed the calculus of the war in air. With the Chinese Air Force in tatters, Chiang dispatched Chennault to the United States in November 1940 to help T. V. Soong, the generalissimo's brother-in-law, with ongoing lobbying efforts for a volunteer fighter group manned by experienced American aviators. Though pessimistic, Chennault departed Hong Kong on the Pan American Clipper on Monday, November 11. Three days later, the flying boat delivered him to San Francisco. By Monday the eighteenth, he had arrived in Washington, DC.

The United States would not enter World War II for another twelve months, but China and Japan had already been locked in battle for three and a half years. President Roosevelt felt America had clear imperatives for helping China, including maintaining freedom of navigation in the Pacific and ensuring China's trade remained open to all nations rather than falling under the exclusive domination of the Japanese. He also envisioned Chiang's

Nationalist government becoming a stabilizing, democratic influence in the Far East. More immediately—and more realistically—the Japanese had one million troops in the country. Should Chiang's government surrender, Tokyo could shift those troops to threaten US interests elsewhere in the Pacific. Roosevelt hoped a volunteer fighter group would serve as a deterrent to further Japanese aggression and gave his verbal authorization to the scheme.[27] It continued a course of steadily increasing diplomatic and economic pressure against the Empire of Japan, including an embargo on shipments of scrap iron and oil, and forward deploying the US Pacific Fleet from San Diego to Pearl Harbor. Against the backdrop of escalating rivalry in the Pacific, only the particulars of the Japanese strike on Sunday December 7, 1941, would come as a surprise to informed observers.

2

Hope for China

July 22, 1941
Pier 23, San Francisco, California

Not much of a crowd had gathered to see off the MS *Bloemfontein*—not like in the movies, anyway. As the ten thousand-ton ship of the Java Pacific Line put out into the harbor, George McMillan looked back to see the city of San Francisco reaching from the water's edge to the tops of distant hills; the Oakland Bridge stretched out to the east. Gazing ahead, he saw Alcatraz and, beyond that, the Pan American Clipper lifting from the water to wing its way toward Hawaii. The enormous, four-engine flying boat epitomized a new age of rapid, luxurious transoceanic travel; the restless young airman wished he were aboard her instead of the old "Bloom."

Bloemfontein passed under the Golden Gate Bridge at about five o'clock in the evening, picking up speed until it reached its full sixteen knots. In addition to crew and cargo, it carried one hundred passengers—twenty-eight of them destined to join the American Volunteer Group (AVG) in Burma. They did not constitute a particularly diverse group; the pilots were, without exception, white and, without exception, male. Most came from middle-class upbringings and had at least a couple years of college under their belts. Many had four-year degrees.[1] McMillan, or "Mac" as his friends called him, had joined the US Army Air Corps in 1938 only six credits short of graduating from the prestigious Citadel Military College in South Carolina. He cut a striking figure; one of his fellow passengers described him as "the kind for whom the expression 'tall, dark, and handsome' might have been coined."[2] Few of the pilots had as much experience in Army fighters as he had. His logbook documented 548 hours in fighters and 794 overall.[3] Some of the others had spent less than six months in the service. He met one pilot with only

Hope for China   13

350 hours total flying time—Mac had flown that much in training alone! The recruits seemed undaunted by their inexperience, lured by promises of adventure, lucrative salaries, and a hinted-at $500 bonus for every Japanese plane they shot down.[4]

Mac thought back to an incident from just before they sailed. Mr. Richard Aldworth, of the Central Aircraft Manufacturing Company (CAMCO), had approached him and inquired about his experience flying fighters and his length of service and rank in the Air Corps. CAMCO was the front company employing the AVG's pilots and ground crews. With America and Japan not yet at war, the US government had to obscure its role in sending men and planes to the aid of embattled China. Mac had resigned his commission as a first lieutenant to join the group. Upon hearing his resume, Mr. Aldworth immediately upgraded his contract to class two, meaning a promotion to flight leader. Mac thought the episode a bit odd: CAMCO's New York office had known all the dope on him for months; they must have been holding out on him, hoping to recruit more experienced men. No bother. He would enjoy the extra $75 a month. Not that it mattered much; he had instructed the company to deposit all but $100 of his $675-a-month paycheck in the bank anyhow. He looked forward to the responsibility of the position, though; he knew he could handle it. After two years as a peacetime fighter pilot while the rest of the world erupted in war, he felt ready to fight for a foreign government in a faraway conflict.[5]

Standing along the ship's rail, shooting the bull with some of the other volunteers, including David Lee "Tex" Hill, Ed Rector, R. T. Smith, and Bill Reed, Mac watched as the West Coast of the United States disappeared from view. Suddenly, he found himself struck by the vastness of the Pacific Ocean. The sheer magnitude of endless water in every direction left him feeling an uncertain emptiness. He looked forward to putting in at Honolulu. They would be there only long enough to take on food and water, but he hoped to see a little of the city and perhaps steal a quick swim at Waikiki Beach.[6]

Before long, rough seas had the ship pitching and rolling. Though never before prone to seasickness, the fifteen-foot swells turned Mac's feeling of uncertain emptiness to one of vague nausea. R. T. Smith, a former Army flight instructor, said he never felt worse than "woozy and uncomfortable" but claimed half the group looked pretty wretched, "even some of the old salts from the Navy!"[7] Former Navy dive-bomber pilot Tex Hill, on the other hand, maintained that all the Navy men did just fine, while those from the Army became "violently seasick to a man!"[8]

14   FALLEN TIGERS

Mac had plenty of time to find his sea legs; *Bloemfontein* finally delivered the volunteers to Batavia, Java, by way of Honolulu, Brisbane, and Manila on August 26. Its sister ship, the *Jagersfontein,* then brought them to Singapore on September 1, and a small Norwegian freighter named the *Haishing* carried them the rest of the way to Rangoon, arriving at about noon on the fifteenth. Bill Pawley, the president of CAMCO, and C. B. "Skip" Adair, the AVG's transportation and supply officer, met them at the dock. The pair took the new arrivals to lunch and then hustled them onto a train bound for Taungoo, 170 miles to the north. The group had secured the use of a Royal Air Force (RAF) airfield there so the pilots and ground crews could learn to fly and maintain their Curtiss Hawk 81A2 Tomahawks, an export model of the Warhawk similar to the P-40B. They reached Taungoo that night at nine thirty.

Three or four days later, a twin-engine Beechcraft arrived from China with the group commander, "Colonel" Claire Lee Chennault. His new rank was an honorary title only and had no relation to his prewar service as a captain in the Air Corps. He gave a short welcome speech to the new arrivals at the pilots' mess that evening and later met with them in his office. He greeted them warmly. "We're glad to have you here," he told them, shaking each of their hands in turn.[9] Bold and dynamic, his hard, angular jaw with its distinctive, defiant set, he seemed the embodiment of the larger-than-life character they expected. Jet black hair topped his deeply lined, weather-beaten face, and dark eyes radiated the intense energy of his active mind.

Every morning at six o'clock sharp, Chennault brought the pilots together in a teakwood shack beside the airfield. He spoke to them about the challenges of fighting in China: the rugged terrain, the poor weather, the meager supplies. He talked about teamwork, about using the strong points of their equipment against the weak points of the enemy's. Teaching came naturally to him. He had taught primary school in rural Louisiana before he joined the Army in 1917. Later, he instructed and managed the curriculum for fighter aviation at the Air Corps Tactical School at Maxwell Field, Alabama. Now he taught his fighter pilots all he knew about the Japanese—the sum of bitter lessons learned during the retreat from Shanghai to Chongqing. Though he had been a teacher all his life, he firmly believed the instruction he gave his airmen in Taungoo to have been the best teaching of his career.

"You will face Japanese pilots superbly trained in mechanical flying," Chennault informed his new arrivals. "They have been drilled for hundreds of hours in flying precise formations and rehearsing set tactics for each

Hope for China 15

situation they may encounter. Japanese pilots fly by the book, and these are the books they use." He passed around captured tactics manuals translated into English. "They have plenty of guts but lack initiative and judgment," he continued. "They go into battle with a set tactical plan and follow it no matter what happens. Bombers will hold their formations until they are all shot down. Fighters always try the same tricks over and over again. God help the American pilot who tries to fight them according to their plans."[10]

For the pilots, it was like being in grade school again; they sat in neat rows in the small shack while the teacher lectured them and chalked out tactical diagrams on the blackboard.[11] "The object of our tactics," Chennault explained to them, "is to break up their formations and make them fight according to our style. Once the Japanese are forced to deviate from their plan, they are in trouble. Their rigid air discipline can be used as a powerful weapon against them."

As he detailed the heretofore unknown performance figures of the deadly Zero, many of the volunteers began to doubt the ability of their P-40s to triumph in air combat. A few disheartened pilots even handed Chennault their resignations. He continued, undaunted. "You must use the strong points of your equipment against the weak points of the enemy," he stressed to those who remained. "Each type of plane has its own strength and weakness. The pilot who can turn his advantages against the enemy's weaknesses will win every time."[12]

"What the hell are our advantages, sir?" one of the pilots asked nervously from the back of the classroom.[13]

"You can count on a higher top speed, faster dive, and superior firepower," Chennault told them. "The Jap fighters have a faster rate of climb, higher ceiling, and better maneuverability. They can turn on a dime and climb almost straight up. If they can get you into a turning combat, they are deadly."

"Fight in pairs," he emphasized. "Use your speed and diving power to make a pass, shoot and break away. You have the edge in that kind of combat. All your advantages are brought to bear on the Japanese deficiencies. Close your range, fire, and dive away. Never stay within range of the Jap's defensive firepower any longer than you need to deliver an accurate burst."[14]

Chennault boiled his instructions down to the most basic tenets: "dive-squirt-pass-run."[15] He reinforced his instructions with simple rhymes: "It's better to fight and run away and live to fight another day."[16] His lectures had the pilots on the edge of their seats. They took copious notes, asked questions,

16   FALLEN TIGERS

and answered his pop quizzes. The low Cajun drawl, fatherly warmth, and charisma of the "Old Man," as they affectionately called him, drew them in. He spoke with the confidence and authority of a wizened old warrior who had been fighting the Japanese longer than they could imagine.[17]

Privately, though, Chennault worried about the quality of his pilots. The idea had been for a volunteer fighter group manned by experienced American aviators. But he did not get the experience he had hoped for. Though McMillan arrived in Burma with hundreds of hours in fighter aircraft, two-thirds of the group's pilots had none. More than half came from the US Navy, where many had flown dive bombers or flying boats, and a few of Mac's fellow Army pilots even came from bulky four-engine strategic bombers. Chennault hoped he could forge his volunteers into a formidable, combat-ready fighter group in time to face the enemy when Japanese bombers returned to Kunming that winter. But while training at Taungoo, the group suffered a plentitude of accidents and three fatalities: John D. Armstrong went down in a midair collision while mock-dogfighting with another P-40 on September 8. Maax C. Hammer crashed in bad weather on the twenty-second. Peter W. Atkinson's fighter disintegrated in a power dive on October 25. The group's chaplain, an ex-missionary by the name of Paul Frillmann, presided over their burials at St. Luke's Church in Taungoo. Although the parson worried over this toll in men and hardware, he also noticed a growing confidence and skill among the group's pilots and ground crews. By the end of November 1941, he judged the AVG to be as ready for combat as it ever would be—and just in time.[18]

"Received news today that Japan had bombed Pearl Harbor and Nichols Field and that the U.S. has declared war on her," Mac wrote in his diary on the morning of December 8, 1941. "Fine business! Maybe we'll see some action now. Everyone is getting tired of sitting around Taungoo. Want to go on to Kunming."[19]

In the wake of the surprise attack, the AVG stood alert. Group headquarters authorized all personnel to carry sidearms and issued gas masks and shrapnel helmets. A flight of P-40s, fully armed and fueled, waited at the south end of the field, ready to take off at a moment's notice.[20] Yet the widening war in the Pacific did little to touch the group during the first week and a half after Pearl Harbor. They continued to train and bide their time, reconnoitering airfields in Thailand, and preparing for the inevitable. Then, on the morning of December 18, bombers of the Japanese Army Air Force renewed

Hope for China   17

their terror attacks on Kunming. Chennault immediately ordered two of his squadrons to move into China. Mac wanted to go, but the 3rd Pursuit Squadron, of which he was now vice squadron leader, remained behind to help the RAF defend Rangoon.

Thirty-four P-40s from the 1st and 2nd Pursuit Squadrons landed at Kunming on the afternoon of the eighteenth. Each of the fighters boasted the group's trademark shark mouth painted on the engine cowling. While training at Taungoo, McMillan, along with pilots Erik Shilling and Lacy Mangleburg, had seen the scheme in a photograph of an Australian P-40 on the cover of the *Illustrated Weekly of India*. They approached Chennault for permission to decorate their fighters similarly. He agreed—on condition that it become the entire group's insignia.[21] Thus adorned, the American fighters remained unchallenged at Kunming until the twentieth.

By December 1941 Chennault could boast that "the Chinese air-raid warning system was a vast spider net of people, radios, telephones, and telegraph lines that covered all of Free China accessible to enemy aircraft." The net in Yunnan Province featured 165 radios at observation posts set in concentric rings around Kunming and other friendly airbases—some in such remote locations that even southwest China's ubiquitous mule trains could not reach them. The observers reported to a central command post, where fighter controllers would plot the raids to determine their target and then marshal fighters to intercept from an advantageous position. This network would allow Chennault to concentrate his meager forces against a numerically superior foe.[22]

Airfields all over China signaled the *jingbao*,[23] or alarm, by raising red, ball-shaped paper lanterns up a flagpole. One ball went aloft when the warning net detected Japanese aircraft airborne. Two balls meant the fighter controllers thought that particular airfield the likely target. Three indicated enemy airplanes directly overhead. To save precious gasoline—every gallon of which had to be trucked in over the Burma Road or flown over the Hump—Chennault directed his men to wait to takeoff until enemy aircraft approached within twenty minutes of the field. That would give them just enough time to climb to altitude and position themselves to ambush the incoming formation.[24]

The morning of December 20 dawned cold and windy. At 9:45 a.m., Chennault received a phone call from Col Wang Shuming, commander of the Chinese Fifth Route Air Force. "Ten Japanese bombers crossed the Yunnan

18   FALLEN TIGERS

border at Lao Cai heading northwest," Wang reported. Chennault hurried to the code room and watched as the warning net updated progress of the raid.

"Heavy engine noise at station X-Ray-One-Zero."

"Unknowns overhead at station Peter-Eight."

"Noise of many above clouds at station Charlie-Two-Three."[25]

The fighter-control board showed the plots slowly inching toward Kunming. Chennault stepped outside and fired off a red flare to send his "Sharks" aloft. He ordered 1st Squadron to intercept the bombers east of the city and 2nd Squadron to remain over the field in reserve. The latter encountered the enemy first—but began firing well out of range. The bombers jettisoned their payloads and hightailed it for the border. First Squadron caught them fleeing the area and dove to attack, wading into the enemy formation with all guns blazing. The Americans claimed four destroyed for no losses, though one P-40 ran out of fuel and had to land off field.

"Three of ten Japanese bombers which tried to raid Kunming on the 20th inst. and were shot down by your group have already been found, according to the reports of the Yunnan Provincial Air Defense Headquarters," Colonel Wang wrote to Chennault on Christmas Day. He cited two reports received from the warning net of seven enemy planes seen returning to Indochina at 11:20 and 11:25, respectively. "There can be no doubt that altogether 4 planes were brought down that day provided that the 4th plane exploded after 11:25 a.m.," he concluded.[26]

The Japanese refrained from striking Kunming for sixteen months after the battle, though they continued to probe Chennault's outlying defenses. Instead, they shifted their weight of effort to Burma, launching massive raids on Rangoon on December 23 and 25. Mac received credit for shooting down three enemy bombers during the fierce air battle on Christmas Day: "I went in to knock off a straggler," he recorded in his diary. "He hit my windshield and shattered it, but bullet-proof glass stopped it. I then closed in to about 50 feet directly on his tail. Opened up on him again and got him, but he hit my prestone cooling system (knocking my engine out). Explosive bullet hit me in left hand and shoulder. Headed down towards shore and made a crash-landing in a rice paddy." Mac returned to the airfield with the help of local police by eight thirty that evening. Despite his injuries, he returned to duty just two days later.

In the two air battles over Rangoon, the Japanese admitted losing seventeen warplanes to the AVG and RAF. Mac and the rest of 3rd Squadron gave better than they got but lost two pilots and five aircraft in the process. "Even

Hope for China   19

though we're getting good results we can't last thru more than a couple more raids," Mac worried in his diary.[27] Chennault rotated the squadron up to Kunming a few days later, sending 2nd Squadron to Rangoon in its place.

It was after the move to Kunming that Mac ran into one of the probing attacks by Japanese bombers. On the morning of January 17, 1942, he sat in the cockpit of his P-40, warming it up for an armed reconnaissance over northern Indochina. At 9:50 a.m. the warning net reported loud engine noise crossing the border near Lao Cai. Mac scrubbed the reconnaissance run and scrambled to intercept, with pilots Chuck Older, Tom Haywood, and Erik Shilling in tow.

Not long after they took off from Kunming, an AVG radioman stationed at Mengzi, 116 miles to the south, reported three Japanese bombers overhead. The rough gravel airfield there appeared to be their target. Fighter controllers in the code room at Kunming relayed this information to Mac, and shortly thereafter he caught sight of the enemy. With the Christmas Day battle still fresh in his mind, he did not hesitate to engage with the odds in his favor. Older quickly shot down the leader; brilliant orange flame trailed from the olive-colored bomber as it fell toward the clouds below, a "very beautiful sight against the white overcast background," Mac noted. The other two bombers split up and headed for Hanoi. In the fifteen-minute running battle that followed, Older, Haywood, and Shilling took on the straggler while Mac attacked the one in the lead. His concentrated fire finally knocked its right engine out of commission. "He disappeared through the overcast badly smoking," he wrote in his diary that night. "Same happened to the other one."[28]

Unaware of the interception taking place, Chennault walked into the operations shack just as the pilots reported the first bomber going down in flames.

"What's going on?" he demanded.

"I was too busy to call you," his executive officer apologized, explaining the situation.[29] That hardly mollified the Old Man, but the results pleased him. Mac's flight made a clean sweep: all three bombers shot down with no injury or damage to the Americans. Mac received credit for one of the kills. "Not a bad day's hunting!!" he wrote. "We received only one hit in my whole flight. I got one bullet thru my left wingtip. Much different from those days at Rangoon, believe me!"[30]

As it happened, the Chinese government made good on the rumor of a $500 bonus for every Japanese airplane destroyed. "Very shortly some bonus

20   FALLEN TIGERS

money should be coming thru," Mac wrote his mother several weeks later. "I got knocked [down] Xmas Day about forty miles from the base [in Rangoon], but only after I'd gotten three of them. Received slight injuries in my left hand and arm which didn't do more than make me mad. Another one paid for that later on [in China]."[31]

Given the defensive posture of his forces early in the war, Chennault put little thought into evasion and recovery of his airmen. Most of his pilots bailed out within a short distance of the airfield and returned without difficulty; their aircraft, even if destroyed, could at least be salvaged for parts. The AVG lost seven men on its few offensive forays deep into enemy territory: two captured and one killed in Thailand, one captured and one killed in Indochina, and one captured and one killed attacking a Japanese field headquarters in Jiangxi Province. Most of these airmen went down well outside the reach of the Guomindang, though three of the four prisoners eventually escaped.

When Erik Shilling crashed in the mountains west of Kunming in December 1941, the local people initially thought him to be Japanese. He spent the night in the cockpit of his demolished Curtiss-Wright Demon interceptor, alone, wrapped in his parachute to keep warm against the cold and drizzle. In the early hours of dawn, he saw two men and a boy approach the wreck along a dirt path. He called out to them. Startled, they turned around and ran away. Alone again, he decided to follow the path in the direction of Kunming. As he gathered his belongings, a crowd of thirty men arrived. Han Chinese often thought of these people, Yi tribesmen,[32] as "hillbillies." Short, stocky, and muscular, they wore loincloths reaching down to their thighs and leather vests that left their chests exposed. One of them began questioning Shilling, though he could not understand the man.

"Meiguo ren!" Shilling announced, motioning to himself. But the frustrated tribesman evidently did not understand Mandarin and began screaming. Shilling had a passport written in Chinese. He pulled it out and handed it to his interrogator. The man took the booklet and, holding it upside down, leafed through it. Apparently he could not read either. Shilling pulled it out of his hands, turned it right-side up, and handed it back. The crowd erupted in laughter.

Humor and his interrogator's loss of face seemed to diffuse the tension, but the suspicious tribesmen nevertheless set about building a stockade around the wrecked fighter. Shilling suddenly realized they thought *he* might be an enemy airman! They had probably never seen a Japanese or a white man before, though they had ample opportunity to observe hostile warplanes overhead. While they built his tree-branch prison, he pulled a Victrola and stack of records that had miraculously survived the crash out of his baggage compartment. The scratchy sound of music made the crowd temporarily forget their work, and they gathered around, talking and pointing excitedly. They kept Shilling under guard that night and carried him down the mountain in a crudely fashioned sedan chair the next morning. Blond haired and blue eyed, he became a curiosity in every village through which they passed. Eventually, they delivered him to Mr. Lu, a radio operator working at a remote outpost of the air raid warning net. Lu did not speak English either, but he had a Chinese-English dictionary. Slowly, painstakingly, Shilling and the radioman communicated one word at a time. They arranged for him to be picked up at a nearby grass airstrip. "I am alright," he radioed Chennault in Kunming that evening. Shilling returned to the AVG three days later, feeling he had barely dodged death at the hands of fearsome mountain tribesmen.[33]

Shortly thereafter, each airman in the group received a cloth chit issued and stamped by China's Aeronautical Affairs Commission. The 7.5-inch by 9.5-inch piece of silk featured the Nationalist flag printed on the top half and a unique serial number and twelve Chinese characters on the bottom. The characters proclaimed, on behalf of the bearer: "This foreigner has come to China to help in the war. Soldiers and civilians, one and all, rescue and protect him."[34] Many AVG pilots had the iconic chit sewn to the back of their leather flying jackets. This later changed less conspicuously to inside the jacket, though many airmen, like Glen Beneda, folded it and carried it in a pocket instead. Formally known as an escape chit or blood chit, aircrews usually referred to it as their "back flag," "identification flag," or simply their "flag." Significantly, it promised neither reward nor compensation for rescuing Americans. In fact, although the Guomindang or Fourteenth Air Force reimbursed many rescuers for their expenses, most never received payment for their services or sacrifice.

The Army Air Forces also eventually issued a booklet called the "pointie-talkie," which featured questions or phrases in English accompanied by Chinese translations. Airmen could point to a phrase, rescuers could read the Chinese version, and then point to a response, which the airmen could then read in English. Seventy percent of evasion reports specifically mention use of the flag and pointie-talkie. According to 1st Lt Walter Krywy, a P-51 pilot

22   FALLEN TIGERS

who fell victim to small arms fire while strafing a train in Anhui Province in early 1945: "The pointie-talkie was the most valuable item I had. I believe it saved my life." During the initial two weeks after he bailed out, Krywy did not encounter a single person who spoke English. "I felt the two most important items of evasion equipment I had were my pointie-talkie and my Chinese identification flag."[35]

In Shilling's case the utility of the flag and pointie-talkie may have seemed limited with illiterate mountain tribesmen. Indeed, 9 percent of evasion reports complained of rescuers who could not read Chinese characters. Nevertheless, the chit eventually became so widely recognized that even the illiterate knew its meaning by sight. Those who could not decipher the characters understood the symbolism of the Nationalist flag and the official chop of the Aeronautical Affairs Commission. Second Lieutenant George Snyder found himself in Shilling's predicament when his P-51 suffered a complete electrical failure in December 1944. Disoriented without his instruments and low on fuel, he made a wheels-up landing along the east bank of the Wuding River in Shaanxi Province. "A single Chinese was by the side of the plane when I climbed out," he reported. "I showed him my pointie-talkie but he was unable to read." A hostile crowd from the nearby village soon surrounded him. The tension quickly escalated. He opened his jacket to show them the identification flag sewn inside. The villagers found one among their number literate enough to make sense of the flag and booklet. After leafing through the pointie-talkie, the man informed them they had an American on their hands. "Immediately the attitude of everyone changed," recalled Snyder. "I learned later that when I first landed, the populace was uncertain as to whether I was Jap or friendly."[36]

The flag and pointie-talkie played a vital role in the recovery of downed airmen. Though some Chinese still could not tell the difference between a Caucasian and a Japanese, they came to see American aircraft as irrefutable proof Japan had not won and that resistance continued. The AVG's decisive engagements over Yunnan Province meant the end of sustained terror bombing against the cities of Free China.[37] Though three-quarters of its aerial combat took place over Burma, in just a couple actions over southwest China, the group made its shark-mouthed P-40s a symbol of vengeance for the United States and hope for China. The Japanese, on the other hand, found the insignia bewildering: "If these markings were found on a submarine, the significance could perhaps be understood," a Tokyo newspaper remarked, "but on a plane?"[38]

3

Doolittle's Raid

December 24, 1941
Tacoma, Washington

Second Lieutenant Everett W. "Brick" Holstrom rushed to preflight his B-25B in the frigid, pouring rain. The rest of his crew had already scrambled aboard the medium bomber or huddled under its wings for shelter. Brick quickly finished his walk-around, climbed aboard, started the engines, and got rolling down the waterlogged runway. Only then did he realize he had forgotten to remove the pitot-tube cover! It was too late now—he would have to get by without his airspeed indicator this time. The twin-engine bomber lifted off the ground at five o'clock in the morning, still nearly three hours before sunrise. Brick flew his crew to their assigned patrol area off the coast of Washington State and descended through the clouds to five hundred feet. The Navy had told them any US submarine in the area would have an escort. If they saw an unescorted sub, they should attack it.

Paranoia had seized the West Coast in the weeks after Pearl Harbor. Brick's bomb group, the 17th, had been overnighting at March Field, near Riverside, California, when they heard the news of the Japanese attack. The B-25s had no guns in their turrets, so the crews flew to Hamilton Field, near San Francisco, the next day to arm their planes. The men had just taken delivery of the guns and had begun installing them when word came down the line to throw the weapons in the planes and take off immediately. The base commander ordered them off the field because he expected a Japanese bombing raid at any moment. "You've got to get out of here!" he bellowed frantically. The bombers hurried aloft and continued to their home base at Pendleton, Oregon, that night. By December 20, Brick found himself on detached service flying anti-submarine patrols out of McChord Field, near Tacoma.

24   FALLEN TIGERS

Though no fleets of enemy aircraft carriers lurked offshore, the paranoia did not prove completely unfounded. The Imperial Japanese Navy had dispatched nine submarines to the Pacific Coast in an attempt to intercept the American aircraft carriers that had escaped destruction at Pearl Harbor. One even eventually shelled the Ellwood Oil Field near Santa Barbara, California, with its deck gun.

Brick's crew flew their prescribed search pattern. For nearly two hours they scoured the featureless expanse of open water. The bombardier, who had partied a little too hard the night before, used the bombsight cover as an airsick bag. Suddenly, the top-turret gunner sounded off:

"Submarine on the surface at 3 o'clock!"

The copilot, "Hoss" Wilder, soon chimed in that he saw it too. Brick doubted that; it was probably a whale, maybe a log. Nevertheless, he began a right-hand turn. Then he saw it in front of them.

"We've got a submarine!" he said, dumbfounded. There was no mistaking it; the sub had surfaced under a rain squall. Brick flew straight for it. The bombardier opened the bomb bay doors, but his groggy eyes had still not made it out. "I'm headed right at it!" Brick exclaimed. The bombardier finally spotted it but too late; he toggled off three bombs, which landed long. Brick pulled into a hair-raising 180-degree turn and made another run. The sub had begun to dive, but the bombardier toggled off their last three bombs as they went by. They felt an explosion as they passed overhead.

"It looks like we scored a hit just ahead of the conning tower!" reported the gunner. Brick circled around, and the crew observed an oil slick and some debris in the water. They reported the engagement to Naval Station Bremerton by radio and received instructions to remain overhead as long as possible. They circled the debris until they were low on fuel and then headed back to the mainland.

Though later credited with destroying a Japanese sub, Brick and his crew never claimed one as destroyed, nor did the Japanese admit to losing one. Submarine *I-25* had been patrolling off the mouth of the Columbia River around this time and, for some unspecified reason, failed to deploy its E14Y "Glen" reconnaissance floatplane, located in a watertight hangar forward of the conning tower. It remains uncertain as to whether this was the boat Brick and his crew encountered.[1]

Such submarine patrols did not last much longer for the crew. By early February 1942, the 17th Bombardment Group began a move to Columbia,

South Carolina, and Brick received orders to fly to Minneapolis for modifications to his bomber. The plant there installed additional fuel tanks in the upper bomb bay, in the crawlway above the bomb bay, and in place of the remote-controlled bottom turret. One evening, Brick's squadron commander, Capt Edward "Ski" York, called everyone together in a hotel room in downtown Minneapolis. He had just returned from meeting with Lt Col James H. "Jimmy" Doolittle. The famed aviation pioneer and daredevil racing pilot wanted volunteers for a secret and dangerous mission that would take them out of the country for a few months. Everyone volunteered—everyone except for Brick, that is. He was visiting his wife's uncle who lived nearby and missed the meeting. Fortunately, one of his friends figured he would want to go and volunteered him on his behalf.

On February 25, Brick and his crew landed at Eglin Field, Florida, to begin a month of training in long-range, overwater navigation as well as operations from extremely short airfields. The men figured their mission must involve taking off from an aircraft carrier—Lt "Hank" Miller, an instructor from Naval Air Station Pensacola, helped them develop a technique to get off the ground in the shortest distance possible. But they could only guess at their objective; by the week after Pearl Harbor, America found itself ensnared in a global conflict, simultaneously at war with Fascist Italy, Nazi Germany, and the Empire of Japan. For all the airmen knew, Doolittle's special project could be destined for anywhere in the world.[2]

During the early months of World War II, the United States scrambled to deal with the realities of a global conflict. On December 22, 1941, President Roosevelt and British prime minister Winston Churchill convened the Arcadia Conference in Washington, DC. Despite American outrage over Pearl Harbor, they agreed on an overarching strategy to defeat Germany first, relegating the war against Japan to second-tier status. They also announced the formation of the China Theater, encompassing China, Indochina (modern Vietnam, Laos, and Cambodia), and Thailand, with Chiang Kai-shek as its supreme Allied commander.[3] Notwithstanding the theater's low priority, Roosevelt decided to send one of his most promising and energetic field commanders to serve as Chiang's chief of staff.

Lieutenant General Joseph W. Stilwell landed at Kunming on March 3, 1942, and remained there overnight so he could confer with Claire Chennault the next morning.[4] Their first meeting went well; it foreshadowed none of the animus that would later define not only their relationship but the

26 FALLEN TIGERS

entire American war effort in the Far East. "To airfield to wait for Chennault," Stilwell jotted in his diary. "Had a talk. He'll be OK. Met a group of the pilots. They look damn good."[5] Immediately following the short conference, the general departed for Chongqing to meet with Chiang.

Stilwell arrived in China without soldiers, weapons, or supplies of any kind. He alone would be the extent of America's contribution to help stop the Japanese advance in Burma. Throughout the war, the resources the Western Allies allocated him would never equal those given to other commanders in the war against Japan—and would not even remotely approach the resources made available to Gen Dwight D. Eisenhower in North Africa and Europe. The nature of the Pacific War has often been overshadowed by comparison— or obscured by false conflation—with the war in Europe. Bundling them together under the banner of "World War II" masks important differences between them. Though the conflicts took place simultaneously, in truth, they bore little resemblance to each other. The struggle against Imperial Japan was, in short, a different war in a different place against a different enemy. The Chinese differentiated their war from the global struggle by calling it simply the "War of Resistance against Japan."[6] But Americans came to see both conflicts through the same generic lens.

The primacy of the European war in Anglo-American strategy and American memory has minimized the shock and anger Americans felt specifically toward Japan after Pearl Harbor. The attack brought forth overwhelming outrage and a dramatic outpouring of patriotism. In the days, weeks, and months that followed, young men lined up outside recruiting stations in the tens of thousands. Few of them had ever before ventured far from their hometowns, let alone traveled abroad. Those who wound up in China brought their parochial perspectives to a geographically, culturally, linguistically, and politically alien land.

Glen Beneda grew up in the small town of McCook, Nebraska. He wanted to be a pilot, but the Army Air Forces required applicants to be at least twenty years of age and have two years of college under their belts. He was only a freshman and had turned eighteen a month after the attack on Pearl Harbor. In the face of dramatic expansion, however, the Army Air Forces dropped those requirements in January 1942, instead mandating prospective airmen take a battery of tests known as the Aviation Cadet Qualifying Exam.[7] Beneda quit school and joined the aviation cadets in March, hitching a ride to Omaha with family friend Ralph Egle to sign the paperwork and take the exams.[8] By

Doolittle's Raid 27

February 1943 he had his wings, graduating with Class 43B at Luke Field, Arizona, before shipping off to a P-40 operational training unit in Florida.

Though born in Bassens, France—just northeast of Bordeaux—Henry Minco grew up in Cleveland, Ohio. His parents, John and Marie, met in France during the Great War, where John had served as a sergeant in the American Expeditionary Forces. After the armistice, the newlyweds lived together in the United States until 1923, when John sent Marie back to live with her family while he established himself in business. She was pregnant with Henry at the time and accompanied by her one-year-old son, John Jr. The family reunited once John Sr. opened a car dealership in Cleveland. When the Depression hit, it ruined him financially. In 1933 he died suddenly at the age of thirty-eight, leaving Marie to raise the two young boys on her own. They had a tough life, but they managed. The US Army drafted John Jr. in 1942 and he deployed to Europe as an aerial gunner. This meant Henry, as the only other child of a widow, had a draft exemption. But Henry had always been a risk-taker and a hell-raiser. He volunteered for the Army Air Forces, earned his wings, and reported to an operational training unit at Perry Army Airfield in Florida to learn to fly fighters. John Jr. resented his brother for leaving their mother on her own. Henry dismissed the criticism; he could not stomach the thought of sitting this one out.[9]

Paul Crawford, the middle child in a family of seven, grew up in Americus, Georgia, a rural town sixty-five miles southwest of Macon. Both his brothers also joined the Army Air Forces. He went on to fly P-51s in China; his brothers Tim and John both flew bombers in North Africa. Paul had never left the South before he joined the Army; he had never seen an Asian or heard the Chinese language. Like his fellow aviators, his preconceptions rested on popular culture and racial stereotypes. Comic strips like *Terry and the Pirates* and folktales about the diseased miasma of slums and opium dens prejudiced their perspectives. For Crawford, dozens of films featuring the exploits of Detective Charlie Chan had left a deep impression. Such movies painted the Chinese in a more benevolent light, with the sly Chan always outsmarting the bad guy. But the character—always played by a white actor—reinforced crude racial clichés.[10] Invariably, most American intelligence reports casually (and probably unintentionally derisively) referred to Chinese civilians who rescued airmen as "coolies" or "natives."

A powerful China lobby in New York and Washington, DC, also helped shape American attitudes. Media magnate Henry Luce's publications, including

28 FALLEN TIGERS

Time and *Life*, paternalistically advocated for the plight of Chiang Kai-shek and Song Meiling in their struggle against the Japanese. In 1938 *Time* named them "Man & Wife of the Year." Early in the war the magazine led news publications all over the country in trumpeting the exploits of the American Volunteer Group. Its tactical victories in the skies over Burma and China shined bright in contrast to the bad news emanating from Wake Island, the Philippines, and the Dutch East Indies. The December 29, 1941, issue included a short piece under the headline, "Blood for the Tigers": "Last week ten Japanese bombers came winging their carefree way up into Yunnan, heading directly for Kunming, the terminus of the Burma Road. Thirty miles south of Kunming, the Flying Tigers swooped, let the Japanese have it. Of the ten bombers, said Chongqing reports, four plummeted to earth in flames. The rest turned tail and fled. Tiger casualties: none."[11]

In addition to the enthusiastic report of the battle, the article contained the first appearance of the name "Flying Tigers" in newsprint. The moniker quickly caught on, though its exact origins became something of a controversy. "How the term Flying Tigers was derived from the shark-nosed P-40s I will never know," Chennault later wrote. "At any rate we were somewhat surprised to find ourselves billed under that name."[12]

Many AVG pilots, including Dick Rossi and R. T. Smith, believed the Chinese press invented the name, though like Chennault, Tex Hill admitted, "I don't know how the term came about."[13] In a 1949 letter to Chennault recently unearthed in the archives of the Hoover Institution, T. V. Soong claimed he came up with it. He had been discussing the idea of a distinctive emblem for the group with his staff in Washington, DC. "Someone suggested using the Chinese dragon," he wrote, "which I rejected as being rather dated. The eagle was next considered, which I turned down as being too distinctively American. Finally I thought of using the 'Flying Tiger.' The boys of course pointed out that the tiger is tied down to the mundane earth. However, I told them of the Chinese saying, 'giving wings to the tiger,' meaning that the tiger, already the most formidable animal alive, became, as it were, endowed with wings, which makes its prowess in good American language, 'super-colossal.'"[14]

After the war, many AVG members argued they were the only "real" Flying Tigers—that the name did not apply to the Army Air Force organizations that followed them. They even attempted (unsuccessfully) to litigate the issue.[15] Whoever invented the name and whether or not they intended it to

Doolittle's Raid   29

continue on with the China Air Task Force and Fourteenth Air Force, it took on a life of its own in both China and the United States. To the Chinese in particular, the title grew to encompass all US air forces aiding them in their fight against the Japanese. Most did not appreciate the nuance between an "American volunteer" and an "American serviceman" anyway.[16] Undoubtedly, the name would have had no weight whatsoever had not the exploits of the AVG made it legendary. But the postwar argument created bad blood between Americans who fought and sacrificed for the same cause in the same place.

Precious few newspapers or magazines made their way out to Burma and China and into the hands of the volunteers in late 1941 and early 1942. "Certainly hope you're saving all the clippings written in the papers and magazines about us," George McMillan wrote his mother on February 29. "Oughta make a pretty good scrap book. So far we haven't seen much in writing. Managed to see a few issues of Time magazine here but they don't give much of an account of things. Most of 'em being too early. All I can say is we've borne the brunt of almost everything without much help or cooperation from our friends."[17]

News of the Flying Tigers did much to shore up American morale in the dark early days of World War II. To the US Army and Navy, however, the group served as a major source of embarrassment. Even though former military pilots and ground crews manned the unit, the fact remained that early in the war a volunteer fighter group, outside the control of any US military command, proved to be one of the only effective American units in combat. Having accomplished little of substance in response to Pearl Harbor, the Army and Navy collaborated to plot their own newsworthy revenge.

On April 2, 1942, the aircraft carrier USS *Hornet* steamed out of San Francisco Bay with sixteen B-25s strapped to its deck. Of the eighty Army airmen destined to fly the bombers, all but five remained ignorant as to their ultimate objective. As the West Coast of the United States disappeared from view, Brick Holstrom heard the ship's loudspeakers crackle to life. "Now hear this. Now hear this," the captain's voice boomed. "This force is bound for Tokyo!" The cheers of two thousand men suddenly thundered from bow to stern of the eight-hundred-foot-long vessel. More cheers rose from across the water as the message reached the other ships of the task force via semaphore.[18]

Later that day Lieutenant Colonel Doolittle called his bomber crews together in the mess hall. "We're going to bomb Tokyo, Yokohama, Osaka,

Kobe, and Nagoya," he told them. He let the news sink in. Alongside elation, a new anxiety filled the Army fliers: They would be the instrument of revenge against Japan. Their strike would be the first to hit the enemy homeland since Pearl Harbor. "We've made arrangements to land at small Chinese airfields not far inland," Doolittle continued. "We'll gas up as quickly as we can and then fly on to Chongqing."[19] Listening to the briefing, Brick could not then have predicted the drama of bailing out in the dark and rain over China, of being rescued by farmers and guerrillas. Nor could he imagine he would remain there another fourteen months, receiving a spot promotion to major and command of a bomber squadron. Before any of that, one of the most dramatic combat missions of World War II lay ahead of him.

The eighty Army airmen spent the intervening weeks aboard the *Hornet* studying target intelligence, pouring over old maps of Japan and China, and losing frequent poker games to their Navy hosts. They planned to take off five hundred miles east of Tokyo on the evening of April 18. That would put them over Japan in darkness and over China in daylight. On the morning of the eighteenth, Brick was sitting in his stateroom below decks when he suddenly heard the deep rumble of naval gunfire followed immediately by the blaring of a klaxon horn. A voice boomed from the loudspeaker: "Army pilots, man your planes!"

He scrambled through the bowels of the ship to reach the flight deck.

"What's going on?" he asked an ensign rushing by through the passageway.

"I don't know," came the brusque reply, "I think they're firing at a submarine!"

He emerged on deck to find the carrier turning into the wind, plowing through rain squalls and pounding waves. A Japanese picket boat had spotted the task force and alerted Tokyo; Doolittle's bombers would have to take off 250 miles farther east than planned. Brick was not happy; the early launch meant his B-25 would arrive over Japan in broad daylight. It also meant he might not have enough fuel to make it to China. His crew quickly stocked the bomber with ten extra 5-gallon cans of gasoline, but as he ran the numbers in his head, the extra distance plus a stiff headwind still brought them up short. "What the hell do we do now?" he contemplated bitterly.

Brick had no misgivings about the takeoff, at least. He had faith in Doolittle and watched as the legendary airman's bomber lifted off the pitching deck at 8:25 a.m., followed by Travis Hoover and Bob Gray. Brick thought

Doolittle's Raid   31

they all appeared to be a little too nose high.

He taxied into position for his turn. Everything went exactly as briefed: feet on the brakes, flaps full down, yoke back, elevator trim full aft. He gave a thumbs-up to the signal officer, who began to wave a checkered flag in a circle above his head, first slowly, then faster and faster. Following the signal, Brick gradually brought the throttles up to full power. The roar of the two Wright Twin Cyclones built to a crescendo until it reverberated in his spine. As the deck began its upward swing, the signal officer dropped to his knee, flag pointing toward the bow. Brick released his brakes and the bomber surged forward. The takeoff proved to be much easier than his training flights at Eglin Field. He quickly discovered why Doolittle, Hoover, and Gray had been nose high; with fifty knots of wind across the deck, the B-25 did not need full aft elevator trim. As his bomber leapt into the air at about eight thirty, Brick had to quickly lower the nose to keep from stalling.

Once safely away, Brick turned the airplane over to his copilot and got out of his seat to confer with 1st Lt Harry McCool, the navigator. Together they studied the maps and evaluated their fuel. They figured their tanks would run dry about a hundred miles short of the China coast. To add to their difficulty, the gunner informed them that a hydraulic leak had rendered their top turret useless.

As the bomber winged its way low over Sagami Bay, just southwest of Tokyo, Brick suddenly saw seven Japanese fighters coming at them. He broke under the first pair and saw tracers zip by over the cockpit. The copilot pointed out two more preparing to attack, but as Brick broke into them, another struck from above and behind; he could see its rifle-caliber bullets raking the left wing. Without a turret, his crew had no way to defend themselves. And with a full load of bombs still aboard, they had no chance of getting away.

"The hell with this!" Brick exclaimed over the intercom. He ordered the bombardier to salvo their bombs into the bay while he took evasive action. "If we can get to China, we will live to fight another day," he told himself; "hopefully with better odds." They sped away, the only one out of sixteen B-25s not to strike the Japanese homeland.

Brick dropped to a mere 150 feet above the East China Sea. The wind shifted to aid their progress, but visibility dropped to nearly nothing as it began to rain furiously in the deepening twilight. His crew made ready to ditch, donning life jackets and preparing the raft. Then an island appeared suddenly out of the storm. Brick jinked to avoid it. McCool suggested they

32 FALLEN TIGERS

climb to six thousand feet to avoid any terrain in case they crossed the coast.

"I think we are over land," he offered helpfully a few minutes later.

"I hope you're right," Brick thought to himself. As the fuel gauges hovered on empty, he ordered the crew to prepare to bail out. "Okay," he instructed them, "when I get up, you guys get out and I'll be right behind you."

Shortly thereafter, one engine sputtered and died, starved of fuel. The crew removed the escape hatch, and Brick crouched to get out of his seat. The left wing dropped instantly. Apparently he had not done a great job of trimming the airplane for level flight. He quickly sat back down and straightened it out. By the time he looked back again, his entire crew had vanished! He scrambled back through the hatch as fast as he could manage. The parachute blossomed over his head, he swung once, and then hit the ground. In the dark and rain, he pulled out the pint of whiskey issued to him on the *Hornet* and drank it all. Then, shivering, he wrapped himself in his parachute to wait out the night.[20]

Fifteen of the bombers managed to reach China that night; one crew proceeded to the Soviet Union instead and landed safely at Vladivostok. The Soviets interred them for thirteen months before they eventually escaped to Iran. The other seventy-five airmen descended on Zhejiang, Jiangxi, and Anhui Provinces, completely unanticipated by the local Chinese or even Chennault and his Flying Tigers; Lt Gen Henry H. "Hap" Arnold, commanding general of the Army Air Forces, thought Chennault too close with Chiang to trust with details of the raid. Army chief of staff Gen George C. Marshall informed Stilwell in the vaguest possible terms so he could prepare airfields near Quzhou to receive the bombers. But Stilwell, preoccupied with the disastrous campaign in Burma, gave it little priority, assigning the project to two officers whom he forbade to communicate with Chennault or the Chinese. This lack of trust resulted in none of the fields broadcasting on their assigned radio frequencies. Consequently, not a single one of Doolittle's bombers landed safely in China.

Eight of the aircraft, including Brick's, crashed not far from friendly airfields. Two others passed well beyond them. Had Stilwell's men succeeded in setting up the radio beacons or had the raiders arrived over China in daylight, as originally planned, it is likely at least those ten could have made it. The crew of the last B-25 to lift off from the *Hornet* bailed out near Nanchang, 180 miles beyond Quzhou. Collaborationist troops reportedly captured those five airmen and delivered them to the Japanese. Three more from the sixth bomb-

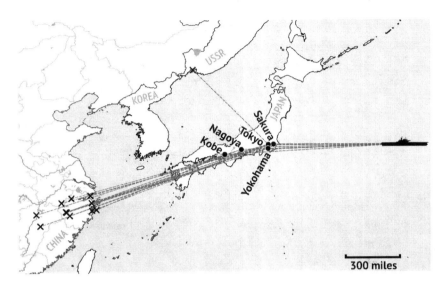

The Doolittle Raid

er fell into enemy hands, and a total of three others died in crashing or bailing out. Without warning or preparation, the Chinese rescued the remaining sixty-four.[21]

Chennault later complained that had he known about the raid, a single AVG radioman could have talked the bombers into friendly fields with the aid of the warning net. He felt betrayed by the lack of trust exhibited by Arnold, Marshall, and Stilwell. It made little sense considering his recent return to active duty in the US Army; he had received word of his promotion from captain to the temporary grade of colonel on April 9. The blatant show of mistrust, along with other slights that followed it, engendered a bitterness that came to define Chennault's relationship with his military superiors.[22]

As dawn broke on April 19, Brick Holstrom found himself isolated on a remote hillside. He kept to the highlands that day and the next, working his way westward. On the evening of the twentieth, he finally made contact with a group of farmers in a small mountain village. They gave him a bowl of rice and allowed him to stay the night. He noted the filth and unsanitary conditions of the place in his diary, though he later reflected he ought to have been grateful.

Brick continued west the next morning. A crowd followed him, and as he arrived at a larger village, they gathered around, talking excitedly. More appeared as if from nowhere until it seemed as if hundreds surrounded him. Aboard the *Hornet* he had learned a phrase to identify himself as an American, but the villagers did not seem to understand. Still, they did not appear to feel threatened and allowed him to pass the night there while they sent a messenger to alert nearby guerrillas. When the irregulars arrived, Brick tried to identify himself to their leader. He drew a map with flags and a figure with a parachute and motioned to himself, then he drew four more parachutes. The guerrilla captain seemed confused. Brick had to admit, the sketch looked pretty terrible! The leader sent out a runner, and they waited awkwardly until he returned with a magazine bearing a photo of Roosevelt on the cover. "Yes," the pilot nodded, gesturing between himself and the photograph, "he and I." That did the trick. The guerrillas soon delivered him to Shangrao, where the local Nationalist commander put him aboard a train for Quzhou, sixty-five miles to the northeast. Brick arrived early on the twenty-second.

Meanwhile, Doolittle's crew bailed out near Tianmu Mountain, one hundred miles north of Quzhou. Scattered in the jump, the five airmen reunited the next day at the headquarters of He Yangling, the Nationalist governor of western Zhejiang Province. After inspecting the wreckage of their bomber, they made their way south, escorted by the governor's secretary. They arrived at Quzhou on the twenty-sixth, helped along the way by a Baptist missionary named John Birch. The fiery young preacher had fled his church in Hangzhou following the outbreak of war between the United States and Japan. Ministering throughout unoccupied Zhejiang and Jiangxi Provinces, he came to hate the Japanese, seeing towns "destroyed several times over" by the crushing weight of their continual bombing raids. He had recently decided to volunteer his services to the US Army when he chanced upon Doolittle's crew. Birch asked the legendary aviator to recommend him up the chain of command.[23]

Doolittle did not remain in Quzhou for long; he and his crew departed for Chongqing the next day. Before he left, he put Brick and another pilot in charge of collecting stragglers. Birch acted as their interpreter.

For their part, the Japanese practiced terrible revenge for the violation of their homeland. They launched a punitive expedition that thoroughly destroyed the airfields near Quzhou and razed every village through which they believed the raiders had passed. In the process they slaughtered more than two hundred thousand men, women, and children. Troops of the Imperial Japanese Army not only killed those suspected of helping the Americans but

Doolittle's Raid   35

also annihilated their families and their villages.

Brick had given his leather jacket and wristwatch as souvenirs to the villagers who had helped him, not realizing the items meant death if discovered by enemy soldiers. Fortunately, the guerrilla captain who walked him out recognized the danger and collected the items to return to the pilot at Quzhou. This did not prove to be the case elsewhere; gifts left in goodwill to willing rescuers meant doom when discovered by Japanese troops. Remarkably, despite the high price ordinary Chinese civilians paid for the raid on Japan, the rescues of over seven hundred China-based American airmen took place after the Imperial Army concluded this punitive campaign. In other words, the Chinese knew the cost, but they chose to help anyway.

Brick Holstrom left Quzhou on May 3, just ahead of the advancing Japanese. He finally reached Chongqing eleven days later, traveling across the country by train, truck, and airplane. On May 19, a Douglas DC-3 carried him over the Hump to India. After surviving one of the most dramatic combat missions of World War II and then escaping the advance of a vengeful Japanese army, Brick looked forward to returning to the United States and reuniting with his beautiful wife.[24]

4

Enemy Occupation

April 8, 1942
Leiyun, China

Eleven-year-old Wu Eyang loved his idyllic life at the Central Aircraft Manufacturing Company factory in western Yunnan Province. The plant and its 2,650-foot-long gravel runway nestled into a nook of densely forested hills bounding the north end of a small plateau. Burma lay not even half a mile to the west, just across the slowly wending Nanwan River. Buddhist temples, their prominent, golden, Burmese-style spires stabbing skyward, topped a few of the nearby hills. More than two thousand Chinese workmen found employment at the bustling factory, including Wu's older brother, who had graduated from a Christian high school in Shanghai and spoke decent English. He managed to secure a job as a mechanic on the assembly line and brought the rest of the family with him. Wu's father served as head of non-military logistics and his two sisters became nursing assistants at the local hospital. Wu had little to do outside his elementary school studies though. "Life in Leiyun was peaceful and enjoyable," he recalled. "Like other eleven-year-olds, I was excited about the natural playground in the woods, hide-and-seek under the living quarters of the stilt houses of the Dai[1] people, and hot springs in the mountains."

Japanese bombs brought the fairytale crashing to an end on the afternoon of October 26, 1940. Without warning, thirty-five enemy warplanes appeared overhead. Amid the rain of bombs, as air raid sirens began to howl, Wu's older brother shouted for him to run and hide in the woods. Several bombs hit a few of the factory buildings south of the runway, but most slammed into the worker housing to the north. One fell only fifty feet from the hospital. When the attack ended and Wu emerged from the trees, he found a maelstrom of flame engulfing more than one hundred of the residences and a fresh bomb crater terrifyingly close to his own home. The raid left forty dead and sixty injured. From then on, the specter of another enemy attack loomed over the factory like a dark cloud.[2]

Then the P-40s of the American Volunteer Group arrived. "These swift planes will defeat the Japanese," Wu's older brother assured him confidently. The youngster found himself mesmerized by the incredible speed of the new machines and by the deafening roar of their Allison engines. He was proud to have them at his airfield. He wanted to see them fight.

The AVG had been fighting frantically for months in Burma—trying to stem the enemy tide. But despite their victories in the air, they could not singlehandedly prevent disaster on the ground. Paul Frillmann, the group's chaplain, led a convoy of ground personnel out of Rangoon before the city fell on March 6.[3] The aircraft retreated to Magwe, more than two hundred miles to the north, and then just across the border to Leiyun. The Japanese Army Air Force dogged them relentlessly. On April 8 and 10, the elite 64th Air Regiment[4] hit Leiyun hard with fighter sweeps by more than a score of its Ki-43 Hayabusas.

At twelve thirty on the afternoon of the eighth, the warning net reported numerous enemy planes heading toward the field. Nine P-40Bs and three newly arrived P-40Es quickly scrambled, climbing out to the south toward Lashio. R. T. Smith had just reached ten thousand feet when his radio erupted with a frantic call from the controller at Leiyun: "Enemy planes strafing the field!" Smith turned back immediately, diving toward the base at three hundred miles per hour.[5]

Wu Eyang's mother yelled for him to run and hide as eight Japanese fighters raced low over the field, machine guns blazing. Filled with giddy enthusiasm and an absolute faith that his side would triumph, Wu instead found a vantage point from which he could watch the air battle unfold overhead. "I was so excited to see one Japanese plane shot down," he explained. "This was real, you know, not like watching movie scenes today. After the sirens became silent and the American pilots returned, they were cheered by crowds and showered with beer."[6]

"We really mixed it up, dogfighting at very low altitude right over the field," Smith recorded in his diary. "It was the most thrilling experience I've ever had. The guys on the ground saw it all and are still raving. They say it looked just like a movie only better. Ha!"[7] In the course of its fighter sweeps, the 64th Air Regiment admitting losing six Hayabusas in two dogfights with the AVG, leaving behind just two P-40s destroyed on the ground and two RAF Hurricanes shot out of the sky. The Americans celebrated their lopsided victory, though they misidentified the army Oscars as navy Zeros.[8]

Unfortunately, the dogfights did nothing to stymie the relentless Japanese ground advance. As enemy troops neared Lashio—the linkage between the railroad from Rangoon and the road to China—panicked workmen at the factory began appropriating any vehicles they could find to evacuate their families and belongings.[9] Lashio fell on April 29; the AVG evacuated Leiyun just two days later. Wu Eyang escaped in a truck bound for Baoshan, arriving just in time to witness a devastating bombing raid on May 4. "Baoshan was like hell on earth," he recalled. "I witnessed some of the most horrific scenes that I will never forget, including a human arm hanging on a wire; a middle-aged woman whose waist was cut open by shrapnel, screaming for help; and a woman holding her baby burned to death inside a damaged vehicle."[10] The bombs hit right where the Burma Road passed through the densely populated city center, killing as many as ten thousand civilians. Among the dead was AVG pilot Ben Foshee, caught in the maelstrom while driving a truck full of equipment evacuated from Leiyun.[11]

Following the fleeing refugees, three regiments of the Japanese 56th Division surged across the border into China, advancing all the way to the steep gorge of the rapid, narrow Salween River, known to the Chinese as the Nujiang, or "Angry River." Only a frenetic series of airstrikes by the AVG and a courageous counterattack by two divisions of the Chinese Seventy-First Army stopped the enemy advance.

Lieutenant General Joseph W. Stilwell proved conspicuous by his absence as the crisis unfolded. In March, the generalissimo had given him three of his best armies to help the British defend Burma. Just two months later, those armies lay eviscerated, Burma had fallen into enemy hands, and Stilwell had gone missing, remaining incommunicado for weeks while he led his staff on foot through the jungles of Burma to India. China already lay at the end of a circuitous fifteen-thousand-mile supply line from the United States, snaking around Japan's conquests in the Pacific and Nazi armies in North Africa. With the capture of the Burma Road, its only remaining link to the outside world consisted of a tenuous airlift from India over the "Hump"—a perilous spur of mountain ranges jutting south from the Himalayas. With only seventy-seven tons of aid delivered in July 1942, the airlift's potential seemed limited.[12] No one knew how long such an emergency expedient could keep China in the war. Upon resurfacing in India, Stilwell immediately began planning to turn around and go back to the scene of his defeat. To break the blockade of China, he would build a road through north Burma.[13]

Caught in the chaotic fighting west of the Salween, a soldier named Pei Haiqing decided to desert the Nationalist Army. Conscripted from his home in Sichuan Province, he had fought with the Fifth Army, first in the defense of Guangxi in 1940, then against the Japanese drive through Burma into China in 1942. As his unit disintegrated in the futile fighting near Tengchong that May, Pei ran. For a poor, slight-framed boy torn from his home and thrown into a doomed battle, what choice existed but to run? Thousands like him deserted. Nothing so consummates hopelessness as the futility of fighting a losing battle.

Over the Gaoligong Mountains he fled as the summer rains gushed in torrents down the thickly wooded, steep, rugged slopes. The tide of Japanese conquest stopped at the base of the mountains on the west bank of the Salween. Pei stopped on the east bank and settled in a small village south of Liuku. He decided to become a fisherman. For two long years, a standoff ensued—the Japanese on the west bank, the Nationalists on the east. The enemy, though only one hundred yards away, could do nothing to Pei. Neither side could cross the perilous river in sufficient strength to challenge the other. Reminders of the war remained frequent, however. Pei often saw warplanes fly by, but he could never tell if they were Japanese or American.[14]

On the morning of October 17, 1943, four P-40s dove into the narrow canyon of the Nujiang to attack a Japanese encampment. Each fighter dropped a set of three 30-pound fragmentation bombs, followed by a five hundred-pound demolition bomb, and then another three frags. As the flight leader released his final volley, the triggering mechanism on the frags malfunctioned; they went off immediately, tearing off his right wing. Engulfed in flames, the fighter spiraled out of control until it hit the ground and exploded. The frags of the last airplane in the formation also prematurely detonated. The leader of the second element watched in horror as his flight leader crashed, then looked back to see his wingman tumbling through the air ablaze. He saw the fighter cartwheel into the river; he did not see a parachute. "I circled [the] target for five minutes and observed no special activity other than [the] plane burning in the river," he reported. He presumed both pilots had perished.[15]

40 FALLEN TIGERS

In fact, the wingman, 2nd Lt Francis Forbes, had managed to bail out of his stricken fighter—only to land on the wrong side of the river. For four days, the injured airman evaded capture on the Japanese-occupied west bank before finally deciding to try his luck at a dangerous river crossing. Buoying himself with a few pieces of bamboo flotsam, he set out.

Standing alone on the east bank, just a mile north of the Japanese camp, Pei suddenly saw the airman struggling in the water. It seemed he could not escape the war after all. He waded into the rapid, dangerous river and, though not even five feet tall, managed to drag the big American to shore. The exhausted pilot collapsed in front of his home, unconscious. Within minutes, Nationalist Army forces arrived to evacuate him. "They carried me until the American air force could get me and then I was brought into a base hospital," Forbes later dictated in a letter to his parents. "I was not hurt badly at all," he assured them, minimizing the extent of his injuries. "Just slight burns on the hands and face. They expect me to recover very quickly." Though Pei's encounter with the pilot lasted only a brief moment, it left an indelible impression. As a deserter from the Nationalist Army he seemed to epitomize the rotten decay that permeated much of wartime China. But something about saving a fallen airman created hope, where before, defeat after defeat had caused utter hopelessness.[16]

Meanwhile, the Japanese consolidated their gains on the battlefields Pei and his comrades had deserted. On May 10, 1942, a column of three hundred troops approached the city of Tengchong. The storied old trading center, once visited by Marco Polo, lay astride the ancient caravan route to Burma and featured markets famous for their jade and gems. With twenty thousand inhabitants, it was the largest population center west of the Salween. It had served as a remote frontier outpost since the late thirteenth century, occupying a mountain valley 5,500 feet above sea level. Still surrounded by its imposing medieval stone wall, the town made a neat square in the valley, its four corners pointing like a compass in the cardinal directions. The wall stood over thirty feet tall and twenty feet thick, each face almost a mile in length.

Lu Caiwen grew up near the wall and climbed it many times as a child. From it, he watched as the column of troops approached the city, the population of which had swollen with wounded soldiers and desperate civilians fleeing from Burma. Long Shengwu, superintendent of the Tengchong Frontier Zone and son of Long Yun, the notorious warlord and provincial governor, had three battalions of provincial troops at his disposal. He ordered

Enemy Occupation   41

them to retreat. They looted all the jade, silk, opium, and artwork they could carry and then departed. The people felt betrayed by these "warlord soldiers," who had bullied and taxed them but, when the enemy arrived, disappeared without firing a shot.

As he lay atop the wall, Lu could hear gunfire and shouting. He felt paralyzed, unsure of what to do or where to hide. Then he saw them: soldiers carrying long rifles tipped with gleaming bayonets, steel helmets atop their heads. "Chinese soldiers don't wear steel helmets," he realized. "The Japanese are here."[17]

Many of the city's residents fled; Lu escaped into the mountains to the north. Japanese soldiers terrorized the countryside in their wake, plundering rural villages of rice and grain and taking any chickens, cows, and pigs they could find. They tortured and killed anyone they suspected as guerrillas or spies and many others besides. In Tengchong County alone, the Japanese murdered more than thirteen thousand civilians, burned down more than twenty thousand homes, and stole more than sixty thousand tons of grain and fifty thousand livestock. They conscripted the men to build fortifications. They raped the women.[18] "In some of the districts through which I passed, every woman caught by the Japanese had been raped without exception," reported *Time* correspondent Theodore White. "The tales of rape were so sickeningly alike that they were monotonous unless they were relieved by some particular device of fiendishness."[19]

Ruthless exploitation by the Imperial Japanese Army left its conquered territories completely devastated. Japan promised a program of Greater East Asian "co-prosperity," of "Asia for the Asians."[20] But its policy of "using the war to feed the war" destroyed any credibility or support such a program may have garnered. In carving out their own exclusive economic zone, the Japanese sought to insulate themselves from another Great Depression. The home islands would become the core of a new economic empire, consuming raw materials imported from the periphery and turning out manufactured goods. Lopsided policies that benefited Japan at the expense of its possessions, though, made it very evident to most that East Asian "co-prosperity" was only a façade for colonial control.[21]

The Japanese did not have the men or material to physically occupy the full extent of their conquests. Though often depicted covering vast areas, their occupation extended little beyond points and lines—strategic ports and cities and the roads, rivers, and railroads connecting them. In western

Europe, by contrast, the Nazis could depend on a much more robust transportation network to aid their occupation of an area less than a tenth as vast.[22] The Japanese sought to facilitate their rule of the space in between their points and lines by establishing collaborationist "puppet" regimes. They instituted one such regime for occupied Yunnan, headquartered in Longling, just as they had created other lackey administrations all across occupied China. Wang Jingwei, former premier of the Nationalist republic, led the most notable of these.

Like Wang, most politicians collaborating at the highest levels had been sidelined by the Nationalist government due to corruption, ineffectualness, or lack of clout. Still others were artifacts left over from defunct warlord regimes. Wang tried to turn this paradigm on its head, claiming himself to be the true heir to Nationalism and declaring Chiang to be nothing more than a regional military usurper in the remote southwest. His "Reorganized National Government of China," headquartered in Nanjing, even used the same flag as Chiang's, though with an added pennant bearing the slogan "peace, anticommunism, and construction." Yet Wang's government only existed with a rhetorical veneer of independence and did not possess any real authority over the multitude of other puppet administrations throughout the country. The Japanese believed in divide and conquer, even when it came to their supposed "allies."[23]

To augment their million-man garrison in China, the Imperial Army depended on large numbers of indigenous troops. The Nanjing government had its own regular army, though of course it remained under Japanese control in the field. Some Nationalist Army units defected wholesale—allegedly with the connivance of Chiang so as to preserve them for later use against the Communists.[24] Elsewhere, the Japanese hired bands of mercenary Chinese to police the countryside in "security brigades." These consisted of anything from local militias to secret societies and even bandit gangs that took advantage of Japanese backing to target rival criminals or plunder local elites.[25]

In the wake of defeat, occupied China thus became a confused intermingling of conquered and conqueror. Lines blurred between collaboration and resistance. Two hundred million Chinese lived under enemy occupation. Though some, like Lu Caiwen, managed to escape and join the Nationalists in exile, most lacked the means to evacuate ahead of the enemy advance— especially since that advance continued unabated for so long.[26] The very act of evacuation impoverished the evacuees and often made subsequent

Enemy Occupation   43

withdrawal impossible. The average Chinese did not have a choice whether to reach some sort of accommodation with the enemy. In many cases collaboration represented an acknowledgment of reality, a circumstance imposed by a lack of choice.[27]

Like Liu Zhenghua, the refugee-turned-officer from Hubei, Lu Caiwen attended the Central Military Academy in Kunming. He graduated as an intelligence officer and led a plainclothes intelligence team behind the lines back to Tengchong County. In the small village of Dadong, he met with Sun Zhengbang, the leader of a security brigade working for the puppet government. Sun's actions may have branded him a traitor, but Lu's contacts indicated he might be willing to work with the Nationalists. Japanese soldiers and puppet troops surrounded Sun's compound, and Lu had to sneak in barefoot for the surreptitious meeting. His heart raced. Coming face-to-face with Sun inside, Lu did not mince words. "The Chinese will one day return to Tengchong," he declared. "You're serving the Japanese; what kind of end will you come to? Think about your family, your property, your life. You cannot protect them!" Sun had probably cooperated with the Japanese for the very reason of safeguarding his family and property. But Lu spoke the truth; if the Nationalists returned, he could be tried as a traitor and possibly executed. He could hedge his bet by remaining in command of the security brigade while passing information to Lu's intelligence team. Sun agreed. Afterward, Lu still had to make it out of the compound. He crept past the guards, then stepped out into the street and walked casually away, expecting shouts or bullets to follow him at any moment. Nothing happened; none of the guards seemed to notice him. Relieved, he wiped the sweat from his forehead and set out to rejoin his team.[28]

As Lu discovered, collaboration proved to be anything but a black-and-white issue. Puppet regimes played an ambiguous role in the war, seeming to cooperate out of convenience, necessity, or pragmatism rather than ideological agreement with the enemy. Motivations ranged from the purely selfish to those desperately trying to prevent another disaster like the Rape of Nanjing. Either way, they found the cost of overt resistance too high.

There is considerable evidence some puppet troops carried out a racket whereby they sold their Japanese-issued weapons to the Communists.[29] Some have claimed Wang's regime secretly reveled in watching the Japanese bombed and strafed at Nanjing later in the war. They alleged that the reorganized government did not intend to resist the United States or the Guomindang, rather

44   FALLEN TIGERS

it served primarily to protect Chinese civilians in occupied regions. The Japanese apparently uncovered a plot by puppet troops in Nanjing to use their anti-aircraft guns to target Japanese, rather than American, warplanes. The Imperial Army promptly repossessed the weapons.[30]

In Tengchong County the occupation government actively undermined the Japanese. Most of the township heads also served as local schoolmasters; they paid lip service to the Japanese-mandated curriculum but secretly encouraged resistance. They developed pamphlets to aid in rescuing American airmen. More than a century of contact with British merchants and missionaries in nearby Burma had exposed many of Tengchong's residents to the English language. In fact, the region prided itself on its early efforts to reform its education system with an emphasis on Western sciences and English language instruction. The pamphlets included different ways to recognize American airmen and a list of helpful phrases. For those who could not speak English, they provided Chinese words with similar pronunciation. Second Lieutenant William Findley reportedly benefited from these pamphlets.[31] In February 1945, he became lost in poor weather while on a reconnaissance mission over northern Burma and managed to belly-land his F-5 Lightning in a paddy field near Jietou, thirty miles north of Tengchong. He had no idea of his location or the identity of the locals that suddenly surrounded him. Pulling a stack of blood chits from his escape kit, he held up one at a time in turn, each printed in a different language. The crowd stared blankly. Eventually, he held up the one covered in Chinese characters. The people began pointing and gesturing excitedly. "This was it!" he realized. He dug through his escape kit again, only to discover it did not contain a Chinese-language pointie-talkie. Fortunately for the young pilot, Yang Yinting, a landlord in nearby Jietou, managed to communicate with him using the pamphlets secretly distributed by the occupation government along with a Chinese-English dictionary.[32]

Missing aircrew, evasion, and intelligence reports contain surprisingly few instances of the Chinese turning over downed American airmen to the enemy. Collaborators purportedly betrayed the five Doolittle Raiders who bailed out near Nanchang, as well as four airmen from a B-25 that crash-landed near Hong Kong later in 1942. Puppet troops also picked up four members of a B-29 crew who bailed out sixty-five miles northwest of Nanjing in late 1944. They apparently had no intention of turning the men over to the enemy but inadvertently ran into a Japanese patrol while negotiating with the Communist New Fourth Army for the Americans' release. The Japanese in-

Enemy Occupation   45

sisted they take control of the prisoners and supposedly shot and killed one of the airmen when he resisted.[33] Remarkably, though, in early 1945, twenty-five puppet troops escorted three US Navy airmen out of Hong Kong and delivered them safely to Nationalist guerrillas.[34]

Ruthless self-policing at both the government and grassroots level probably helped account for relatively few instances of betrayal in China. After returning to American control in early 1945, 1st Lt Fred McGill reported that the Nationalist commander at Guhezhen, a small town fifty miles west of Nanjing, had ordered stern reprisals against anyone who failed to immediately bring him American airmen who went down in his sector. "I personally saw this order and know that General Bai threatened to obliterate any village which did not comply with it," McGill confirmed.[35]

Loyal townspeople recovered Capt Donald Burch when he crash-landed his P-40 near Yanshi, Henan Province, in September 1944. The villagers hid him in their homes and gave him a change of clothes and shaved his head to disguise his appearance. After two days of helping him evade capture, they brought him to a local official to facilitate his handover to Communist guerrillas. The official gave him over to the enemy instead. The guerrillas had offered a reward of $50,000CN (Chinese National currency) for the airman's recovery, but the Japanese offered $200,000CN. The official's betrayal provoked a visceral reaction from the enraged townspeople; they attacked and killed him when he returned to the village with his reward. The pilot spent the rest of the war as a prisoner, enduring beatings, interrogations, and malnutrition until finally liberated from a prison camp on the Japanese island of Hokkaido in September 1945.[36]

In July 1945 Chinese commandos trained by the US Office of Strategic Services (OSS) reported rescuing a downed airman from collaborators. The commandos had only recently parachuted in behind enemy lines near Hengyang. Local residents came to the hilltop temple serving as their base and reported the capture of 1st Lt Charlie Tapp by two men intending to sell him to the Japanese. The commandos immediately dispatched a fifty-man team to rescue the pilot and arrest the traitors. Sergeant Li Yuntang recalled both collaborators receiving death sentences for treason. He escorted them from the temple for their execution.

"See you in the afterlife," one of them remarked to him bitterly.

"Screw you," Li replied without pity. The commandos shot both men without ceremony.[37]

46   FALLEN TIGERS

It is certainly possible that collaborators betrayed or murdered some of the 418 airmen still listed as missing in action. However, sixteen of them are known to have already been in Japanese custody when they disappeared. Plotting the last known position of the others reveals as many as 175 lost at sea while transiting overwater or engaged in antishipping sweeps. Another eighty-one probably went down in the rugged terrain of mountainous Yunnan Province. Altogether, that accounts for 64 percent of those still listed as missing in the China Theater. It seems unlikely many of the remaining 146 survived their crash or bailout without any mention in American, Chinese, or Japanese records.

As compared to China, collaboration in Europe had a distinctly different character. After the war, Dr. Herman Bodson, a former Belgian resistance fighter, decided to make a scientific study of evasion. He found collaboration to have been an even greater obstacle to evading airmen than Nazi policing. Admittedly, the scope of the air war there was enough to overwhelm resistance networks. The US Army Air Forces reported twenty-three times as many aircraft lost on combat missions over western Europe as it did in China; yet only four times as many missing airmen there returned to Allied control.[38] In western Europe the Germans found many more ideological converts than did the Japanese in China. Though few welcomed outright Nazi occupation, not everyone disagreed with their politics. In nations still struggling with the economic and political malaise of the Depression, left-wing communism and right-wing authoritarianism vied for primacy. Many supporters of the latter respected Hitler's domestic agenda. Before the German invasion, the Netherlands even boasted a small but active Nazi Party of its own.

"I explored . . . the world of awakening against oppression, the world of rebellion that never stopped growing with occupation," wrote Bodson. "Sadly enough, I was also led to dig into the world of collaboration and treachery. . . . And sadder to say, I discovered fifty years after the fact, that those people had been far more numerous than those fighting for freedom." Such widespread collaboration existed that, after the war, Belgium's civil and military authorities found themselves inundated with more than four hundred thousand case files dealing with traitors.[39]

The Japanese did not have a domestic political program comparable to that of the Nazis. State-controlled Shintoism elevated the Japanese race and its godhead emperor above all others—even other East Asians. This racial chauvinism limited political and economic participation to an extent not felt in western

Europe.[40] Exclusivist racial politics and a brutally oppressive occupation thus made it extremely difficult for the Japanese to garner ideological converts.[41]

If the ambivalent, or even sympathetic, attitudes of collaborators confused the nature of occupied China, agents working for the Japanese did the same in so-called Free China. In January 1944 an assassin stabbed an inebriated American sergeant in the crowded streets of Kunming. Local authorities found him bleeding out by the side of the road and rushed him to the hospital. He died shortly thereafter.[42] On November 27, 1944, a Fourteenth Air Force intelligence officer reported signal fires in the shape of an arrow pointing toward the American airbase at Yunnanyi. The next night Japanese bombers raided the field.[43]

Similarly, 1st Lt Malcolm Rosholt, an intelligence officer in command of Dog Sugar Eight, a forward radio post at Changsha, reported an instance of a lantern less than one hundred yards east of his station guiding single-engine bombers onto his position. He and his men heard two such aircraft overhead but could not see them in the darkness. One of the Americans shot at the lantern, and it flicked out. Rosholt ordered everyone out of the post and into the slit trenches. As they ran across open ground, a third bomber roared overhead. "Take cover!" Rosholt yelled. Most of his men made it to the trenches, but the lieutenant could not get there in time. He jumped behind a low stone wall as the bomber strafed the area. "Please God, not yet," he prayed silently in desperation, clutching his legs to his body to make himself as small as possible. The attack ended as suddenly as it began; the bomber climbed away, and Rosholt's men rushed over to see that he had survived.[44]

In a country devastated by war and reeling from crushing poverty and hyperinflation, few found it surprising the Japanese could buy off some individuals. When a dozen Hayabusas ambushed two flights of P-38s on a river sweep near Jiujiang in October 1943, the Americans assumed some traitorous Chinese had leaked word of the mission.[45] Though this proved to be erroneous, it was telling that the knee-jerk reaction was to blame an imagined collaborator. The airmen found themselves in a country not only where enemy agents could assassinate their servicemen and light signal fires directing hostile bombers to their bases deep in "free" territory but also where partisans could smuggle out American airmen who crashed or bailed out deep in "occupied" territory—even from the most heavily garrisoned cities and towns. Somehow, in China every place was enemy territory and yet no place was enemy territory.

48   FALLEN TIGERS

Despite the ambiguous nature of the country—both occupied and free—the data clearly show an overwhelming number of downed American airmen rescued. A key example from Yunnan Province may help explain why. When an air raid alert went up at about 2:45 p.m. on December 26, 1942, the people of Xiangyun piled out of their shops and homes to watch. Japanese bombers had refrained from striking Kunming after the AVG had intercepted them a year before. Yet, as with the three bombers shot down by McMillan's flight in January 1942, they continued to probe Chennault's outlying defenses. This included the airfield at Yunnanyi, 130 miles west of Kunming. Xiangyun lay astride the Burma Road in the next valley west of the airfield. The villagers looked skyward in curiosity and wonder, unafraid of an enemy sent to bomb a military base ten miles distant; their small town featured nothing of interest to the Japanese airmen. They could hear the distant growl of engines as two flights of P-40s lifted off from Yunnanyi and took up station south of the field. Then at three o'clock the enemy formation hove into view: nine bombers, three elements of three, flying in a V of Vs, like a flock of mechanical geese. Ten blunt-nosed Hayabusa fighters flew escort. As the shark-mouthed P-40s dove into the fray, a lone fighter rocketed aloft from the dusty airfield, sailing past the other Americans to plunge into the enemy formation. The people talked excitedly as the melee sprawled across the sky above them.

"Look!" one of the villagers shouted, pointing to a Japanese fighter low over the town, squaring off for a head-to-head pass with the lone American. They watched as flames erupted from the wings of the Shark and the nose of the Oscar. A split second later the crackle of machine-gun fire reached their ears. Guns blazing, each pilot found his mark. The Japanese fighter exploded; the American began to smoke and sputter. The townspeople witnessed the P-40 plummet from the sky, its engine frozen, a plume of smoke trailing behind it. They could see the pilot had rolled back the canopy, but he did not jump. Why? They watched in horror, so riveted by the scene they could hardly move—even though the fighter could drop into their midst as soon as the pilot bailed out. But the American stayed with his aircraft, keeping it under control until clear of the town. The crowd saw the fighter disappear behind a hill, then a geyser of flame shot skyward as it impacted the ground. The spell suddenly broken, they ran pell-mell through fields of winter wheat toward the crash site.

They found the pilot lying in a cemetery, his body broken, his head bleeding from a gash where it had hit a gravestone. A half-opened parachute lay limply on the ground beside him. He could not have been more than four hundred feet above the ground when he had finally jumped. A few of the villagers rushed off and returned with a door torn from its hinges. Gently, they lifted the American aboard and carried him into town. An elder led them, dressed in a black cotton robe, a scraggly beard reaching to his chest. As they hurried along, a jeep roared up in a cloud of dust. An American pilot vaulted from the front passenger seat and joined the crowd of villagers. The old man led them to Dong Qiyuan, a local doctor who had attended a British medical school in Shanghai before the war.

The doctor examined the injured airman and found bruising around the gash on his head. "He has a concussion," he told the downed pilot's comrade. He pulled a medical book from its place on the shelf. "I need to give him an injection to counteract the effects," he said, pointing out the applicable section of the text. "I would like your permission to give it to him."

The American seemed reluctant. "Our flight surgeon went out to another crash," he explained. "I have no idea when he'll get here."

"This is urgent," the doctor pressed.

Anxiety showed in the pilot's tortured expression. He had no reason to distrust the doctor, who had attended a modern medical school and spoke fluent English. But without the flight surgeon on hand, he felt responsible for the ultimate fate of his friend. "Go ahead and give him the shot," he finally acquiesced.

The doctor's wife held the injured airman's tongue to keep it from blocking his airway; she sat with him for hours, cradling his head between her arms. He died just before midnight. Ten minutes later, the flight surgeon arrived. The other pilot explained what had happened, distraught at perhaps having done the wrong thing in authorizing the injection. "It was the only thing you could do," the surgeon reassured him.[46]

The denizens of Xiangyun felt profound sadness at the death of a man they had never known. His name, they learned, was 1st Lt Robert Mooney, an aggressive young fighter pilot from Kansas City, Missouri. The Chinese people already felt genuine gratitude for the Americans who came to their country to fight the Japanese. But Mooney had done something different and wholly unexpected. He could have bailed out over the town, saving himself and leaving his fighter to crash into the watching crowd—killing dozens of them—and they still would have hailed him as a hero. But he did not. Mooney stayed with his stricken plane, valuing the villagers' lives above his own.

50   FALLEN TIGERS

In wartime China the value of an individual human life did not seem to matter in the slightest. The Imperial Japanese Army certainly did not care about the lives of Chinese civilians, as evidenced by the great slaughters it carried out at Shanghai and Nanjing and by its campaign of terror bombing deliberately directed at the civilian population. Yet even China's own leadership seemed to prize the collective over the individual. When Chiang ordered the Yellow River dams breached to halt the enemy advance in north China, the resulting floods killed at least half a million of his own people and displaced millions more.[47]

The people of Xiangyun took up a collection. Five months after the tragic combat, they invited the pilots of Mooney's squadron to a ceremony; at the intersection of the Burma Road and the highway to Dali, they unveiled a monument to the deceased hero. It stood twelve feet tall, a monolith atop which sat a five-pointed star of the same design that decorated the wings and fuselages of American fighters. Four panels at the base exhibited a carved portrait of Lieutenant Mooney and recounted his sacrifice in both English and Chinese.[48] The ceremony proved an emotional event for villagers and airmen alike. In that moment, Mooney's comrades glimpsed what their shark-mouthed fighters symbolized to the Chinese, what they themselves symbolized. American politicians and generals forged the policy that sent them to China. American industry produced the aircraft they flew. American taxpayers funded it: $49,449 for each Curtiss P-40 Warhawk.[49] But to the Chinese people, the airmen who animated those machines epitomized America itself—values, policies, and weapon personified.

What began with the AVG's plucky defense of Kunming in December 1941 quickly spread. Across the length and breadth of China, the Americans made evident their daring with mighty proofs: staging audacious raids on heavily defended and seemingly inaccessible targets such as Hong Kong, Taiwan,[50] and Shanghai. The morale boost from these raids should not be underestimated. To the inhabitants of embattled China, the sight of American planes aggressively taking the fight to their shared enemy rekindled a hope they had barely dared to whisper during the years of Japanese ascendancy. In the United States the shark-mouthed fighters of the Flying Tigers came to symbolize vengeance for Pearl Harbor. Most Americans did not realize the much deeper emotional impact sparked by the arrival of Allied warplanes in China. In the remote interior of Japan's wartime empire, American aircraft and American airmen became the irrefutable proof Japan had not won and that resistance continued.

"The ruthless bombardment of our unfortified cities by the Japanese have been fortunately and effectively checked by your highly esteemed Air Force," the citizens of a district in Guizhou Province wrote to Chennault in August 1942. "Your brilliant and unsurpassed bravery has not only driven the Japs into the sea and killed them in the air, but also signaled the final victory of the United Nations."[51]

Before the arrival of the Americans, Japanese army and navy air forces maintained complete air supremacy. The Chinese Air Force lay in ruins. The Nationalist Army did not have the means to push back the invaders. Millions of refugees fled in terror and lived in squalor, ever fearful of coming under the guns of enemy planes as they ranged across the country unopposed. "The Japanese had full advantage in the air. They were extremely arrogant," recalled Lu Caiwen, the refugee–turned–intelligence officer from Yunnan. "They occupied the entire sky. The sky," he reiterated, "was entirely their territory. After the Flying Tigers came, the sky was *our* territory."[52]

5

China Air Task Force

June 3, 1942
Dinjan, India

Forty-one airmen walked to the flight line through spitting rain. Six B-25s, parked wingtip to wingtip, waited motionless in the predawn darkness for the men who would animate them. Their flight that day signified the culmination of a fifteen-thousand-mile journey from the far side of the world; in April 1942, as the *Hornet* bore Jimmy Doolittle's bombers west toward Tokyo, another twenty-six B-25s prepared to depart Morrison Field, West Palm Beach, Florida, in the opposite direction—across the Atlantic, sub-Saharan Africa, and the Middle East—to India. Originally designated Project 157, the first flight of six now formed the recently reactivated 11th Bomb Squadron, under the command of Maj Gordon "Gordie" Leland, a gung-ho West Point graduate eager to get into combat. Theirs would be the first US Army warplanes in China—the promised offensive punch to augment Claire Chennault's volunteer fighter group. The perilous mountain ranges of the Hump remained their only obstacle.

Twenty-two veterans of the raid on Japan eventually joined the newly reconstituted squadron. By early June almost half the rescued airmen had already left the China-Burma-India (CBI) Theater. Fearing itself short of bomber crews, Tenth Air Force received permission from the War Department to hold on to the rest. Since Doolittle had left him in charge of collecting stragglers at Quzhou, 1st Lt Everett W. "Brick" Holstrom found himself caught in this embargo. He remained at Karachi for the time being, but five other raiders joined Leland's thirty-six airmen to ferry the first B-25s to China.[1]

With his crew and extra passenger, 1st Lt Robert Klemann readied his B-25C, "Texas Tornado," for takeoff. He had been trying to get into the war since before Pearl Harbor, even going so far as to sign up for a second American

China Air Task Force   53

Volunteer Group (AVG)—all to no avail. The Japanese attacked Hawaii before the group got underway and Klemann found himself back in the Army Air Forces awaiting reassignment. He felt relieved and excited to finally get a chance to see some action with the 11th Bomb Squadron.

Klemann had assumed they would fly directly over the Hump to Kunming. Since the Japanese conquest of Burma, DC-3s from the China National Aviation Corporation (CNAC), a subsidiary of Pan American, had been flying fuel and cargo over the mountains to relieve the blockade. A small contingent of US Army Air Force transports had only recently joined them. After arriving at Dinjan on the evening of June 2, Major Leland conferred with Col Caleb V. Haynes, the officer in charge of the airlift. Returning to his men, the major informed them they would bomb the airfield at Lashio on their way to China the next morning. Japanese fighters had been using the field to harass Allied transports on their supply runs. The bomber crews would get their first licks in at the Japanese on their first flight in theater.

The crews scrambled to throw together a last-minute plan. They would make a minimum-altitude attack, each aircraft carrying six 500-pound bombs in addition to baggage, tools, spare parts, and extra crew members. The diversion turned a five-hundred-mile direct course into a seven-hundred-mile dogleg, putting the overloaded bombers at the edge of their range. They used what maps they had, but much of the flight would take them over literally uncharted territory. The intelligence officer at Dinjan briefed them that the terrain between Lashio and Kunming reached up to nine thousand feet above sea level. Leland's men planned to fly that leg at eleven thousand feet to remain well clear.

The added complexity unnerved Klemann. A simple ferry flight had suddenly turned into a short-notice, unescorted, low-altitude attack on an enemy fighter base in unfamiliar terrain at the edge of their bomber's range on their first mission in theater. But Leland pressed them enthusiastically. They would arrive in China as the nucleus of a new American strike force after having flown fifteen thousand miles from the United States and having already hit the Japanese with a surprise raid, making the airlift route safer by striking the enemy's forward airfield. The plan represented the kind of audacious thinking that, if it succeeded, Army Air Force leaders would hail as bold and inventive.

As the men readied their ships that morning, the weather injected an extra layer of complexity; the spitting rain portended something far worse farther east. A few of the CNAC pilots recommended the bomber crews wait

54   FALLEN TIGERS

a day for the storm to pass. Leland ignored them. What did a bunch of broken-down old transport pilots know about tactical military aviation?

The rising whine of inertial starters soon broke the morning calm, giving way to the coughing, stuttering splutter of fourteen cylinders on each of twelve Wright Twin Cyclone engines. The surrounding tea plantations reverberated with a low rumble, gradually building to a full-throated roar as the bombers rolled down the field at six o'clock. Within minutes the sound faded, and silence reigned over the countryside once more.

The six bombers winged southeast in two flights of three. Major Leland led the first flight; Klemann flew in the number three position off his right wing. The second flight formed up behind and to the right of the first. They maintained strict radio silence. The weather continued to thicken so that by the time they were forty-five minutes out of Dinjan, they had to fly completely on instruments.

"This is eerie, flying blind," thought Klemann. He stayed glued to the commander's wing, holding tight formation to keep from losing him in the mist. Suspended in cloud, with Leland's bomber as his only reference, the lieutenant could easily become disoriented. His body could play tricks on him, making him unsure whether he flew level or in a turn. He glanced at his instruments to calibrate himself. They must be close to the target; he noticed his altimeter unwinding through five thousand feet as they descended. He also noted his fuel gauges dropping at an alarming rate; all this throttle jockeying to stay in close formation used up a lot of gas. The glance inside lasted only a moment, and his eyes returned to their vigil out the left window. Major Leland's bomber remained fixed there, slightly indistinct in the soupy whiteness. Then the lush green of the hilly Burmese jungle, first in spasmodic glimpses, then in totality, emerged from beneath the ragged clouds. Only five bombers appeared; 1st Lt Bill Gross, flying the last airplane in the second element, must have lost the others in the weather.

"There!" the copilot tapped Klemann on the shoulder, motioning to the airfield off their right wing. Leland must have seen it too; he banked hard to line up on the target. Inside the major's turn, Klemann dove and banked tight, throwing the throttles forward to keep from stalling out and spinning in. Their wings practically overlapped as they lined up for the bomb run. On cue from the commander, the five B-25s opened bomb bay doors, overflying the airfield at fifteen hundred feet and laying their five-hundred-pound bombs along its length. Two fixed-gear fighters scrambled from the field and gave chase. Le-

China Air Task Force   55

land turned eastbound and climbed. Just before the five ships reentered the weather, Gross's crew in the missing sixth bomber appeared far behind them to make its attack alone. The fighters turned to intercept this new intruder.

Meanwhile, the five continued up to eleven thousand feet in and out of broken clouds. Worried about his fuel consumption and remembering the near disaster of being too close inside Leland's turn on the approach to Lashio, Klemann edged out to the right to give himself more room to maneuver. As they plunged once more into the thick white veil, he found he could barely see the major's airplane to his left—a mere shadow in the mist.

The flight became tedious, cruising at eleven thousand feet, in the weather, maintaining formation off the indistinct impression of his commander's bomber. Then, in an instant, the shadow turned to a flash of orange light, followed quickly by another. Something like distant thunder buffeted his airplane. In that same instant the copilot punched Klemann's shoulder and pointed to a blur of rocks, scrub, and trees whizzing by underneath the wing. He pulled back violently on the yoke, clearing the top of the unexpected mountain by mere feet. Then nothing again—whiteness. His heart pounded. Continuing the climb, he soon broke out into blue, sunlit skies.

It took Klemann a moment to fully register what had happened. Leland, his crew, and the men flying in the bomber on the major's left wing were all gone. Unbeknownst to him at the time, the leader of the second element had also crashed—a total of twenty-one airmen lost in a split second. Their charts and briefing had it all wrong; several mountain ranges between Lashio and Kunming rose above nine thousand feet. In fact, a direct route threaded the needle between two massive peaks over eleven thousand feet tall. Twelve miles north of their course stood Great Snow Mountain at 11,482 feet, while only three miles to the south, Red Flower Mountain rose to 11,220 feet. Three miles is no great distance considering the bombers flew in the weather, without navigation aids, on a dead-reckoning course for Kunming.

Weather and terrain made for a deadly combination. At the time, much of China's remote interior remained unmapped. Crude aeronautical charts often depicted a river or lake where airmen found none—or found several. Terrain elevation could be missing or misrepresented by thousands of feet. "Any resemblance between those maps and the terrain would be a coincidence," declared AVG pilot Tex Hill.[2] Poor weather frequently made it much worse; a common motif in Chinese landscape paintings shows precipitous mountains enshrouded in clouds and mist, imagery that engenders awe in the casual ob-

56 FALLEN TIGERS

server but, from a knowing airman, elicits a sharp draw of breath through the teeth. Throughout the war, weather-related incidents accounted for at least 108 combat aircraft reported missing in the China Theater, only twenty-five fewer than fell to enemy planes. After surface-to-air fire and enemy aircraft, weather represented the third deadliest adversary, accounting for the loss of almost 16 percent of all aircraft types and more than one in four B-25s.

"Texas Tornado" flew alone in the burning blue, an unbroken field of white stretching to the horizon in every direction. Silhouetted against the clouds out ahead, Klemann caught sight of "Yokohama Express," the only other survivor of their encounter with the mountain. He began to follow it, but after a few minutes, his navigator, 1st Lt Alton Peck, climbed into the cockpit.

"Do you want to go with them, or do you want to go to Kunming?" Peck asked sardonically.

"Well Peck," Klemann replied, "you got us this far from the States; just tell me where to go." The navigator gave him a new heading, and they soon lost sight of the other plane as they plunged into a bank of clouds.

Before long the sky grew ominously dark and the fuel gauges hovered on empty. Peck climbed back into the cockpit.

"We should be over Kunming," he informed the pilots. "Find a hole in the clouds."

"What if we're not?" Klemann shot back.

"Then it's up to you," he retorted wryly.

Klemann found a hole and let through to find the city of Kunming directly beneath them. Ignoring any other traffic, he made a straight-in approach to the single runway. As he taxied clear, the engines coughed and died, starved of fuel. The seven crewmen climbed out through the fore and aft hatches to find another B-25 landing and taxiing toward them. It turned out to be Gross's bomber, which had made its run on Lashio alone after losing the rest of the formation en route from Dinjan.[3] The two Japanese fighters that scrambled from the field had filled it full of holes. One broke away after Staff Sgt James Burge hit it with a burst of fire from the top turret. The other persisted; in a thirty-minute running battle, it made attack after attack, hitting and killing Sgt Wilmer Zeuske, lying in the tail to operate the finicky, remote-controlled ventral guns.

They saw no sign of "Yokohama Express." The pilot, 1st Lt Johnny Ruse, ordered his crew to abandon ship when it ran out of gas fifty miles north

China Air Task Force 57

of Kunming. The men walked in with the help of Chinese rescuers twelve days later.

General Chennault grilled Klemann on all the details of the mission, understandably upset only one bomber out of six arrived at Kunming unscathed; Gross's ship required extensive repairs due to the damage inflicted by Japanese fighters. The utter stupidity of Leland's last-minute raid infuriated Brick Holstrom: "He lost all the damned airplanes!" he fumed. Brick knew most of the men lost in the awful tragedy; 1st Lt Bob Martin, one of the copilots, had been a classmate of his in pilot training and a close friend to him and his wife.

Six more B-25s arrived at Kunming over the next two weeks, all flying direct from Dinjan. Promoted to captain and appointed a flight leader, Brick accompanied the new squadron commander, Maj William E. Bayse, in a flight of three Mitchells crossing the Hump on June 16. Not all the Project 157 bombers went to the China Air Task Force (CATF), however; three never made it across Africa, and two remained on detached service in India. The remaining six formed the nucleus of the 22nd Bomb Squadron, the 11th's sister squadron based in India for operations in Burma. With little reinforcement, Chennault's bomber force remained pitifully small. It became further diminished when, in poor visibility, AVG pilot Freeman Ricketts mistook "Texas Tornado" for a Japanese bomber and shot it down thirty miles north of Lingling on July 15. Fortunately, Capt Joe Skeldon and his crew managed to bail out safely.[4]

Chennault found himself newly promoted as a brigadier general in charge of barely more than a couple squadrons' worth of airplanes. His task force boasted only forty-two worn-out and abused old P-40s and six B-25s— forty-eight planes arrayed against as many as 250 Japanese aircraft. The CATF reported to Brig Gen Clayton Bissell's Tenth Air Force, headquartered more than fifteen hundred miles away in New Delhi, India. Bissell and Chennault had known each other before the war and had an antagonistic relationship, constantly clashing over priorities, tactics, and administration. Chennault blamed him for the bungled reception of the Doolittle Raiders. And despite the AVG's notable successes against overwhelming odds, Bissell did not like the idea of a mercenary fighter unit defending China. He pressed to have the group inducted into the US Army.[5]

The AVG ceased to exist on July 4, 1942, replaced by the inexperienced and untested 23rd Fighter Group and one squadron of the 51st Fighter Group. In just over six months of operations since December 1941, the AVG

58 FALLEN TIGERS

had lost only fourteen aircraft in air-to-air combat and twenty-nine to ground fire, accident, navigation error, or malfunction. By contrast, US Army airmen in the Philippines, flying newer model P-40s, lost sixty-eight fighters—almost 60 percent of their fighter force—in the first three days of the war. The AVG claimed 297 Japanese aircraft destroyed,[6] whereas Army fighters in the Philippines only managed to down thirty.[7]

Only five AVG pilots accepted immediate induction into the Army. Chennault appointed three of them to command the squadrons of the 23rd: Maj Frank Schiel Jr. to the 74th Fighter Squadron, Maj Tex Hill to the 75th, and Maj Ed Rector to the 76th. Colonel Robert Lee Scott Jr., the colorful author of *God is My Copilot,* took charge of the group.[8]

Not a single pilot from the 3rd Pursuit Squadron accepted induction. Exhausted after more than six months in combat, they wanted to go home on leave before returning to the war. They also took offense to the Army only offering reserve commissions. When one pilot stood and told Bissell he wanted a regular commission, the slight-framed, sallow-faced general exploded in rage. Why did these damn civilians think they deserved special treatment? He rejected their demands outright. "For any of you who don't want to join the Army," he remarked acidly, "I can guarantee to have your draft boards waiting for you when you step down a gangplank onto US soil." That did it—not one man elected to stay.[9]

George McMillan hated to abandon Chennault but, weary like his comrades, emaciated at only 130 pounds, and still aching from the wound inflicted to his shoulder on Christmas Day, he went home. He wanted to see his four siblings, especially his brother Malcolm, soon to ship off to Maxwell Field for training, and his little sister, Sarah Elizabeth, now fifteen, whom he affectionately referred to as "Sissy." Mac reckoned she had "graduated from cotton to silk" in his absence. "Only wish it were possible for me to take a few days off and come home!" he penned in a handwritten note to his mother. "I've seen enough of this old world to last me quite a spell." Mac also had romance on his mind. He asked his mother to call Jean Guernsey and tell her he was okay. "Guess you remember meeting her at the station the day I left," he reminded her. "Damn sweet girl in my way of thinking. Maybe you'll get to know her better when I get home, ha!" He left China that July, a vice squadron leader with four and a half kills to his credit.[10]

The passing of the AVG made room for a new cast of characters around Chennault. Colonel Scott (Chennault called him "Scotty") originally arrived

China Air Task Force 59

in CBI in April 1942 as part of a strike force of eight heavy bombers and nine transport aircraft under the command of Colonel Haynes. Hardly had they landed at Karachi when they learned the Army Air Forces had reassigned the bombers elsewhere. Left with only their nine Douglas C-47s, Haynes and Scotty aided the Allied evacuation of Burma and, alongside CNAC, pioneered the airlift over the Hump. Both men longed for combat assignments. Scotty finagled his way into command of the 23rd Fighter Group, while Haynes took charge of Tenth Air Force's nascent armada of medium and heavy bombers. In October 1942 Bissell made him commander of the India Air Task Force, Chennault's counterpart on the other side of the Hump.[11]

Haynes's deputy, Col Merian C. Cooper, had to fend for himself. In April he flew to Chongqing to debrief the Doolittle Raiders and afterward composed a report for Gen Hap Arnold. He tried to put together a rescue mission for the crew captured near Nanchang, but to no avail, unfortunately. For weeks after that, he sat idly in Chongqing until it became clear he would have to do some finagling of his own to get involved in something interesting. Cooper had a talent for finagling, though, and a lifetime full of interesting adventures. Expelled from the US Naval Academy during his senior year in 1914, he nevertheless learned to fly and served as a bomber pilot with the Army Air Service during the Great War. Shot down over enemy territory, he spent the last six weeks of the conflict as a German prisoner. A year later he returned to action, founding a squadron of American volunteers to fly for the Polish Air Force in its war against the Soviet Union. Again, his plane went down behind enemy lines, but this time, after spending nearly nine months in a Soviet gulag, he managed to escape.

Cooper spent the interwar years first as a traveling correspondent, then as a documentary filmmaker. His greatest claim to fame, however, came from his time in Hollywood; Cooper conceived of, cowrote, coproduced, and directed the 1933 blockbuster *King Kong*, which shattered barriers in special effects. During the film's climactic scene, as the enormous ape clings to the top of the Empire State Building, Cooper himself is at the controls of the biplane that delivers the lethal burst of machine-gun fire. A close friend and confidant of both the commanding general of the Army Air Forces, Hap Arnold, and the director of the Office of Strategic Services, Col William "Wild Bill" Donovan, he had returned to military service in June 1941.[12]

Cooper arrived at Chennault's office in Chongqing at the beginning of August 1942, a bedroll under his arm, his untucked shirt stained with pipe ashes, and his unkempt hair ringing the bald spot on his head. "I want a job

60   FALLEN TIGERS

with an outfit that's fighting," he announced. Amused, Chennault made him his chief of staff, sensing in the forty-eight-year-old colonel the boundless energy and imaginative creativity that could make his badly outnumbered task force a formidable offensive instrument.[13]

As evidenced by his prewar writings and remarkable successes with the Chinese warning net and AVG, Chennault's expertise lay in defensive operations. Like any good fighter pilot, though, his heart yearned to go on the offensive. However, his task force did not possess enough equipment—quantitatively or qualitatively—to carry out a conventional air campaign. The later mission to Hankou, during which Glen Beneda and Lee Gregg both went missing on May 6, 1944, involved fifty-four airplanes—one of the largest aerial armadas ever assembled by the Americans in China. On that same day over western Europe, 336 heavy bombers and 185 fighters of the Eighth and Ninth Air Forces hit multiple targets across France.[14] In land warfare the weak can often offset the advantages of a more powerful adversary by resorting to guerrilla tactics. As unlikely as aerial guerrilla warfare sounds, airpower has many characteristics that are inherently irregular, such as tactical mobility in three dimensions and the employment of lightning raids on enemy positions.

Cooper helped Chennault refine a four-phase approach to this innovative mode of warfare: first, preparation; second, a strategic defensive to secure base areas; third, tentative expansion with offensive guerrilla raids; and fourth, a conventional air campaign to annihilate the enemy. Coincidentally, this four-phase approach proved remarkably similar to that of Chinese Communist leader Mao Zedong. With the creation of the warning net and construction of airfields throughout China, Chennault had largely accomplished the first phase before the United States even entered the war. The AVG carried out the second phase over Yunnan from December 1941 through the first half of 1942, rendering airfields there free from sustained Japanese bombing. By the time Cooper arrived in China, Chennault had set his task force to making pinprick raids on Hankou, Nanchang, Hai Phong, Guangzhou (Canton), and targets in north Burma.[15]

Strategically, Chennault's air force lay at the end of the world's longest supply line. Operationally, though, his airfields in China worked along interior lines of communication. This meant that while the Japanese operated on a broad arc from Manchuria to Indochina, the CATF could easily move its planes from one base to another in an aerial shell game that kept the enemy guessing. Chennault's warplanes could strike out from their string of fields at

Hengyang, Lingling, and Guilin in central China and then fall back to the relative safety of the interior when the enemy retaliated.[16] Owing to the subsequent lack of American planes at the forward fields, retaliatory attacks accomplished little more than to blow craters in gravel runways. After each of these raids, local workers quickly repaired the damage. China's advantage in manpower negated any damage the Japanese inflicted on its airfield infrastructure.[17]

Unlike ground-based guerrilla warfare, Chennault did not have to restrict himself to hitting soft targets on the periphery of Japan's East Asian domains. "No line of trenches, no geographical barrier, and no type of fixed fortifications can bar the operations of aircraft moving in the three dimensions of space," he had noted years before the war.[18] Rather than attack the fringe, he would use surprise and mobility to attack the center and therefore reach a level of efficiency—in terms of damage caused to the enemy versus the meager size of his force—impossible to attain in traditional guerrilla warfare.

In October 1942, Cooper set about planning the raid that would become the template for the greatest missions of America's China-based air forces: the first attack on occupied Hong Kong. Japanese warships and transports used Victoria Harbor as an important waystation en route to Southeast Asia and the Southwest Pacific. Intelligence predicted it would be packed with shipping.[19] This promised to be a mission as cinematic and full of drama as any of the legendary director's movies—Hong Kong instead of King Kong, this time with Cooper as the "guerrilla." Just like in the movie, it would be airplanes delivering the coup de grâce.

The colonel worked around the clock to perfect every detail. First, he built up a stockpile of ammunition, bombs, and gasoline at Guilin, in Guangxi Province, 470 miles east of Kunming. Supplies flown in over the Hump had to travel east by truck, train, and oxcart—a journey that often took weeks. To maintain the element of surprise, he planned for the strike force to fly a dog-leg course that passed west of Guangzhou, avoiding Tian He airdrome and other Japanese airfields in and around the city. The P-40s would need external fuel tanks to make the long round trip. Cooper maintained strict operational security, only providing details to a few key leaders and spreading misleading rumors throughout Guilin's bars and brothels. The fleet of nineteen warplanes staged through Guilin on the morning of the raid. Only then did Colonel Cooper and newly promoted Brigadier General Haynes brief the airmen on their mission.[20]

6

Hong Kong

October 25, 1942
Hong Kong, China

First Lieutenant Howard C. Allers piloted the last of the twelve B-25s on the big mission. Each flight of four maintained a tight diamond, with the three diamonds stacked up and back in a "javelin" formation. Brigadier General Caleb Haynes led the vanguard. Allers tucked in behind Brick Holstrom, his flight leader, as the low man at the tail end of the last diamond. He and most of his crew had arrived in the Far East with Project 157. Two crews on the mission, his and Wilmer McDowell's, actually hailed from the 22nd Bomb Squadron, then based in India. They had flown over the Hump to augment their sister squadron for this "maximum effort" mission.

Cruising at seventeen thousand feet, the formation reached its initial point seven miles north of Hong Kong. Allers kept in close as they turned toward the target. His crew functioned as a team, each man trusting the others to do their jobs. The copilot, 1st Lt Nick Marich, glanced over the engine instruments and then looked out the cockpit window: Not a single cloud marred the afternoon sky; no flak or fighters greeted them. Meanwhile, standing in the electrically powered upper turret, Sgt Paul Webb watched as two flights of P-40s carved gentle arcs through the air three thousand feet above them. He tracked the "Sharks" for a moment in his optical sight, then resumed his scan for enemy fighters. As his ship's engineer, he had a thorough knowledge of its systems, its engines, and its armament. Normally, he helped the copilot monitor the engines and fuel consumption and troubleshot mechanical issues. But when it came time to go into action, Webb manned the twin .50-cals in the Bendix turret. Similarly, Sgt Jim Young, the radio operator, left his compartment to man the .30-caliber gun mounted through a hole in the floor. (Since arriving in the China-Burma-India Theater, squadron armament crews had removed the clunky and unreliable remote-controlled bottom turret.) Though on his thirty-fifth mission, Young had never before flown as a member of Allers's crew. Neither had the navigator, 2nd Lt Murray Lewis. The only member of the crew not to have arrived in India with Project 157, Lewis was on his very first combat mission. From the navigator's compartment, he monitored their position in case they became separated from the formation. In the greenhouse nose of the bomber, 1st Lt Joe Cunningham waited to drop the bombs. This would be a formation drop; all twelve bombers would release with the lead aircraft.

The greenhouse gave Cunningham an excellent view as they approached Hong Kong. He did not see the promised convoy in the harbor—in fact, it looked completely empty. Haynes's ship adjusted course ever so slightly toward the docks at Kowloon instead. Anti-aircraft fire belatedly began to burst around them. Then Cunningham saw the lead bomber open its bomb bay doors. Reaching down to the handle on his left, he opened theirs. He quickly inspected the bomb control panel once again to make sure their five demolition bombs would salvo all at once, then moved his thumb over the release switch, just left of the Norden bombsight. There! He jammed down the button as the first bombs fell clear of the lead B-25. He felt his ship lift perceptibly and watched as the formation's thirty thousand pounds of demolition and nearly two thousand pounds of fragmentation bombs slammed into the docks and warehouses below.

Haynes began a left-hand, diving turn to break away from the anti-aircraft fire.

"Bandits ahead—Zeros! Eleven o'clock!" the radio erupted. Allers looked to his left, but Haynes abruptly reversed his turn in a steep bank to the right. At the end of the whip, Allers reacted quickly to maintain his position.

Marich, the copilot, saw at least a dozen Oscars in front of them now—the general had turned into them to spoil their attack![1] The enemy fighters began shooting at the lead flight and continued through the formation, firing as they passed. Two of them dove between Allers's ship and Brick Holstrom's in front of them, barely missing a collision. The air exploded with tracers as the bombers returned fire. Three groups of Japanese fighters—at least twenty-one in total—engaged the Americans, quickly overwhelming the small fighter escort. Marich watched as the disciplined enemy reformed and began making methodical, diving passes from out of the sun.

64   FALLEN TIGERS

"I've got six planes climbing and closing on us fast from about two o'clock," Webb announced over the intercom. He kept up a steady fire with his .50-cals, trying to track one of the fighters high and to his right. The turret could not move fast enough; the Oscar riddled the bomber with bullets from engine to tail.

Young fired with the .30-cal as the fighter passed underneath. A flickering glow caught the corner of his eye, and he stood from his gun to look out the side window. "The right engine is on fire!" he told the crew, the alarm in his voice carrying through on the intercom.

Marich looked at the engine instruments; the attack had severed an oil line. "The emergency system is working," he told Allers. "The engine is still working, but it's throwing oil. Pressure is zero." Allers watched grimly as they began to fall behind the rest of the formation. A swarm of fighters singled out their wounded bomber.

Seven Oscars attacked them now. In the nose, Cunningham fired his single .50-cal at one making a head-on pass. He could see his tracers pouring into it. Webb soon joined in from the top turret. Shot and shrapnel from the fighter hit all around the bombardier, bouncing off the armor plate. The enemy dove out to sea, smoking. Cunningham took the opportunity to change ammunition belts.

"Three enemy pursuits directly behind us!" Young's voice came over the intercom again. Webb slewed his turret aft and opened fire. A bullet blasted through, showering him with Plexiglas, and streaked down into Young's ammunition can. Powder and brass exploded everywhere. Three P-40s dove in to help the stricken bomber, but more Hayabusas piled into the dogfight; one of the Sharks fell away flaming.

The next attack hit the bomber's left engine, which quit immediately. The right engine continued sputtering for a time but soon gave out as well. Allers glided for land and told the crew to prepare to bail out. Three fighters followed them down, continuing to pelt them with machine-gun fire.

With both engines out, Webb no longer had power for the turret. He climbed down to find Young's .30-cal had jammed. The intercom was dead.

"What do you think about bailing out?" Young asked him. Webb glanced forward. They had no way to communicate with the four officers up front, and the bomber continued losing altitude fast.

"Let's jump," he confirmed.

The two sergeants helped each other into their parachutes and opened the rear hatch. The green-brown waters of the Pearl River raced beneath

Hong Kong   65

them. Young went first. Webb jumped after him and pulled his ripcord barely a thousand feet above the ground.

Meanwhile, as soon as Allers instructed them to prepare to bailout, Cunningham crawled back from the greenhouse into the navigator's compartment. Marich helped him don his parachute. Lewis, the young navigator, managed to pull on his own pack but could not seem to fasten the leg straps; Cunningham tried to lend him a hand. Marich looked back to the flight deck and saw they had less than two thousand feet of altitude. He noticed Allers lining up on a dry rice paddy.

"It's too late to bail!" he told the others. "Allers is going to crash land!"

They braced for impact. Allers set the B-25 down as gently as possibly, but the men bounced around the compartment as the airplane skidded to a halt. The four officers scrambled out through the escape hatch above the cockpit.

"We have to burn the plane," Allers insisted immediately. He walked to the nose, drew his .45-caliber pistol, and fired seven bullets into the Norden bombsight. Then shots began raining down from the sky and a blunt-nosed fighter roared overhead. All four airmen hit the deck. Bullets pinged off the aluminum skin of the airplane as two more Hayabusas strafed the wreck. Allers, Marich, Cunningham, and Lewis ran for some brush near the edge of the rice paddy, but the Japanese followed them with their guns, continuing to strafe for another fifteen minutes. Marich lost his pistol in the mad scramble; Allers took a bullet to his left foot.

Then the fighters disappeared. Cunningham ran back to the bomber and retrieved the first-aid kit. He also grabbed the bombing tables and threw them into a muddy ditch nearby. He returned to his comrades, and the three of them helped Allers hobble to a small village about four hundred yards away. A crowd gathered around them. The crew did not see any Japanese, so they paused to dress Allers's foot. Marich asked some of the villagers if they had a doctor, but none seemed to understand. With the foot bandaged, the Americans set out for the hills. Before long, a few villagers who spoke a little English caught up with them and offered to help—for a price. Later, this would have been a clear warning sign to an evader. Very few Chinese rescuers ever accepted money from American airmen: A third of evasion reports specifically mention Chinese refusing any sort of payment; only one in five describe rescuers accepting money, and many of those instances proved troublesome. The four officers had no idea, however, being the first China-based airmen to have

66   FALLEN TIGERS

gone down so far from a friendly airbase. Later, aircrews received extensive briefings from squadron intelligence officers and participated in late-night bull sessions in which they discussed what they would do if they went down. But Allers, Marich, Cunningham, and Lewis had no such preparation. Theirs would be the first test case.

Marich gave each of the men $1,000CN. The locals guided the four Americans to an old temple, where they exchanged jackets and flight suits for traditional Chinese garb. The villagers promised to take them upriver by boat later. While they waited, Cunningham purchased food and tea for another $1,600CN. A doctor arrived to look at Allers's foot.

Meanwhile, the two sergeants had landed in an irrigation ditch. Extricating themselves from the muck, they walked to a nearby village. A man there told them he would try to get them to Macau, still in the hands of neutral Portugal, on the opposite bank of the Pearl River. In the meantime, he needed them to hide in the brush along the water's edge. The men huddled there until dusk, when a young boy arrived and motioned for them to follow. He led them away from the bay up a dirt path into the countryside.

Back at the temple, Cunningham had become suspicious. One of their pistols had gone missing. He caught a villager trying to steal his wallet. Then a woman arrived, dressed in a fine silk gown. The locals showed her deference. "You will await the coming of Japanese authorities," she announced in clear English. "We intend to hold you here."

Not all the villagers were in accord, apparently. The moment she stepped out, an old man discretely drew a picture of a Japanese flag and motioned to indicate enemy soldiers nearby. Cunningham drew his .45—the only one the airmen had left. He brandished it as they exited the temple, threatening to shoot anyone who tried to stop them.

The four of them started for the mountains to the northeast. Allers's injured foot slowed them down and he became progressively more delirious from exhaustion and loss of blood. Before long, shots and yelling rang out from the village and they saw torches and flashlights moving toward them through the gathering night. The men took cover in some long grass on a steep ledge. One of the collaborators found them there and ran back for the main body of pursuers. Cunningham and Marich scrambled over the ledge and shouted for Allers and Lewis to follow; receiving no reply, they ran. Shots rang out from those in chase. Cunningham returned fire on the move and the two of them escaped into the night.

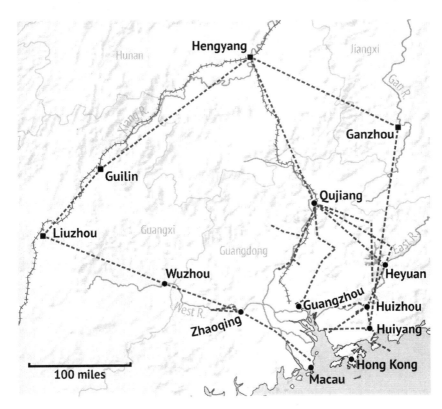

Evasion Ratlines from Hong Kong

In the meantime, Webb and Young continued to follow their young guide downhill along the path toward a small village. Suddenly, as they stepped through a brick gateway, four Japanese soldiers sprang from the shadows and surrounded them. The soldiers quickly disarmed the two and marched them with bayonets at their backs to a bombed-out house nearby. The sergeants found Allers and Lewis there, already in enemy custody. The four airmen then boarded a truck to begin their six-week stay in Guangzhou's city jail, where Japanese intelligence officers tortured and interrogated them before eventually sending them to the Jiangwan prisoner of war camp in Shanghai.

Marich and Cunningham continued moving into the interior for two days, dodging Japanese patrols, until finally they met a band of friendly guerrillas. These men refused their money. Their commander sent a squad to look

68   FALLEN TIGERS

for the other four crewmembers but could find no trace of them. The guerrillas escorted the two airmen to Waizhou, delivering them to Major Douglas Clague of the British Army Aid Group (BAAG), a unit from Military Intelligence Section 9 (MI9) established to help British soldiers and civilians escape Hong Kong after the Japanese conquest in December 1941. The group proved a boon to Chennault's airmen, running stations at Waizhou, Qujiang, and Wuzhou that became collecting points for nascent ratlines out of occupied Hong Kong and Guangzhou; every single evasion report in the archives for airmen who went down in this area mentions use of these lines. From Waizhou, Marich and Cunningham traveled by boat up the East River and then by truck and train to the American airbase at Guilin.[2]

The success of BAAG influenced the setup of America's own burgeoning evasion organization in China; Major A.R. Wichtrich arrived in late October to organize a local branch of Military Intelligence Service-X (MIS-X). Just as Britain's MI9 obscured the secret nature of its work in China by operating under the name BAAG, so Wichtrich decided to ambiguously title his organization the Air-Ground Aid Section (AGAS). Eventually numbering some three dozen personnel, several of whom could speak Chinese, Wichtrich's officers and men quickly spread throughout China, briefing airmen at their bases, and traveling behind the lines to establish safe areas, build ratlines, and hire local agents.[3]

The Hong Kong strike force lost two aircraft: Allers's bomber and a P-40 flown by 1st Lt Morton Sher. Like Marich and Cunningham, Sher successfully returned to friendly territory with the help of BAAG. The eleven remaining B-25s landed at Guilin and immediately loaded up for two night missions. In the first of these, six B-25s returned to Hong Kong to bomb the North Point power plant in CATF's first night raid of the war. "All of Hong Kong brightly lighted during the bombing run," the mission commander noted in his report. "All lights flashed out at the same instant as the bombs of the lead flight exploded on target. This would indicate direct hits on the objective—at least the main distribution and control station of the power plant." Three other bombers targeted gasoline storage tanks at Tian He airdrome in nearby Guangzhou. All nine aircraft returned to Guilin without incident and the strike force departed for the safety of Yunnan the next morning.[4]

Chennault optimistically informed Tenth Air Force headquarters that the raids on Hong Kong caused widespread damage to docks, warehouses, administrative buildings, the North Point power plant, and the China Gas

Company. "Two direct hits registered in [Whitfield] Barracks, more than one hundred Japanese soldiers killed," he added in a personal radiogram to Brig Gen Clayton Bissell.[5] Newsreels boasted, "American airplanes are striking at the enemy in China in ever-increasing numbers—white stars a familiar sight where once, only the rising sun of Japan was seen overhead." Audiences learned that the raids on Hong Kong had devastated harbor installations and shipping in an effort to "smash the Jap base."

Over the next several days, Japanese newspapers countered this narrative, claiming the Americans had merely "dropped a few bombs haphazardly when chased by Nipponese fighters." In response to Chennault's rosy appraisal of damage inflicted, the papers bragged: "As can be seen by the public themselves, all these stories are absolutely false. It can be seen that all the shipyards are continuing work as usual and that the electric system is still functioning." The raids "caused only slight damage to property but great suffering to the Chinese."[6]

A telegram sent to the Chinese National Military Commission by Cao Xingren, a liaison staff officer with the Seventh War Area, confirmed that bombs hit Hong Kong Island at Causeway Bay, Sai Wan, Stanley, and Deep Water Bay and on the Kowloon side at Tsim Sha Tsui, causing large fires and killing hundreds of people. "One of our aircraft was shot down during the battle," it continued. "Four of the crew were captured, but the other two escaped. Both of them arrived safely at Dongguan."[7]

In addition to facilitating the rescue of Cunningham, Marich, and Sher, BAAG produced its own intelligence assessment of the raids. The station at Waizhou reported that the Japanese issued no air raid warnings in advance of the attacks, nor did they enforce blackouts. "The raids could not be regarded as successful from the military point of view," the report continued, "of the main targets of the docks, power stations, gas works, as well as Whitfield Barracks; only Whitfield Barracks received successful hits." In spite of Japanese claims of great suffering inflicted on the Chinese, BAAG found that residents "took it that only military installations were targeted, except for strays."[8]

In Chennault's estimation the series of raids had the desired effect, demonstrating the increased reach and audacity of his small task force. Indeed, the Japanese Army Air Force wasted a good deal of effort maintaining standing fighter patrols over Hong Kong and bombing the empty airfield at Guilin. The mission provided extra impetus to the establishment of an evasion organization, as recovery of downed aircrews would become more of an issue as

70   FALLEN TIGERS

Chennault set his forces increasingly on the offensive. It also provided a template for even more audacious raids later in the war: On November 25, 1943, fourteen B-25s and fifteen long-range fighters would stage through Suichuan, 250 miles east of Guilin, for a Thanksgiving Day raid on Taiwan. The strike force would claim forty-six Japanese aircraft destroyed. On January 17, 1945, seventeen P-51 Mustangs would stage through Nancheng, an additional 150 miles east of Suichuan, for an attack on Shanghai, claiming seventy-three Japanese aircraft destroyed. Neither of these spectacular missions would result in any American losses.[9]

Lieutenant Colonel Clinton D. "Casey" Vincent, a staff officer stationed in Karachi, desperately wanted to get in on the action in China. The ambitious young West Point graduate had been destined for the Philippines as commander of the 35th Pursuit Group when the Pearl Harbor attack forced his ship to turn around. By the time he finally left the United States again aboard the USS *Mariposa* on January 12, 1942, the Japanese had cut off the Philippines, invaded Malaya, and besieged the Dutch East Indies. Casey ended up diverted to India where he became executive officer of the Karachi Air Base Training Center. He feared he would sit out the war behind a desk without having an opportunity to serve in combat and petitioned any general who would listen for a frontline assignment. He hated marking time in Karachi. "What a place!" he penned in his diary. "The wind blows hard all day and everything is covered with dust—at least everything in my tent is covered. The food is terrible." Good news finally came on October 1, when he received a letter from General Bissell telling him he would take over as Chennault's chief of staff. "Whoopee!" Casey wrote that evening.[10]

Of course, Chennault already had a chief of staff, Col Merian Cooper. It seemed Bissell wanted to push out Chennault's man in favor of his own—probably in an attempt to clean up the rough informality left behind by the AVG and replace it with some West Point discipline. Despite his group's effectiveness in combat, Chennault had earned a reputation at theater headquarters in New Delhi as a narrow-minded air-power enthusiast with only a tenuous grip on matters of staff, command, and logistics.[11] Inspections of his headquarters that fall catalogued a litany of discrepancies, citing violations of Army regulations for care, condition, and maintenance of arms, transportation, combat equipment, and personnel records. Officers and men apparently disregarded Army dress and appearance standards, including not wearing proper uniforms or shaving or bathing regularly. Brick Holstrom, who took

Hong Kong   71

command of the 11th Bomb Squadron that January and received a promotion to major in February, complained he did not even have paper for his required reports. "When you ran out of Form 1s on the airplane, you were out," he said. "The crew chief just had a piece of scrap paper to write things on." He kept the squadron's morning reports chalked on the walls of the alert shack. Only six months later could anyone transfer the information to the proper forms.[12]

"The CATF is not operating according to our ideas of a military air force organization," complained one of the Tenth Air Force inspectors. "It is continuing as a one-man show. This is due to the prior organization and functioning of the AVG and the fact that proper staff officers, especially a capable executive, have not been assigned. General Chennault is somewhat rusty on Air Force and Army procedures and customs due to his long separation from our service and close association with the Chinese forces during the past seven years."[13]

Chennault angrily rebutted this report. "Operations of the US Air Force units in China are limited by a number of factors which are not present in other theaters," he wrote. He blamed the high operations tempo and minimum of trained personnel. He blamed shortages of supplies, aircraft, and fuel. He blamed overcrowded bathing facilities and dirty, odorous water. "Although separated from the regular Army for some time, I feel that I am perfectly capable of operating air force units in regular Army style," the Louisianan assured Bissell. "My methods here are deliberately planned because of the situation in China and I believe that the results attained in Burma and China since December 7, 1941, fully justify my methods. I have repeatedly requested an adequate number of staff officers and enlisted personnel for the work in China, but my requests have not been approved."[14]

Nothing irritated the Old Man more than what he perceived as Bissell's misplaced emphasis on "meticulous staff work and detailed reports" when he had a war to fight. The only staff officer Bissell offered him was for a position he had already filled with an exceptionally capable officer for whom he had great respect. Chennault pushed back against the appointment of a new chief of staff. Casey Vincent had unwittingly become a pawn in a bureaucratic battle between old rivals. Five days after receiving the good news of his transfer, he learned it had been indefinitely postponed.[15]

A flurry of passive-aggressive radiograms shot back and forth across the Hump. Bissell implied the disorganization of Chennault's task force was

72   Fallen Tigers

"embarrassing to the Theater Commander," though he assured him that "Tenth Air Force is anxious to help you in every way possible. Your difficulties are fully realized."[16]

Chennault pointed out again that he had asked for more staff officers, noting the table of organization provided by Tenth Air Force was "insufficient to carry on the duties of my headquarters. It will be necessary to draw both officers and enlisted men from the tactical organizations. This necessity has been for years acknowledged throughout the Army as undesirable. This is particularly true where the squadrons are understrength as is the case here."[17]

"These recommendations are currently under consideration in the War Department," Bissell replied dismissively. "You must draw to a limited extent on the tactical units for some assistance. This procedure is necessary in almost all Army units."[18]

In Chennault's performance report Bissell downgraded him as an officer who "does not render generous and willing support to plans of his superiors regardless of personal views. Separation prevented Chennault from getting service in field grades and denied him experience and opportunity to know and understand administration and logistical requirements of larger forces."[19]

"Only directive received was one governing ops of CATF," Chennault countered. "Rendered most willing support of this directive although severely handicapped by reason of fact that tonnage of supplies required by plan was not furnished or closely approached. The commanding general, 10th Air Force, had approved the supply plan and was responsible for its execution, but failed completely in delivering even 50% of the tonnage required."[20]

Amid this heated bureaucratic battle, Casey saw his chance to serve in a combat zone slipping through his fingers. He visited China in late October to make his case personally. He made a strong impression on Chennault, who decided he could use the young officer—just not as his chief of staff. After returning to Karachi, Casey received word on November 1 that Bissell and Chennault had finally agreed on his transfer. This time Bissell rewrote his orders, specifying he would report for duty as executive officer, CATF. Chennault already had an executive officer, though—Col Robert Scott filled that role while also commanding the 23rd Fighter Group.

Bad weather delayed Casey crossing the Hump until the twelfth. That afternoon he landed at Wujiaba Field in Kunming, leading a formation of eleven P-40s to reinforce Chennault's fighter forces. The husky, even-tempered twenty-seven-year-old climbed from the cockpit of his personal fighter, "Peggy I," and immediately set out for the headquarters building. When he finally found Chennault, the brigadier general informed him he would be neither executive officer nor chief of staff; instead he appointed him his operations officer, or A3.

"This is a helluva job," Casey decided within a few days. "General Chennault doesn't need an A3—he runs his own operations." Though he had never thought of himself as a staff man, he quickly became frustrated with the administrative mess he found in Kunming. "Administrative practices are poor here," he observed. "The group just runs by itself." Nobody used the prescribed forms or routed anything through proper channels. Casey had to send numerous reports back to their authors for corrections. He had no idea how Chennault had been so successful with such a lackluster staff. "What an outfit!" he groaned. "Any similarity between the China Air Task Force and a military organization is purely accidental."[21]

Chennault needed staff officers, but he had no intention of letting Clayton Bissell or Casey Vincent change his way of doing business. He would not allow them to convert the CATF to West Point parade-ground discipline. Instead, he intended to convert Casey to the combat traditions of the Flying Tigers. He ordered his new operations officer out of the office: "Casey," the Old Man told him, "you better go out east and find out how it's done before you begin telling other boys how to do it."[22]

Though disappointed at not having received the job he had been promised, Casey jumped at the opportunity to get into combat. He proved only too willing to take advantage of his position as operations officer to fly on some of the missions he planned. The first would be a strike on enemy shipping in the Indochinese port of Hong Gai.

Japan depended on merchant shipping to import raw materials from China and Southeast Asia to the home islands. Those same ships carried troops and military hardware from Japan out to its conquests. Much of this shipping traveled along the China coast and used Chinese and Indochinese ports as waystations. Hong Gai boasted a six-hundred-square-mile bay dotted with hundreds of karst islets just one hundred miles northeast of Hanoi. In designing his first raid, Casey used the same logic that guided Cooper in his attack on Hong Kong: by attacking shipping, the CATF could strike at targets of real strategic importance and hopefully inflict disproportionate damage with their puny fleet of warplanes.

74   FALLEN TIGERS

Poor weather held up the mission for several days, but finally, on November 22, 1942, nine B-25s and ten P-40s staged through Guilin for the raid. Casey flew with the fighter escort, hoping to see some action.[23] The bombers split into three flights over the target. The first went after a large steamer heading for the open sea and reportedly sank it. Brick Holstrom led the second flight in a minimum-altitude attack on a ship in the harbor. He released his bombs right on the deck and heaved back on the yoke as they slammed into the side of the ship; it quickly sank to the bottom.[24] Johnny Ruse, the pilot who had bailed out north of Kunming when he became lost on his way to China in June, led the third flight in a bombing run on an army barracks in Hai Phong. Casey did not run into any aerial opposition, but he did drop some bombs into the mix. He missed the ship he targeted, but his bombs landed among the dockyard warehouses and added to the destruction there.[25] All the aircraft returned safely to Guilin.[26]

Casey planned and personally flew on six missions between November 22 and 27. The last of these, a raid on Guangzhou, finally brought him his first air-to-air kill and an award of the Silver Star. "This was the day I shot down my first enemy plane!" he enthusiastically jotted in his journal that night. Chennault's plan to convert the young ring knocker appeared to be working. Casey fully bought into the Flying Tigers' way of war—even if the lack of proper administration still bothered him. "Combat flying is fun!" he wrote to his wife, Peggy. Unfortunately, his personal fighter, which bore his wife's name, went missing on December 14 when another pilot could not find the airfield and had to make a wheels-up landing on a dirt road.[27]

Chennault had converted Casey, but Lt Gen Joseph Stilwell—now installed in his New Delhi headquarters after the disastrous campaign in Burma—objected to the increasingly offensive posture of the CATF. He believed the airlift over the Hump to be an emergency expedient. To break the blockade of China, he wanted to build a road through north Burma.[28] Stilwell wanted the air forces in China to remain on the defensive, protecting the airlift and supporting his road construction campaign. His plan called for flying one hundred thousand Chinese troops to India, where, unhindered by the blockade, he would provide them lend-lease equipment and mold them into the core of a new Chinese army. This "X-Ray Force" would then invade north Burma from India while twenty divisions of a "Yoke Force" would invade from Yunnan. Joining in the middle, they would reopen an overland supply route to China and then march across the Guizhou Plateau and

Hong Kong   75

Hunan in an attack on Hankou. The plan, though logical and linear, would mean years without most of occupied China seeing any evidence of Allied aid. The Chinese had already been at war for five years. Stilwell's methodical approach addressed the military situation but not the sociopolitical crisis of China's sagging morale.[29]

Chennault wanted to fight an air campaign in China, not a ground war for Burma, but the phased plan he had developed with Cooper did not make much sense to a traditional old foot soldier like Stilwell. The airman never intended his phases to be strictly linear, and, in fact, several could be in progress simultaneously. For example, Chennault's fighters could be conducting a strategic defensive to secure bases from enemy air attack in central China while at the same time, fighters and bombers used airfields in east China to carry out offensive guerrilla raids, and fighters, bombers, and transports could be supporting the Chinese army with a conventional air campaign in southwest China—all while he continued to expand the warning net and build new runways even farther afield. He did not understand Stilwell's obsession, as he saw it, with returning to the scene of his defeat.

Stilwell, of course, blamed others for the disaster in Burma: the British for abandoning their positions, the Chinese for not strictly following his orders, and Chiang Kai-shek for meddling from Chongqing. In all fairness, all his charges had some basis in fact. But for a post that required him to be as much a diplomat as a soldier, Stilwell was quickly proving unequal to the task. The wiry, cantankerous infantryman began to believe the stalemate in China owed entirely to the corruption and ineptitude of Chiang. The generalissimo, he presumed, planned to use the Americans to fight the Japanese for him while he hoarded lend-lease supplies for a future showdown with the Communists. Stilwell began to refer to Chiang as "the Peanut" to his staff and in his personal writings. His lack of respect and tact began to show in his dealings with the Nationalists.[30]

Chennault chafed under Stilwell, whom he saw as indifferent to his problems. He made an end run around his boss when Wendell Willkie visited China in October. Willkie had once been a political opponent of Roosevelt's, running against him in the election of 1940. Just two years later, however, he served as the president's personal envoy on a tour around the world. Chennault took advantage of the occasion to press his case and ended up writing a memorandum for Willkie to deliver to the president personally, though he later claimed it had been Willkie's idea. The blatant breach of protocol and

76   FALLEN TIGERS

disregard for chain of command only heightened the bad blood between the CATF commander and his superiors.[31]

Cooper, meanwhile, decided to make his own case against Stilwell. He sent a bitterly critical letter to his friend "Wild Bill" Donavan. The OSS director circulated it around Washington, DC, much to the horror of Gen George Marshall, Stilwell's old friend and stalwart supporter. The Army chief quickly demanded Cooper's recall. Chennault delayed as much as possible: "I have [not] had nor do I have any intentions of evading your orders concerning Cooper. My sole interest is the fighting efficiency of my command," he radioed to Bissell in late November. "I considered it essential that Vincent get to know officers and men and he was on constant combat duty with them. Will immediately relieve Cooper from his official duties if you insist though I think it unwise but vital to this command that he work with Vincent and A-2 [Intelligence] for minimum time necessary to explain what I consider their complex China operational conditions."[32] Bissell did insist. Chennault delayed as long as he could, but he eventually gave in to the weight of the chain of command. Merian Cooper, the brilliant planner, legendary pilot, and fearless adventurer, returned to the United States at the end of November.[33] Colonel Scott departed not long after him. Both the positions of chief of staff and executive officer went unfilled for the time being.

7

Aerial Offensive

April 24, 1943
Karachi, India

The big, four-engine transport took off across the Arabian Sea and droned west toward the drab brown landscape of the Middle East and North Africa. Inside, Lt Gen Joseph W. Stilwell and Maj Gen Claire Lee Chennault sat at opposite ends of the cabin, an air of icy indifference between them. Neither man—either in personal diaries or later biographies—mentioned speaking a word to the other on the long flight to America. Their professional relationship had long since lost any pretense of cordiality.[1]

The two made for an interesting study in contrasts. Stilwell possessed the pedigree of a West Point graduate from an upper-middle-class family in upstate New York. He looked almost professorial, with close-cropped gray hair, wire-rimmed spectacles, and a long cigarette holder clutched between his fingers. The largely self-taught Chennault chain-smoked his way through a pack of Camels, his dark eyes narrowed in a perpetual squint. He had spent his youth in the backwoods of rural Louisiana and had the deeply lined, tanned features of a frontiersman. Now the two of them traveled to Washington, DC, to present their competing visions for the war to President Roosevelt and the Anglo-American Combined Chiefs of Staff. Using his briefcase as a desk, Chennault refined his plan en route.[2]

Reluctant to commit more troops to another Stilwell-led misadventure in Burma, Chiang Kai-shek had advocated for Chennault's vision and asked for an American air force in China free from the interference of Tenth Air Force in New Delhi. Chennault's recent promotion signaled some level of agreement or accommodation on the part of the Roosevelt administration. On March 10, 1943, the Fourteenth Army Air Force had taken the place of

78   FALLEN TIGERS

the old CATF. Though Chennault no longer answered to General Bissell, his new command remained under Stilwell's jurisdiction. The same basic disagreement remained: Stilwell wanted to focus on a ground offensive to retake Burma; Chennault wanted to fight an air campaign in China.

The C-87 transport touched down in Washington on April 28, two weeks before the start of a major Allied planning conference code-named Trident. Chennault had several private audiences with the president before and during the conference. Standing before him in the Oval Office, he passionately pitched his ideas for the conduct of the war: "The Japs don't want to fight in China, particularly in the air, and therefore should be made to do so," he began. "China is the only place from which the Allies can gnaw at Japan's vitals. We've already been hitting the Yangzi River ports, as well as Hong Kong, Hankou, Guangzhou, and French Indochina. The Japanese life line through the Taiwan Strait and South China Sea is within range of medium bombers based at Guilin. The Japanese industrial cities of Kobe, Tokyo, Nagoya, Nagasaki, Osaka, and Yokohama are all within range of heavy bombers at new, far-eastern fields." He had the president's attention.

"My timetable," he continued, "calls for a two-month operation against the Japanese Air Force in China beginning in July. The Japanese don't want to expend a major air effort in China, but if strongly challenged, they will be forced to, or else face a crippling blow to their war economy. During the final month of counter-air-force operations, B-25s will begin pounding the China coast ports, Hainan Island, and the Gulf of Tonkin. The second phase, beginning in September, will extend their range to cover the Taiwan Strait and the South China Sea. Heavy bombers will move into east China fields and begin bombing Taiwan and the Shanghai-Nanjing area. By the end of November, at the earliest, it will be possible to bomb Japanese shipping from Korea to Cam Ranh Bay and to begin operations against the industrial cities of Japan."

Chennault seemed to be promising a shortcut to the war in the Pacific— a shortcut that would allow Roosevelt to pursue the defeat of Japan while still maintaining his Europe-first policy.

"To begin," the general explained, "I need three more fighter squadrons and three more B-25 squadrons than I have in China right now. And I need the immediate flow of 4,700 tons over the Hump each month. After three months, I will need just 150 fighters, seventy medium bombers, thirty-five heavy bombers, and 7,129 tons over the Hump."

His shortcut seemed to come at a minuscule cost.

"Merchant shipping is the key to the enemy war effort," Roosevelt mused. "Could a China-based air force sink a million tons of Japanese shipping a year?"

"Sir," Chennault answered, "if we receive ten thousand tons of supplies a month, my planes will sink a million tons."

The president banged his fist on the desk. "If you can sink a million tons, we'll break their backs!" he exclaimed.

Stilwell had his own private audiences with the president. But in contrast to Chennault's passionate evangelism, the infantryman remained reserved, lamely mumbling his Burma plan while sitting hunched over in a chair.

"Is he sick?" Roosevelt asked General Marshall.

"The Chinese show an increasing tendency to neglect their obligation of furnishing the manpower we are to equip and train," Stilwell groused to the president. He explained he wanted to withhold lend-lease supplies to coerce Chiang into sending troops to Burma. He thought Chennault's plan dangerous. "As we found out last spring," he asserted, referencing the aftermath of the Doolittle Raid, "any attempt to bomb Japan is going to bring a prompt and violent reaction on the ground." Stilwell's acerbic aloofness and penchant for understatement fell flat against Chennault's dramatic exaggeration. His idea of withholding lend-lease supplies to strong-arm the generalissimo disturbed the president. And to his point about Japanese retaliation for air action, Chiang had already promised his troops could hold the eastern airfields.[3]

"My first thought is that Stilwell has exactly the wrong approach in dealing with Generalissimo Chiang," Roosevelt commented to Marshall. "All of us must remember that the Generalissimo came up the hard way to become the undisputed leader of four hundred million people—an enormously difficult job. . . . One cannot speak sternly to a man like that or exact commitments from him the way we might do from the Sultan of Morocco."

It did not take long for Chennault's ideas to take hold at Trident. "The difficulties of fighting in Burma are apparent," Prime Minister Winston Churchill told conferees at the White House during their first meeting on May 12. "The jungle prevents the use of our modern weapons. The monsoon strictly limits the length of the campaigning season, and there is no means of bringing sea power to bear." Even if Stilwell's plan opened a road through north Burma, Churchill pointed out, it would not be operational until 1945, and even then, it would be unable to deliver more than twenty thousand tons a month. Instead, the Allies should focus on an operation against Sumatra or Malaya and support China by improving the airlift over the Hump.

Roosevelt agreed. "I don't think we can overlook the possibility of a Chinese collapse," he told the conferees. They simply could not build a road through Burma fast enough. "The question resolves itself to assisting China by air," he concluded.

Chennault and Stilwell attended the second meeting at the White House on May 14. Both Roosevelt and Churchill restated their decision to support China from the air and asked Field Marshal Sir Archibald Wavell, the British commander in chief in India, for his analysis. "When I was asked to produce a plan to conquer Burma in the next dry season, I had prepared what I thought was the best plan possible," Wavell replied. "Even so, it is a hazardous one and difficult of accomplishment."

"There are many naval problems involved in the capture of Rangoon," commented Roosevelt. "Can sufficient carriers be made available?"

"The Rangoon operation is not attractive," answered Admiral Sir James Somerville, commander in chief of the British Eastern Fleet.

"Carriers cannot be made available until they can be released from the Mediterranean," added Admiral of the Fleet Sir Dudley Pound.

Only Stilwell advocated for the immediate recapture of Burma. "The weight of opinion is apparently against me," he complained. He again harped on the necessity of opening land communications to China, but his words amounted to little. The president instructed him to limit his operations in north Burma and to give priority to Chennault's air force. By all appearances, Chennault had won; his ideas would govern the conduct of American operations in China.[4]

On his last day in Washington, Chennault reported to the president for a third and final audience. Roosevelt sent for detailed maps of the China coast and went back over the airman's plans in detail. He wanted to know exactly which ports his fighters would dive-bomb, which sea lanes his bombers would sweep, and which channels they would mine. Finally, satisfied with the discussion, the president leaned back in his chair.

"Now I want you to write me from time to time and let me know how things are getting along," he told the general.

"Do you mean you want me to write to you personally?" Chennault asked incredulously.

"Yes, I do," Roosevelt replied.[5]

Aerial Offensive 81

The president was offering him an end around to bypass the chain of command. Using a private channel would only further tax his relationship with his superiors, but Chennault had always believed in doing what he must to get the job done. It seemed the legendary leader of the Flying Tigers had captured the president's imagination.

The Fourteenth Air Force's new chief of staff, Brig Gen Edgar "Buzz" Glenn, met the Old Man when he touched down at Kunming on June 5. With Glenn's assignment, the chief of staff post had eluded Casey Vincent once more. Promoted to full colonel in January, he had departed for Guilin on May 28 to take command of the Fourteenth's new forward echelon. He was only too happy to escape headquarters and get away from General Glenn, whom he found "officious, stubborn, and too damn ambitious."[6]

Chennault intended the forward echelon to advance the strategic defensive to his central China bases at Guilin, Lingling, and Hengyang ahead of the two-month air-superiority campaign he had promised the president. Previously, these airfields had served as temporary staging bases for guerrilla raids—as in the case of Merian Cooper's attacks on Hong Kong. Two squadrons of P-40s from the 23rd Fighter Group moved forward and Brick Holstrom brought his B-25s out to Guilin on May 15.[7] Casey also had occasional use of the new 308th Bomb Group's B-24 Liberators. General "Hap" Arnold sent the unit to China as an experiment to see if the heavy bombers could fly their own bombs, fuel, and supplies over the Hump. He hoped to put the concept into practice a year later to bomb Japan with B-29 Superfortresses based in China.[8]

Unbeknownst to Chennault, while he geared up for his summer air offensive, the Japanese Army Air Force devised its own plans for China. Lieutenant General Moritaka Nakazono, commander of the 3rd Air Division, resolved to wipe out the American air force before it built up enough strength to raid the home islands. His three-phase offensive would focus first on the airfields in central China from the end of July until mid-August, then shift to the Nationalist capital at Chongqing for two weeks before finally aiming to wipe out the bases in Yunnan Province in September.[9]

Nakazono had two new arrows in his quiver to challenge the American fighters: an upgraded Ki-43-II Hayabusa, with a new engine, rudimentary self-sealing fuel tanks, and strengthened wings. He also had an entirely new menace: the Nakajima Ki-44 Army Type 2 "Shoki" (Demon) Fighter, known by its Allied codename, "Tojo." The Shoki looked more like a P-47 Thunder-

82   FALLEN TIGERS

bolt than a Zero, with a large radial engine; short, tapered, cigar-shaped fuselage; and elliptical wings. It had a tighter turning radius, faster level speed, and higher ceiling than a P-40. It could out dive it, too, and had better armament and armor than a Hayabusa. The Shoki's only notable weakness seemed to be its limited range.[10]

Coincidentally, Nakazono's offensive kicked off at the same time as Chennault's campaign. The two sides parried inconclusively for nearly a month, often disrupted by long bouts of terrible weather. American pilots caught fleeting glimpses of the new "Tojo," but on August 20, 1943, they encountered the new fighter in force. Fourteen Sharks took off from Guilin that morning when the warning net reported unknowns inbound. At 9:15 a.m. the enemy formation appeared overhead—at least twenty Ki-44s from the 85th Air Regiment. Captain Yukiyoshi Wakamatsu led them in between thirty and thirty-five thousand feet—high above the waiting P-40s. Rather than lure the Americans into dogfights, the Japanese turned their own tactics against them, abandoning the usual three-plane elements in favor of fighting in pairs, and diving out of the sun to make hit-and-run attacks before zooming back to altitude. The outmatched Americans could only fly along line abreast and try to turn into the attacks before the enemy closed into range. Two P-40s went down in short order, both pilots killed in action; Captain Wakamatsu's fighters reported no losses. The Japanese appeared to have a decisive technological advantage.[11] Suddenly, the American effort in China seemed to hang in the balance.

Second Lieutenant Glen Beneda had arrived in China that May. The nineteen-year-old joined the 76th Fighter Squadron in central China, moving between Hengyang and Guilin as they defended against marauding Japanese planes. The squadron commander, Maj Grant Mahony, passed on Chennault's instructions to use hit-and-run attacks and not to turn with the Zeros—lessons Mahony had learned the hard way fighting in the Philippines and Dutch East Indies early in the war. Beneda put the advice to good use in an air battle over Hengyang on July 25, claiming a Japanese fighter as "probably destroyed."[12]

Meanwhile, 2nd Lt Lee Gregg had arrived in North Africa in the spring of 1943, too late to take part in the fighting against Field Marshal Erwin Rommel's Afrika Korps in Tunisia. Axis resistance had ended there on May 13, the second day of the Trident Conference. Though the Combined Chiefs of Staff had debated courses of action for China and Burma, most of their

Aerial Offensive   83

discussion centered on the trajectory of the war in Europe. The next step after Africa would be the invasion of Sicily in July. In the meantime, an uneasy quiet had descended on the Mediterranean. Allied air forces focused on bombing airfields and ports on the islands of Sicily, Sardinia, and Pantelleria. These raids encountered sporadic opposition, but the Luftwaffe and Regia Aeronautica had become shadows of their former selves. Flying from Algeria with the 1st Fighter Group, Gregg shot down a single Italian fighter—a Reggiane Re.2001—while covering a raid on shipping at Golfo Aranci on the northeast coast of Sardinia. The increasing rarity of contact with the enemy left Gregg feeling a sense of anticlimax; his squadron claimed only three enemy aircraft destroyed during the entire month of June.[13] Then he heard about Maj Robert Kirtley recruiting from the training command and three veteran P-38 groups in North Africa to form a squadron for China. The young lieutenant decided to volunteer. Kirtley's new unit had no designation; Gregg received orders assigning him to "Squadron X."

Twelfth Air Force transferred Kirtley to the 1st Fighter Group the day before Squadron X departed, but Capt Sam Palmer took charge in his stead.[14] At four thirty in the morning on July 6, 1943, twenty-five Lockheed P-38 Lightnings took off from Algeria into the burning red of the rising sun. To their left, the vibrant blue of the Mediterranean stretched into the distance, while to their right lay the drab brown of the rugged Saharan frontier. Twenty-five airmen left one war to join another; behind them, Fascist Italy and the Nazis still clung to the Mediterranean basin, while ahead, across more than six thousand miles of desert, ocean, and mountains, loomed the fight against the Imperial Japanese Army in China.[15]

Chennault had been clamoring for modern interceptors to replace his aging fleet of P-40s even before the combat debut of the Tojo. "It is essential that I be supplied with the most modern pursuits, preferably the P-51 in increasing increments," he had radioed his superiors in August 1942. "Strongest representations should be made to Washington that the fighter group in this area [is] now having to fight greatly superior numbers with outmoded and worn out aircraft and this condition will certainly grow worse unless increasing numbers of modern type fighters in steady flow [be] supplied to me."[16]

Chennault preferred the P-51 Mustang because of its speed, agility, high-altitude performance, and low fuel consumption—only seventy-five gallons an hour. At 130 gallons an hour, he argued, the twin-engine P-38 simply used

84   FALLEN TIGERS

too much gasoline for his supply starved command. In July 1943, however, the Army Air Forces had 1,421 P-38s in the inventory against only 327 P-51s.[17] Additionally, General Arnold prioritized the Mustangs for the war in Europe. In his estimation, P-38s certainly met the measure of a modern, high-altitude interceptor, and he had a squadron conveniently available second-hand after the fighting ended in North Africa. Ultimately, Chennault would take what he could get.

The first flight of Lightnings landed at Kunming on July 23—the same day General Nakazono's 3rd Air Division launched its offensive. Lieutenant Gregg ended up stuck in Karachi for a few extra days, though; a crew chief at the maintenance depot there had been performing an engine run on his fighter when it jumped its chocks and went through the side of a shed. The young pilot had to wait while maintenance personnel changed out the ruined engine. Gregg flew the Hump with the second flight of Lightnings early the next week. Shortly after he arrived, Squadron X received a new designation: the 449th Fighter Squadron.

Chennault sent the new fighters to the front piecemeal to help in the desperate fighting against Nakazono's Oscars and Tojos. Two Lightnings scrambled alongside the 74th Fighter Squadron on July 26, when eight Ki-44s from the 85th Air Regiment attacked Guilin. First Lieutenant Walter Smith led the pair, the 74th selecting him to introduce the new unit to combat in China because of his prior P-38 experience. Unfortunately, the Tojos caught Smith right off the end of the runway; his Lightning pancaked in, and he barely escaped with his life. Meanwhile, 1st Lt Lewden Enslen rocketed aloft in the other Lightning and scored the unit's first victory, claiming one enemy fighter destroyed.

With only a handful of new American fighters trickling in, the Japanese held the initiative. Using its powerful new aircraft and deadly new tactics, the 3rd Air Division set the tempo for air battles over the central China fields. Chennault decided it was time for a change of pace. He radioed Casey Vincent to hit the Japanese airfields at Hankou, Hong Kong, and Guangzhou with everything he had to force the enemy to engage on American terms. To secure his bases in central China, Casey would turn the forward echelon's strategic defensive into an offensive.[18]

The first two missions failed miserably. Casey was supposed to furnish fighter escort for B-24 Liberators sortieing from bases in Yunnan. But on August 21 a skirmish over Hengyang in the late morning made his fighters

Aerial Offensive   85

miss their rendezvous. Major Walter Beat decided his fourteen B-24s would press on to Hankou without escort. An intense air battle developed over the target, with some bomber crews counting as many as sixty enemy fighters attacking en masse. Two B-24s went down in flames, including the commander's; Beat and his crew are still listed as missing in action.[19]

The fighters managed to make their rendezvous for the next mission on August 24. Six P-40s flew close escort for seven B-24s from the 425th Bomb Squadron, while ten P-38s flew top cover at thirty thousand feet. Over Hankou an estimated forty enemy fighters from the 33rd and 25th Air Regiments intercepted the bombers. Though some of the Lightning pilots heard the commotion on the radio, they could not contact their flight leader and therefore did not intervene. The 425th lost forty men on four aircraft, with twenty-three killed outright, six still listed as missing in action, and eleven rescued by the Chinese.

"Jumped by Zeros again," Casey complained. "Four B-24s are missing. God knows where they are—shot down, I guess."[20]

"Enemy fighters snatched the cheese without springing the trap," Chennault fumed. "Four out of seven Liberators went down in flames while the P-38s buzzed along at 30,000 feet oblivious to the fight raging below."[21]

The forward echelon finally hit its stride over the next several days, running four big missions to Hong Kong, Guangzhou, and Yichang by the end of August. Casey continued to sneak out on the occasional mission himself, scoring his sixth confirmed aerial victory on the twenty-sixth.

Despite several tactical successes, Nakazono had to admit the failure of phase one of his plan; he did not drive the Americans out of central China. Poor weather and the attacks on his air bases also caused phase two to flounder; his warplanes only managed to mount one raid on Chongqing. He decided to initiate phase three anyway and wipe out the American bases in Yunnan. This time he would direct the effort personally. On the early afternoon of September 9, 1943, he and his staff boarded two Mitsubishi twin-engine transports to move his headquarters from Chiayi, Taiwan, to Guangzhou. At 2:05 p.m. that day, four P-38s took off from Lingling to bomb the Huangpu docks south of the city. First Air Brigade issued a warning for all Japanese aircraft to remain clear of the area because of enemy action; Nakazono's transport either did not receive the warning or failed to abide by it.

Climbing away from his dive-bombing run, 2nd Lt Billie Beardsley spotted the transport six miles southeast of Guangzhou. He and his wingmen gave

86   FALLEN TIGERS

chase. According to eyewitnesses on the ground, at three thirty in the afternoon, two P-38s came alongside Nakazono's aircraft while a third dove from behind and let loose with guns and cannon. The stricken transport crashed onto an island in the Pearl River; Beardsley received credit for its destruction. Japanese medical personnel later examined the bodies pulled from the wreckage and determined Nakazono had died from gunfire before his plane had hit the ground. The general's timely demise occurred less than five months after Rex Barber shot down Admiral Isoruku Yamamoto over Bougainville. The 3rd Air Division feared the United States had broken its codes and knew all its plans. Division headquarters cancelled phase three after only one attack on Kunming. Initiative passed decisively to the Americans. Ironically, Beardsley had no inkling as to the strategic consequences of his actions and did not find out until forty years later. Nakazono's death owed entirely to happentance. This time, the fog and friction of war played to the advantage of the Americans.[22]

Nakazono's air offensive represented the fiercest fighting yet in the air war for China. The summer of 1943 saw the opposing forces closest to parity in terms of number of aircraft, technology, and experience. It proved to be a tipping point that swung the air fighting in favor of the Americans. It could easily have gone the other way.

Fourteenth Air Force did eventually receive fifteen P-51s in October, but like the P-38s, these arrived secondhand. Each had accumulated at least a hundred hours of "city miles" at an operational training unit in Florida. With only small numbers of pre-worn replacements, the P-40 remained the backbone of the Fourteenth's fighter fleet until well into 1944. The Ki-44 Shoki, however, proved troublesome even for the early model Mustangs. On December 1, 1943, Tex Hill led six P-51As on a mission to Hong Kong. He had arrived for his second combat tour in October, taking command of the now veteran 23rd Fighter Group just as it received its first Mustangs. A squadron of Tojos bounced Tex and his flight over the target, quickly shooting down Capt James M. Williams, leading the second element, along with his wingman, 1st Lt Robert T. Colbert. Under heavy attack, Tex flew with manic desperation, twisting, rolling, and diving for the ground. The Tojos filled his fighter full of holes, but he managed to escape and limp home. He immediately reported to Chennault in Kunming.

"Sir, they've got a new fighter down there," he told the Old Man. "It whipped our P-51s pretty good. I don't know if we're going to be able to beat them in the air!"

Ever the pragmatist, Chennault told him the same thing he had told Casey Vincent when the Tojos first appeared that summer: "Get them on the ground. Then you don't have to fight them in the air."[23]

Both Williams and Colbert successfully evaded with the help of friendly Chinese and returned to American control—Williams through Wuzhou, Colbert through Huizhou and Qujiang. Both noted odd behavior on the part of Colonel Hill leading up to the disastrous dogfight. For starters, he did not climb above ten thousand feet until just before reaching the target. Then he did not respond when Williams called out "Zeros" on the radio. "I waited," reported Williams, "thinking that Col. Hill was waiting until they got almost there but he did nothing and then it was too late."[24] Perhaps Tex's fighter suffered some sort of radio malfunction, or perhaps he overestimated the capabilities of the P-51—or underestimated the Tojo. Whatever the reason, he found his narrow escape a sobering experience.

Subsequent combat showed the Shoki and Mustang relatively evenly matched, with pilot skill and tactical advantage often proving the critical factors. The P-51 could fly faster than the Shoki and turn with it at indicated speeds greater than three hundred miles per hour. The Shoki, on the other hand, still had a greater service ceiling than the early model Mustang and could easily outclimb it. Compared with four .50-caliber machine guns mounted in the P-51's wings, the Shoki had two in the wings and two on the cowling. Firing through the propeller arc restricted the cowling guns to a slower rate of fire, giving the Mustang a slight edge in overall firepower. But the Mustang's guns had to be mounted diagonally in its slim, efficient wings, which frequently caused the feeding mechanisms to jam when fired under the high g-forces of a typical dogfight.[25]

Altogether, enemy aircraft accounted for more than 19 percent of American warplanes reported missing on combat missions in the China Theater. This included twenty-nine P-51s—slightly over 12 percent of the total number of missing Mustangs. Predictably, P-40s suffered worse—a total of sixty-four aircraft, or just over 29 percent of the total number of missing Sharks. Surprisingly, P-38s, known as Zero-killers in the Pacific, suffered the greatest percentage lost: twelve out of twenty-three reported missing—over 50 percent! Perhaps even more surprising is that few, if any of them, fell to Ki-44s.[26] In most cases, Hayabusas from the 25th Air Regiment ambushed the Lightnings from greater altitude, shooting down multiple P-38s in each of four

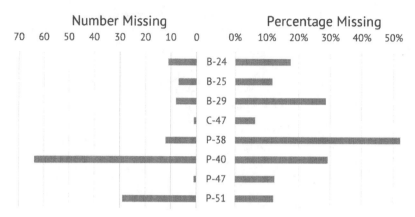

Aircraft Missing Due to Enemy Aircraft

engagements. Such was the case when Lee Gregg, John Opsvig, and William Jones went down southwest of Hankou on May 6, 1944.

This trend greatly frustrated Chennault. The P-38 had a clear advantage over the Hayabusa in terms of speed, rate of climb, ceiling, and firepower; it lacked only in maneuverability. "They arrived from North Africa with a fondness for dogfighting and without spare parts," the general grumbled. "These pilots refused to believe a P-38 couldn't turn with an Oscar, Zero, or Tojo. As a result, the 449th became the only American fighter squadron in China against which the Japs approached an even break."[27]

October 30, 1943, marked a low point for the troubled squadron. The 25th Air Regiment caught two flights of P-38s at low altitude while dive-bombing shipping at the Yangzi River Port of Jiujiang. Four Lightnings went down in short order, including that of Capt Lewden Enslen, the new squadron commander. Two pilots managed to return to friendly territory; one remains missing in action. The men blamed imagined collaborators for leaking word of the mission. Enslen, though rescued by the Chinese, died from his wounds ten days later in the small village of Huangmei. His loss devastated the squadron. Chennault realized he needed someone he could count on to fix both the unit's tactical deficiencies and their low morale. He had just such a man in mind.[28]

8

Shipping Is the Key

September 27, 1943
Gulf of Tonkin

At 6:50 a.m. they spotted a lone Japanese steamer forty miles southwest of Weizhou Island, its wake illuminated by the early morning sunlight. Captain Lloyd Murphy banked the B-25 around to the left and made a diving strafing attack. The steamer's crew scrambled to their battle stations as the bomber roared low overhead, guns blazing. Murphy pulled up into a tight 180-degree turn and made another pass from the rear quarter. The small vessel took evasive action and began to return fire with its compliment of light anti-aircraft guns. In the bomber's nose, 1st Lt Robert Kroll opened the bomb bay doors as they set up for a third run. In the back, Staff Sgt Richard Betts readied his camera equipment to record the bomb run. Suddenly, smoke began pouring from the left engine.

"Oil pressure falling off," the copilot, 2nd Lt James Funk, announced. "The prop won't feather!" The wind-milling propeller blades, flat to the airstream, acted as giant airbrakes. The bomber began losing speed and altitude. Murphy salvoed the bombs to lighten the load; all fell wide of the steamer. He managed to pull up to eight hundred feet, but the speed kept bleeding off and he could no longer hold altitude. The B-25 crashed into the water at a hundred miles an hour. Funk quickly opened the cockpit escape hatch and scrambled out on top of the bomber with Murphy and 2nd Lt Fred Breese, the navigator, right behind him. The nose had already filled with water and the aircraft rapidly began to sink. Murphy waded aft to help the enlisted men while Funk and Breese donned their life vests and retrieved the raft. Within two minutes, the plane disappeared from sight, taking Kroll and Betts, the bombardier and photographer, to a watery grave.

90   FALLEN TIGERS

Murphy helped the two gunners, Tech Sgt Robert Chiarello and Staff Sgt William Holtz, into the raft. Chiarello had a deep gash over his right eye exposed to the bone. Lieutenant Breese had a laceration on the right side of his head and was suffering from shock. Situating themselves in the small raft as best they could, the five survivors began paddling north. They alternated in half-hour shifts, fighting against a gentle swell pushing them toward Japanese-occupied Indochina. At nightfall, they rigged up a small triangular sail from one of their parachutes to take advantage of favorable winds blowing toward China. As dawn broke the next day, though, a squall blew up and choppy waves began breaking into the raft. Chiarello, Breese, and Murphy all became violently seasick. Then, around ten thirty in the morning, they caught sight of a sail on the western horizon.

"Should we try to signal it?" one of them asked. They discussed their options and decided not to attempt contact, since they did not know whether it was friendly or enemy. Soon, however, the ship spotted them and altered course in their direction. By noon, it had overtaken them—a large, three-masted wooden sailing junk, one hundred feet long from bow to stern. It seemed more like an anachronism from the age of buccaneering than something they expected to encounter in the twentieth century. The crew of fifteen Chinese sailors launched a small boat to retrieve the airmen and brought them aboard. After more than twenty-four hours in the small raft, they felt weak and found it difficult to stand on cramped legs. The sailors treated them cautiously at first until they saw the Nationalist flag sewn to the lining of Sergeant Holtz's flight jacket. Murphy used his pointie-talkie to communicate with the captain, a Mr. An, who explained that his ship had been carrying a cargo of rice from Hai Phong to Guangzhou when a storm blew them off course. He announced he would take them to Beihai, a port on the China coast about a day's sail north. His crew brought what medicines they had to treat the airmen's cuts and bruises. Lieutenant Breese poured sulfa powder in the gash on Chiarello's head and bandaged it. The sailors then gave the airmen warm milk, beer, cigarettes, and a change of clothing and hid away their life raft and uniforms below decks. That evening, they shared a meal of rice, eggs, sweet beans, noodles, and dried beef.

A storm blew up in the night, driving the junk west, toward Indochina. All the next day and night, the Americans remained out of sight in the cabin while the ship tacked tediously to the northeast. On the morning of September 29, they sighted the Indochinese port of Mong Cai. This put them square-

Shipping Is the Key   91

ly in Japanese-controlled waters. They expected to encounter enemy patrol boats at any moment. The ship remained in sight of land throughout the next three days, still tacking east. The aircrew helped stand watch at night, alert for danger and eager to ease the burden on their rescuers. On the night of October 1, they alerted the sailors to a passing boat.

"Pirates," one of the Chinese told them. The ships passed silently in the night, the Americans tensely expecting an attack from the ruffians. They finally arrived at Beihai at three thirty in the morning. Mr. An took Captain Murphy and Sergeant Holtz ashore to meet with the customs agent. Surprisingly, the agent already knew of the junk's American passengers and had a translator on hand. He went aboard to inspect the ship's cargo of rice and brought the rest of the bomber crew ashore with him. By then, an enthusiastic crowd had gathered to welcome them.

The customs inspector, though very hospitable, would not give his name to the Americans and seemed very anxious to send them on their way. He feared the Japanese would discover them and retaliate. Beihai had actually been occupied by the Japanese since 1940. They had a garrison only thirty miles away and their patrol boats frequented the port. Technically, the customs inspector worked for the puppet government. Fortunately, this in no way disposed him against helping American airmen and, in fact, he evidently maintained strong ties with Nationalist officials in southern China. He rented five bicycle rickshaws and riders, and the local magistrate provided an escort of two officers and two enlisted men. They departed Beihai at ten thirty on the morning of October 3. The ship captain, Mr. An, went with them.

They traveled north to Lianzhou[1] on narrow dirt paths between rice paddies.[2] The Chinese had systematically destroyed the main road by digging ditches every hundred feet or so, each about five feet deep by six feet across. In Lianzhou, they met with the magistrate and a group of fifteen government officials, including a major general from the Nationalist Army.

"Tell us the facts of your mission—in detail," they insisted.

"It was a secret mission," Murphy told them, trying to beg off. This only piqued their curiosity, however, and they continued to grill him. Eventually, the officials gave up for the night and released the crew to go to a dinner hosted by local police. They remained overnight at a hospital, though they refused medical treatment due to the unsanitary conditions.

On the morning of October 4, the major general met them at the hospital and continued to press them for information. The crew urged him instead

92   FALLEN TIGERS

to muster the bicycle rickshaws so they could return to their base as soon as possible. He finally relented. As they departed Lianzhou, the magistrate met them at the gate and introduced them to Chung Ho-keng, a guide he had entrusted with their safety and to whom he had given money to cover their expenses.

"The road from Lianzhou direct to Nanning is bandit country," Chung told them as they departed. "We will spend the nights in Zhanghuang and Lingshan."

As they proceeded via this circuitous route to the north, their escorts wired ahead to prepare food and accommodations at each stop. At Lingshan, Mr. Chung handed them over to Captain Cheng Ku-wan of the Nationalist Army and an interpreter named Joseph Chan. They left early the next morning for Nanxiang and from there traveled by boat up the Yu River. On the eighth, they finally arrived at Nanning; Captain Cheng delivered them to the American airbase there the next morning.[3]

Captain Murphy and his crew may as well have come back from the dead. No Allied surface vessels or submarines combed the sea lanes for downed aircraft off the China coast. In fact, only one other Fourteenth Air Force airman survived a crash farther out to sea: Capt George K. O'Neil parachuted from his B-24 when Japanese night fighters shot it down near Taiwan in August 1944. As he floated among the wreckage, Sergeant Masayoshi Kakimoto, a Japanese military policeman, approached in a small boat. O'Neil fired his revolver at him, but the sergeant fired back and took the American captive. He spent the rest of the war in a prison camp near Tokyo. None of the rest of the crew survived the crash.[4]

Murphy and his men had been extremely fortunate to have been picked up by Mr. An's sailing junk. However, their rescue from the middle of the Gulf of Tonkin, though remarkable, illustrated many of the problems with shipping interdiction. Despite his helpfulness, Mr. An had been carrying a cargo of rice from one enemy-controlled port to another. Did that constitute enemy trade? Colonel Jesse Williams, director of Fourteenth Air Force intelligence, recommended against attacking small boats in the area. "Friendly natives may be responsible for saving more US personnel operating in this section," he argued.[5]

Since the beginning of the war, Chennault had envisioned China-based warplanes cutting Japan's ocean-borne trade. Phase two of the plan he had briefed to Roosevelt had his B-25s conducting sea sweeps beginning in

Shipping Is the Key   93

September 1943. Though he believed the downfall of Japan ultimately lay in burning its wood-and-paper cities from the air, he yielded to the president's emphasis on the importance of interdicting sea lanes for the time being.[6]

The 11th Bomb Squadron had been hitting merchant shipping since Casey Vincent's mission to Hong Gai in November 1942, but they initially restricted their attacks to enemy ports and river traffic. The mission on September 27 represented the squadron's first counter-shipping sweep over the open sea. Brick Holstrom no longer commanded the squadron; he and the other holdovers from the Doolittle Raid finally received their orders home on May 25. Lieutenant Colonel Morris F. Taber, the new commander, led this first sweep with the squadron's operations officer, Captain Murphy, flying a second B-25.

The loss of Murphy's aircraft on the squadron's very first sea sweep did not bode well. Nevertheless, they ran three additional missions before the end of the month and began sending flights of two or three B-25s on river or sea sweeps almost daily through April 1944. These operations put the medium bombers at the edge of their range and beyond the reach of friendly fighter cover. Typically, the B-25s flew in pairs five hundred feet above the water. Once they sighted an enemy vessel, they used their forward firepower to suppress anti-aircraft guns and then bombed from minimum altitude, using low-level skip-bombing techniques learned from Lt Gen George Kenney's Fifth Air Force in the South Pacific.[7]

It was dangerous work. Fourteenth Air Force reported fourteen B-25s missing on river and sea sweeps throughout the war. When the 22nd Bomb Squadron finally moved from India to Yangjie, China, in early 1944, it lost seven aircraft on missions to Indochina and the South China Sea in just seven weeks of operations.[8] The squadron commander Maj Edison Weatherly led the unit's first sea sweep on February 3. While strafing a 200-foot vessel in the Ca River near Vinh, the major came in so low that he collided with the ship's mast. It tore a gaping hole in the leading edge of his bomber's right wing inboard of the engine, severed hydraulic lines, and damaged the right elevator and stabilizer. Weatherly had to crash-land his crippled bomber at Kunming—fortunately with no injuries to the crew. Two of the squadron's bombers flew a second sea sweep on the fifth but returned due to poor weather without expending their bombs.

On February 6, Major Weatherly led three B-25s to attack shipping near Da Nang (called Tourane by the French). The squadron grew worried when

94   FALLEN TIGERS

none of them had returned to Yangjie by nightfall. It turned out that poor weather had separated the flight, and each aircraft independently attacked targets of opportunity down the Vietnamese coast. Low ceilings and poor radio reception made it impossible to return to their home airfield. Weatherly managed to land once again at Kunming. The squadron reported the other two aircraft as missing. One crew later walked in minus its radio operator and with a severely injured gunner. The other had simply disappeared. That same day, another of the squadron's aircraft went missing on a weather reconnaissance, though that crew managed to bail out and return without further incident.[9]

A B-25C piloted by 1st Lt James H. Gardner vanished on an anti-shipping sweep to the Gulf of Tonkin on the fifteenth. Eleven days later, Fourteenth Air Force learned from sources in Indochina that the bomber had crashed near Do Len with the loss of all aboard. French colonial authorities buried the crew near the crash site. Not quite a month later, on March 13, Capt Elmer Thompson led four of the squadron's B-25s to attack Qiongshan Airdrome on Hainan Island in a joint mission with the 491st Bomb Squadron. The two squadrons planned to attack simultaneously but became separated in poor weather en route. The flight from the 22nd first bombed a seaplane base to the west before hitting the airfield with clusters of incendiaries. One crew reported seeing the control tower on fire. They could also see enemy fighters taking off in every direction—probably A6M Zeros from the 254th Kokutai. The fighters attacked them as they raced for home north across the Qiongzhou Strait at 250 miles per hour. The four bombers formed into a tight diamond and descended to just three hundred feet above the waves. The Zeros made a few ineffectual passes from the sides but then one pulled ahead of the formation and winged over into a head-on attack. Thompson watched as the fighter's tracers tore into the cockpit of 1st Lt Hampden Harding's bomber off his left wing. The ship burst into flames, staying level for a few precarious moments before pitching forward into the water. At that moment, the flight of bombers from the 491st suddenly appeared from the mist with an escort of four Sharks. The Zeros pulled away to deal with the new intruders.[10]

The 22nd's sixth and seventh losses happened on March 18 and 26, respectively, when they lost a B-25H to ground fire at Vinh and another to navigation error southwest of Kunming. The crew of the former went down with their ship. The five members of the latter crew survived and returned to

Shipping Is the Key   95

Fourteenth Air Force Counter-shipping Search Zones

Allied control. The relentless string of losses crushed morale. Many B-25 crews wondered if the risks they took merited whatever effects they managed to achieve.[11]

In June 1944, Fourteenth Air Force halted daytime visual sweeps by medium bombers in favor of nighttime radar sweeps by SB-24s. Flying search patterns between twenty-five hundred and five thousand feet above the sea, specially equipped Liberators used an SCR-717 sea search radar to detect targets as far as fifty miles away. Once one of these SB-24s located a vessel, it dropped down to four hundred feet and made up to three radar-guided bomb runs. Because the airmen could rarely identify their targets visually, they had to deconflict search zones with US Navy submarines. The zones dedicated to Chennault's bombers included a semicircle radiating one hundred miles from Shanghai as well as a corridor beginning one hundred miles northeast of Xiamen and running due east to Taiwan, then down the west coast of the island to a point south of Kaohsiung, then west-southwest to

96   FALLEN TIGERS

a point one hundred miles east of Hainan Island, and finally southwest to Indochina just south of Da Nang.[12]

Flying in pitch blackness on instruments, probing the dark ocean with radar, these "snooper" missions, as the crews called them, could be both tedious and terrifying. Many aircraft did not return. At 5:15 p.m. on the evening of October 26, 1944, eleven airmen from the 374th Bomb Squadron lifted off from Chenggong in an SB-24J under the command of Maj Horace S. Carswell Jr. to attack a convoy reported in the South China Sea southwest of Hong Kong. They could see the full moon reflecting brightly off the ocean surface as they crossed the coast. Three hours into the flight the radar operator detected twelve enemy vessels. Carswell caught sight of them in the moonlight. He dove to six hundred feet above the water and made a run on one of the escorting destroyers. The bombardier toggled off six 500-pound bombs, but all missed. They encountered no anti-aircraft fire; the attack had been a complete surprise.

Carswell departed the area and circled for thirty-five minutes in an attempt to deceive the convoy into thinking he had left for good. Then he barreled in once more at six hundred feet, this time scoring two hits on a freighter. The Japanese were ready for him, putting up heavy anti-aircraft fire. Silhouetted against the full moon, the B-24 made an excellent target. Shells and shrapnel holed the bomber like a sieve, knocking out the hydraulics system and punching a hole in the number two fuel tank. Carswell had to shut down and feather the number one and number three engines. Fortunately, number four seemed to be in good condition and number two kept sputtering for a time. The crew jettisoned their remaining bombs and threw everything they could overboard: toolboxes, ammunition cans, flak vests, and machine guns. Still, as the bomber limped away toward China, Carswell knew he would not be able to clear the terrain between him and the Allied airfields in the interior.

Second Lieutenant James O'Neal, an extra pilot aboard as an observer, came up to the flight deck and found the copilot bleeding profusely from a shrapnel wound through his right hand. He lifted him from the seat and took his place to help Carswell, fighting to maintain control of the crippled bomber. Three other crewmembers tended to the copilot's wounds.

As they neared the border of Guangxi Province at 11:15 p.m., Carswell could see mountains rising above them on all sides. It was time to bail out. Eight crewmembers jumped, but the bombardier, 2nd Lt Walter Hillier, discovered that shrapnel had riddled his parachute. He would have to stay with the ship. Carswell and O'Neal remained at the controls, determined to bring the bomber down safely with the three of them aboard. As the rest of the crew parachuted to the ground, they saw the overcast light up with an explosion as the B-24 collided with a mountainside. For giving his life in an effort to save all the members of his crew, Horace Carswell posthumously received the Medal of Honor—the only China-based airman to do so. Six crewmembers survived the bailout and returned to Allied control with the help of Chinese guerrillas.[13]

The loss of Carswell's bomber represented just one of over a score of grievous losses suffered by the 308th Bomb Group in its anti-shipping campaign. Between May 24 and October 31, 1944, SB-24s attacked 222 ships and claimed sixty-seven as sunk, an estimated 248,665 tons of shipping. Despite the hazards, nighttime radar bombing appeared to be much more effective and efficient than daytime sweeps by medium bombers. Yet a postwar joint Army-Navy assessment showed just the opposite to be true. Instead of the sixty-seven ships claimed during the May through October timeframe, SB-24s sank only ten. The total tonnage amounted to just 11 percent of that estimated.

A multitude of factors accounted for the gross exaggeration of claims. Crews could mistake radar returns from rocks or reefs as ships, for example. Though Fourteenth Air Force required visual confirmation of a sinking, this could include seeing large fires, lifeboats, or even the disappearance of a target blip from the radar scope—intelligence analysts interpreted the rules liberally. Additionally, aircrews routinely overestimated the size of their targets. Many vessels claimed as Japanese merchant ships may in fact have been wooden sailing junks, like the one that rescued Murphy's crew from the Gulf of Tonkin.

Twenty-three Liberator bombers failed to return from sea sweeps, resulting in the loss of thirty dead, 131 missing, and seven captured airmen. Instead of the eighty-three ships claimed throughout the war, they sank only twenty-two. This meant Fourteenth Air Force traded B-24s nearly one-for-one with enemy merchantmen or warships and lost more than seven airmen per ship sunk. Meanwhile, B-25s sank twenty-five of the forty-eight merchant vessels they claimed throughout the war against fourteen losses—a rate a little worse than two ships sunk for every aircraft lost and three airmen for every two ships.

98   FALLEN TIGERS

Ironically, then, the B-25s proved much more effective and efficient than SB-24s at shipping interdiction, even managing to halt daylight movement of large vessels on the Yangzi River by the end of 1943. A postwar report suggests the SB-24s would have been more useful working in concert with US Navy submarines in a purely reconnaissance role or in mining enemy harbors instead of attacking shipping. Mines not only sank ships but also confused schedules, closed harbors, and prevented delivery of cargo. Just a limited number of mines closed Hai Phong to Japanese shipping by the end of 1943 and prevented movement in and out of Hong Kong and Shanghai for weeks at a time. Ultimately, submarines proved to be a much more devastating menace to the Japanese merchant marine than Chennault's planes.[14]

Though the CATF and Fourteenth Air Force reported losing more than three times as many fighters as bombers throughout the war, the large crew sizes—five to seven in a B-25 and nine to eleven in a B-24—meant the vast majority of airmen reported missing in the China Theater went down in bombers. Including those from Twentieth Air Force B-29s, this totaled an astounding 1,221 airmen from just 150 planes. Sadly, 167 of those bomber crewmen probably went down at sea—unfindable—forever missing in the depths of the Pacific.

9

Thanksgiving Day

November 22, 1943
Hsinchu, Taiwan

"Marjorie J." cut a solitary pair of contrails across the afternoon sky above the Taiwan Strait. At her controls, 1st Lt Winfree Sordelett prepared to photograph the airfield at Hsinchu, a major training and modification depot for Japanese bombers. The unarmed Lockheed F-5A, a photo-reconnaissance version of the P-38G Lightning, had four aerial cameras in its nose in place of the usual cannon and machine guns. Its only defense lay in speed and altitude. Fortunately, at speeds of over four hundred miles per hour and altitudes up to forty thousand feet, it could fly faster and higher than most anything in the Japanese inventory. None of the sixteen F-5s reported missing in the China Theater are known to have fallen to enemy aircraft, though one once returned with five bullet holes from an encounter with a Tojo over Hainan Island.[1]

Fourteenth Air Force needed accurate intelligence to pit its limited resources against the weak points of the enemy. Though the air raid warning net performed brilliantly in a defensive role, it had little utility in offensive operations. Likewise, General Chennault could not depend on information from the Chinese War Ministry since it often took up to six weeks to reach his headquarters. He therefore relied a great deal on photo reconnaissance. In the early days of the AVG, Chennault directed pilot Erik Shilling to modify one of the group's P-40s into a jury-rigged photo ship. This sort of improvisation remained the order of the day until November 1942, when a flight of three F-4s (modified P-38Es) from the 9th Photo Reconnaissance Squadron in India arrived at Kunming for detached service in China. The twin-engine Lightnings immediately captured the imagination of Maj Frank Schiel, the

100   FALLEN TIGERS

AVG veteran in command of the 74th Fighter Squadron. He checked out in the new aircraft and began flying reconnaissance missions in early December. On the fifth, he flew the first photo mission to Taiwan. Unfortunately, he encountered adverse weather upon his return to Kunming and fatally crashed into the side of a mountain.

As Chennault increased the tempo of his offensive operations, it became apparent he needed more than a single flight of reconnaissance planes. On August 12, 1943, the 21st Photo Reconnaissance Squadron took over for the 9th's detachment, with A Flight at Kunming covering Burma, Thailand, and French Indochina and B Flight at Guilin covering Hankou, Guangzhou, and Hong Kong.

That summer, while American fighters fought their strategic defensive for the bases in central China, Chinese workers completed a new field for aerial guerrilla operations at Suichuan, in Jiangxi Province, 250 miles east of Guilin. The 21st Photo Reconnaissance Squadron established C Flight there on October 29 to begin regular coverage of Shanghai and Taiwan. Winfree Sordelett demonstrated the potential of the new base two days later when he flew a nine-hour mission to reconnoiter Sasebo and Nagasaki—a round-trip of over two thousand miles; "Marjorie J." became the first American warplane over the Japanese home islands since the Doolittle Raid, a feat for which Sordelett received the Distinguished Flying Cross. Without modern navigation aids, long-range missions like this depended entirely on pilotage and dead reckoning. Flying "unarmed, alone, and unafraid" left reconnaissance pilots without the mutual support of a wingman or a witness if something went wrong. Unsurprisingly, the cause of loss remains unknown for eight of the sixteen F-5s reported missing in the China Theater—compared to fewer than 9 percent of aircraft overall.

The field at Suichuan finally put Taiwan within reach of the forward echelon's long-range fighters and medium bombers. Having only recently returned from a short leave to the United States, Casey Vincent immediately began planning a mission to Hsinchu. He ordered C Flight to maintain regular photographic coverage. The strike force he assembled consisted of fourteen B-25s: eight from the veteran 11th Bomb Squadron and six from the new Chinese-American Composite Wing (CACW). The latter organization grew from a novel idea to build a new, modern Chinese Air Force that could hold its own against the Japanese by having Chinese airmen fly in joint squadrons alongside American counterparts. Each leadership position had

Chinese and Americans working in tandem, such as Chinese and American co-squadron commanders. Captain Xu Hua-jiang, survivor of the Chinese Air Force's first encounter with the Japanese Zero in 1940, co-commanded the CACW's 7th Fighter Squadron alongside AVG veteran Maj Bill Reed, for example. Once the Chinese aviators gained enough experience to stand on their own, the Americans planned to withdraw from the organization.

Half the Chinese officers attended training programs in the United States. All the aviators and ground crews—Chinese and Americans alike—went through P-40 or B-25 transition at an operational training unit in Karachi. The unit taught navigation, gunnery, radio use, medium-altitude and skip bombing, armament, fighter and bomber tactics, line maintenance, and technical supply methods.[2] As could be expected, the CACW had considerable obstacles to overcome in terms of differing language, culture, and experience.[3] An aircrew-attrition study found the wing's fighter losses to be two-and-a-half times higher per one hundred sorties than the Fourteenth Air Force's other fighter units; bomber losses averaged one-and-a-half times higher.[4] The CACW's 2nd Bomb Squadron (Provisional) completed its training and flew to China in late October 1943. The unit did not get off to an auspicious start. "The first mission by the Chinese-American Composite Wing was not so good," Casey noted in his diary on November 4. "We lost two planes."[5]

Fighter escort for the mission to Hsinchu would include eight of the P-51As only recently arrived in China and assigned to the 76th Fighter Squadron as well as eight P-38s from the 449th. On November 9, in the aftermath of the 449th's disastrous mission to Jiujiang, General Chennault had appointed a new squadron commander, someone he believed could fix both the unit's tactical deficiencies and its low morale: Lt Col George "Mac" McMillan.

When Mac had returned home after the AVG disbanded in July 1942, the small citrus town of Winter Garden, Florida, gave him a hero's welcome. The *Orlando Sentinel* dedicated the entire front page to him. The mayor pulled him on stage in the local theater to tell the assembled crowd about his adventures with the AVG. Mac hated it; although confident in his abilities as a fighter pilot, he did not like being the center of attention. He wanted to spend time with his family. He needed to decompress. The jubilation of the crowd and his success at shooting down four and a half enemy planes clashed with his feelings over the death of his friends, his injury in combat, the loss of

102   FALLEN TIGERS

Burma, and the job left unfinished in China. He knew he had more of a part to play in what promised to be a long and bloody war.[6]

Shortly after coming home, Mac rejoined the Army Air Forces as a first lieutenant. He promptly received a promotion to captain and departed on a brief trip to the Southwest Pacific, where he educated American fighter squadrons on the tactics that had made the AVG so effective. Promoted to major on his return, Mac reported to the Army Air Forces Proving Ground at Eglin Field, Florida. Between December 1942 and September 1943, he tested new equipment, weapons, and tactics—flying attack aircraft, bombers, transports, observation planes, and trainers. He piloted every frontline fighter in the Army Air Force inventory as well as US Navy Hellcats and Corsairs—even a British Spitfire. In just ten months, he added another 272 flying hours to his resume. His assignment at Eglin overlapped with that of his brother, Charles, a technical sergeant with a crash-boat company. Mac also made a handful of flights to Orlando to visit his family. He went out several times with Jean Geurnsey, the girl he had written home about in 1942. She was smitten. But he had begun to think of a career in the military, while she wanted him to get out and settle down after the war. Before long, a breakup was in order; he had to let her down easy.

Mac's stateside interlude could only last so long. Chennault wrote to him personally to ask that he return to China. He left the States in October, promoted to lieutenant colonel just before his departure.[7] Another old China hand, Col Tex Hill, went with him. Tex had also spent his interlude at the Proving Ground and returned to China to command the 23rd Fighter Group.

In Lieutenant Colonel McMillan, Chennault knew he had the commander he needed to turn around the 449th. Ironically, of all the frontline Army fighters at the Proving Ground, Mac had flown the least number of hours in P-38s (only seventeen, compared to thirty-six in P-51s, forty-three in P-40s, and seventy-six in P-39s). Still, his time with the AVG meant he had more combat experience than the rest of the squadron combined. Certainly, he had more flying time: a whopping 1,221 hours. Most young fighter pilots in China had barely a third as much.[8]

Mac could have stepped into the 449th and immediately shaken things up—taken charge, led from the front, and inundated the men with lessons learned from his time with the AVG. But he chose a different approach. For several weeks he flew as wingman to the interim operations officer. He listened and learned, observing the squadron carefully until he knew it from top

Thanksgiving Day   103

to bottom, every intimate detail of maintenance, armament, intelligence, and operations. He even washed floors, dug gun emplacements, and did everything he asked his sergeants, lieutenants, and captains to do. His changes came quietly and collaboratively. The men respected his humility and appreciated his careful handling of their raw nerves.[9]

"Mac was an old China hand who knew the country and hated the Japs," wrote 1st Lt Robert Patterson in the squadron's official historical report. "He had flown under General Chennault with the AVG in Burma and he knew from experience where the enemy's strength and weaknesses lay. A tall, rangy man, he was the essence of all fighter pilots and he had the respect and admiration of the entire squadron from the start."[10]

The squadron chaplain, Father Joseph Cosgrove, could not help but admire how the veteran fighter pilot handled his new command. Cosgrove had been a Catholic priest in China before the war, running a mission just south of the 449th's base at Lingling. Chennault frequently leveraged the experience of old China hands and missionaries. Paul Frillmann had been a Lutheran preacher in Hankou before joining the AVG as chaplain and later returning to China as an intelligence officer. Malcolm Rosholt, a newspaper reporter in Shanghai, and John Birch, the Baptist missionary who had helped Jimmy Doolittle, also joined Fourteenth Air Force intelligence. These men brought with them a rare familiarity with the country, the people, and the language that proved invaluable to the American air force in China.[11]

Father Cosgrove valued Mac's ability to show unselfish care for his men without coddling them. The priest also marveled at his utter fearlessness in combat. "McMillan was first to roar down the runway and first to turn into enemy fighters when sighted," he wrote. "I never saw a pilot who so relished combat with the enemy." One day the chaplain kidded him about his aggressive flying.

"George, you must be Irish!" he joked.

"Irish be damned, Padre," Mac retorted. "I'm Scotch, and a Scotsman will lick a Harp any day!"[12]

Meanwhile, when the photos from Sordelett's reconnaissance mission on November 22 hit Casey Vincent's desk, the eyes nearly bulged from the colonel's head. He had one of the photos enlarged and tacked it to the wall in his office. He immediately convened his staff.

"Gentlemen," he began, "you see before you a photograph of Hsinchu Airdrome on the island of Taiwan. There are eighty-eight bombers of the

104   FALLEN TIGERS

Imperial Japanese Navy lined up here, wingtip-to-wingtip." He looked directly at Tex Hill, who had only recently taken command of the 23rd Fighter Group and also served as second in command of the forward echelon. "Tex, do you have any suggestions?" he asked with a wink.

"Let's get 'em!" Tex replied enthusiastically.

After the meeting, Casey pulled Tex aside. "I want you to take charge of this mission," he told him. Casey would have liked to lead it himself, but Chennault had grounded him after his sixth air-to-air kill in August. "It's got to be a secret," he continued. "Don't even tell the men where you're going until you're about to take off. This one can't leak out to the Japs." As with Merian Cooper's attack on Hong Kong a year earlier, operational security would be paramount. The strike force would also have to maintain strict radio silence until over the target. "When you get close to home, give me a call on the radio," Casey directed. "If the mission fails, the code will be 'New York.' If it succeeds—"

"How about 'San Antonio'?" Tex suggested.

"San Antonio it is."[13]

On November 24, Mac gathered his pilots in the alert shack at Lingling and told them to prepare for an overnight stay at an undisclosed airbase. He made sure to mention that they needed to bring their Mae West life jackets. Eight P-38s departed for Suichuan at dusk. Eight P-51As and fourteen B-25s joined them from Guilin. At eight thirty the next morning—Thanksgiving Day—Tex collected the crews together and briefed them on their mission. All thirty planes took off between nine thirty and ten o'clock, though one of the Mustangs returned to base with a hydraulic malfunction.[14] Two days before, Casey had staged a strike force through Suichuan to attack Hankou. Tex led his armada of twenty-nine warplanes on a feint to the north to trick any watchful enemy agents into thinking he was repeating the earlier mission before finally turning east.

Over the strait, the formation dropped to a mere hundred feet above the water to avoid detection by Japanese radar. When the coast of Taiwan came into view, the warplanes climbed to one thousand feet. The P-38s charged ahead to clear the way for the bombers; the P-51s held back as close escort. Mac flew on the mission but did not lead the Lightnings, deferring instead to Maj Sam Palmer, the group operations officer and the man who had brought Squadron X to China in July.

The Lightnings crossed the coastline at about noon, careening into a gaggle of Japanese bombers preparing to land at the field. Many enemy airmen

Thanksgiving Day   105

went down in flames before they knew what hit them. The P-38s then dove to strafe the parked aircraft; Japanese air and ground crews scattered, diving for cover. Behind the Lightnings, the B-25s roared in, line abreast. Their fragmentation bombs tore through aircraft, hangars, and barracks across the length and breadth of the field. Tex Hill's P-51s followed, downing a couple of enemy fighters that launched to intercept. As the formation wheeled around to the west, the Lightnings came in for one last strafing run, expending the rest of their ammunition into the murky, smoke-filled inferno.[15]

Tex radioed Casey on his return to Suichuan: "San Antonio—in a big way."

Fourteenth Air Force claimed forty-six Japanese planes destroyed on the raid. The Imperial Japanese Navy reported losing two A6M Zeros and two G3M "Nells" in the air and twelve Nells on the ground. The Japanese Army Air Force did not report its losses, though it almost certainly had aircraft at the field.[16] A reconnaissance mission later that day seemed to corroborate American claims, though billowing smoke obscured much of the photograph. The mission cost the Americans a single bullet hole through the tail of a P-38, minor damage to three of the B-25s from small-arms fire, and minor damage to a P-51's wing where it had hit a tree while strafing. The raiders returned to their central China bases the next day, leaving little behind to bear the wrath of Japanese retaliatory bombing at Suichuan.

"Thanksgiving. Finally got our 'dream' mission off," Casey wrote in his diary. "Fourteen B-25s, eight P-38s, and seven P-51s led by 'Tex' Hill. Cleaned House—shot down fourteen Japanese planes over their own field and destroyed or damaged fifty to sixty Japanese bombers on the ground. We lost not a plane! The Chinese-American Bomber outfit got in it with six of their B-25s and did admirably. I'm thinking they're going to be a damn good outfit. We took a big risk, but it turned out well. Sent them in low— right on the water—and achieved 100 percent surprise. A very lovely Thanksgiving Day!"

Chennault visited Suichuan himself on February 4, 1944. The transport carrying him and Casey landed safely despite battling low ceilings and stormy weather the entire way from Guilin. The Old Man was on an inspection tour of his eastern airfields; in addition to the base at Suichuan, the Chinese had finished fields at Ganzhou and Nanxiong, forty and ninety miles to the south, respectively. All fell within Casey's area of responsibility. His forward echelon had become the 68th Composite Wing at the end of December 1943,

106   FALLEN TIGERS

responsible for operations in central and eastern China. Colonel John Kennedy's 69th Composite Wing covered operations in the south and west.[17]

Up to this point in the war, the eastern fields had served primarily as forward staging bases for guerrilla raids. But Chennault felt it was time for the Fourteenth Air Force to take its next step forward. Suichuan put his medium bombers within easy reach of the lower Yangzi, the Taiwan Strait, and the South China Sea. Touting the inflated claims from frequent sea sweeps, he had written to President Roosevelt that his airmen sank 56,900 tons of shipping in January 1944 alone. He promised even better results if he could get just ten thousand tons of supplies over the Hump each month. "Your figures on results of operations against Japanese shipping are excellent," Roosevelt replied. "You are the doctor and I approve your treatment."[18]

Air Transport Command had finally crossed the ten thousand tons a month threshold in December 1943, but this included supplies destined for the Nationalist government and American-trained Chinese troops in addition to the Fourteenth Air Force's allotment. Nor did the complexity of Chennault's logistical problem end once supplies made it over the Hump.[19] The tenuous road and rail links, known as the eastern line of communications, often took months to move fuel, equipment, and ammunition to his forward airfields. It could take weeks to build up enough of a stockpile for a substantial mission. Operations from Suichuan had to be continually balanced against the meager resources available.

Nevertheless, Casey had moved a mixed detachment of fifteen Sharks and Mustangs from the 76th Fighter Squadron to the field on December 26, 1943. A Japanese bombing raid the next day hit the alert shack, burning up everything inside—including all of Glen Beneda's clothes![20] A strafing attack three days later destroyed "Marjorie J.," the storied reconnaissance Lightning that had been the first Allied warplane over Japan after Doolittle's bombers and had brought back the photos that prompted the Thanksgiving Day attack on Taiwan.[21]

The 449th's improved performance and morale under the leadership of Lieutenant Colonel McMillan gave Casey confidence to move a detachment of eight Lightnings to Suichuan on January 6, 1944. Two days after Chennault's visit in February, he moved the rest of the squadron forward. In a sense, this put all his eggs in one basket—all the Fourteenth Air Force's long-range fighters at the same exposed forward base. Not only could the newer Mustangs and Lightnings better handle marauding Japanese fighters, though, the eastern

Thanksgiving Day   107

field also amplified their greater range. American aircraft flying from Suichuan often struck at important targets like Jiujiang, a port on the Yangzi River only 250 miles to the north-northeast that served as a waystation for shipping into Hankou. The Japanese had captured the port in November 1938 and pressed south along the railroad to take Nanchang, the capital of Jiangxi Province, in May 1939. They had since heavily fortified both cities with flak and fighters. Raids on these enemy strongholds often encountered fierce resistance.

This meant Mac's squadron would be in the thick of it, and he became particularly concerned with the problem of how to build his pilots' skill and confidence. With every ounce of gasoline having to come by airlift over the Hump and then down the eastern line of communications, he did not have fuel for training. He decided to give novice pilots time to build experience by assigning them less hazardous missions; only battle-tested veterans would visit tough targets like Hankou and Jiujiang. Mac always led the most dangerous missions personally; he never asked his men to go on one he would not fly himself.[22]

He frequently discussed the situation with his new operations officer, Maj Rex Barber, the man who shot down Admiral Yamamoto. Chennault had subverted War Department policy in allowing Barber to fly combat missions in China. Because of his role in the attack on Yamamoto, the major knew something about American code-breaking activities. If he were shot down and captured, the consequences could be catastrophic for US intelligence operations. But Chennault constantly struggled to keep his small command adequately manned with experienced aviators, and it irked him to see a perfectly good fighter ace going to waste; he decided to risk it.

On February 10, 1944, Mac led an escort mission from Suichuan, with Barber on his wing. Captain Earl Helms, a North Africa veteran, led the second element, while 2nd Lt Keith Mahon, a young, inexperienced new pilot in the squadron, flew tail-end Charlie—the last fighter in the formation. Half an hour into the mission, they sighted a flight of three Type 99 "Lily" light bombers headed in the opposite direction, slightly above them and to their right.[23] McMillan attacked, firing a short burst that sent one of the bombers down in flames. A second bomber escaped up-sun, but the third continued on course.

Rather than let any of the veterans run up their personal scores, Mac held them off to the side and gave Mahon a crack at the third Lily. The young aviator, his mouth dry and fingers fumbling with switches, closed on the twin-engine warplane until he could feel the buffet from its prop wash. He opened fire, tracers flying wildly, bullets hitting all over. The clumsy attack

108   FALLEN TIGERS

had no apparent effect. Mahon focused, trying to tighten his aim, and finally noticed a spray of oil jetting back. Then the bomber slowed and yawed sideways—the young lieutenant had to break hard to keep from ramming it! When he rolled out, he saw the bomber plummeting toward the earth in flames. With that, the young novice had one confirmed aerial victory to his credit. Mac's choice to develop his new pilot rather than add to his own score set the lieutenant on a path to eventually become an ace himself.[24]

Two days later, on February 12, the Japanese Army Air Force put the outcomes of Mac's leadership philosophy to the test when it attacked Suichuan in strength. Major Tougo Saito led eleven Ki-44 Shokis from the 85th Air Regiment and fourteen Ki-43 Hayabusas from the 11th Air Regiment toward the base at twenty thousand feet. The Americans launched everything they had: Captain Stewart with a total of ten P-40s and P-51s and Lieutenant Colonel McMillan with fourteen P-38s. They met the enemy south of the field. Captain Wakamatsu, the ace who had participated in the attack on Guilin on August 20, led the top cover. He dove in and immediately shot down a Mustang, killing its pilot. Other Americans hit his fighter in turn, and Wakamatsu had to leave the fight, nursing his damaged Shoki back to Guangzhou. There he waited for the other ten planes from his regiment; only two returned. The survivors told him the Americans had been so aggressive it had been nearly impossible to break away—even when they ran low on fuel. Two of their number, including the wounded regimental commander, Major Saito, crash-landed, out of gas, on their way back to Guangzhou. The remaining six Ki-44s all fell in combat with the American fighters. Just six months before, the Shoki seemed to have offered Japan a decisive technological advantage in the skies over China; the dogfight on February 12 made it clear that advantage had disappeared.[25]

The battle saw Lee Gregg claim his third confirmed and second probable aerial victories in just over six months of combat in China—quite a change of pace from his time in the Mediterranean. Overall, Mac's Lightnings claimed six enemy fighters destroyed for the loss of only one of their own. Second Lieutenant Art Masterson bailed out south of the field; he walked into Suichuan just two days later. The decisive air battle showed just how complete a transformation Mac had brought about in the 449th. For their part, the Japanese did not make any major daylight raids against the base for the next three months.

10

Ambush at Jiujiang

April 29, 1944
Jiujiang, China

Rex Barber pulled his Lightning around in a climbing turn toward his wingman's attackers. "Dive for the deck!" he ordered. He had thought this would be a "milk run." The weather had finally lifted enough for a pair of B-25s to patrol north from Suichuan on a river sweep. Barber had decided to accompany them with an escort of nine P-38s. With Lieutenant Colonel McMillan on detached service in India for several weeks, the major had temporary command of the 449th. Figuring it would be an easy mission, he flew with 2nd Lt Fred Roll, a recent arrival, on his wing. They had stayed low under the scud as the B-25s began combing the river for enemy shipping. Six miles west of Jiujiang, however, Japanese fighters had set upon them in a classic ambush from above. Ten Hayabusas from the 25th Air Regiment and four fixed-gear Ki-27 "Nates" from the 118th Flying Training Regiment dove to attack. Barber ordered the B-25s to head for home and brought his Lightnings in to cover them. Then he noticed his novice wingman had fallen behind.

The major pulled into a steep climb, taking aim at Roll's attackers. They had too much of an altitude advantage; his speed quickly bled away and his fighter mushed into a stall. Tracers filled the sky around him as an enemy fighter set fire to his right engine. Barber jettisoned the canopy and jumped clear only four hundred feet above the ground.

Second Lieutenant Robert Campbell followed Barber into the fight; he shot an Oscar off the major's tail and then turned to help Roll. Another Oscar hit him from behind in turn. His left engine quit and smoke began pouring into the cockpit. He dove away toward Suichuan.

110 FALLEN TIGERS

Meanwhile, Billie Beardsley had just scored his first confirmed kill since unwittingly ending the enemy's summer air offensive the previous September. Exiting the melee, he spotted Campbell's crippled fighter ahead of him, flying south along the Jiujiang–Nanchang railway. Overtaking it, he noticed the feathered prop on the dead left engine. He did not think the shot-up Lightning would make it back to Suichuan. Instead, he figured the best course of action would be for Campbell to get as far from enemy territory as possible.

"Fly west!" Beardsley directed.

"I can't climb over the mountains to the west," Campbell replied.

Beardsley stuck with him, circling the mountain ahead of them until they got pointed in the right direction. Then Campbell's right engine began cutting out. He kept the Lightning under control down to eight hundred feet. Then Beardsley saw the fighter suddenly flip onto its back. A moment later he saw the pilot bail out. The airplane crashed and exploded; Campbell landed on a hillside, his parachute tangled in the trees. Beardsley marked the position—two miles south of Tianzhu—and then headed home.

Despite his proximity to the enemy strongholds at Jiujiang and Nanchang, Campbell had fallen into good hands. Civilians in the area had an excellent track record of immediately moving downed American airmen from harm's way. Captain Kenneth George, for example, had crash-landed twenty miles to the south when ground fire crippled his P-51 on February 7. After seeing his identification flag and pointie-talkie, villagers sent a runner to alert nearby guerrillas. Two soon arrived, indistinguishable from the civilians save for their rifles. They hired a sedan chair and carried the pilot into the hills.[1]

When 1st Lt Jack Blanco bailed out of his P-40 on March 18, the Hayabusas that had shot him down came around for a strafing pass. Machine-gun fire came within ten feet of him as he jumped into the underbrush. He remained hidden for several minutes after the enemy fighters departed. Hearing murmurs from the other side of the scrub, Blanco emerged with his identification flag in hand. Several civilians who had gathered around his parachute motioned for him to hurry over. One took off his overcoat and exchanged it for Blanco's flying coveralls, another gave him pants, and a third a straw hat and a pair of rope sandals. Then they hurried him into the hills.[2]

Once Lieutenant Campbell extricated himself from his parachute harness, he called to a nearby farmer and showed him his pointie-talkie. The man quickly led him to a village and hid him in a small hut. The pilot remained there alone for a few minutes until the farmer returned with a small man dressed in black; a button on his tunic had Chinese writing and a number. Using the pointie-talkie, he identified himself as a guerrilla and made it clear the two of them had to hurry to stay ahead of the Japanese.[3]

Guerrillas such as this one professed allegiance to the Guomindang in Jiujiang District. Some of the irregulars had been businessmen or government officials who fled when the Japanese took the city. Still others had been farmers, chased from towns along the railroad between Jiujiang and Nanchang. Many wore tattered gray uniforms with ammunition belts around their waists and across their shoulders. Most carried old German pistols. Some had ancient bolt-action rifles, many French made but some German, Belgian, American, and even Japanese models. They had also captured a few light machine guns, some grenades, and other equipment.

The guerrillas claimed not only to challenge Japanese patrols in the countryside but also to infiltrate occupied towns and villages to create chaos for the occupiers. One fighter told Captain George about a time he had snuck into town with an automatic pistol concealed in his clothing. At an opportune moment, he pulled it out, shot an unsuspecting Japanese soldier, and then disappeared into the crowd. Another said he carried dynamite with two-to-three-minute fuses, which he inconspicuously dropped into concentrations of Japanese and then walked away. One pilot reported meeting "a good looking Chinese boy who claimed his hobby was to dress and act as a woman and entice the not unwilling Japanese soldier to some secluded location and then slit his throat. She (he) claimed quite a number of successful conquests."[4]

Rex Barber also soon found himself in the care of friendly guerrillas. After bailing out only four hundred feet above the ground, he hit hard, landing on a small, wooded hill, breaking his right arm in two places and severely injuring his right ankle. Too hurt to move, two civilians dragged the major several miles to safer ground. As soon as they left the main trail, a squad of Japanese soldiers hurried by, quiet and grim. Only later did Barber learn that guerrillas quickly liquidated any small groups of Japanese that ventured into the hills. A few of these partisans arrived soon after the soldiers passed. They constructed a crude sedan chair from bamboo and enlisted the help of some nearby farmers to carry the American away. They sent a runner ahead to prepare relays of fresh carriers.[5]

112 FALLEN TIGERS

The guerrillas had to move fast; enemy troops aggressively pursued them into the mountains. Those who had rescued Captain George brought him to a small hut in a remote valley. Just twenty minutes after he crash-landed, a company of 150 Japanese soldiers arrived at the wreck and began questioning the locals. Their inquiries met with stony silence. The troops offered a cash reward for any information, also to no effect. Then they threatened to behead the reticent townsfolk and set fire to their homes. Still, no one said a word, even when the soldiers began to make good on their threats. Many civilians died to protect a foreigner they had only glimpsed in passing. The soldiers nevertheless managed to track George to the valley and established blocking positions across the two trails leading in and out. The guerrillas gathered what forces they could—three hundred men eventually—and for three days attacked the enemy positions until the Japanese finally withdrew.[6]

Mr. Yiu, the guerrilla captain who took charge of Blanco's rescue, told the American about Japanese agents dressed as civilians who spread throughout the countryside to determine his whereabouts. They offered a $35,000CN reward for information leading to his capture. Yiu claimed to have personally shot a Chinese traitor trying to gather information for the enemy. After learning of Japanese troops shooting several civilians they suspected of helping Blanco, the guerrilla captain decided to publicize details of the rescue in several local newspapers. These accounts included his name and the names of several of his key lieutenants. The breach of security perplexed Blanco, but Yiu explained he wanted the Japanese to focus their efforts on his resistance fighters, rather than on innocent civilians.[7]

Regardless of Yiu's efforts, civilians in the countryside experienced frequent reprisals for helping Americans and harboring guerrillas. As he progressed west into the mountains, Campbell reported that the Japanese had destroyed every town through which he passed. Syphilis sores covered many of the people he saw. The locals told him about a few enemy commanders who had tried a more conciliatory approach; their troops continued to plunder the countryside for food and supplies, but they issued receipts promising future payment. These efforts, far too little and far too late, did nothing to change the attitudes of the occupied.

In contrast, the Chinese gave the very best of their meager food and accommodations to their American guests, usually meals of rice and chicken, sometimes fruit. Campbell reported eating 173 eggs before returning to Suichuan. His rescuers brought him south and west through the mountains to the small foothill town of Jing'an. There he met Mr. Chen, the exiled magistrate of Anyi County. Chen spoke a little English and, after Campbell told him all the details of his bailout, dispatched three hundred troops to find and, if possible, destroy the aircraft. He offered the lieutenant use of a bed in his office. It consisted of little more than boards covered by a quilt, and, as the pilot discovered, was infested with bedbugs. Chen had decorated the office walls with paper banners proclaiming in English, "Long Life of American," "Long Life of China," and "We Will Bring the Japanese Imperialists to Their Knees."

The next day the town held a parade in Campbell's honor, and Chen gave a speech. "Yesterday you came to here," the magistrate began, addressing the aviator:

> It is very celebrated, for we became acquainted with you at this place. You are an officer in the Fourteenth Air Service of USA. But you came to our country seven months ago, having no regard for your very life. You are fighting life and death against the Japanese for a real and lasting peace and for achieving the goal of the final victory. We rejoice to see you here and we must learn your good and gallant spirit.
>
> Today in devout gratitude we are celebrating that you are safely coming back, but we apologize, for we have no good things to greet you, because this place is at the front. We are allies, your country gives us effective and immediate aid, but we will wage this war while there is strength in our bodies and blood in our veins! Your President Roosevelt said we are making sure, absolutely and irrevocably sure, that this time the lesson will be driven home to them once and for all. We are actually going to be rid of the outlaws this time. Every one of the United Nations believes in a real and lasting peace, and justifies the sacrifices we are making, and our humanity is as confident in seeking that goal.
>
> We must fight! We repeat it sir, we must fight! We alike again worked with the wise, and good and gallant gentlemen, the brave officers of Fourteenth Air Service of USA. Now on behalf of the eight hundred thousand [sic] Chinese of Anyi, I simply want to say to you that we love you. At last, I deliver a prayer for your arriving at the destination safe and sound and please accept my best wishes for your happiness on the way back.
>
> God be with you.[8]

114 FALLEN TIGERS

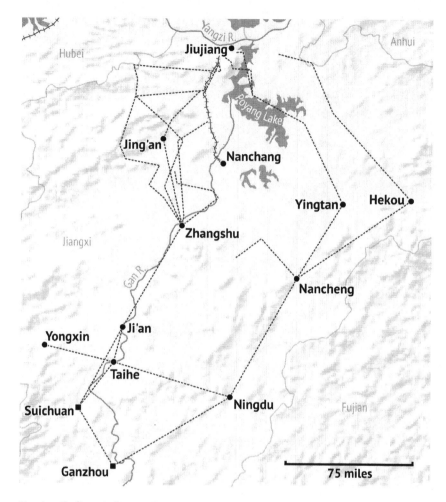

Evasion Ratlines in Jiangxi Province

The heartfelt speech touched Campbell deeply. He owed his life to these people and yet they celebrated him as some sort of hero—he who had been shot down by the enemy! He mumbled a few words of thanks.

Campbell rested in Jing'an for two days before continuing his journey. Soldiers from the Nationalist 183rd Division brought him south to Zhangshu, on the Gan River, on May 5. Two days later, he boarded a river steamer south through Ji'an, arriving at Taihe on the eleventh. At each stop, his hosts kept careful track of any expenses incurred and had him sign the receipts so they could secure compensation from the Nationalist government—a practice mentioned in a handful of evasion reports. A car picked him up the next day and drove him to Suichuan. Barber followed almost a month behind. Because he had bailed out so much closer to Jiujiang, his rescuers had to swing much farther west through the mountains before they could bring him south. The two young men who had dragged him out of harm's way stayed with him. Both had escaped Shanghai after the Japanese took over and wished to leave occupied Jiujiang at the earliest chance; an American pilot landing in their backyard provided just such an opportunity. When they arrived at Ji'an on June 7, Barber found Lieutenant Colonel McMillan waiting to drive them to Suichuan in his Jeep. Barber made sure the young men both got jobs at the Fourteenth Air Force hostel there.[9]

The journey back to American control gave evading airmen a rare opportunity to coordinate with Chinese forces in the field. Barber's rescuers informed him they no longer operated east of the railway between Jiujiang and Nanchang; the Japanese had made it too difficult for them. They asked him to tell other airmen, if possible, to head west of the tracks before bailing out or crash-landing.

Passing through the headquarters of the New Third Army in Caofang, Captain George had seen a multitude of troops—apparently well trained and well equipped—moving into defensive positions in the hills. Their commander, General Yi, seemed to think the Japanese would make a move soon. He asked if the Americans would be able to help. "Yes," George told him, "if at all possible. But you'll have to use markers of some sort to designate areas to be hit. Mark the flanks of any area to be attacked with large, light-colored panels with an arrowhead pointing in the direction to attack."[10]

Evaders also brought back valuable intelligence from their time behind the lines. Squadron intelligence and Air-Ground Aid Section (AGAS) officers debriefed them, learning that Japanese influence extended little beyond points of occupation; outside their blockhouses and garrisons, their influence melted away with the passing of their patrols. The debriefings also uncovered crucial information about enemy air defenses. Blanco reported that the 25th Air Regiment maintained standing patrols over the docks and city of Jiujiang. When they judged the weather favorable, they launched a flight very early in the morning, increasing their strength aloft until at least eighteen Hayabusas patrolled during peak hours of American attacks, between

116   FALLEN TIGERS

ten thirty in the morning and two o'clock in the afternoon. Afterward, they gradually decreased the patrols until the last flight landed at dusk. Barber reported enemy fighter patrols taking off regularly each day at six thirty, eight thirty, and ten thirty in the morning, and two thirty and four thirty in the afternoon. According to Mr. Yiu, the guerrilla captain, the Japanese had also constructed a crude imitation of Chennault's warning net, giving them twenty minutes' notice of planes approaching from upriver.[11]

Suddenly, the ambushes over Jiujiang made sense. After losing four P-38s on October 30, 1943, the demoralized 449th had assumed some traitorous Chinese had leaked word of the mission. In reality the Japanese warning system had probably detected the Lightnings as they approached down the Yangzi and alerted patrolling Hayabusas. The same thing had probably happened to Blanco on March 18 and Barber and Campbell on April 29.

In addition to intelligence about the enemy, evaders also brought back information gleaned from Chinese sources on the fate of their fellow airmen. Guerrillas told Barber what had happened to 1st Lt Tommy Taylor, the pilot still missing from the ambush on October 30. His squadron mates had heard "the epitome of a fightin' Texan" had crash-landed and "shot it out with the Japs on the ground."[12] According to the guerrillas, however, when civilians appeared on the scene to rescue him, he mistook them for the enemy and shot several of them. They withdrew and shortly thereafter, a Japanese patrol arrived and captured him. The troops beat Taylor severely and then dragged him away. The guerrillas claimed the enemy subjected him to the "sun treatment" before he died in captivity.

Captain Maxwell Becker, the AGAS officer debriefing Barber, believed this to be just one in a rash of incidents of downed airmen becoming trigger happy. "Our airmen must learn to recognize their friends, the Chinese," he concluded. "In some cases, there may be a question but I should venture to say in 999 cases out of a thousand the Chinese may be instantly recognized by their actions and by their clothing."[13]

The question of whether to carry a firearm on combat missions proved surprisingly contentious among Americans in China. Blanco did not have a gun on him when he flew, believing it would have done him little good. Captain James Williams, shot down by Tojos near Hong Kong in December 1943, had a similar opinion. When asked by the debriefing officer if he had a gun, he replied: "No sir, I didn't. I feel like this about carrying a gun: I think if I met a small group of people, they would be Chinese because any small band of Japs would be wiped out or quickly gotten rid of. A large number of Japs would probably get me anyway. To shoot Chinese would be equally serious. If I had a gun and they wanted it, I would give it to them."[14] In contrast, Lieutenant Cunningham, the bombardier from Howard Allers's B-25, swore by his sidearm. "If it hadn't been for my pistol," he asserted, "the Chinese villagers would have taken me . . . and later in the pursuit they would have been far bolder if I had been unarmed."[15]

Some airmen ventured another reason for carrying a sidearm. One fighter pilot recalled that when he reported to his squadron in China, the commander handed him a pistol. "You count the number of bullets in that gun," he told him. "If they shoot you down, you kill as many of them as you can. But save one for yourself."[16] This shocking advice reflected a considerable anxiety many felt at the prospect of being captured by the Japanese. The Americans knew all too well the enemy's brutality, whether in strafing airmen when they crashed or bailed out or in mistreating or murdering prisoners. Indeed, though less than 5 percent of missing airmen in the China Theater became prisoners of war, a startling 29 percent of those did not survive the experience. While with the guerrillas, Blanco learned that the Japanese had captured Maj Lee P. Manbeck and paraded him through the streets of Jiujiang. Manbeck had been missing in action since February 10, 1944. Either because of injuries suffered in the crash or at the hands of his captors, he died two days later.[17]

The case of Sgt Carl K. Cannon became infamous in the Fourteenth Air Force, with new details and rumors emerging in successive evasion reports. Cannon served as aerial photographer on a B-25 lost over Jiujiang on January 10, 1944. Witnesses reported that the bomber took fire from a river gunboat, dropped its bombs on the docks, circled twice around the city—apparently out of control—and then crashed three miles to the southwest. "I believe that it is very improbable that any members of the crew survived the crash and explosion," reported 2nd Lt Albert Vavrick, navigator for another B-25 on the mission. Second Lieutenant Robert Thompson agreed: "I would say it would have been impossible for anyone to have gotten out."[18] But one crewmember did get out; guerrillas told a bomber crew walking out in September that Sergeant Cannon had bailed out and landed in a pond, surviving despite his parachute failing to fully deploy. A bandit gang immediately began firing at the airman, attracting the attention of nearby Japanese troops. The enemy rolled him up before friendly guerrillas could get to him.[19]

118   FALLEN TIGERS

Blanco's rescuers told him the Japanese troops paraded Cannon through the streets of Jiujiang and even offered money to a group of schoolboys to beat him. The kids apparently took the money and tore it up, outraging the soldiers. Later, the occupiers decided to seize on the propaganda value of Cannon's capture by compelling the city's civilians to attend a mass rally. A Japanese official railed against the British and Americans and extolled the virtues of Japan's Greater East Asia Co-Prosperity Sphere and its vision of "Asia for the Asians." The audience listened without enthusiasm. After his speech the official condescendingly offered Cannon a cigarette. The battered airman tore it to bits and threw it away. Enraged, the official ordered the guards to beat him.

In another story, the sergeant's captors made him stand for three days in river water up to his waist, not permitting him to sit down or rest. Yet another tale held that Cannon's father had been a missionary in Jiujiang before the war. When the Japanese paraded him through the streets, he came face to face with the old woman who had been his nurse.[20] A final story had that the Japanese walked the sergeant through Jiujiang for three days with a rope around his neck. He continually cursed the enemy in Chinese for the townspeople to hear. Then the soldiers pulled out his teeth, cut off his legs, and dragged his torso through the streets. The sergeant still lived, however, so they cut off his arms and left him to die.[21] There is no telling whether any of these stories are true. The last certainly proved to be false—or at least became conflated with that of another captive. The Japanese informed the International Red Cross of Cannon's capture on October 30, 1944, and American forces repatriated him from the Shinjuku prison camp near Tokyo on October 15, 1945. Regardless, the rumors required no exaggeration to add to the anxiety many airmen harbored at the prospect of being captured by the Japanese. According to Cannon's former commander, his time as a prisoner of war left him so traumatized that he eventually committed suicide.[22]

For those evaders who managed to return to Allied control, War Department policy limited their influence by prohibiting them from flying over enemy territory again. The policy further directed that personnel who could not be useful in noncombat posts return to the United States without delay. The underlying reasoning had that an airman could divulge information harmful to friendly underground organizations if shot down a second time and captured. This annoyed Chennault, but he had already subverted War Department policy when he allowed Barber to fly in China in the first place. His gamble came close to disaster when the major went down near Jiujiang.[23] Jack Blanco, Kenneth George, Rex Barber, and Robert Campbell thus all departed for the United States soon after they returned to American control. Their evasion experiences uncovered a dedicated and surprisingly active guerrilla movement deep in enemy territory that fought out of all proportion to its meager equipment, manning, and training. The presence of American airmen in occupied China gave a needed boost to the long-suffering Chinese and created a rare opportunity for coordination. Their return from behind the lines brought critical intelligence information to the American command.

11

Operation Ichi-Go

May 6, 1944
Hengyang, China

Casey Vincent watched as twenty-five P-40s and fourteen B-25s took to the air. They drew into formation over the field and rendezvoused with the top-cover element of fifteen Mustangs and Lightnings that had taken off from Lingling. Six of the bombers hailed from the veteran 11th Bomb Squadron, the other eight from the Chinese-American Composite Wing (CACW). They followed the Xiang River to the north-northeast at fifteen thousand feet, driving deep into enemy territory to strike supplies stockpiled at Hankou for a massive Japanese offensive. The Sharks packed in tight around the bombers as close escort. Tex Hill led the top-cover element above them at twenty thousand feet. His Mustangs—seven new "B" models—boasted Packard-built Merlin engines with more power and a higher service ceiling than the old P-51As; Casey had gone to India to lead the first flight over the Hump personally at the end of February.[1] Glen Beneda had gone with the colonel but ended up stuck in Karachi for a month, suffering from a relapse of malaria. The lieutenant returned to China on his own when he got out of the hospital and now led the last element of the last flight of Mustangs.[2] With Lieutenant Colonel McMillan still on detached service in India and Major Barber missing, 1st Lt Lee Gregg led the eight Lightnings.

This motley collection of fifty-four warplanes represented the greatest aerial armada yet assembled by the Americans in China. Casey had scraped together every airplane he could find for the big mission and flew up from Guilin to brief the Shark pilots and bomber crews himself. The rapidly growing emergency in the hinterland north of Hankou demanded a maximum effort response; he hoped it would make a difference.

Since January 1944, Fourteenth Air Force intelligence had reported enemy troops and supplies massing on the Yangzi at Hankou and north of the Yellow River bend near Kaifeng. The reports began as unverified rumors from Chinese sources, but downed airmen also brought back clues from behind the lines, such as when Kenneth George learned about the New Third Army's preparations to meet the enemy offensive.[3] John Birch, the former Baptist missionary who had helped the Doolittle Raiders, set up radio observation posts overlooking the Yangzi which reported on the uptick of river traffic into Hankou. He took a team north of the river to organize radio intelligence nets in Henan Province and witnessed large numbers of troops preparing to move south along the Beiping–Hankou Railway.[4]

Then on the night of April 17, the Japanese 37th Division crossed the Yellow River and began a drive toward the rail junction at Zhengzhou. Chinese resistance crumbled; the city fell within just two days. With the cork out of the bottle, 148,000 Japanese troops surged south along the railway.[5] The Imperial Army had timed its offensive to take advantage of seasonal bad weather as a screen against airpower. Casey could neither determine the enemy's movements nor divine their intentions. "I'd like more information on this new Japanese offensive," he vented in his diary.[6]

The Japanese called it Operation Ichi-go ("Number 1"). Their anxiety over the prospect of American warplanes bombing the home islands had only increased since the summer of 1943, when the 3rd Air Division had failed to dislodge Chennault's airmen from their central China bases. The situation became truly alarming with the Fourteenth Air Force's expansion east to Suichuan in the fall and the imminent arrival of the first B-29s that spring. On January 24, 1944, Imperial General Headquarters issued orders to General Shunroku Hata, commander in chief of the China Expeditionary Army, to prepare to destroy important Allied airbases in central and southwest China. The Japanese army would attempt to accomplish on the ground what it had failed to achieve in the air: final destruction of the American air force in China.[7]

The Japanese had other motivations besides just wiping out the airbases. They had estimated they would lose 1.8 million tons of shipping in the first two years of war with the United States. By the end of 1943, however, the Allies had destroyed 3.8 million tons, reducing Japan's merchant fleet to 77 percent of its prewar capacity. US Navy submarines accounted for more than half these losses, while aircraft operating from the South Pacific and China accounted for a

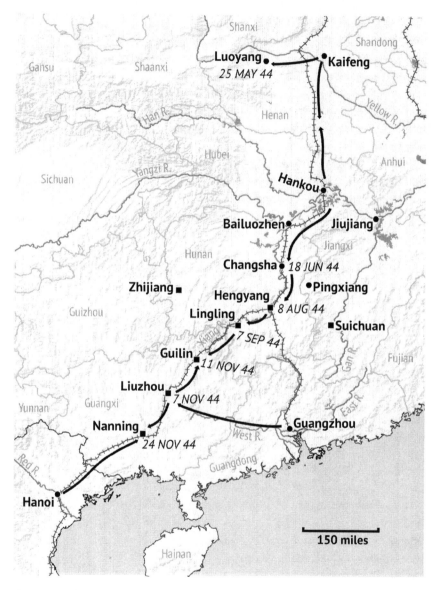

Operation Ichi-Go

quarter. A massive ground offensive through central China would not only eliminate the American airbases there but also complete the old railway corridor from Beiping to Indochina, establishing an inland line of communications safe from submarine attack.

Imperial General Headquarters specified its objectives for Ichi-go in a subsequent outline of operations sent to General Hata:

> Important areas along the Hunan–Guangxi, Guangzhou–Hankou, and southern Beiping–Hankou railways will be captured and maintained and vital enemy airbases will be destroyed, thus neutralizing enemy air activities.
>
> In late spring of 1944, the China Expeditionary Army will commence its operation from north China and from the Hankou area and, in summer from the Hankou and Guangdong areas.
>
> The China Expeditionary Army will destroy the enemy, particularly those units under the direct command of the Central Government. It will capture and secure first the southern sector of the Beiping–Hankou railway south of the Yellow River and then the strategic areas along the Hunan–Guangxi and Guangzhou–Hankou railways. If circumstances permit during subsequent operations, the Beiping–Hankou and Guangzhou–Hankou railways will be repaired.

The offensive thus had two main phases, each consisting of a vast pincer movement from opposing ends of the defunct railways. Phase one, which had begun in mid-April, sought the capture of the Beiping–Hankou line south of the Yellow River. The Japanese already controlled the line north of the river, which connected to rail networks throughout Manchuria and into Korea. Phase two would begin at the end of May and complete the connection between Hankou and both Guangzhou and Indochina, eliminating the Allied airbases in central China in the process. With nearly half a million troops committed to the operation, Ichi-go would be the largest Japanese ground offensive of World War II.[8]

The Japanese reinvigorated their air strength for the offensive, but air power took a back seat to ground operations. In mid-February, the 3rd Air Division became the Fifth Air Army, with four regiments of fighters, two of light bombers, one of attack aircraft, and one of reconnaissance and direct-cooperation aircraft—a total of 183 warplanes. General Hata tasked it with

124   FALLEN TIGERS

supporting his troops in the field. After mid-May the Japanese would no longer send big fighter sweeps or massive daytime bombing raids to challenge the Americans at their bases; the warning net gave the defenders too much of an advantage. Instead, the point of contact for the opposing air forces would be over the front lines of the ground battle. Fifth Air Army Headquarters issued a directive to its units: "Type 99 light bombers will assault and destroy enemy planes in night attacks on enemy airfields while the fighter units will shoot down enemy planes over the operational zone."[9]

With Nationalist forces unable to stop the Japanese offensive, Casey Vincent had to focus his efforts on the enemy's army instead of its air force. But most of the fighting north of Hankou took place outside the range of his bases in central China. Four squadrons of fighters and one of bombers from the CACW deployed to a handful of bases north of the Yangzi; however, poor weather and the chaotic situation on the ground hampered their ability to support Chinese ground troops. Unable to stop the enemy armies in the field, Casey endeavored to hit their concentration of supplies with the strike force of fifty-four planes he sent to Hankou on May 6.

The Fifth Air Army detected the fleet of warplanes approaching their supply base and launched twenty-four Ki-43-IIs from the veteran 25th Air Regiment to intercept. Major Toshio Sakagawa led the Hayabusas in an aerial ambush on the Americans over Dongting Lake, 120 miles southwest of the city. Major Charles Griffith, leading the Mustangs, called out on the radio when he saw the enemy fighters appear from the haze above and to the right of the formation.[10] Suddenly, the air filled with Oscars, and the fight devolved into utter chaos. Three P-38s went down in short order. One of the Japanese pilots, Lieutenant Morita, ran into 2nd Lt William Jones after the American bailed out.[11] The collision severely dented the wing root of Morita's Hayabusa and probably killed Jones.

"Lieut. Gregg was last seen by the undersigned leading his flight in a head on attack on approximately twenty enemy fighters," wrote Fred Scudday in a terse report filed two days after the mission.[12] He wrote almost identical statements for Jones and 1st Lt John Opsvig. Scudday barely made it back himself. Having become separated from the rest of Black Baker Flight, he continued to Hankou, coolly maneuvering his P-38 in and out of the mass of Oscars. The unflappable Texan had flown as a volunteer with the Royal Air Force Eagle Squadrons in 1941 and already had two confirmed aerial victories to his credit before he arrived in China.

When he finally disengaged from the fight, Scudday realized the enemy fighters had shot out his compass. He had no idea which way to go, so he circled a small town about sixty miles north of Suichuan. The warning net eventually reported his position, and a fighter controller guided him home over the radio. As his P-38 touched down, both his engines quit, starved of fuel; he coasted to a stop in the middle of the runway.

Back at the alert shack, one of the other pilots gave him a hard time: "Boy, are you lucky, Scud!" he kidded.

"Luck?" Scudday leaned casually against the wall with a sandwich in his hand and a big grin spreading across his face. "Brothers of the 449th, one and all, that was skill. Had my fuel supply figured out to the last drop!"[13]

Meanwhile, 1st Lt Wendell Stoneham made a somewhat more detailed statement on June 11 concerning the disappearance of his element leader: "I was flying Lt. Beneda's wing, the last element of the last flight," he wrote:

We were flying P-51Bs. About 15 minutes out of the target we were jumped by 30 Zeros. Lt. Beneda and I dropped our belly tanks with quite a bit of trouble. He was unable to drop one of his, the left one. He then called out three Zeros above us and said for us to go down. He rolled over on his back and suddenly snapped or a similar vicious maneuver. I split s'ed and tried to follow. It is my belief that he was hit when he snapped. I pulled up after about 5,000 ft. and couldn't see his plane. Before I had time enough to look carefully, I spotted two Zeros 2,000 ft. above at 10 o'clock coming at me so I pulled into them and made [a] head on pass with the leader. After that I looked for Beneda again and I saw a parachute [at] about 8,000 ft. I saw no other planes close to the chute and started over to look at it. Before I got there I see two P-38s diving on one Zero and they had four Zeros on their tails. I went over and got the four off their tails and we fought for a few minutes. I never saw the chute again. It is my belief that Lt. Beneda was lost due to enemy action.[14]

Casey Vincent waited at Hengyang for the strike force to return from the mission. All the P-40s and B-25s landed safely, but the loss of four of his long-range fighters frustrated him greatly. "Big mission today—we put fifty-four planes over Hankou," he journaled that evening. "Bombing was excellent—fighters disappointing. Formation was jumped fifteen minutes from target.

126   FALLEN TIGERS

Only one Zero confirmed. We lost three P-38s and one P-51. Zeros did not get to either the bombers or P-40s—all of which returned. I came back to Guilin in the late afternoon."[15]

According to Japanese sources, on May 6 a force of approximately forty-five fighters and bombers carried out an attack on Hankou, "inflicting heavy damage."[16] The 25th Air Regiment reported no losses, though three Hayabusas returned to base severely damaged and one pilot suffered serious injury.[17] Major Sakagawa's men could rightly claim to have won a tactical victory in their dogfight with the American fighters. But the top cover had done its job, occupying the Japanese interceptors so the bombers could escape and hit their target. Despite "inflicting heavy damage," though, fourteen B-25s could hardly stop half a million Japanese ground troops. By May 25, General Hata's forces had completed phase one of the Ichi-go offensive, securing the full length of the Beiping–Hankou Railway at a cost of just 1,061 killed, compared to 21,643 dead Chinese defenders.[18]

The Japanese embarked on phase two on May 27; eight divisions of the Eleventh Army marched south from Hankou toward Changsha while two divisions of the Twenty-Third advanced north from Guangzhou toward Qujiang. Casey decided he needed to visit the front personally. On June 1, the twenty-nine-year-old colonel ducked into the old schoolhouse serving as headquarters for the Ninth War Area. He had traveled incognito, without staff or entourage, to meet with General Xue Yue, the war area commander. Though he did not yet know the full extent of Japanese ambitions, what Casey did know troubled him greatly. Hundreds of thousands of enemy troops were pouring into central China; he believed his bases fell squarely in their crosshairs.[19]

Inside the schoolhouse, the young wing commander found General Xue bent double over a large table covered with maps. A single kerosene lamp provided the only illumination in the dim, humid space. The general stood erect to greet his guest. His slight frame seemed to vibrate with an impatient energy. He wore an immaculately pressed uniform complete with a Sam Brown belt and polished, knee-high riding boots.

Diminutive, articulate, and soft spoken, the forty-seven-year-old seemed the very model of courtesy and decorum—hardly the image of a great warrior in the American way of thinking. Casey had met him once before, though, and knew he had proven himself time and again in combat. Xue had attended the first class of the Central Military Academy in 1924, during

Chiang Kai-shek's tenure as commandant. He fought to great effect during the Northern Expedition, rising to command the Fourth Army. His operations in Jiangxi from 1933 to 1934 helped to propel the Communists on their Long March. He fought in Shanghai in 1937 and throughout the withdrawal up the Yangzi. But Xue cemented his reputation as Nationalist China's most effective battlefield commander by thrice defending the city of Changsha against Japanese attack, earning himself the nickname "Tiger of Changsha." Now, in the late spring of 1944, five columns of enemy troops stretched south from Hankou in a fourth attempt on the city. Casey depended on the "Tiger" defending it once more to block the Japanese from advancing on his airfields in central China.

Xue's armies lacked any sort of armored vehicles or heavy weapons, possessing only a handful of mortars and just fifty light artillery pieces. These the general positioned in the hills around Yuelu Mountain, on the west bank of the Xiang River. "It is our intention to draw the enemy into our city where we can use our small arms fire more effectively," he explained to Casey through an interpreter. "Over here," his finger jabbed down on the map, "across the river, our artillery batteries will open up as soon as the enemy reaches the outskirts of the city and we will cut them to pieces just the way we did it three years ago."[20]

"General, I'm afraid the Japanese are going to bypass Changsha and I will have to evacuate Hengyang," Casey cautioned. He doubted the Japanese would fall for the same trap as before. He thought the general's confidence unwarranted, that he underestimated Japanese capabilities and intentions.[21]

The sputtering of an old motorcycle outside interrupted the conversation. A moment later 1st Lt Malcolm Rosholt walked in. "I'm sorry sir," the intelligence officer mumbled to Casey. "I was totally unaware you were coming." With Rosholt's arrival, the meeting began to wind down. Xue explained he would count on American warplanes to cut the enemy's supply lines from Hankou. Close cooperation would be vital. He asked who would represent his armies to the American air force. Casey nodded in the direction of the young lieutenant. Rosholt would pass whatever information his airplanes required to operate in direct support of Chinese ground troops.

With the meeting concluded, Casey accompanied the lieutenant three miles south to the old Buddhist temple housing Dog Sugar Eight, the Fourteenth Air Force's forward radio post in Changsha. They drove through a ghost town; Xue had ordered the civilian population evacuated two days

128 FALLEN TIGERS

earlier. The colonel looked around as Rosholt led him into the U-shaped courtyard of the temple. Chennault had intended these posts to serve not only as a liaison with the Chinese ally but also as a node for collecting intelligence—even though General Stilwell officially forbade him from building his own intelligence organization. Dai Li, the chief of Chiang's secret police, had offered a helpful alliance, but Chennault rebuffed him, knowing a deal with Dai would limit his ability to work with anyone outside the Nationalist regime. So he got around Stilwell's order on a technicality by organizing Fourteenth Air Force intelligence teams within the framework of the warning net—something over which he did have authority. Rosholt led a team of three radio operators and two code clerks. Plugged into the warning net, they could alert American aircraft in the area to any plots of enemy planes. They also encoded intelligence reports for transmission to Kunming and to Casey's headquarters in Guilin. In addition to passing information from General Xue's Ninth War Area Headquarters, they trained Chinese agents to carry hand-cranked V-100 radios behind the lines to report on enemy movements. These agents, reporting to Fourteenth Air Force intelligence teams at forward radio posts, had provided the first warning of the Japanese buildup at Hankou.[22]

After conferring with Rosholt, Casey boarded a launch to travel back to Xiangtan, thirty miles to the south. Thousands of refugee boats crowded the river, most pulled by laborers walking along the bank. The Chinese had long since destroyed Changsha's airfield and the road and railroad south. Xiangtan had a small field, pockmarked by bomb craters, without a control tower or even a windsock. Its exposed, forward position left it vulnerable to enemy attack. Aircrews spent as little time on the ground there as possible.[23]

The launch took seven and a half hours to make the journey, leaving Casey plenty of time between dozing to mull over what had taken place. He did not share Xue's confidence, nor did he think Chennault understood the gravity of the situation. The Old Man believed the Japanese could not beat a combination of American warplanes and Chinese ground troops, pointing to successes at the Salween River in May 1942 and at Changde in December 1943. But both of those instances involved a limited number of enemy troops pursuing limited goals. In the case of the former, only three regiments advanced to the river, with no clear imperative to cross. In the case of the latter, the enemy had intended to hold Changde only long enough to seize the rice harvest and then fall back in a preplanned withdrawal. Neither case

Operation Ichi-Go   129

involved a determined attempt by the Imperial Japanese Army to advance in force and hold ground.[24]

"Headquarters doesn't seem to realize that we are about to lose eastern China and all the beautiful bases we've been building for so long," Casey mused. His fuel reserves had already dwindled to a minimum, requiring him to pull his B-25s from Suichuan and limit operations elsewhere. The plan for B-29s to bomb Japan from airfields in China—code named Operation Matterhorn—as well as the recently begun offensive on the Salween Front, diverted supplies from his forces.

After cajoling Chiang and President Roosevelt for over a year, General Stilwell had finally secured a commitment for his two-pronged attack on north Burma. Forty thousand troops of the Chinese Expeditionary Force crossed the Salween River at midnight on the early morning of May 11, advancing over the Gaoligong Mountains toward Tengchong and Longling. Stilwell required Chennault to support this offensive with fighters, bombers, transports, and reconnaissance aircraft. "While I can't get what I need, General Stilwell is using twelve-and-a-half divisions across the Salween River against a couple of Japanese battalions!" Casey fumed. "Everybody is crazy out here! I haven't received much I've asked for lately—so we'll fight with what we've got—and then fall back."[25]

The launch finally arrived at Xiangtan in the predawn darkness of June 2. The colonel climbed aboard a UC-64, a single-engine utility plane small enough to take off and land from the bombed-out field. The pilot had waited anxiously through the night and was eager to go. They took off, lights out, into the darkness.

Just as Casey had feared, everything soon fell to pieces. The Japanese bypassed Changsha, outflanking Xue and forcing him to retreat. Rosholt packed up his radio station and moved across the river to Yuelu Mountain on June 4.[26] Four days later, Xue evacuated his headquarters and decamped for Zhuzhou, thirty miles to the southeast. American fighters and medium bombers swept north along the Xiang River to attack the advancing Japanese and interdict their supply lines, but the critical fuel situation and terrible weather conspired against them. Casey's airmen frequently contended with ceilings as low as one hundred feet. "Even the birds are walking!" he complained. The Japanese moved at night and in poor weather, bypassing Nationalist defenses and dispersing to minimize the danger from air attack. "If only the Chinese would put up a decent fight—even a half decent

130   FALLEN TIGERS

one—we could hold them," he vented. "The Chinese ground forces won't fight worth a damn!"[27]

The Nationalist armies actually did fight, but against one of the most lethal, well-trained, battle-hardened armies in the world, they could respond with little more than ragtag conscripts armed with ancient bolt-action rifles. The Chinese did not have heavy weapons, tanks, or artillery. They did not have modern communications or logistics. In short, they were outmatched. The armies in central China did fight—and upward of 750,000 Nationalist soldiers died, disappeared, or suffered serious injury.[28]

A sense of unreality pervaded the entire situation. Stilwell tied up Nationalist China's best-trained and best-equipped forces in Burma and on the Salween Front. The vast majority of American advisors, training, and supplies went to them. The general responded to any suggestion of drawing from these troops to reinforce central China with frantic threats to end all lend-lease aid. Casey told Chennault that unless they implemented emergency measures, all would be lost. "My recommended emergency measure is to put the B-29s on Hankou—with P-47s flying cover—and clean out that rat's nest," he penned in his journal.[29]

In the Twentieth Air Force's inaugural mission to the Japanese home islands on June 15, 1944, seventy-five Superfortresses took off from airfields near Chengdu, in Sichuan Province, to attack the Imperial Iron and Steel Works at Yawata, in northern Kyushu. The huge bombers could level Hankou in a single mission, and yet Chennault had no influence over their operations: The B-29s remained under the control of Gen Hap Arnold and the Joint Chiefs of Staff in Washington, DC. Stilwell halfheartedly forwarded the suggestion to target Hankou but refused to declare the situation an emergency. As far as he was concerned, Chennault and Chiang had brought it on themselves. Their air campaign provoked the response he had predicted in 1943—and he gloated. The Joint Chiefs refused to release the airplanes or their stockpiled supplies from the strategic mission to bomb the Japanese homeland. "Instructions understood and exactly what I hoped for," Stilwell wrote in reply to General Marshall. "As you know, I have few illusions about power of air against ground troops."[30]

The callous response was consistent with Stilwell's long-held personal and professional prejudices. But his genuine belief that using the B-29s would be an unsuitable response had some validity; air action alone could not stop Ichi-go. Yet, in denying their use, Stilwell offered no alternative. He and

Chennault had stark ideological differences. His failure as a leader in this circumstance, though, had nothing to do with ideology; he disengaged. Stilwell's area of responsibility as American theater commander encompassed China, Burma, and India. While ten divisions carried out the largest Japanese ground offensive of World War II in central China, he spent the vast majority of his time at the front in north Burma focused on the remnants of one division defending Myitkyina. Stilwell seemed content to chalk Ichi-go up to the self-critiquing consequences of Chennault's myopic advocacy and Chiang's disregard for his advice. While the situation in China barreled toward disaster, Stilwell's handling of it brought the Allied command to a crisis point.

12

Collateral Damage

June 1944
Suichuan, China

Lieutenant Colonel George McMillan assembled his men in the squadron ready room. "Boys, you've always known I've never held anything back from you," he began. "The Japs are getting closer. They are pressing down on Changsha and now they're starting a squeeze play by moving on us from the south. The jig is up. Our stay here now depends entirely on the Jap movement. Maybe it will be a day longer, maybe a week or more, but it's pretty sure sooner or later we shall have to move and move quickly."[1] Though the situation remained tenable at Suichuan for the moment, Casey Vincent ordered the airfield at Hengyang evacuated on June 16. Japanese troops reached the gates of the city on the twentieth, and the colonel ordered the airfield demolished the next day. He warned Mac that Suichuan would be next. The first truck convoy of parts and maintenance equipment departed the base on the twenty-second.[2]

The fighter squadrons at Suichuan, Lingling, and Guilin flew mission after mission against the enemy's troops and supply lines. Between May 26 and August 1, the 68th Composite Wing flew an astonishing 5,287 sorties— more than four thousand of them by fighters. Many planes and pilots averaged a blistering three to four sorties per day.[3] But it became increasingly difficult to pinpoint the forward elements of the enemy advance. The warning net disintegrated. General Xue Yue lost contact with many of his forces in the field and asked for American aircraft to reconnoiter the front. But even when weather permitted aerial reconnaissance, it proved of limited value; the Japanese advance soon merged with the flood of fleeing refugees.[4]

As the enemy continued south, the American air force had less and less information to go by. "We are out of touch with our liaison teams in the

Collateral Damage   133

field—no information for the last twelve hours," Casey journaled on June 20. "I'm not getting any information from the field—no telling where the Japanese are," he wrote the next day. "The warning net has gone to hell." The young colonel felt a growing alienation between his forces in central China and headquarters in Kunming. "I can't get any support from the people at 14th Air Force Headquarters," he complained. "Either they don't know how serious the situation is—or they don't care."[5]

Despite his very vocal frustration with General Stilwell's lack of support, Chennault projected an obnoxious sense of confidence, believing unto the end in the messianic power of air to pull victory from the jaws of defeat. "I take a rather broad view on the use of air," he told *Yank* magazine. "I've found that air can be used as infantry, as machine guns, and as artillery."[6] Casey disagreed. He hated using his fighters and bombers as frontline troops. Instead he advocated for cutting Japanese supply lines. But until serious Chinese resistance developed, the Japanese did not have to use much in the way of supplies, making interdiction efforts largely ineffective. The colonel had no choice but to keep sending his airmen into the breach. Headquarters, meanwhile, kept sending him "nasty wires." He felt unable to convince Chennault of the seriousness of the situation. "He hasn't admitted that an air force cannot by itself hold back a determined ground drive," Casey griped. "I think my people have done more than expected—without support, without supplies, and without replacements."

The young colonel became increasingly pessimistic and overwhelmed. "It's too damn bad we have to sacrifice American youngsters for a cause as hopeless as this one," he lamented. "I feel deep down that no matter what we do—no matter how many Japanese we kill—how many trucks we destroy or boats we sink—the end will be the same! But we won't quit." As the enemy advance continued unabated, Chennault grew cantankerous and clashed frequently with his commanders at the front. "General Chennault and his staff are 'Sunday morning quarterbacking' again," Casey protested. "I am concerned about General Chennault—he's becoming very irritable," he commented later. "Damn this Theater!" he penned shortly after that. "The flight surgeons are shirking their duty in not recommending General Chennault for rotation. He's definitely 'war weary.'"

Casey worked tirelessly to fight a battle he could not win. Despite the growing tension with headquarters, Chennault recognized his efforts and recommended him for promotion to brigadier general. Congress confirmed

134   FALLEN TIGERS

the grade, making him the second youngest general officer in the history of the Air Force. "Became a brigadier general. Broke out the bourbon," he recorded on June 23.[7] The next morning, suffering from the worst hangover of his life, he flew to Suichuan in "stinko" weather and found Mac getting ready to lead a bombing mission against Japanese supply lines. He told him to cancel it. Chinese intelligence reported ten thousand enemy troops less than twenty miles north of Pingxiang, a small town in the mountains sixty-five miles southeast of Changsha. He wanted Mac's Lightnings to check it out. If they could find the column, he wanted them to strafe it and hit it with fragmentation bombs.

Mac refused. He thought the idea asinine and told Casey as much. It would be a damned awkward mission; the low ceilings meant his fighters would meet a murderous reception from enemy small-arms fire. The newly minted brigadier flew into a rage! He, least of all, believed in the value of sending his airplanes out as infantry scouts on these hopeless sorties, but what choice did he have? He had his orders and expected his subordinates to follow the orders he gave in turn. The two men had it out on the flight line in full view of the squadron, venting on each other their mutual frustration at fighting a losing battle.

"If you don't fly the mission," Casey finally blurted out, "I'll court-martial you!"

"Fine!" Mac shouted back. "I'll fly the damn thing. But this isn't over!"

Squadron armament crews quickly unloaded the five-hundred-pound bombs slung under the P-38s' wings and replaced them with fragmentation clusters. Before long, eleven of the twin-engine fighters winged their way to the north-northwest, scud running under the clouds, low over hilly terrain. Mac led the formation. If there was to be a damned awkward mission, he would lead it. He never asked his men to go on one he would not fly himself.[8]

The Lightnings arrived over Pingxiang to find the town bursting with thousands of troops. "Are those Chinese or Japs?" someone asked over the radio. Nobody knew. The report from Chinese intelligence had the enemy column miles to the north. Mac faced a dilemma: if he attacked straightaway, he risked killing friendly troops. If he decided to take a closer look, he sacrificed his tactical advantage, risking himself and his men by putting them at the mercy of enemy small-arms fire. There was no decision, though. Not really. Lieutenant Colonel George B. McMillan had earned the respect of his

Collateral Damage   135

officers and enlisted men by always playing it straight. He believed in doing the right thing and expected the same of his subordinates. He would protect them until hell froze over as long as they were straight with him. "You could rob a bank," they would joke, "and if you told him you did it, he'd probably try to get you out of it—just so long as you didn't lie to him about it!"[9]

"Hell, let's get it done," Mac whispered under his breath. He led his flight in for a closer look.

They circled the town three times at less than two hundred miles per hour. The troops below them did not break ranks. They still could not identify them as Japanese or friendly. On the fourth pass, all hell broke loose; instead of diving for cover, ten thousand Japanese soldiers stood their ground, shouldered their 9-millimeter rifles, and fired en masse. Mac turned and dropped his frags. As each canister left its rack, a small parachute deployed. The bombs dropped straight down, exploding on contact with the ground, ripping through the crowd of men.[10]

Mac's right engine began smoking badly.[11]

"Those little slant-eyed bastards got me," he announced coolly over the radio. "I'm going to have to bail out." He turned east. "I'm going to get out of the target area as far as I can first." His wingman stayed with him, shutting down his own damaged right engine.[12] "All of the coolant in my right engine is leaking out," Mac told him. "Left engine oil pressure is dropping fast." Ten miles east of Pingxiang, they crossed the Yuanshui River. Still flying low beneath the weather—dangerously low for bailing out—he suddenly had an idea.

"How do these things land on water?" he asked his flight.

"Climb out of your parachute," one of them advised. As Mac removed his shoulder straps, his left engine froze and he began losing altitude rapidly.

"My left engine's gone," he told them, "and there goes my right," he added a moment later. "Well boys, we'll see how these crates land in the water." But Mac never made it to the river. His wingman saw a fireball erupt as the fighter crashed two hundred yards to the south.[13]

"Dear Mr. and Mrs. McMillan and family," wrote Father Cosgrove two days later.

I do not know of a more difficult task I have had to perform than to write to you expressing my sentiments upon the loss of your boy. My sincerest and deepest sympathy to you all! Your keen bereavement is also felt by each and every boy of the 449th Fighter Squadron.

136   FALLEN TIGERS

You gave back to God your splendid son. We lost a friend, the best this squadron ever had, a great and competent fighter pilot and commanding officer whose coolness and leadership were evidenced even in the last minute of his life. . . . To Colonel George's younger sister, [Sarah] Elizabeth, I offer my sincere condolence. He was mighty proud of her. Early in June I went with Colonel Mac to a certain Chinese city where I helped him buy silk cloth. "My kid sister is going to college, Padre," he said, "and I've got to pick out the finest silk there is for her."

Great leaders like Colonel George come only once in a blue moon. The news of his regrettable death shocked us all and those in his flight that day were stunned beyond words. The boys lost a pilot's pilot and every one of us an idol. "It'll never be the same squadron again without the 'Old Man,'" I heard one enlisted man say.

Indeed it will not. Colonel George was a superb pilot and fighter and commanding officer. Be assured that there are many, many others who share your grief and the burden which Almighty God has seen fit to bring into your lives.[14]

Chennault followed with his own letter to Mac's father three days later. "Dear Mr. McMillan," he began.

You have no doubt been advised officially of Mac's death. I realize and understand how much you must feel the loss of a son like Mac. We over here know that Mac, both as a leader and a man, is irreplaceable.

I personally feel Mac's loss—he was one of my best squadron commanders—his understanding, aggressiveness, and fine spirit made him tops where his officers and men were concerned and I was always confident that whatever Mac did for his squadron would be right; his judgment and final decisions at times when it was necessary for a level-headed judgment were invaluable and I know I speak for his officers and men when I say that they would have followed Mac anywhere he told them to.

Mac was shot down in combat—he was on a strafing mission and ground fire was encountered—his engine was hit and he attempted to make a forced landing; unfortunately, his engine blew up on landing and Mac was killed instantly.

His personal effects have been collected and will be shipped to the Quartermaster Depot, Kansas City, Missouri, for forwarding to you. You realize that this may take considerable time. Should you consider it desirable to make inquiry, your letter should be addressed to the Quartermaster General, Washington, DC.

Please convey my sincere sympathy to Mac's family. If ever there is anything I can do for you, please do not hesitate to let me know.

With kindest personal regards, I am, most sincerely yours,

C. L. Chennault.[15]

For his part, Casey Vincent wrote no letter, nor did he mention Mac's death in his journal—odd for such a faithful and detailed diarist, especially considering that he had written of him a number of times before. Besides mention of his own promotion, the entry for June 24 makes only the quixotic (and erroneous) record: "The weather here was 'stinko' all day and I couldn't get a plane off the ground. Lucky Japanese!"[16]

The governor of Jiangxi Province informed Fourteenth Air Force that an American pilot perished while attempting to crash-land near the village of Linjiafang. Policemen from the nearby town of Luxi buried him close to the wreckage and posted a guard to watch over his grave. They would be unable to return the body to American control; the considerable number of Japanese troops in the area made that far too dangerous.[17] For their part, the men of Mac's squadron had little time to mourn his loss. Just two days after the crash, with Japanese troops less than forty miles from the field, they evacuated Suichuan.[18]

Japan's armies succeeded where its air forces had failed, plucking plane after plane from the sky and smashing them to the ground. Throughout the war, surface fire accounted for nearly 37 percent of American warplanes reported missing in the China Theater—more than any other single cause. The massive Ichi-go offensive left the corridor between Hankou and Guilin a veritable graveyard of US planes—at least ninety-five in all, 88 percent of which were fighters. Mac's P-38 actually represented the only Lightning lost to ground fire during the campaign.[19] The big fighter had several advantages over its peers: Having a second engine meant it could often limp home after suffering significant damage. It also made little noise when approaching low and fast—its long exhaust pipes muffled engine noise and directed it upward, away from the ground. Enemy troops often did not hear the distinctive, high-pitched whine of a P-38 until it arrived right on top of them.[20]

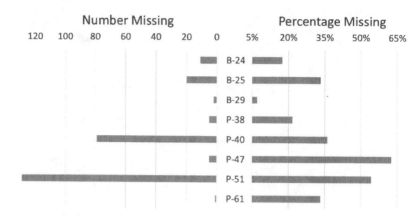

Aircraft Missing Due to Enemy Surface Fire

Throughout the war, Fourteenth Air Force lost only five Lightnings to surface fire, less than 25 percent of the total reported missing. Predictably, P-40s suffered worse—36 percent of those reported missing, or about seventy-nine planes. Perhaps surprisingly, more P-51 Mustangs fell to surface fire than any other aircraft. Actually, America's "wonder fighter" fell in greater numbers than all others combined. Of the 252 warplanes reported missing due to surface fire, 129 were P-51s.[21] The Mustang proved to be incredibly vulnerable in this regard. When it came down to it, any liquid-cooled engine was vulnerable, whether in a P-38, P-40, or P-51; the P-38 packed a spare, though. The Mustang's particular weakness came from the placement of its radiator. To hit a P-40 in the radiator, located in its distinctive "jaw," enemy troops had to shoot at it head on, staring it down while it came at them firing its six .50-caliber machine guns. The P-51, in contrast, housed its radiator in the underside scoop beneath the cockpit; enemy troops could shoot at it from any angle. A hit to the radiator—or just one bullet in an oil or coolant line—and the mighty Mustang had about two minutes of flying time remaining.[22]

"My plane was hit while swinging around a mountain by a single rifle bullet in the oil line," reported 1st Lt Harold Miller, a pilot from the 26th Fighter Squadron who bailed out of his P-51 eighty miles west of Guangzhou in November 1944.[23]

"I ran into difficulty, in the form of enemy ground-fire, 20-mm cannon fire," stated Lt Edgar Headley, another pilot from the 26th on a mission fifty miles south of Changsha. "It made a direct hit on the motor, hitting the coolant jacket, and evidently damaging the cylinders. I was just clearing the trees at 25 feet. I pulled up, as the engine was running badly, and barely got 400 or 800 feet, when the engine absolutely quit. In the meantime, I had jettisoned the canopy, and bailed from not more than 500 feet up. The chute popped just before I hit the ground, fortunately."[24]

Despite the fighter's vulnerability, most Mustang pilots claimed they trusted the greater speed of the sleek P-51 as better protection than the old P-40's rugged construction. The 25th Fighter Squadron proved a notable exception to this mode of thinking. Providing close air support to the Chinese Expeditionary Force on the Salween Front, the 25th elected to keep its Sharks for as long as possible. They made a wise choice; an analysis of mission reports shows the 25th lost one P-40 for every 258 ground-attack sorties. A P-51 squadron flying similar missions in north China lost one Mustang for every 95 ground-attack sorties.[25]

While American warplanes took grievous losses, the enemy advance finally hit a roadblock at Hengyang: Gen Fang Xianjue determined to hold the walled city with the sixteen thousand men of his Tenth Army. It was the kind of stand for which Casey Vincent had been begging. For forty-seven days they held out against more than one hundred thousand Japanese. Casey sent everything he had—fighters, bombers, and transports—to attack the enemy and resupply the besieged Chinese. The Fourteenth Air Force thus found itself supporting two vastly different sieges simultaneously, each of which proved a turning point of sorts for the war in China. While Casey's 68th Composite Wing supported the Tenth Army in its defense of Hengyang, Col John Kennedy's 69th Wing supported the Chinese Expeditionary Force on the Salween Front as it laid siege to the walled city of Tengchong.

The five divisions of Maj Gen Huo Kuizhang's XX Army Group faced off against 1,850 experienced, well-entrenched, highly determined, but vastly outnumbered Japanese defenders at Tengchong. Huo's troops had American training, equipment, and advisors. American warplanes provided close air support and battered the city walls to clear the way for Chinese soldiers to scale the rubble with bamboo ladders. On August 2, 1944, nine flights of P-40s and P-38s and one flight of B-25s hammered five breaches in the southeast wall, allowing the infantry to finally flood into the city. Among the Warhawk pilots that day was 2nd Lt Henry Minco, the French-born hell raiser who grew up with his brother and widowed mother in Cleveland, Ohio. Minco had joined

140   FALLEN TIGERS

the 25th Fighter Squadron in July at Yunnanyi and flew three sorties on August 2; the first, a patrol over Longling and Mangshi in the late morning. Shortly after noon, he took off to bomb the southeast wall of Tengchong. The flight of four Sharks circled overhead, waiting for the B-25s to finish their run, before commencing a shallow dive from ten thousand feet, strafing, and releasing their five-hundred-pound demolition bombs just five hundred feet above the ground. One of the bombs scored a direct hit, blowing a hole next to the gate in the middle of the southeast wall. A burst of heavy black smoke erupted in the air as the last P-40 pulled off the target, but all four Sharks returned safely to Yunnanyi. Minco took off on another patrol that afternoon, flying wingman to 1st Lt Roger R. Vadenais, and landing just before dark.[26]

House-to-house fighting raged in the city for weeks. Chinese troops finally cleared out the last pocket of defenders on September 14; after fifty-one days of siege, only fifty Japanese soldiers remained. It represented the first time a Chinese army had gone on the offensive and successfully removed the Japanese from conquered territory. It proved that properly trained, supplied, and led, Chinese soldiers could defeat a modern enemy.[27]

Meanwhile, the defenders of Hengyang held out heroically but in vain. They had no American training, no advisors, and only what meager supplies Casey's planes could deliver by air. The city fell on August 8. After forty-seven days of siege, only 1,200 defenders remained. General Fang's men inflicted an estimated sixty thousand casualties on the attacking troops—almost half the Japanese casualty count for the entire Ichi-go campaign. But having captured Hengyang, Gen Shunroku Hata continued south. His forces took Lingling on September 7 and Guilin on November 11. The central China bases from which Chennault's airmen had so daringly attacked the enemy in 1942 and 1943 had fallen.[28] Casey returned to the United States in December, having served nearly two years overseas. His tenure had seen the highest heights of victory and the lowest depths of defeat.

The chaotic, fluid front throughout the Ichi-go offensive imposed all manner of new challenges on evading airmen. Oftentimes, they bailed out or crash-landed in close proximity to the Japanese troops they had just been strafing, troops who, in many cases, had just shot them down. On June 15, Maj Arthur Cruikshank led a flight of Sharks to bomb and strafe the advancing enemy at Zhuzhou, thirty miles south-southeast of Changsha. His P-40 took a hit to the engine accessory compartment and another to the radiator. Cruikshank turned west. Two miles from the target, his cockpit filled with smoke; he bailed out only three hundred feet above the ground, landing in no-man's land. A farmer quickly appeared on the scene and led him to his home. Thirty minutes later, a Nationalist patrol arrived. The platoon leader, an officer by the name of Ming Zhongyi, spoke some English. "It is not safe here," he told the American. "We must start at once for the south."

As they left the small village, a flight of five Sharks roared overhead. Cruikshank climbed a small hill to watch them bomb and strafe the Japanese positions. "I could see the Jap ground fire and it seemed rather heavy, either 20- or 37-millimeter," he related in his evasion report. "I believe this was the same fire that scored hits on my plane."[29]

Cruikshank commanded the 74th Fighter Squadron, then flying out of Hengyang. He rejoined the squadron but fell to enemy ground fire again on June 25. This time the opening shock of the parachute sprained his neck and pulled the ligaments holding his kidneys. He landed in a rice paddy ten miles south of Hengshan. The incredible pain left him barely able to move. Two men dressed in peasant garb grabbed him, confiscated his pistol, and began carrying him north. The major found their appearance and behavior a bit odd. As they hauled him toward Japanese lines, he realized they must be plainclothes scouts, such as the enemy often sent ahead of its main body to collect intelligence and sow chaos. He fumbled through his jungle kit as they dragged him along. In a flash he drew his machete and brought it crashing down on the head of one of the men, killing him instantly. The other fled, leaving the injured airman to hobble off by himself.

Cruikshank walked west, toward the mountains. After several hours of dodging enemy patrols, he came across an injured Chinese soldier. The man lay dying from a bayonet wound to his chest. Feebly, he raised a hand with his waning strength, pointing first to the pilot, then south—toward safety. Cruikshank nodded his thanks and started in that direction. Any doubt about the intentions of the plainclothesmen vanished from his thoughts. A short time later he found a group of three other wounded soldiers and joined them, the four allies limping along as best they could until they reached a Nationalist Army post two days later.[30] As the general there bundled him off to Lingling in a sedan chair, Cruikshank bid farewell to his injured companions, giving each $1,000CN with which to buy food and medicine.[31]

Like Cruikshank, most downed airmen fell in with small bands of Nationalist troops. These soldiers, seeking to make their own way out from enemy territory after their units had been destroyed, proved only too willing

142   FALLEN TIGERS

to take on an extra charge. Instead of forming ratlines then, evasion routes radiated in every direction away from the Japanese advance. To the east, evaders journeyed through the mountains to the Gan River in Jiangxi Province. To the west, they went to Baoqing, then either south to Guilin or later, one hundred miles farther west to Zhijiang. To the southeast, they went to Chenxian, where Xue Yue had reconstituted his headquarters and Malcolm Rosholt had established a new radio post, Love Zebra Five. The lieutenant often hosted evading airmen there as they waited for a UC-64 to fly them out of the town's small airfield.[32]

A surge of friendly fire and collateral-damage incidents accompanied Ichi-go. The confusion sown by the enemy's rapid advance meant many American airmen faced Mac's dilemma; intelligence simply could not keep up with the pace of battle. Even if airmen could pinpoint the forward line of troops, the leading Japanese elements often merged with crowds of fleeing soldiers and civilians. Additionally, the enemy bypassed many Chinese positions and left numerous fragments of defeated units in their wake.

When 1st Lt Oswin "Moose" Elker bailed out of his stricken P-40 north of Xiangtan on July 29, he found the civilian population there incredibly frustrated with the American air force. "In this area including the river, the road, and the railroad, the Chinese were pretty well riled up against the Americans for the strafing," he reported, "claiming that it was mostly Chinese killed in that district." On the evening of the thirtieth, he and his escort of fifteen Nationalist soldiers stopped for dinner along the Lianshui River, a tributary of the Xiang. One of the soldiers got into a fight with a civilian there.

"What was that about?" Elker asked his interpreter.

"He is one of the people who suffered from your strafing," the interpreter replied. "He wanted to turn you in."

A few days later, while staying the night in the small village of Jieling, he learned of an errant bombing raid that had unintentionally killed seven residents there.[33]

Earlier that month, on July 5, 2nd Lt George Denton had bailed out of his P-40 fifteen miles south of Pingxiang. Landing on the side of a mountain, he injured his foot and lost consciousness for a short while. "When I came to, I saw that the plane had crashed into a house and completely destroyed it," he reported. "The women and men who owned the house were crying and wailing about the loss of their home. One man was badly burned, so I gave these people $3,000CN to help them."[34]

Collateral Damage   143

After bailing out northeast of Qiyang on September 5, 2nd Lt Gordon Berven joined a battalion of six hundred Nationalist troops trying to make their way south to Guilin. They holed up outside the town of Guiyangzhen, awaiting nightfall so they could cross the Xiang River under cover of darkness. While they waited, two flights of P-40s roared overhead—four fighters low to strafe, four high as top cover. The Sharks thoroughly worked the area over, concentrating their fire on any boats in the river and on a compound across from the town. Fortunately, the town's residents had been evacuated, but the strafing killed a Chinese soldier.[35]

The sad fact of the matter was that in the frenzy of retreat and hopelessness of defeat, American warplanes frantically struck at anything that appeared to be a target. Liu Zhenghua, the infantry officer from Hubei who had attended the Central Military Academy in Yunnan, led a platoon in the attack on Tengchong on the Salween Front. Several of his men drowned while crossing the river guarding the city's northern walls. As bullets and shells streaked out from the Japanese defenses, hitting all around him, American planes dove into the fray and strafed the enemy positions. Some of his men got caught in the crossfire. "Well, this is war," he said simply, "and shit happens in war. For this reason, we don't blame the Americans. Whenever we saw American planes fly over, we were still very happy about it." Only seven of Liu's men survived the assault. He never made it into the walled city himself; an enemy mortar shell hit nearby, sending shrapnel into his back and head. Liu spent the next several weeks convalescing in a military hospital near Baoshan.[36]

The war claimed the lives of so many millions of Chinese soldiers and civilians, it became increasingly abstract to those higher up both the Chinese and American chains of command. The human cost, especially in civilian life, no longer seemed to enter into the strategic calculus. The tragic destruction caused by collateral damage and friendly fire reached a climax during the bombing of Hankou on December 18, 1944.

Two months earlier, on October 18, President Roosevelt had finally recalled General Stilwell, whose disrespectful attitude, disengagement from Ichi-go, and attempts to coerce Generalissimo Chiang by manipulating lend-lease aid had boiled over. The general's treatment of the Nationalist government was the sort of condescension one expected from a nineteenth-century colonial official. Chiang demanded he be removed as a matter of China's national sovereignty. Lieutenant General Albert Wedemeyer took command of American forces in the China Theater and immediately set about doing

144 FALLEN TIGERS

everything possible to staunch the as-yet unstoppable Ichi-go offensive. He began airlifting Chinese troops from Burma to the front in China and finally secured use of the B-29s for an attack on Hankou.[37]

Chennault had long advocated the value of incendiary attacks on the wood-and-paper cities of Japan. High-altitude bombing of its steel industry had thus far proven ineffective, making only a 2 percent dent after six months of operations. Chennault and Maj Gen Curtis LeMay decided to experiment with low-altitude firebombing on Hankou as a proof of concept. To Chiang, the attack represented another necessary sacrifice, just like the order he gave to breach the Yellow River dams in 1938. On December 18, 1944, eighty-five Superfortresses joined two hundred Fourteenth Air Force fighters and bombers in the largest aerial armada ever to darken China's skies. The B-29s dropped more than five hundred tons of incendiary bombs; Hankou burned for three days. The smoldering ruin of the once great city pleased LeMay and provided a template for his systematic destruction of Japan. No one remarked on the civilian toll: as many as forty thousand died. The raid may have wiped out an important Japanese supply hub, but it came too late to save central China. The devastating attack seemed a cynical act of wanton destruction for destruction's sake.[38]

Collateral damage and apparent insensitivity to civilian casualties is the obvious counterpoint to the gratitude most Chinese felt for American air support. As Liu pointed out, they understood mistakes happen in war. For the most part, the Chinese appreciated American air support despite suffering from friendly fire and collateral damage. Yet it is difficult to ignore the emotional response of individuals who suffered from American strafing or who endured injury or lost their homes to airplanes falling from the sky. The Americans arrived in 1941 as humanitarians, bringing an end to Japanese terror bombing. Robert Mooney's selfless sacrifice to avoid killing or injuring onlooking villagers in Xiangyun exemplified their idealism. But with Ichi-go, things began to come unglued. Chinese soldiers and civilians got caught in the crossfire as American warplanes frantically lashed out against an enemy their intelligence could not adequately target. Yet it was the bombing of Hankou and the seeming disregard for civilian casualties there that proved the hardest to reconcile with the idealistic early days of 1941 and 1942. China would never be the same.

First Lieutenant Glen E. Beneda arrived in China in May 1943 and flew with the 76th Fighter Squadron through some of its toughest months of combat. Japanese fighters shot him down southwest of Hankou on May 6, 1944, but the Communist New Fourth Army carried him to safety. *Ed Beneda*

Vice Squadron Leader George McMillan of the American Volunteer Group climbs aboard his shark-mouthed fighter. By the time he returned to the United States in the summer of 1942, he had four-and-a-half kills to his credit fighting in Burma and China. *Janet McMillan Alford*

Blood Chit, also known as the "back flag" or simply the "flag." Stamped by China's Aeronautical Affairs Commission, the chit identified its bearer as fighting on behalf of China and asked soldiers and civilians to give him aid. This chit belonged to 2nd Lt Francis Forbes, who bailed out over the Salween River in October 1943. *William Forbes*

Captain Everett W. "Brick" Holstrom, commander of the 11th Bomb Squadron, with the crew of his B-25 "Tokyo Jo" in February 1943. Right to left: Holstrom, Lt L. J. Murphy, Capt Clayton Campbell, Lt George A. Stout, Tech Sgt Douglas V. Radney, Staff Sgt Robert T. Schafer. *National Archives*

Second Lieutenant William Findley belly-landed his F-5 Lightning in a rice paddy in southwest China after becoming lost in poor weather. Local Chinese eagerly helped him return to American control. *Findley Family*

After witnessing his heroic sacrifice in December 1942, the people of Xiangyun built a monument on the Burma Road honoring 1st Lt Robert Mooney. *National Archives*

Japanese troops inspect the wreckage of 1st Lt Howard Allers's B-25C. Allers managed to crash-land north of Hong Kong after enemy fighters knocked out both his engines. *22nd Bomb Squadron Association*

Left to right: Second Lieutenant Joe Cunningham, Col Merian Cooper, Lt Col Herbert Morgan Jr., 2nd Lt Nick Marich, and Maj Ed Rector. Cooper planned the raid on Hong Kong, Morgan flew as lead bombardier, and Marich and Cunningham were the only members of 1st Lt Howard Allers's downed B-25 to successfully evade capture. *National Archives*

Major General Claire Lee Chennault (right), legendary commander of the Fourteenth Army Air Force, presents Brig Gen Clinton D. "Casey" Vincent with the Oak Leaf Cluster to his Air Medal, December 12, 1944. *National Archives*

Japanese aircraft burn on Hsinchu Field, Taiwan, during the Fourteenth Air Force's raid on Thanksgiving Day 1943. *National Archives*

Major General Claire Lee Chennault (left) confers with Maj Art Cruikshank (center), commander of the 74th Fighter Squadron. Ground fire forced Cruikshank to bail out over the front lines twice in June 1944. *National Archives*

Lee Gregg with the 449th Fighter Squadron after returning from his ordeal behind enemy lines. The Communists who rescued him gave him a Japanese uniform, flag, and swords. Standing, left to right: Dave Williams, Lee Gregg, Billie Beardsley, and Gerry Hammond. Seated: Keith Newnom and Tom Pugh. *Carl Molesworth*

A Chinese and an American pilot discuss tactics in a P-40N from the 5th Fighter Group (Provisional). Chennault conceived of the Chinese-American Composite Wing as a way to rebuild the Chinese Air Force with American mentorship and shared Chinese-American leadership. *Clay McCutchan*

Americans and Chinese inspect the wreckage of the C-47 that brought the Dixie Mission to Yan'an in June 1944. When the propeller broke free, it narrowly missed Captain Champion in the cockpit. *From the American Geographical Society Library, University of Wisconsin-Milwaukee*

First Lieutenant Paul Crawford with his P-51 "Little Rebel." Crawford bailed out when surface fire hit his Mustang on July 14, 1945. Surprisingly, Fourteenth Air Force lost more Mustangs than any other type of aircraft—most of them to ground fire. *Paul Crawford*

The wreckage of AVG pilot Jack Newkirk's P-40 after he crashed in Lamphun, Thailand, in 1942. Of the five AVG and Fourteenth Air Force airmen reported missing in Thailand, two were captured and later escaped, one was killed (Newkirk), and two are still listed as missing in action. *Royal Thai Air Force Museum*

French Foreign Legion pilot Lt Hubert Cochard evacuated Maj Ed Witzenburger from Indochina in this Potez 25A2 biplane after the Japanese coup in March 1945. *Bruce Carnachan*

The US Army recovered George McMillan's body from a grave near Linjiafang and moved it to the Hongqiao Road Cemetery in Shanghai. On March 12, 1948, his family reinterred him at Arlington National Cemetery. *Author's Photo*

The people of Luojia enthusiastically greet Glen Beneda and his family, September 9, 2005. He did not want to return to China, but his curiosity got the better of him. *Sino-American Aviation Heritage Foundation*

Glen Beneda in a bamboo chair on the way to the excavation site for his airplane. The trip helped him put his wartime experiences into perspective. *Sino-American Aviation Heritage Foundation*

13

With the Communists

June 4, 1944
Dawu Mountain, China

The two fighter pilots greeted each other with heartfelt relief. It had been nearly a month since they had bailed out a hundred miles southwest of Hankou. Neither had seen another American since then.

"I thought you would have left already," remarked Lee Gregg. "They told me you were two days ahead of me."

"I heard that they had you and that you were following behind me," Glen Beneda replied. "They decided to stop somewhere safe and wait for you so we can get out together."

Beneda had spent the last seven days awaiting Gregg's arrival at the mountain headquarters of the 5th Division, New Fourth Army. It had been his first reprieve after three weeks of evasion. Both airmen had been on the run and both looked a sorry sight indeed, wearing a hodge-podge of American, Chinese, and captured Japanese clothing, with long hair, scraggly beards, and ankles swollen from the long journey and relentless mosquitos. Both still suffered from serious injuries sustained in their bailouts and beyond.

"I had been riding a horse and he threw me and kicked me," explained Beneda. "They fixed a stretcher and carried me ever since."

"Either it's my imagination, or my back bone is crooked as hell," complained Gregg. "I'll be glad to get an X-ray of it!" In addition to his fractured vertebra, the P-38 pilot still limped from his wounded ankle, had significant bruising on his back and hips, a blood clot in his eye, and suffered from chills, fever, and a cough that made him think he might have malaria.

Though exhausted, the two lieutenants talked late into the night. "I never saw so many Zeros in the air at one time," Beneda remarked. He did not

146   FALLEN TIGERS

make much mention of the ambush beyond that. The young Mustang pilot had been flying and fighting in China ever since the desperate days of the Japanese air offensive in the summer of 1943, but he had not seen much air-to-air combat personally—only three or four dogfights. He claimed a probable once: He did not see it hit the ground but saw his tracers knocking pieces off of it; it did not explode before he lost sight of it. Beneda still felt very young in a lot of ways, having earned his wings only a year and a half prior—just after his nineteenth birthday—before reporting to China with just thirty hours in P-40s at an operational training unit in Florida. The young Nebraskan looked up to Gregg, five and a half years his senior and a fighter ace, with six victories scored in two theaters of war. He figured Gregg would not want to talk about getting shot down any more than he did. "Did anyone else make it?" he asked instead.

"About ten days after I bailed out, they showed me a parachute, pointie-talkie, some morphine, sulfa powder, and an AGO card belonging to Jones," Gregg replied. "They told me he drowned. They didn't see any blood stains on his parachute." There would have been no way for them to know that Jones had probably been killed in the collision with Lieutenant Morita's Hayabusa. Beneda had watched three P-38s fall from the dogfight in flames, but neither he nor Gregg had heard anything more about other survivors. Their conversation turned to the action they had seen since bailing out.

"I had forty or fifty soldiers with me and we were traveling at night," Beneda related. "It was really dark, it was a moonless night with an overcast. They carried me in a stretcher and we walked along this trail and the Chinese took turns carrying me. It took four guys to carry me in that stretcher. We had just stopped to rest—they had just laid me down—when someone opened up with a machine gun. I heard that 'tat-tat-tat-tat-tat.' I looked over my left shoulder and I could see the muzzle flash. Like I said, I wasn't able to walk, but my legs worked a little better then! I got off of that stretcher and I started running in the opposite direction. We got kind of scattered. I ran for about an hour and when I stopped there were only three soldiers with me. We traveled in circles all night long and stopped at a small farmhouse at daylight. Later in the day, the rest of the escort showed up there. I don't think we lost anybody!"

Gregg had a few similar experiences, such as when he and his escort of seven soldiers ran into a Japanese patrol six days after he bailed out. The Chinese picked up his stretcher and ran, but he slowed them down too much. They ducked behind a house and, finding a haystack there, hid him

With the Communists   147

underneath. The Japanese started shooting, and for about three hours the two sides fired back and forth, occasionally lobbing grenades at each other over the haystack. Finally, the Chinese feigned retreat. The Japanese followed, and the Chinese shot two of them, forcing the remainder to withdraw.

He had another run-in with the enemy about two weeks later. This time Gregg traveled with a battalion of four hundred troops equipped with six light and two heavy machine guns. As they prepared to cross a road under cover of darkness, they met an enemy patrol. The first shot barely missed Gregg, who bailed off his horse and landed knee deep in a water-filled rice paddy. A few more rounds passed close by. The Chinese troops charged the enemy head on, using hand grenades and rifle mortars. Gregg remounted his horse and galloped across the road into a wheat field. After an hour, the enemy withdrew, and he and his escort continued onward.

Beneda asked how he had managed to ride a horse with his injured back. "I rigged up a kind-of brace on the saddle," Gregg answered. "I fixed up a Rube Goldberg arrangement with the rubber part of my jungle kit for a back rest. It helped some, but not too much."

The two got to talking about the events immediately preceding their meeting at 5th Division headquarters. Whereas Beneda had no trouble crossing the Beiping–Hankou Railway, Gregg had a much more dramatic time of it. He had an escort of two hundred troops, "one hundred soldiers in front, one hundred in the rear," he narrated: "As we started crossing the railroad, about half the escort got across when here comes a train hell bent for election. It had two engines, one in front and one in the rear, with four cars, loaded with Japs. Our men had time to setup their machine guns and station riflemen beside the railway. When it got in range, they really let them have it! The Japs in the train were firing back. The engines put full steam ahead and it was a hot short battle. When the train passed we ran like hell while the soldiers stayed to cover us. We got about a mile from the railroad when I heard what I thought was a flight of geese. Just as I looked up, there was a hell of an explosion about a hundred yards ahead and to the right of our column. The bastards had come back and set up a heavy mortar! The second one hit even with me and fifty yards to the right. We were going east and had a strong north wind and I think that wind saved us. We traveled fast for half an hour. They continued to lob them at us but we were out of range with no casualties."

"Have you been keeping notes?" Beneda queried. Gregg handed him his journal, and Beneda leafed through it. "You have been writing a lot more

148   FALLEN TIGERS

than me," he commented. "I'm just going to get a copy of your diary and I'm going to quit."

"Ok," Gregg agreed.

The next morning the two airmen met with Gen Li Xiannian, commander of the 5th Division. He gave them each a captured Nambu pistol with two magazines and forty rounds of ammunition. "Really ding hao!" exclaimed Gregg, giving a thumbs-up and a big grin.[1]

The general explained that he would send the Americans on their way again in a few days. First, he wanted the two of them to visit his division's military academy and officer school. He asked them to speak to his troops about their common cause against Japan. Official American policy supported Chiang Kai-shek's Nationalist government; de facto cooperation with the Chinese Communist Party (CCP) rested on little more than the age-old principle of "the enemy of my enemy is my friend." The CCP wanted more formal recognition. Most airmen knew little about the Communists save for rampant rumors and official propaganda put out by the Nationalists. Nobody knew quite how they would receive Americans before Gregg and Beneda's serendipitous arrival. The generalissimo had actually ordered the New Fourth Army to disband in early 1941 after a dispute over jurisdiction between the Communists and Nationalists devolved into open combat. Chiang branded them as "insubordinate," while they protested his "treachery." The incident contributed to a significant chilling in relations, engendering a mutual suspicion that put a damper on the United Front against Japan. By sending two American airmen deeper into New Fourth Army territory, General Li not only sought to boost the motivation and morale of his fighting men but also wanted to gain exposure and enhance his legitimacy with the US military.[2]

On the morning of June 6, 1944, the same day the Allies landed on the beaches of Normandy, Lieutenants Gregg and Beneda trekked deeper into the mountains with Mr. Huang, a political commissar for the New Fourth Army, who spoke a little English and wore an officer's uniform bare of any rank or insignia. After a grueling journey up precipitous, twisting trails—Gregg in a sedan chair, Beneda on horseback—they arrived at a pine-bough arch under which hung a sign that read, "Welcome to our alliance Lt. Gregg and Lt. Beneda." A bugle corps of twenty boys presented the colors, and two hundred soldiers and students snapped to attention and saluted. After an introductory speech, their hosts asked them to address the assembled crowd. Beneda stepped forward; Commissar Huang interpreted for him: "From the

Nationalist government in Chongqing, we heard the Communist Party of China doesn't resist the Japanese," he began. "They said the New Fourth Army is actually a bunch of rebels and had fooled a lot of foreigners, including myself. But through our own observations over these last few weeks, we witnessed the New Fourth Army standing strong against the Japanese. They are not traitors to China. Their officers and men stand united. They work closely with the local people and have good relations with them. I have seen that every officer and soldier has a pen and that all are being educated. This shows me you are an army striving to act with wisdom. Everyone knows why they must fight against Japan and how they can do their best to win the war."

The audience applauded warmly.

"The Americans are also fighting the war in China," Gregg added, "a fact which I know you doubt as you seldom see an American soldier." Seldom might have been too generous. Thus far, Gregg and Beneda had been the first and only US fighting men they had encountered. These two battered, scruffy-looking young men gave the first tangible proof the Chinese Communists had an international ally in their war against the invader. "We are going to bomb Japan proper from Chinese bases!" Gregg concluded enthusiastically. The crowd clapped and cheered their approval.

The two airmen gave several speeches over the next two days and endured hours of questions, such as: "What does the Guomindang think of the Chinese Communists?" and "What do the Americans think of the Chinese Communists?" Neither pilot documented their answers, though Gregg made a cryptic entry in his diary: "We are now Gregg and Beneda, 'Foreign Diplomats,'" he wrote. "These people can sure ask embarrassing questions and if any of the answers go beyond here, it's going to be our necks!"

They visited thousands of troops, all appearing better trained and equipped than any Nationalists they had seen, with higher morale and superior discipline. During their visit to the academy, they also encountered a fascinating organization called the Japanese People's Anti-War League. Twenty Japanese soldiers, all wearing the same khaki uniforms as the rest of the New Fourth Army, saluted smartly and greeted them. They learned a number of prominent communists from Japan had journeyed to the interior of China. These men worked to convert captured soldiers and help the CCP fight the Imperial army, particularly with propaganda aimed at their countrymen.

"What does the United States think of Japan?" one of them asked through an interpreter. "Do the Americans hate all Japanese? The Japanese

150   FALLEN TIGERS

people—the farmers and the ordinary people of Japan—do not want war," he stressed. "It's just the militarists causing the war."

The whirlwind speechmaking tour of the 5th Division's mountain redoubt exhausted the two fighter pilots. "I was really tired out," Gregg journaled. "Both of us were." They wanted to get moving again. They wanted to go home.

The two of them returned to 5th Division headquarters on the evening of the seventh. Commissar Huang and several other representatives of General Li met with them the next morning and gave them each $5,000CN for expenses as well as a Japanese flag and saber. For General Chennault, they entrusted them with a letter from General Li, a map, a secret document on enemy air defenses, and a beautiful, two-handed Samurai sword that had belonged to a Japanese major general slain in battle. The two departed division headquarters with five Japanese prisoners and an escort of one hundred troops. A bugle corps led the procession. Soldiers lined the trail for miles cheering and clapping, wishing them well on their journey.

They crossed the Beiping–Hankou Railway just before midnight. A long train rolled through fifteen minutes after they passed, but they experienced none of the drama that had attended Gregg's crossing at the beginning of June. For four days they trekked northwest toward Nationalist lines through territory presumably occupied by the Japanese. Much of it had been under Nationalist control before phase one of the Ichi-go offensive. Now it seemed largely barren of Nationalists and Japanese alike. The Communists seemed to thrive in this sort of interstitial space.

The trip proved grueling for the exhausted airmen. Beneda came down with a cold, while Gregg's cough grew worse. They both took quinine, and Gregg put hot packs on his back. The ace also developed a bad toothache, and a rural dentist tried unsuccessfully to pull the offending tooth. Meanwhile, the two airmen waited while the Communists sent messenger after messenger to the Nationalist Sixty-Ninth Army; none ever returned.

They remained in limbo on June 15, spending the night in a prosperous-looking village in northern Hubei Province. Early the next morning a strange sound disturbed the predawn quiet. Gregg's eyes snapped open. His mind slowly swam back to wakeful consciousness. He looked around—darkness. Then he became aware of a low rumble, a pulsating, rich reverberation that woke him. It sounded like an airplane passing overhead—a big one. He rolled over and tried to go back to sleep, but the sound returned again and again. He stepped outside as dawn broke. An enormous, silvery four-engine warplane

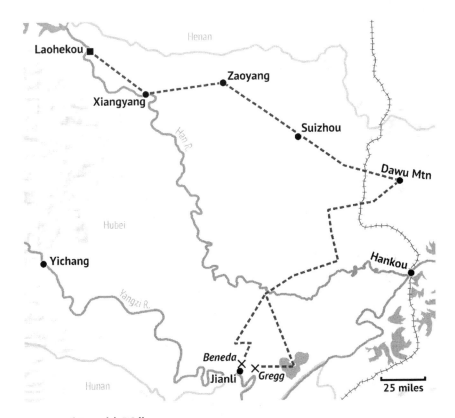

Gregg and Beneda's Walkout

roared overhead—a B-29 Superfortress. As he stood there, six of them flew by, one by one.

"Many of them passed in the night," the interpreter told him and Beneda at breakfast.

"Maybe they bombed Tokyo," Gregg uttered almost in disbelief. His prediction to the troops at the academy had come true in just over a week. The planes he watched cruise overhead had bombed the Imperial Iron and Steel Works at Yawata, on the southern island of Kyushu. Seventy-five of the gargantuan aircraft took part in the raid. Their flight path to and from Japan took them across the length of China, mostly over territory heavily influenced by the Communists. A new phase of the war had begun.

Gregg and Beneda marveled at the thought of the massive bombers repeatedly pummeling the home islands. But the immediate concern of returning to

152   FALLEN TIGERS

American control still remained foremost in their minds. After sending four messengers to Nationalist lines and hearing nothing in return, their escorts informed them they had decided to use an intermediary, an ex-bandit by the name of Mr. Yen.

"He used to be a robber," they told them, "but is now very rich—a gentleman. He will turn you over to the Nationalist troops." The New Fourth Army paid Yen $13,000CN to make the transfer. When Gregg and Beneda arrived at his compound on the morning of June 17, they found he had a small army of his own: men armed with swords, knives, spears, and a handful of firearms that appeared to be at least a hundred years old. Yen was the sort of robber baron who flourished in the contested space between Nationalists, Communists, and Japanese. His ambiguous status made him a useful go-between.

The two airmen set out with the bandit army at two o'clock in the afternoon. Their escorts handed them over to another group of soldiers at eight thirty that evening. These men were not wearing uniforms but were well equipped with machine guns, rifles, grenades, and bandoliers of ammunition over each shoulder.

"These guys are pretty rugged looking," Beneda mumbled. "I wonder whether we'll make it to the other side."

"Yeah," Gregg agreed. "They are a motley-looking crew, but well gunned." An hour later they met a squad of troops dressed in blue cotton uniforms. They marched a short distance farther with these men and then stopped for the night.

As they set out across the rice paddies again early the next morning, lookouts stationed on the surrounding hills alerted them to the approach of Japanese troops. Gregg and Beneda looked back to see a platoon of twenty enemy soldiers advancing down a hillside just half a mile away. The Japanese started shooting; the airmen started running. Six of their escort stayed with them while fourteen peeled off to delay the enemy. The airmen crested a hill and heard the sporadic gunfire erupt into a fierce firefight. They never learned what happened to the troops who stayed behind to cover them—they never even found out who they were. Now, with only a half dozen fighters left to escort them, they continued on. Five hours of walking brought them to a hilltop sentry post. Their escort argued with the sentries for some time; without an interpreter, Gregg and Beneda had no idea what they discussed. After a while the sentries let them pass. An hour after that they came to a river. Machine-gun positions lining the opposite bank barred their way. Again

With the Communists   153

their escorts negotiated with the troops there for half an hour before they finally allowed them to cross. On the other side they learned they had reached a forward command post of the Nationalist 28th Division, Sixty-Ninth Army.

Over the next four days, various units of the Sixty-Ninth relayed Gregg and Beneda to the airfield at Laohekou. They arrived on June 22, the day after Gregg's twenty-sixth birthday. Two days later the pilots jumped aboard a B-25 making a reconnaissance run to Yichang, a Japanese-occupied city near the mouth of the Yangzi River gorges. After making its photo passes, the bomber winged west over the epic chasms to Liangshan, an airbase in Sichuan Province 120 miles northeast of Chongqing. There the two of them caught a transport that eventually delivered them to Kunming. Gregg went to the hospital. Beneda reported to Chennault, delivering the sword, intelligence, and letter from General Li.[3]

The sudden appearance of the two missing fighter pilots at a remote American airbase came as a great surprise—everyone assumed they had been killed. By then, nearly two months had passed since the ambush southwest of Hankou. A month after the battle, the Adjutant General's Office had sent a telegram to Glen Beneda's mother:

THE SECRETARY OF WAR DESIRES ME TO EXPRESS HIS DEEP REGRETS THAT YOUR SON FIRST LIEUTENANT GLEN E BENEDA HAS BEEN REPORTED MISSING IN ACTION SINCE SIX MAY OVER CHINA PERIOD IF FURTHER DETAILS OR OTHER INFORMATION ARE RECEIVED YOU WILL BE PROMPTLY NOTIFIED

General Chennault followed up with a letter of his own, telling her: "Every effort has been made to locate your son and our efforts will continue. However, there is very little hope for his safe return." After meeting with the Old Man, Beneda finally sent a telegram of his own on July 1:

AM WELL AND SAFE PLEASE NOTIFY FRIENDS AND RELATIONS LETTERS WILL FOLLOW ALL MY LOVE GLEN BENEDA[4]

Mrs. Beneda received this last telegram with unimaginable relief. Her friends the Egles had received a similar notification from the War Department when

154   FALLEN TIGERS

their son Ralph went missing. He flew as copilot for one of the 177 B-24 heavy bombers that attacked the oil refineries at Ploiesti, Romania, on August 1, 1943. Fifty-three bombers and 660 airmen did not return from that raid. Unlike Glen's case, as the months wore on, no good news followed. Ralph's loss devastated his family. The Benedas thanked God for their son's miraculous return from behind the lines.[5]

The unexpected resurrection of Gregg and Beneda not only proved a relief for their families but also for their fellow airmen. Chennault did not miss the fact that the New Fourth Army brought them safely through territory "conquered" by the Japanese during phase one of the Ichi-go offensive. Since the defeat of the Nationalist armies there, it had become terra incognita for the Americans. But the Communists thrived in the vacuum left by Chiang's defeated forces. The Japanese could not deny them freedom of movement, despite their frequent patrols. It had been the goal of the Imperial Army to establish a rail corridor from Beiping to Indochina. Chennault sought to deny them that corridor by arraying his warplanes to attack along its entire length. This meant the Fourteenth Air Force had to operate with increasing frequency over territory lacking any Nationalist presence. Though the general did not agree with their political philosophy and remained devoted to Chiang, he saw no alternative to working with the New Fourth Army. Without them, he had no effective way to gather intelligence or recover his fallen airmen.

"I dealt with Chinese of all political shades including Communists, independent guerrillas, and anti-Guomindang dissidents," he later wrote. "This was done with full permission of the Generalissimo, who trusted me to confine my efforts to prosecution of the war and abstain from local political manipulations." His efforts at cooperation proved worthwhile; the 5th Division alone rescued five more of his men, including Capt Armit W. Lewis, whose P-40 quit on him sixty miles southwest of Hankou on October 27. "Guess I'm following the same route Gregg and Beneda used five months ago," he journaled during his forty-three-day walkout.[6]

The New Fourth Army's rescue operations also proved a boon for the Twentieth Air Force. On August 20, Communist troops picked up five airmen from a B-29 that went down in coastal Jiangsu Province, 180 miles north of Shanghai. Seven of the crew ended up captured or missing, but the return of Lt Col William Savoie and four others from his bomber demonstrated the impressive reach and expanding influence of the New Fourth Army.

14

The Secret Airfield

July 24, 1944
Zhijiang, China

Twenty-two shark-mouthed P-40s roared down the field and took off against the backdrop of the rising sun. Gong Kaibing smiled. He worked at the airbase now. When his father had died, Gong left the family farm to look for employment. He ended up joining the War Area Service Corps, a Chinese organization that provided all the food and lodging for every American in China at the incredible rate of just one dollar per person per day.[1] Gong worked at Hostel Number 4, home to several pilots and maintenance crews. He knew a little English and how to read and write, so he served as a clerk, recording the names of visitors, particularly those delivering vegetables or fresh meat. Because of rampant hyperinflation, the job paid in commodities instead of cash; the Service Corps provided his meals and issued him 750 kilos of grain each month, enough to take care of his entire extended family. Additionally, some of the airmen who did not smoke gave him their cigarette rations to sell on the black market; they fetched a small fortune in blockaded China.

The airfield at Zhijiang initially served as a temporary staging base for American planes. Its location in the far reaches of Hunan Province, 180 miles west of Hengyang, made it increasingly important as the Americans evacuated central China. Then, in June 1944, the 5th Fighter Group of the Chinese-American Composite Wing (CACW) made the field its permanent home. Gong loved the excitement of working at the busy airbase. For a young man who had watched Japanese bombers pummel his home with impunity, it felt good to see modern warplanes carrying the twelve-pointed star of the Nationalist republic charge down the runway to challenge the enemy. The

156 FALLEN TIGERS

Japanese no longer dared attack in daylight. Despite some carousing by a few of the less disciplined Americans, Gong and his fellow townspeople felt extremely grateful.[2]

The twenty-two fighters that took off that morning remained low over the hilly terrain to the northeast. Seventy-five miles from the Japanese airfield at Bailuozhen, they sighted Dongting Lake and descended to just above the water—so low their prop wash kicked up a spray behind them. One of the Chinese pilots, 1st Lt Feng Pei-chian, got too low and his propeller caught the water; the belly tank broke free and his fighter slowed dramatically as it first skipped off the surface and then careened into the lake at about one hundred miles per hour. As the rest of the formation sped past, the other pilots could see the empennage sticking out of the water. Though the crashed fighter looked intact, the impact had undoubtedly killed Lieutenant Feng.[3]

Over the massive, featureless lake, the pilots flew purely by dead reckoning, navigating by compass heading and time. "Flying that close to the ground is almost like trying to read a book with your nose only an inch from the page," one of the pilots noted. "You can see the word directly ahead of you, but you don't know what the next word in the sentence happens to be. That was our position: we knew what the ground looked like under us, but we couldn't get any reference points at all. We pulled up and we were not more than three or four miles from the airfield. We could see it clearly."

The Chinese and American pilots of the 5th Fighter Group were about to spring an elaborate trap. Earlier that day, sixteen P-40s from the 23rd Fighter Group had escorted fifteen B-24s to a target south of Hankou. The Americans knew the Japanese had radar and a crude early warning network in the area. They counted on enemy fighters intercepting the mission as they had on May 6, when Lee Gregg and Glen Beneda had been shot down. Sure enough, a force of about thirty Oscars and Tojos dove on the bombers but broke away when they encountered the fighter escort. The twenty-one P-40s out of Zhijiang had timed their arrival to hit Bailuozhen just after the Japanese fighters landed. Their minimum-altitude approach over the lake would ensure the enemy had no advance warning.

The P-40s pulled up to one thousand feet and peeled off in echelon, firing as soon as they closed within range. They strafed and dropped parafrags as they swept across the field. The Sharks made just one pass and then turned for home. "The place was literally ablaze," one of the pilots remembered. "There must have been many, many airplanes burning. We must have cut it

The Secret Airfield 157

to ribbons."[4] They claimed twenty-six Oscars destroyed on the ground for the loss of just the one P-40 that had gone into the lake.[5] Lieutenants Wei, Chou, and Zhou claimed to have destroyed three enemy fighters apiece—the combined wing had come a long way since its first missions the previous November. Indeed, Chinese airmen ended up making significant contributions to the Allied air campaign. Throughout the war, Chinese fighter pilots flying with American squadrons and the CACW claimed 112.5 aerial victories—more than 10 percent of the total number of claims made by American air forces in the China Theater. Of the 1,513 airmen reported missing on combat missions by the China Air Task Force and Fourteenth Air Force, seventy-five were Chinese. Of those, the Japanese captured two, twenty-five died, and forty-eight successfully returned to friendly airbases.

The day after the raid on Bailuozhen, Casey Vincent flew to Zhijiang in his stripped-down B-25 "Silver Slipper" to congratulate the men and award medals to the deputy group commander and two other pilots.[6] Incredibly, the 5th Fighter Group repeated the feat just four days later, claiming another eleven enemy planes destroyed. Realizing Bailuozhen was too vulnerable to use as anything other than a forward staging base, the Japanese withdrew their fighters.[7]

Fourteenth Air Force claimed an astonishing 451 enemy aircraft shot down from the beginning of Ichi-go in mid-April until the end of the year—very likely more aircraft than the Japanese had in China. As with crew claims for counter-shipping sweeps, aerial victory claims could be problematic. For example, in his 1991 book *Flying Tigers,* author Daniel Ford used Japanese accounts of the war to calculate the American Volunteer Group's kills at only 115 instead of the 297 they had claimed. Given the fragmented nature of Japanese records, such a precise figure raised some eyebrows. Predictably, it also generated considerable anger from veterans of the group, though that may have had more to do with the tone of the book than with its content: Ford characterized the Americans as rowdy playboys "downing whisky-sodas" while the serious Japanese fought with discipline and professionalism.[8]

Most airmen actually acknowledged kill claims could sometimes be inaccurate. During the week of the second Schweinfurt raid in October 1943, for example, Eighth Air Force gunners claimed to have shot down 702 German fighters—more than twice as many as the Luftwaffe actually had in Germany at the time. In reality, the Germans reported losing between eighty and 125 interceptors.[9] In China, fighters seldom carried gun cameras, and confusion

158   FALLEN TIGERS

abounded in violent, fast-paced dogfights; often more than one pilot unwittingly shot at the same target, and damaged aircraft trailing smoke and flames frequently dove away from a fight, looking for all the world like they were going down.[10] The emotion of the issue and patchy nature of Japanese records make it unlikely anyone will ever calculate a definitive number.

From a strategic standpoint, though, it hardly mattered. Even if the Americans traded warplanes one-for-one with the Japanese, the latter would still have lost a war of attrition. A number of factors contributed to this. First of all, American industry far outproduced that of Japan. The Nakajima Aircraft Company manufactured 5,919 Ki-43 Hayabusas, the Japanese Army Air Force's standard frontline fighter. The company built just 1,227 of the excellent Ki-44 Shoki.[11] At the same time, 13,738 P-40 Warhawks rolled off the assembly lines of the Curtiss-Wright Corporation, while North American Aviation produced 14,501 P-51 Mustangs, and the Lockheed Corporation churned out 9,536 P-38 Lightnings.[12] Additionally, American mechanics could better return damaged aircraft to combat, partly due to the standardization of assembly line manufacture and partly because of the intentional production of spare parts. The Japanese practically hand built each of their aircraft, making repair difficult.

Second, the US Army Air Forces also had a much more robust pilot training program. At the beginning of the war, the typical Japanese army pilot was a formidable opponent, having graduated from a two-year program as a noncommissioned officer and possessing an average of five hundred flying hours. But flight hours dropped dramatically as the Japanese increased the number of trainees. Forty-six thousand pilots graduated from these programs throughout the war, averaging only one hundred hours of flight experience per man by the end of 1944.[13] The United States, by contrast, mass-produced airmen like any other commodity in the "arsenal of democracy." American pilots graduated as officers after accruing two hundred hours through seven months of primary, basic, and advanced training. Though fighter pilots only averaged forty hours in operational training units at the beginning of the war, this increased to one hundred hours by the end of 1944.[14] Thus, the experience level of new American pilots slowly increased, while the experience level of new Japanese pilots dramatically decreased. From 1940 to 1945, the US Army Air Forces trained 193,440 pilots, including 81,024 in 1944 alone—nearly double the Japanese total for the entire war.[15]

Finally, the United States did a much better job of preserving experience by rotating airmen from combat units to training commands. In contrast,

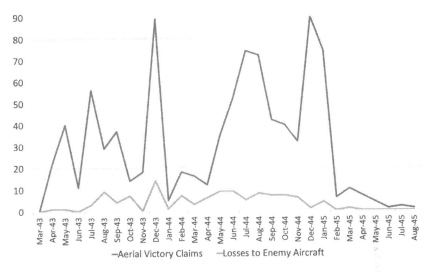

Fourteenth Air Force Aerial Victory Claims vs. Losses to Enemy Aircraft

most Japanese aviators remained in combat until injury or death removed them. The relationship between the Americans and their Chinese allies meant that 90 percent of airmen who survived a crash or bailout in the China Theater returned to American control. Even if they could no longer fly in combat, they could pass on their experiences training replacement pilots. Japanese airmen who crash-landed or parachuted from their aircraft fell into a hostile land, where angry mobs sometimes exacted retribution for terror bombing; many chose to go down with their planes, instead.[16]

Although aerial victory claims are not particularly useful in determining strategic outcomes or the actual number of aircraft destroyed, they do serve as a useful measure of contact with the enemy. A graph of monthly claims shows a spike during Lt Gen Moritaka Nakazono's air offensive in the summer of 1943 as well as a spike in December 1943, when the 3rd Air Division supported ground troops in a limited offensive near Dongting Lake. During the Ichi-go offensive from April 1944 to January 1945, there is a prolonged surge—the death throes of the Fifth Air Army—with a peak of ninety aircraft claimed shot down in December 1944 alone. Meanwhile, the number of American aircraft reported missing due to enemy air action steadily decreased from fourteen in December 1943, to an average of seven a month from May through November 1944, only one in December, four in January 1945, and then just

160 FALLEN TIGERS

one in March. Clearly, the Americans eventually gained air supremacy—just not by as much a margin as their kill claims suggested.

As war-weary veterans rotated back to the United States, new products of the American training system arrived in China. First Lieutenant Paul Crawford earned his wings at Napier Field near Dothan, Alabama, in March 1944. He went on to learn the rudiments of fighter aviation in P-40s and then reported to Pinellas Field in Saint Petersburg, Florida, to fly the Mustang. "I never will forget walking out on the ramp and seeing that great big beautiful P-51," he recalled. "Everybody wanted to fly the Mustang—that was *the* airplane. It was a great airplane to fly. It would do anything you wanted it to." After sixty to seventy-five hours practicing formation flying, dogfighting, dive-bombing, and aerial gunnery, Crawford reported for duty in China with the 311th Fighter Group.

On his first combat mission, he ranged across the Gobi Desert into Inner Mongolia, looking for Japanese trains. His flight leader gave him first crack at one: "I got too close," he admitted. "Hell, if they had a bb gun they could have shot me down!"

The Mustangs operated from Xi'an, the ancient former capital of China located in southern Shaanxi Province. The airfield there allowed P-51 fighter-bombers to range out and relentlessly attack Japan's robust rail network north of the Yellow River. These missions took them over vast areas lacking any appreciable Nationalist presence. As Gregg and Beneda had discovered, the Communist New Fourth Army generally operated in the area north of the Yangzi River in central China. North of the Yellow River, fallen airmen often found themselves in the hands of the Communist Eighth Route Army. Twentieth Air Force Superfortresses also frequently overflew the Eighth Route Army's area of influence on their way to and from targets in Japan and Manchuria.[17]

Cooperation with the Communists would prove vital to operations in north China. But whereas Chennault sought approval from Chiang to work with the New Fourth Army, doing so purely to aid in the fight against Japan, General Stilwell had used the threat of American support for the Communists as a way to bludgeon the generalissimo into acquiescing to his plans. During the spring and summer of 1944, Stilwell had increasingly insisted on establishing an American mission to Mao Zedong's headquarters at Yan'an, deep in remote Shaanxi Province. When Chiang demurred, the general delayed the departure of thirty Chinese airmen destined for pilot training

The Secret Airfield   161

programs in the United States. President Roosevelt added weight to the issue when he sent Vice President Henry Wallace to China in June 1944. Although Roosevelt appreciated China's sacrifices, he thought the Allied cause would benefit from Chiang directing all his resources against Japan instead of devoting a good deal of it to containing (and sometimes fighting) the Communists. Between Stilwell's aggressive coercion and some convincing by the vice president, Chiang finally gave in.

A solitary C-47 approached the airfield at Yan'an around noon on July 22, 1944. The pilot, Capt Robert Champion, spotted the hilltop pagoda his instructions told him would serve as a landmark. He began his descent. A large crowd had gathered to meet the transport, the first US military aircraft to visit the headquarters of the Chinese Communists. Champion touched down smoothly, but as the aircraft trundled down the crude field, its left landing gear dropped into an old grave. The plane suddenly lurched to the left. Champion leaned forward to cut the engines, and just in time—the left propeller hit the ground and sheared off at the shaft, spinning into the cockpit. Had the pilot not been leaning forward, he probably would have been killed. Colonel David D. Barrett rushed forward to find Champion shaken but unhurt, standing beside the jagged hole in the side of his airplane.

Colonel Barrett commanded the US Army Observer Group, also known as the "Dixie Mission," because it would operate deep in "rebel" territory. An intelligence officer by trade and training, the fifty-two-year-old Coloradan had spent much of his twenty-seven-year Army career in China. He spoke and read Mandarin fluently. Barrett had served a short time as military attaché to the US embassy in Chongqing and, most recently, as the chief intelligence officer for the American advisory mission to the Nationalist armies at Guilin. When he took over the Dixie Mission, his instructions from headquarters directed him to solicit information on the order of battle for the Japanese and their puppets; to report on the strength, composition, disposition, equipment, training, and combat efficiency of Communist forces; to ascertain the nature of Communist intelligence in occupied territory; to compile a "who's who" of Communist officials; to provide target intelligence, bomb damage assessment and weather information for American air operations; and to determine the extent of Communist control of Chinese territory along with an evaluation of their current and potential contributions to the war effort.

At least one of his tasks would be made easy by the fact that many of the most prominent Communist officials had shown up to meet the airplane. As

162   FALLEN TIGERS

the nine initial members of the Dixie Mission disembarked from the wreck, Zhou Enlai hastened forward to greet them. Zhou, more than any other individual, had become the public face of the Chinese Communist Party. As its chief representative with the United Front, he had been in Chongqing liaising with the Nationalists until 1943, when worsening relations forced him to return to Yan'an. He introduced the Americans to the other officials at the field before loading the newcomers aboard a truck and taking them to their quarters—tunnels dug into steep hillsides and lined with blocks of hewn stone.

Zhu De, commander in chief of the Red Army, gave a brief speech at a welcome lunch later that day, after which Zhou called Colonel Barrett and Captain Champion forward. "Captain," began Zhou, speaking through Barrett as an interpreter, "a hero has been wounded. We consider your plane a hero. Fortunately, another hero, yourself, was not injured. Chairman Mao has asked me to convey to you his relief that you came to no harm." To Barrett, it seemed the inauspicious nature of the Americans' arrival had been brushed aside by the graciousness of their hosts. He felt a cautious optimism take hold as he set the Dixie Mission about its long list of tasks.[18]

Though Chennault disagreed with Stilwell's strong-arm political tactics, he made sure an officer from the Air-Ground Aid Section accompanied the mission. Captain Henry C. Whittlesey immediately set about coordinating with the Eighth Route Army to rescue downed American airmen.[19] He crisscrossed north China to set up evasion lines and even worked with Eighth Route Army engineers to construct an emergency airfield perilously close to enemy lines in the mountains of southeast Shanxi Province, near the Henan-Hebei border. Local workers expanded a road through a narrow valley, oriented northeast to southwest, into a five-thousand-foot-long packed dirt airfield. On December 30, 1944, Whittlesey met eleven evaders in a tiny village eighteen miles north of the secret airfield. Captain George Varoff and his crew had taken part in a twelve-plane raid against an aircraft modification center in Shenyang on December 7.[20] Though in some respects a marvel of American engineering, the Superfortress earned a reputation as a mechanical nightmare. Varoff's aircraft proved no exception. Shortly after takeoff, the tail gunner discovered his guns did not work. Then, as the plane approached Shenyang, the windows began icing over; the crew had to don oxygen masks and depressurize just so they could see. Over the target, enemy fighters hit their number one engine. Varoff headed for Xi'an to make an

The Secret Airfield   163

emergency landing. The damaged engine caught fire as they crossed the Beiping–Hankou Railway, and Varoff ordered the crew to bail out.

Only a week before the mission, Lt Col William Savoie had lectured Varoff's squadron on his rescue by the New Fourth Army, giving the pilot and his crewmen confidence in the competence and dependability of Communist forces. Twentieth Bomber Command MIS-X officers had also briefed them on the Eighth Route Army specifically. The downed airmen not only knew how to identify themselves as Americans—"Meiguo"—they knew how to ask for the Eighth Route Army—"Balujun." Staff Sergeant Frank Broussard, the radio operator, even remembered the hand sign for the number eight, his thumb and forefinger spread and pointed downward. Communist troops collected all eleven airmen within hours of their bailout and had them reunited by December 13.[21]

Whittlesey wanted to evacuate them from the nearby airfield rather than travel another 220 miles west through Japanese-occupied territory to Yan'an. It had never been done before, though, and communication with the American airbase at Xi'an proved difficult from such a remote location. While Whittlesey worked to arrange a pickup, Varoff and his crew stayed about eight miles away at the home of Minister Zhang Gewei.[22] The minister's gated compound appeared as an oasis among the stark, arid mountains of northern China. Tall stalks of corn and ripe watermelons grew in the yard; a small herd of Holsteins grazed nearby.[23]

Zhang greeted the airmen enthusiastically in perfect English. In conversations with him, they learned he had studied at the University of Chicago in the 1930s and earned a master's degree in agriculture at the University of Minnesota. He married an American from Saint Paul, Eleanor Ingalls. They moved to Beiping and had three children together. Zhang had been away from home when the Japanese captured the city in 1937. The last news he had of his family, the enemy had interned them with other civilians in Beiping. His efforts to rescue them came to naught, and he had heard nothing in the intervening years. Traveling through north China one day, Communists captured the train in which he rode and detained him. Zhang ended up staying with them and putting his agricultural expertise to good use. Now he served as minister of production for the district. The Americans enjoyed chatting with him and very much appreciated the fresh milk and butter from his cows.

As the weeks passed without any word on arrangements to fly the crew out, Whittlesey decided not to wait with them any longer. He had learned

164   FALLEN TIGERS

from Communist intelligence sources that the Japanese planned a campaign to capture Xi'an in the spring. The captain urgently needed to pass this information to American authorities, so he set out on horseback for Yan'an. He traveled fast, arriving at a small village near a railroad junction ten miles southeast of Taiyuan on the evening of January 19, 1945. That night, one thousand Japanese troops converged on the town from seven directions, apparently looking for an officer of theirs who had been captured. They attacked just before dawn and took Whittlesey unawares, still in his bed. The Eighth Route Army promptly counterattacked with a brigade-size force of 4,500 troops. Forced to withdraw, the Japanese executed Whittlesey with a bullet to the head and bayonet to the back. They took the secret documents he had been carrying, leaving behind only his journal and mangled corpse.

Varoff and his crew learned of his death about a week later. An officer from the Eighth Route Army told them the captain had only been captive for a matter of hours. There appeared to be no indication the Japanese had been looking for him specifically; the whole thing had been an unhappy accident. Whittlesey was the Dixie Mission's only casualty of the war, and his death hit Barrett hard. "He was one of the finest young officers I ever knew and I not only esteemed him for his professional qualities, but held him in the highest personal regard," the colonel later wrote. Quixotically, Barrett erroneously reported that the Communists sacrificed almost an entire battalion in an attempt to recover his body but proved unable to do so. In fact, they retrieved the body and transported it south for eventual evacuation from the secret airfield.

Meanwhile, on January 26, Varoff and his crew saw two P-51 Mustangs overfly Minister Zhang's house at about two o'clock in the afternoon. They tried signaling the fighters with pocket mirrors but to no avail. As it turned out, the Mustangs flew escort for a stripped-down B-25 from C Flight of the 2nd Weather Reconnaissance Squadron. The flight had been working out of Xinjin Airfield near Chengdu since November 1944, gathering meteorological data to help forecasters make weather reports for the B-29s. When the flight commander, Capt Robert C. Kunz, heard about Varoff's crew waiting for evacuation from a secret airfield, he volunteered to fly them out. A few minutes after seeing the Mustangs, the B-29 crew received a phone call; Kunz had landed at the field. He had waited for a time but eventually had to depart when they did not show. He left them a few containers of D rations, medical supplies, bedrolls, and winter jackets and promised to return at the same time the next day.

The Secret Airfield 165

Unfortunately, the weather did not cooperate. Every day for the next ten days, the airmen trudged eight miles to the airfield to await Kunz's arrival, but low clouds and haze prevented his return. Searching for the field in soupy weather on February 6, the captain had to send his fighter escort back to Xi'an, low on fuel. He almost turned back himself when he happened to catch sight of the field through the mist. Kunz buzzed it several times, taking photos. The flag north of midfield showed the wind out of the southwest—straight down the runway—and he landed without incident. Though appearing to be 150 feet wide, only the runway's middle twenty feet had been tamped down enough for the bomber. Kunz almost got stuck turning around on the soft shoulder, but he goosed the throttles and pulled through. He picked up the eleven airmen and flew them out to Xi'an. For flying an unarmed medium bomber alone, deep into enemy territory, without fighter escort, and opposed by adverse weather, Kunz received the Distinguished Flying Cross.[24]

He returned less than a month later, on March 3, to pick up another nine airmen awaiting rescue: five from a B-29 and three from a C-46, along with a single P-51 pilot. The Superfortress crew had taken off on a mission to bomb an aircraft factory on Kyushu on November 11, 1944. Major Francis Morgan, visiting from XX Bomber Command Headquarters, accompanied the crew as an observer. They missed their rendezvous, but the pilot, 1st Lt Richard Vickery, decided to proceed to the target anyway, accompanied by just one other B-29. En route, the radio operator received orders to divert to the tertiary target at Nanjing because of prohibitive weather over Kyushu. They saw a formation of fourteen other bombers heading that way, but rather than join them, Vickery decided to circumnavigate Shanghai out over the water before turning west. He made his run on Nanjing alone at twenty-two thousand feet. Anti-aircraft fire hit the warplane as it dropped its bombs. One of the gunners reported a fire burning in the aft bomb bay, which soon grew out of control. Another crewman announced the number-four engine had caught fire, with flames extending out beyond the tail. The B-29 began losing altitude rapidly and lurched to the right.[25]

"Bail out!" the flight engineer ordered. The crew scrambled to abandon ship; Major Morgan watched as the navigator and flight engineer jumped through the forward wheel well. He lined up behind the bombardier, pilot, copilot, and radio operator, but before they could jump, another lurch sent him and the radio operator sprawling into the engineer's compartment. He

166   Fallen Tigers

pushed the man off of him and stood to find himself on the flight engineer's window, looking up at the nose wheel as the big plane dropped sideways out of the sky. Then the bomber rolled and exploded in midair. Morgan regained consciousness free-falling just 2,500 feet above the ground. He quickly pulled at his ripcord. It took several yanks before the parachute finally deployed. Morgan floated to the ground not far from two large sections of burning wreckage, bits of aluminum and burning debris falling all around him. He soon met up with the engineer, radio operator, and one of the gunners. They took stock of the situation. Morgan had several cuts across his face, some broken teeth, and a ragged gash on his right wrist. The radio operator appeared to be suffering from shock. The gunner limped. Only the engineer appeared uninjured. Before they had a chance to tend to each other's wounds, one hundred Chinese guerrillas appeared over a nearby ridge and took them into custody.

They soon found out they had been rescued by the New Fourth Army. The Communist troops also picked up the navigator. They reported finding three bodies in the B-29 wreck—the pilot, copilot, and bombardier. These they buried at the New Fourth Army Memorial Cemetery. The other three gunners and the radar operator fell into the hands of puppet troops. Unfortunately, before the Communists could negotiate with the puppets to secure the Americans' release, the party inadvertently ran into a Japanese patrol. The enemy insisted on taking control of the prisoners and supposedly shot and killed the radar operator when he resisted. The three gunners ended up at the Jiangwan prison camp in Shanghai.

The New Fourth Army transmitted the names and serial numbers of the five airmen they rescued to Yan'an and arranged to take them out via the same route Lieutenant Colonel Savoie's crew had been traversing since August. On December 12, however, they received a message from XX Bomber Command by way of the Dixie Mission: Savoie's crew had returned safely, but the Nationalists refused to accept any more US airmen from the New Fourth Army. Generalissimo Chiang would no longer cooperate with his political rivals to aid his American allies. The last vestige of the United Front had crumbled away. The Communist soldiers expressed frustration at Chiang's intransigence. They decided to head north and hand the airmen over to the Eighth Route Army for evacuation from Whittlesey's secret airfield.[26]

Meanwhile, 1st Lt Walter Krywy's P-51 had taken a bullet to a coolant line while strafing a train near Guzhen, Anhui Province, on January 1, 1945.

He bailed out only seven hundred feet above the ground. The airplane hit a short distance away, exploding in flames. The pilot quickly gathered what he needed from his jungle kit, buried his parachute, and set out toward a cluster of three villages a short distance to the west. Throughout their areas of influence, the New Fourth and Eighth Route Armies organized local villages into "People's Militias." Sometimes these augmented military operations, but usually they simply gathered intelligence and alerted Communist forces to enemy movements. People's Militias controlled two of the villages in the cluster Krywy approached, while Japanese-aligned puppet troops controlled the third. As he neared the villages, fifty puppet troops formed up outside their town, while a pair of militiamen stood outside theirs. Both sides watched Krywy silently as he passed, neither making a move. Suddenly, the two militiamen hurried forward, waving their guns and calling for him to halt. They grabbed him before he could get too close to the puppets. The platoon of collaborators stood and watched as the two militiamen disarmed the airman and confiscated his watch, pen, and money, and then took him to their village. The entire population turned out to see who they had caught. They read the pilot's pointie-talkie and inspected his identification flag. Afterward, the village headman returned all of Krywy's personal possessions—except the cash—and the next day turned him over to the New Fourth Army.

Major Morgan heard about the Mustang pilot and sent him a telegram on January 5, asking that he wait for the B-29 crew to catch up with him. He erroneously addressed it to "Major Waters." Apparently, Krywy's name had become garbled in transmission:

> TO MAJOR WATERS DO NOT LEAVE YOUR BAG TILL YOU GET THE SIGNAL BECAUSE THE SQUEEZE PLAY IS ON AND WE ALL WANT TO STEAL MORGAN

Krywy stayed put, and the major's group joined him nine days later. Together they rode northwest, crossing the Longhai Railway into Eighth Route Army territory on the seventeenth. "Our mounts from now on were of poorer quality," journaled Krywy, "as the 8th Route Army area is generally much poorer than that of the New 4th. We usually had to walk the horses for three or four miles each day to rest them."[27]

On the twenty-fourth, the group of evaders grew one last time when 2nd Lt Al Fisher, Staff Sgt Peter Kouzes, and Sgt Elon Patterson from Air

168   FALLEN TIGERS

Transport Command joined them. Krywy found the transport crew ill prepared for evasion. "The briefing the ATC had had was feeble," he reported. "They knew nothing about the safe areas, proper procedure, or anything." Flying a C-46 full of gasoline barrels from Luliang to Laohekou on December 10, 1944, Fisher had become hopelessly lost in poor weather and somehow ended up overshooting his destination by 220 miles. When they finally broke out of the weather near Kaifeng, a Japanese fighter attacked, setting fire to their right engine. Fisher ordered the copilot, crew chief, and radio operator to bail out. As they ran for the cargo door, the fighter made two more passes, firing into the stricken plane. The bullets sounded like hail on a tin roof as they tore the fuselage to shreds. Fuel covered the cabin floor. The copilot did not make it. The other three crewmen parachuted safely to the ground and took cover in the woods until the fighter departed. Later in the day a patrol of Nationalist soldiers under the command of Gen Wang Dagong picked them up and took them to a small village near the border of Henan and Hebei Provinces, north of the Yellow River.[28]

The transport crew had been there for a week when, on the night of December 20, Communist troops attacked. The battle lasted for thirty-two hours. The Americans sheltered in the attic of a mud building through the night while the Communists fired machine guns, mortars, and light artillery all around them. At about eleven o'clock on the morning of the twenty-first, soldiers climbed atop the building and tore a hole in the slate roof, dropping grenades into the room. Fisher immediately led his crew out the front door into the middle of the firefight.

One of the Communist officers recognized them as Americans. "Meiguo!" he yelled. His troops stopped firing long enough to bring them safely behind their lines. The battle then resumed and lasted until four o'clock the next morning. The Communist troops wiped out the entire Nationalist garrison, including General Wang himself. The Dixie Mission reported speaking about the incident to an Eighth Route Army general, who bizarrely told them his forces had attacked the town to rescue the Americans. He alleged that General Wang had connections to a traitor and that the Communist troops liberated the airmen before they could be handed over to the Japanese. In his evasion report, however, Fisher related that the Communist force was surprised to find them in the village and had not attacked to rescue them. Perhaps the general concocted the story to obscure the fact his forces had attacked a Nationalist garrison. Regardless, by that point in the war, the

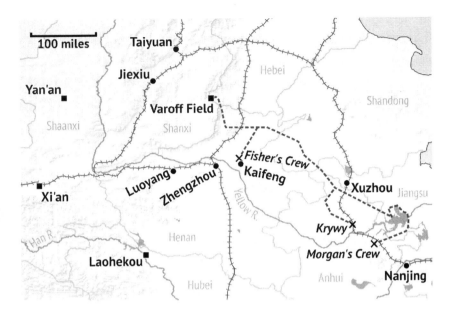

Evasion in North China

Americans knew full well that Nationalists and Communists engaged each other in open combat.[29]

Over the next month, the Eighth Route Army relayed the nine airmen to Minister Zhang's house. Captain Kunz landed his weather reconnaissance B-25 at the secret airfield on March 3, 1945. The airmen climbed aboard while Chinese troops loaded Captain Whittlesey's body into the bomb bay. Kunz took off just nine minutes after he landed. The fighter escort peeled off to land at Xi'an, but the bomber continued to Xinjin, where it touched down to find a senior member of the Nationalist secret police waiting to debrief the rescued airmen on their experience with the Communists. Major Morgan was shocked to learn that during his 113 days behind the lines, XX Bomber Command had ceased operations in China. After six months, the Superfortresses had made only a 2 percent dent in the Japanese steel industry. Major General Curtis LeMay moved most of the aircraft to the Marianas and, following the grisly demonstration at Hankou in December 1944, switched from high-altitude daylight precision bombing to low-altitude nighttime incendiary attacks.[30] For his part, Kunz kept flying special operations between his weather reconnaissance duties. On June 19, he took off from Xinjin with

170   FALLEN TIGERS

a bomb bay full of material for the Office of Strategic Services. He and the other four members of his crew never returned; they remain listed as missing in action.

Until the end of the war, the secret airfield in southeast Shanxi proved useful for evacuating P-51 pilots who went down on their frequent missions out of Xi'an. With bombs and napalm, they supported Nationalist troops pushing back against the Japanese offensive Captain Whittlesey had learned about in January. They also ranged throughout northern China, attacking trains from the Gobi Desert to the Yellow Sea. On July 14, 1st Lt Paul Crawford and his wingman, 2nd Lt Eric Armstrong, strafed a railroad yard outside the town of Jiexiu. They came across the target low and fast to limit their exposure to small-arms fire. Nevertheless, Crawford heard a loud bang and felt his airplane shudder. He looked over his engine instruments—everything appeared to be working normally. Soon he could not see much at all though as smoke filled his cockpit; ground fire must have hit something electrical. He pulled up into a steep climb and prepared to bail out.

Following his element leader in the rapid ascent, Lieutenant Armstrong saw Crawford's canopy separate and tumble away. He immediately tried to contact him on the radio, but to no avail. As he came abreast of the stricken fighter, Armstrong noticed thick black smoke pouring from the right side exhaust stacks. Crawford jumped clear of the doomed Mustang at about four thousand feet, quickly deploying his parachute. Armstrong circled overhead until the lieutenant landed safely four miles south of Jiexiu. Luckily, the Eighth Route Army picked him up almost immediately and began relaying him east to the secret airfield.

During his walkout, Crawford met an old man who lived in Jiexiu. Tom Hill, another lieutenant in his squadron, had gone down in the same area the day before. The old man had watched the fighter crash and reported that the pilot's left arm and right leg had been torn off. The Japanese recovered the body, decapitated it, and hung the severed head over the south gate of the city as a warning against helping Americans. According to the old man, Chinese villagers buried what remained of the body. It sounded to Crawford as if Hill had died in the crash, but the story of his decapitation and the exhibition of his head served as a grisly reminder of the enemy's brutality. He did not want to be captured.[31]

A twin-engine Beechcraft UC-45 picked him up from the secret airfield and flew him to Yan'an in early August. Whether at the request of Mao, who

The Secret Airfield   171

wished to have stricter control over Americans coming and going from his territory, or at the behest of the Americans with the Dixie Mission, who desired to debrief pilots who evaded with the help of the Communists, airmen evacuated from the secret airfield no longer flew directly back to US airbases: everyone had to funnel through Yan'an. Mao himself actually made an appearance at a breakfast Crawford attended. The young lieutenant knew Mao led the Chinese Communist Party and that he opposed Chiang Kai-shek, but when he saw him in 1945, he had no idea how consequential the chairman would become in the history of China and the world. Crawford returned to his unit at Xi'an on August 7, just a week before the Japanese surrender.[32]

Despite the contentious political situation in China and the fact that official American policy supported the Nationalists, the informal relationship between the US Army Air Forces and the Chinese Communists proved immensely beneficial. The CCP claimed to have lost approximately five hundred men while rescuing eighty American airmen. Of ninety-seven evasion reports on file at the Air Force Historical Research Agency, 12 percent detail the experiences of airmen rescued by Communists. If the evasion reports are a representative sample, eighty is a good overall estimate. Even though the CCP and the Guomindang fought each other while also fighting the Japanese—and even though Mao may have had fundamentally irreconcilable political differences with the United States—the rescue of scores of American airmen by the New Fourth and Eighth Route Armies underpinned the ad hoc "enemy of my enemy" alliance with real feelings of gratitude and friendship between individual Americans and Chinese.[33]

15

Thai Fighters

October 25, 1944
Yunnanyi, China

Two North American P-51C Mustangs touched down on the dusty, drab airfield set amid a patchwork of freshly harvested rice paddies. Each of the new fighters presented a beautiful vision of shimmering polished aluminum, adorned with stars and bars on the wings and fuselage and a distinctive black checkerboard pattern applied to the empennage and tail. The men of the 25th Fighter Squadron turned out when they heard the throaty rumble of the Packard-built Merlin engines and watched as the sleek fighters taxied in. These represented the first two Mustangs the squadron had recently learned would replace its aging fleet of P-40s. A training team on detached service from headquarters set up a two-week transition course for the squadron's engineering section and crew chiefs. The pilots, however, received no formal instruction on the new fighter.[1]

The 75th Fighter Squadron at Zhijiang also received its first Mustangs about this time. Like the 25th, its pilots received no formal transition course. First Lieutenant Donald Lopez, an experienced P-40 pilot in the unit, recalled sitting in the cockpit for a time to familiarize himself with the controls. Then he started up the engine, taxied to the end of the runway, and took off. He climbed to ten thousand feet over the mountainous countryside and began to put the new fighter through its paces. He had no idea the Mustang's high-capacity fuselage fuel tank caused the center of gravity to shift dangerously far aft. "The pilot's manual—which, unfortunately, I had never seen, since there was not one with the plane—prohibited aerobatics with much fuel in the fuselage tank," he recalled. "Standard procedure in a Mustang called for using the fuselage tank first." He pulled into an Immelmann maneuver and the airplane stalled violently and snapped into an inverted spin. Hanging upside down in the cockpit, he struggled to regain control as the fighter spun around and around and the mountains grew closer and closer. Finally, he cut the throttle; the spinning stopped and the Mustang fell into a dive. He pulled out, landed, parked, and shut down.

"What in the hell was that, Lope?" one of the other pilots hollered as he climbed down.

"That was a new maneuver I just invented called the Tootsie Roll," he quipped. He never lived that one down.[2]

The 25th Fighter Squadron had a leg up on Lopez's unit; five days before its first Mustangs arrived, it received a new commanding officer, Lt Col John Habecker, who had previously led a P-51 squadron in north Burma. On November 2 he sent a dozen pilots to Calcutta to ferry the next consignment of new fighters over the Hump. The group included 2nd Lt Henry Minco, the French-born hellraiser from Ohio, along with his friends Cliff Long and Thomas Ankrim. The next day, the squadron's first two Mustangs flew their first combat mission on the Salween Front, bombing and strafing fortified Japanese positions in Longling.[3]

During the ferry flight, the squadron lost one of its new aircraft to a landing accident at Mohanbari, India—later attributed to the pilot's lack of training in the type. The rest arrived at Yunnanyi without incident on November 9. Though more vulnerable to ground fire, the greater operating radius of the Mustang would allow the 25th to range into Thailand and Indochina to sweep Japanese lines of communication alongside the P-38 Lightnings of the 449th Fighter Squadron. Despite their inexperience, most of the pilots bubbled with enthusiasm for their new mounts. But Henry Minco had become morose over the preceding weeks. One night, he told Cliff Long that he had a premonition of his own death. Long worried about his friend, but Minco kept his depression buried deep and carried on with the business of war.[4]

The sweeps into Thailand and Indochina would bring the 25th into unfamiliar territory. The United States officially considered both countries to be friendly nations forcibly occupied by the Japanese. The political realities of both proved to be much more complicated. Japanese troops had invaded Thailand on December 8, 1941, en route to objectives in British Malaya and Burma. With fighting already underway, the Japanese ambassador presented the Thai government with a stark choice: either grant their troops free passage or risk further bloodshed from a continued invasion. Feeling it had no

174   FALLEN TIGERS

choice in the matter, the Thai government acceded to Japanese demands. Within two weeks, it bowed to further pressure and signed a formal alliance granting them full use of Thai facilities and airfields. The Japanese 5th Air Division soon had more than two hundred aircraft stationed in the country. In fact, the dramatic Christmas air raids on Rangoon in 1941 had launched from Thai airfields.[5]

The administration of Prime Minister Phibun Songkhram decided to make the most of a difficult situation and reap what rewards might result from a Japanese victory. On January 25, 1942, Thailand formally declared war on the United States and Great Britain. Four months later, on May 10, three divisions of the Royal Thai Army invaded the Shan States in northeast Burma to protect the Japanese right flank. This course of action produced many skeptics, including Seni Pramoj, the minister in charge of the Thai Legation in Washington, DC. Seni refused to deliver the declaration of war to the US government and, in turn, the State Department encouraged him to remain in his post as if he represented an occupied state rather than a belligerent. Seni eventually became one of the leaders of a Free Thai Movement working with the Office of Strategic Services (OSS) and British Special Operations Executive to establish resistance cells across the country. Thailand would, he affirmed, seek US assistance "at opportune times in the future to emancipate itself from Japanese control."[6]

Meanwhile, the Thai government asserted its right to maintain custody of downed Allied airmen captured in its territory, rather than hand them over to the Japanese. The six Army Air Force fliers interned on the campus of Thammasat University in Bangkok enjoyed a much kinder fate than their compatriots subject to the brutal conditions of Japanese prison camps.[7] They ate ample portions of rice porridge, curried rice, beef, chicken, vegetables, and eggs—some of the men even claimed to have gained weight in the course of their confinement. The Thais did not force them to work, gave them plenty of reading material, allowed them to move freely about the campus, and even tried to teach them how to play cricket. According to one captured airman: "The Thais couldn't do enough for Americans." Another said his imprisonment was a "welcome rest."[8]

Free Thai partisans working with the OSS rescued both of the AVG pilots captured in Thailand: Charlie Mott and William "Black Mac" McGarry. In the case of McGarry, the director general of police in Bangkok produced an obviously forged release order to provide plausible deniability of official

Thai Fighters   175

collusion. He then escorted the airman from the internment camp to an OSS safehouse. On the night of April 21, 1945, operatives smuggled him aboard a customs vessel, which motored him out to the Gulf of Thailand for evacuation by a PBY Catalina flying boat.[9]

But even as Thailand played this double game with the Axis and Allies, the Royal Thai Air Force (RTAF) sought to defend the nation's sovereign airspace from Allied attack. In fact, Prime Minister Phibun had justified his January 1942 declaration of war in part as a response to AVG and Royal Air Force (RAF) raids on Japanese forces based in Thailand.[10] The RTAF had traditionally flown American-built aircraft, employing Curtis Hawk 75 fighters and twin-engine Martin 139 bombers, for example, in its 1940 border war with French Indochina.[11] The United States halted the sale of arms and aircraft to Thailand following the border war, but Japan stepped in to fill the gap. In November 1941 the RTAF took delivery of the first of twenty-four Ki-30 "Anns" and nine Mitsubishi Ki-21 "Sallys" (known as the Type 26 and Type 61, respectively, in Thai service) and in January 1942, took delivery of the first of twelve Nakajima Ki-27b "Nates" (known as the Type 15, or "Ota" after the hometown of the Nakajima factory). Japanese airmen provided training in the new types at Don Muang airfield, just north of Bangkok. The RTAF assigned all twelve of the Otas to No. 16 Squadron at Lampang in northern Thailand. The Ki-21s went to No. 62 Squadron stationed nearby at Ko Kha. In place of the traditional red, white, and blue roundels—which looked too similar to those of the RAF—Thai airmen painted the nineteenth-century Siamese flag on the wings and tail of their planes: a charging white elephant on a red field.

As the Royal Thai Army advanced toward Keng Tung in the eastern Shan States, the fighters of No. 16 Squadron flew escort for RTAF bombers striking Chinese positions and troop concentrations. Supplies flowed up the railway from Bangkok through Lampang to Chiang Mai and up the road north from Lampang through Chiang Rai to reach the Thai divisions in the field. For their part, the Thais had no intention of proceeding beyond the limited objectives mandated by the Japanese. Though Thailand had declared war on Britain and America, it had made no such declaration against the Republic of China. In January 1943, it sent envoys to arrange for a truce along the Chinese border. Chiang agreed, issuing a statement on February 26 that he believed the Japanese had coerced Thailand into declaring war on the Allies.

An uneasy quiet descended on the country; the RTAF assumed a defensive posture, the Japanese 5th Air Division moved west to Burma, and Thailand

176   FALLEN TIGERS

suffered few Allied air attacks for nearly two years.[12] But in late 1943, with General Stilwell's X-Ray Force fighting its way toward Myitkyina and the Chinese Expeditionary Force soon to advance on the Salween Front, the Allies grew concerned the Japanese would make use of the road and rail lines in northern Thailand as a means of supplying their divisions in Burma. On December 21, 1943, thirty-two B-24s from the 308th Bomb Group struck the railroad station at Chiang Mai. Ten days later, another two dozen Liberators bombed the railyards at Lampang. Number 16 Squadron launched six Ki-27s to intercept, but the obsolescent fighters could not keep pace with the American formation as it departed the area.[13] An attack on the airfield at Chiang Mai by nine B-25s from the 341st Bomb Group on March 5, 1944, encountered no aerial opposition, but did run into 20-millimeter anti-aircraft fire. One of the bombers failed to return to China. The next encounter with No. 16 Squadron occurred on September 26 when 2nd Lt Frank McKinney reported encountering two of their warplanes climbing toward his F-5E Lightning over Lampang. He pushed the throttles forward and turned for home, too high and too fast for the little fixed-gear fighters to catch up with him.[14]

Lieutenant McKinney hailed from G Flight of the 35th Photo Reconnaissance Squadron. The unit had recently arrived in China to augment the overstretched 21st, and G Flight had three F-5Es, five pilots, and a small photo lab at Beitun Field—a five-thousand-foot grass strip two miles east of Yunnanyi. McKinney did not want to be a reconnaissance pilot; he wanted to fly fighters. He hated having to fly high and fast and run for home when he encountered hostile aircraft. Though he flew his first sortie to Thailand at a textbook thirty thousand feet, he increasingly began to take unnecessary risks. Sometimes he returned with photos taken as low as nineteen thousand feet—well within the reach of enemy interceptors. First Lieutenant Sterling Barrow, his friend and bunkmate, and 2nd Lt Arthur Clark, the flight's intelligence officer, counseled him to follow the rules. They worried about him. At 10:15 a.m. on November 5, 1944, they saw him off on another mission to reconnoiter the roads and railroads of northern Thailand and northeast Burma. His route of flight would take him over more than a thousand miles of unpopulated, dense tropical forests to photograph Uttaradit, Chiang Mai, and the Wan Lai Kam bridge. He never returned.[15]

At about 1:40 p.m. that afternoon, in the midst of a fierce thunderstorm, twenty-one-year-old Fong Inma and her young children suddenly heard the ear-splitting howl of engines roar overhead, followed by an earth-shattering explosion. Several buffalos in the village became so frightened they broke the ropes tied through their noses and scattered. Fong stepped out into the driving rain and saw a column of smoke rising to the northeast. Her father, the village headman, rushed out with her brother to investigate. According to a report filed by district police, lightning had struck the aircraft and set it afire. It crashed in the forest less than one-and-a-half miles from the village of Mae Kua, (about twenty miles south of Lampang). Fong and her curious son visited the smoldering crash site the next day. They saw aluminum debris spread across a small clearing in the forest and the charred torso of the pilot lying on the ground nearby. Fong's father, brothers, and husband loaded the wreckage in buffalo carts and brought it back to the village, storing it underneath one of their stilt houses.

The sheriff of Sop Prap District arrived two days later with several RTAF officers, including Flight Lt Chalermkiat Wattanangura, the commander of No. 16 Squadron. The fighter pilot identified the wreckage as belonging to an American Lockheed P-38, noting the insignia of a white star superimposed on a blue circle and the number "811" on the tail. He told the sheriff the RTAF did not want the wreckage. Two large trucks carted it away. The sheriff consulted with the village headman and together they decided to burn the pilot's remains over a woodfire and bury his ashes near the crash site. Chalermkiat returned to Lampang on November 9, the same day Henry Minco and his compatriots landed their brand-new P-51 Mustangs at Yunnanyi.[16]

McKinney's friends waited in vain for his return. "Mac was overdue at 4:15," Lieutenant Barrow journaled that evening. "Haven't any word on him yet. God grant he be safe—please!" Barrow held out hope that McKinney had landed elsewhere due to weather or malfunction. But as the days passed with no news from other bases within range, he began to wonder if enemy fighters had caught the daredevil flying too low and had shot him down. Lieutenant Clark, however, correctly supposed that McKinney had crashed while trying to push through a thunderstorm on his way back to China. The squadron finally submitted a missing aircrew report on November 7. "Still no word of Mac," Barrow jotted in his diary that day, still optimistic. "Probably take a couple months to walk out."[17]

One week after the disappearance of McKinney and two days after the 25th Fighter Squadron received its new batch of P-51s, Fourteenth Air Force fighters made a sweep of the railroad in northern Thailand. The mission included a heavy top cover element—possibly due to the belief that McKinney's

178   FALLEN TIGERS

reconnaissance ship had fallen prey to enemy fighters. Lieutenant Colonel Habecker led nine P-51s aloft from Yunnanyi at 9:20 a.m., accompanied by eight P-38s from the 449th. Habecker's flight of four Mustangs dropped down on the deck to reconnoiter and strafe, while just above, 1st Lt Roger Vadenais covered them with four more Mustangs. The P-38s flew top cover at fifteen thousand feet. One of the Lightnings returned to base with engine trouble soon after takeoff; the ninth Mustang took its place in the leading top cover element.

Habecker swept low over the airfields at Chiang Rai and Chiang Mai and then followed the railroad southeast toward Lampang. His flight did not pass unnoticed. Similar to Chennault's warning network in China, observers stationed on water towers, rooftops, and in treetop stands reported via hand-cranked wireless telephones when they spotted the Allied warplanes. The RTAF alerted No. 16 Squadron to intercept. At eleven thirty a pair of Ki-27s flown by Pilot Officer Kamrop Bleangkam and Flight Sgt 3rd Class Chuladit Detkunchorn took off from Lampang to patrol to the north, expecting the Americans to sweep down the road from Chiang Rai. Fifty minutes later, though, the observer network reported the intruders attacking Chiang Mai and following the railroad instead. With no radio sets in its Ki-27s, the squadron had no way to recall Kamrop's element. Flight Lieutenant Chalermkiat led Flight Sgt 1st Class Wad Sunthornkomol and Sgt Tada Biewkhaimuk aloft in three more Nates, climbing rapidly to fifteen thousand feet. They caught sight of the eight Allied fighters in the top cover element to the distant northwest over the Khun Tan Range. Though outnumbered and outgunned, Chalermkiat elected to attack them head-on.

The flight of three Lightnings and one Mustang led by Capt Dale Desper all opened fire simultaneously, scoring multiple hits on Chalermkiat's Nate, tearing into the left landing gear, ripping away the cowling, and causing the engine to erupt in flames. The Thai squadron commander hit 2nd Lt Leonard Flomer's P-38 in turn, setting its right wingtip fuel tank on fire. Chalermkiat dove away to make an emergency landing at Lampang, and Captain Desper left the fight to escort Flomer back to Yunnanyi.

Chalermkiat jumped clear of his damaged plane as soon as it rolled to a stop, but he ran back to retrieve his parachute. Just then, Habecker's flight came in low and fast, diving toward the field at 350 miles per hour. The lieutenant colonel saw the Nate on the north end of the runway. Holding the pip of his optical gunsight just above the fighter, he opened fire, unleashing the

Thai Fighters   179

destructive power of his four .50-caliber machine guns as he closed into range. Chalermkiat slumped to the ground, grievously wounded. An enlisted man dashed out and carried him to safety before the plane exploded. Roaring overhead, Habecker's flight continued its sweep down the railroad.

Meanwhile, Kamrop and Chuladit had arrived overhead the field to find a cloth panel with an arrow pointing to the northwest. Chuladit looked to where the railroad tunneled through the Khun Tan Range and, just above, saw four black spots that gradually resolved into the three P-38s and single P-51 of the leading top cover flight. He glanced over at Kamrop who nodded; the two of them throttled up and maneuvered to intercept.

By this time Wad and Tada had charged headlong into the second top cover flight. The flight leader, 1st Lt Dick Conway, shot at one of the Nates, which dove away smoking. Enemy fire then knocked out Conway's left engine and he had to leave the fight to make an emergency single-engine landing at Simao, an auxiliary field near the China-Burma border. Lieutenants Grover Stubbee, Robert Jones, and Joe Fodor remained in the chaotic furball, shooting, maneuvering, and chasing enemy fighters off each other's tails. Fodor made a pass on one of the Nates from the rear quarter and scored hits on its wings and engine. Flight Sergeant Wad intervened, putting himself on Fodor's tail and forcing him to break off the attack as the other Nate rolled and dove away. Jones then came to Fodor's rescue, hitting the Thai warplane and setting it on fire. Severely burned, Wad bailed out of his stricken fighter and parachuted into the woods near a suburb north of Lampang. Villagers eventually brought him to the local hospital where he died in agonizing pain at ten o'clock that night.

Flying on Vadenais's right wing in the middle flight of Mustangs, Henry Minco saw the battle taking place several thousand feet above them. "Do you see them, Vad?" he asked on the radio.

"Affirmative," Vadenais replied as he began a climb toward the dogfight. Fixated on the air battle overhead, he did not see Pilot Officer Kamrop and Flight Sgt Chuladit somehow emerge from the furball unscathed and dive to the northeast.

"I see two below, am going after them," announced Minco, peeling off by himself. By then, Vadenais was engaged, making a head-on pass with Sergeant Tada. Neither scored any hits, and Vadenais repositioned to attack from the rear quarter. His .50-caliber rounds slammed into the Nate's oil tank and guns, barely missing Tada's forehead. With oil spraying into the cockpit,

180   FALLEN TIGERS

the Thai aviator shut down his engine and glided away, his propeller slowing to a stop. He tried to make a dead-stick landing in a rice paddy near the Lampang-Chiang Rai road, but hit hard, completely demolishing his airplane. Soldiers from an infantry unit nearby pulled him from the wreck and took him to the hospital. While this was going on, 1st Lt Otto Miller, the second element leader in Vadenais's flight, dove to assist Minco in his pursuit of Kamrop and Chuladit. Miller took on Chuladit while Minco kept after Kamrop. Chuladit turned into the attack, the opposing fighters firing at each other as they closed. The Thai pilot heard a loud noise from the front of his aircraft. His fighter shuddered twice and then the engine quit. He glided toward the airfield, Miller in pursuit. The American continued to fire, blowing a hole in the Nate's right wing. An anti-aircraft gun opened up and the Mustang pulled away. Chuladit crash-landed in a rice paddy just short of the runway; the landing gear snagged on a termite mound and the fighter cartwheeled, throwing the pilot clear. Though suffering a broken collarbone, he somehow miraculously survived.

Minco kept after Kamrop, diving toward the mountain range northeast of town. "I've got one trapped in the valley down here!" he radioed as he raced eastbound up a narrow draw. According to Joe Fodor, "That was the last we heard of him." Kamrop thought he was doomed; a bullet tore into his seat and parachute. Another blew a big hole near the right rudder pedal, sending shrapnel into his leg. He saw tracers streaking overhead. But Minco had misjudged his rate of closure with Kamrop's Nate and overshot underneath, simultaneously having to pull up to avoid the rising terrain. The Thai pilot suddenly found Minco's Mustang filling his gunsight. Instinctively he opened fire; the P-51 crashed with a fiery explosion into the steep ridge to his right. "Please go to a better place," Kamrop prayed silently. "Don't think of revenge if we meet in the next life."

Leaking oil and with only ten minutes of fuel remaining, Kamrop made for the airfield. As he approached, he saw a column of smoke rising from the burning wreck of his squadron commander's fighter on the runway and what he took to be a P-38 Lightning high overhead—likely a photo recon F-5E. He bypassed Lampang and landed instead at Ko Kha, eight miles to the southwest. Wounded and fatigued, he remained in his damaged plane until workers from a nearby sugar plant lifted him from the cockpit and took him to the hospital. "Maybe our Lord Buddha protected me and my friends," he later reflected. "We survived even though the enemy aircraft were better in quality

Thai Fighters   181

and quantity and manned by well-trained pilots with high morale. It was pure luck that I shot down the Mustang before it shot me down."[18]

None of the Mustang or Lightning pilots knew what had happened to Henry Minco. Lieutenants Stubbee and Miller both reported seeing a plane crash in the mountains but assumed it to be a Nate. However, none of the Thai fighters crashed in the mountains; three of the five managed to make emergency landings at Lampang and Ko Kha and the other two crashed on the outskirts of Lampang. Stubbee and Miller must have unwittingly witnessed the crash of Minco. Back at Yunnanyi, Cliff Long learned the sad news about the loss of his friend. Minco had been an experienced pilot on his seventy-first combat mission. But he had no formal training and no more than twenty hours in the P-51. Whether or not he gave any credence to the premonition of his own death, it became a self-fulfilling prophecy when he recklessly broke away from his flight leader and attacked two enemy airplanes by himself.[19]

The RTAF reported all five Nates as written off or destroyed. The American fighters claimed six, double counting Flight Lieutenant Chalermkiat's as destroyed in the air and on the ground. The Thai fighters had proved challenging: "They were maneuverable as hell, but slow as hell," Joe Fodor recalled. The audacity of the pilots surprised the Americans. They assumed them to be Japanese and had become accustomed to the declining quality of enemy airmen. In its mission report for November 11, 1944, the 25th Fighter Squadron noted: "The Japanese pilots were very aggressive and eager to fight and would press the attack."[20]

For its part, No. 16 Squadron had only four serviceable Ki-27s remaining. Shocked at the lopsided combat and wary of further antagonizing the Allies, the RTAF began pulling its squadrons back into central Thailand. Thai fighters intercepted a few more Allied raids on Bangkok, but the November battle over Lampang marked the last air-to-air confrontation with the Fourteenth Air Force. The situation had changed dramatically since the declaration of war in January 1942; the Allies had reversed the tide of Japanese ascendancy and had begun the steady march toward victory. Prime Minister Phibun had resigned in July 1944, replaced by Khuang Aphaiwong, secretly one of the founding members of the Free Thai Movement. The new prime minister set the RTAF to supporting the resistance with supply drops and transport missions right under the nose of their Japanese "allies."[21]

On November 11, 1944—the same day Henry Minco went missing in Thailand—1st Lt Rudolph Shaw's P-51 ran out of fuel over Indochina after

182 FALLEN TIGERS

the fighter pilot became separated from his flight in poor weather. He bailed out and landed in a rice paddy northwest of Cao Bang, a Vietnamese town about fifteen miles from the China border. "I took my jungle supplies out of the kit and ran for the hills," he later reported.[22]

As proved to be the case in Thailand, the situation in Indochina turned out to be much more complicated than a mere Japanese occupation; the region had a long, difficult history of conflict and colonialism. France had conquered the Red River Delta by 1884 and the rest of Vietnam, Laos, and Cambodia by 1893. When France fell to the Nazis in June 1940, the colonial authorities in Hanoi aligned themselves with the collaborationist Vichy government. Taking advantage of the situation, Japan demanded the use of four airfields and the right to station up to six thousand troops in northern Vietnam. To underscore the weakness of the French position, the Imperial Japanese Army attacked colonial garrisons at Lang Son and Dong Dang on September 22, 1940, and carrier- and land-based aircraft bombarded the port of Hai Phong on the twenty-sixth. Governor-General Jean Decoux quickly acquiesced to their demands. By July 1941, the Japanese had tens of thousands of troops in the region and had occupied southern Vietnam without resistance.[23]

Though clearly undermining French sovereignty, the Japanese appreciated the efficiency of allowing the colonial regime to administer its colony for the benefit of Japan. French officials enforced the law and collected taxes; French troops maintained garrisons and border forts; and French gunners fought back against Allied air raids. French soldiers even captured AVG pilot Lewis Bishop near Lao Cai when anti-aircraft fire brought down his P-40E on May 17, 1942. They made a show of trying to maintain custody of Bishop but eventually turned him over to the Japanese. He endured extensive beatings and interrogations and months of solitary confinement before finally arriving at the Jiangwan prisoner of war camp in Shanghai on March 27, 1943. However, the situation in Indochina began to change irrevocably with the liberation of France in the summer of 1944; the position of the colonial authorities grew increasingly untenable as the Japanese occupiers became wary of growing pro-Allied sentiment.[24]

Yet another factor further complicated this tangled picture: the Vietnamese themselves. Throughout the war Japan progressively squeezed Indochina for more rice and other agricultural products to feed its war machine. This predation, combined with destructive flooding in 1943 and a poor harvest in 1944, caused a severe famine. As many as two million Vietnamese peasants perished. An organization calling itself the League for the Independence of Vietnam, also known as the Viet Minh, sought to unite disparate insurgent factions to overthrow both the French and the Japanese. One of the movement's leaders, a middle-aged revolutionary by the name of Nguyen Tat Thanh, aptly described the situation: "The Japanese become the real masters," he wrote. "The French become kind of respectable slaves. And upon the Indochinese falls the double honor of being not only slaves to the Japanese, but also slaves of the slaves."

Nationalist Chinese authorities arrested Nguyen in August 1942 when they caught him traveling with false documents under the assumed name of Ho Chi Minh. He remained in prison until September 1943, when a Guomindang general decided the revolutionary might prove useful to Chinese interests in Vietnam. By the time Lieutenant Shaw bailed out of his Mustang in November 1944, Ho had established a guerrilla base in the hills near Cao Bang. Shaw spent the night of the eleventh hiding in a clump of bushes on a mountainside. The next day, he decided to give himself over to a group of Vietnamese civilians who appeared to be searching for him. They disguised him in local garb and, over the following days, relayed him to a guerilla camp in the hills.[25]

"The leader of the anti-fascist group came to see me," Shaw journaled on November 15. "He could speak some English and assured me that I would be safely conducted to the border."[26] This leader turned out to be none other than Ho Chi Minh himself, who personally escorted the pilot all the way to Kunming. He refused a cash reward, instead requesting an audience with General Chennault. But the French Military Mission in Kunming strenuously objected to the meeting and so Chennault declined for the time being. The entire affair would have amounted to little more than a curious historical footnote had it not come to the attention of Charles Fenn, a former reporter and self-described leftist then serving as a first lieutenant in the OSS. After hearing the story of Shaw's rescue in early 1945, he decided to try to track down Mr. Ho.[27]

Meanwhile, the pro-Allied activities of the French in Indochina became ever more brazen. On March 5, 1945, Maj Ed Witzenburger bailed out forty-five miles northwest of Hanoi after anti-aircraft fire crippled his P-51K during a railroad sweep by four Mustangs of the 26th Fighter Squadron.[28] French army troops watched him bail out and cordoned off the area until they found him and took him into custody. He had hurt his ankle when he hit the ground but proved otherwise uninjured. The next day a pair of officers disguised him

184   FALLEN TIGERS

in the uniform of a foreign legionnaire and drove him to the Citadel in Hanoi—the not-so-secret headquarters of the Resistance. He spent considerable time in conference with the leaders of the underground, asking and answering questions and making arrangements for his escape to China. One of the leaders, a Captain Bertrand, even drove him around the city to assess damage done by Allied air raids.[29]

Then, at 9:21 p.m. on the night of March 9, 1945, the commander of Japanese forces in Vietnam flashed the code "777" to his sixty-seven thousand troops stationed in the country. From Hanoi to Saigon Japanese soldiers carried out a coordinated coup d'état to overthrow the French administration.[30] Captain Bertrand took charge of the Citadel's defenses, issuing guns, ammunition, grenades, and dynamite to the embattled defenders. Witzenburger found himself armed to the teeth with a carbine, pistol, and five grenades. As the situation became increasingly desperate, Bertrand decided to make a break for it. Witzenburger followed him over the north wall of the fortress and into the city of Hanoi. Bertrand led Witzenburger and a group of ten French and Vietnamese refugees up the Black River toward Son La, a town 135 miles from Hanoi in the remote reaches of northwest Vietnam. The Japanese pursued them doggedly. At one point, a squad of enemy soldiers caught them crossing a road and advanced on them at a run, firing their rifles. Witzenburger and three others had remained behind the main group to cover them as they crossed. As the Japanese entered their kill zone, Witzenburger and company opened fire, leaving no survivors. The gunfire attracted a truck full of even more Japanese troops, which sped toward them down the road. The major tossed a grenade at the front of the truck, stopping it, and then threw another in the back. The enemy soldiers scattered and Witzenburger and his companions sprinted across the road and escaped.[31]

The party finally arrived at Son La at about noon on March 15. The commander of the Foreign Legion garrison there arranged for Lt Hubert Cochard to fly Witzenburger to Mengzi, China, the next day in a rickety Potez 25A2 biplane. Upon delivery of the major, an Air-Ground Aid Section officer gave Cochard a portable radio to coordinate the rescue of eight other airmen in the hands of the French underground. The vintage biplane crashed in bad weather on the return trip, however, killing the pilot and destroying the radio.[32]

The coup proved devastating to Allied activities in Vietnam. On the morning of March 10, 1945, Lieutenant Fenn received a six-word transmission from one of his agents: "Japanese seized all posts throughout Indochina."

Thai Fighters   185

From that moment, Vietnam went dark—the OSS had no dependable sources of intelligence and Fourteenth Air Force had no viable way to rescue its downed airmen. General Wedemeyer urged the establishment of a new intelligence network employing friendly Vietnamese, if necessary. Fenn queried his friend Albert Ravenholt, a United Press correspondent, and learned that Ho Chi Minh had remained in Kunming after rescuing Lieutenant Shaw. He managed to set up a meeting at the Dragon's Gate in the hills west of Kunming at eleven o'clock on the morning of March 17.

Ho and Fenn talked about the League for the Independence of Vietnam. When the OSS lieutenant asked if the group leaned communist, Ho replied: "Some of our members are communists and some aren't. The Chinese and French call all of us communist who don't fit into their pattern."

"Are you against the French?" the young American asked.

"Certainly not," said Ho. "But unfortunately they are against us." Fenn found the distinction amusing.

"Would you like to work with the Americans?" he asked.

Ho looked puzzled. "What kind of work?" Fenn described his plan for the revolutionary to return to Vietnam with a radio and a generator to collect intelligence and rescue more downed airmen. In return, Ho asked for medicine and arms for his league and once again requested a meeting with Chennault.

"Why are you so keen about that?" Fenn inquired.

"He's the Westerner we most admire," Ho replied. "I'd like to tell him so myself."

Fenn knew Chennault well from his days covering the AVG as a correspondent for the Associated Press and he knew the general did not give a damn about the political affiliations of groups willing to help his airmen. He arranged for a meeting on March 29. At the appointed hour, Doreen Davis, the general's secretary, ushered them into Chennault's office. The legendary leader of the Flying Tigers opened the proceedings by expressing his gratitude for the rescue of Lieutenant Shaw.

"I'm always glad to help the Americans," Ho told him.

"That's great," replied Chennault, "because now we'd like your help against the Japanese. I think Lieutenant Fenn has already told you how. Is there anything you'd like to ask about?"

"No, thank you, general," Ho answered. "But there's one small favor I should like to ask." Fenn held his breath in anticipation of hearing something outlandish. "May I have your photograph?" The lieutenant exhaled with relief.

186   FALLEN TIGERS

"With pleasure!" the general beamed. With the press of a button, Ms. Davis returned with a stack of eight-by-ten glossies. Ho took his pick and Chennault duly signed it, "Yours sincerely, Claire L. Chennault." Before heading back to Vietnam, Ho also asked Fenn for six .45-caliber pistols, which the lieutenant produced from OSS stocks.

The fifty-year-old revolutionary's return to Vietnam surprised many of his colleagues, some of whom had believed him to be dead. He moved swiftly to consolidate his leadership over the Viet Minh. He told a meeting of revolutionary leaders he had secured the help of the Americans, including General Chennault. When they expressed skepticism, he produced the autographed photo. He then gave each of them a .45-caliber pistol as a gift—sent to them personally by Chennault, they presumed. From that moment on, Ho Chi Minh's position became unassailable.

At Ho's direction, the Viet Minh did provide intelligence and weather reports to the OSS.[33] However, they assisted in the rescue of only one other Fourteenth Air Force airman: 1st Lt Palmer Foss, a P-38 pilot from the 449th Fighter Squadron brought down by surface fire twenty miles north-northwest of Hai Phong on July 7. Throughout the war, the outlook for missing airmen in Indochina remained grim. The AVG, China Air Task Force, and Fourteenth Air Force reported 115 airmen missing there. Nearly 68 percent of them did not survive the crash or bailout—compared to 54 percent overall in the China Theater. Against the figure of 5 percent of fallen airmen in the theater captured, 20 percent of those downed in Indochina became prisoners. By the end of the war in August 1945, only 12 percent had been rescued.

On September 2, 1945, the day of the surrender ceremony in Tokyo Bay aboard the USS *Missouri,* two P-38 Lightnings from the 449th flew an armed reconnaissance mission to the Red River Delta. The pilots observed large crowds gathered in Hanoi and swooped low for a closer look. It just so happened that the pair of twin-engine American fighters buzzed overhead just as Ho Chi Minh declared Vietnamese independence. He pointed to the chance flyover as further proof of American support for his fledgling government. Ho had certainly realized a remarkable return on his investment of rescuing a single American airman in the fall of 1944.[34]

16

The Final Offensive

January 17, 1945
Shanghai, China

The internment camp adjacent to Longhua Airdrome on Shanghai's south side brimmed with American merchant sailors and Allied civilians taken from the city's International Settlement. Every day they endured unpredictable guards, near-starvation diets, and scant supplies and clothing. For three long years after their internment in December 1941, they saw no indication of the turning tide of war—save for the increased skittishness and spasmodic brutality of their guards. Three small radios brought news of the war clandestinely into the camp, but their operators kept the circle of trust small to protect against discovery. Most of the interned population remained suspended in limbo, held in perpetual defeat by their captors, fantasies of food foremost on their minds.

British novelist J. G. Ballard, then fourteen, lived with his parents and sister at the Longhua camp. He later described his experiences in a 1984 semiautobiographical novel, *Empire of the Sun*. He remembered vividly the Japanese airfield next door, its rows of aircraft parked in front of vast machine shops and hangars, and the seven-story-tall Buddhist temple converted into a flak tower on its north end, its octagonal balconies soaring more than a hundred feet above the ground, sandbagged fighting emplacements positioned around its base.

That Wednesday afternoon, seventeen sleek P-51 Mustangs swept down on three of Shanghai's airfields to destroy scores of planes staging to support the Japanese defense of Luzon, the crucial northern anchor of the Philippines. Ballard stood on the first-floor balcony of the men's washroom when a flight of American fighters suddenly roared past the camp barely twenty feet

188 FALLEN TIGERS

above the paddy fields, barreling toward the airdrome. They rose to clear the perimeter fence, a flash of shining aluminum, then dove, guns blazing, at the rows of parked aircraft. He stared in awe as the beautiful Mustangs opened fire with their .50-caliber machine guns, racing up and down the field, leaving a trail of fire and destruction. The guards scattered. An air raid siren belatedly began to wail. The top story of the pagoda lit up with machine-gun fire as anti-aircraft crews sprang into action. Bits of shrapnel fell on the roofs and in the courtyards of the camp. Then, as suddenly as it began, it ended. The roar of engines dissipated; the staccato of machine-gun fire slackened. Smoke from burning fuel and planes filled the air. To the young British prisoner, the P-51 Mustang embodied power, speed, and destruction. "However brave the Japanese soldiers and pilots, they belonged to the past," Ballard realized. "America, I knew, was a future that had already arrived. I spent every spare moment watching the sky."[1]

Prisoners of war at the Jiangwan camp, on Shanghai's northeast side, greeted the raid with even greater enthusiasm. They too had illicit radios with which they kept abreast of the war's progress. But like the Allied internees at Longhua, and indeed like millions of beleaguered people throughout Japan's wartime empire, the harsh reality of daily life under the thumb of enemy imprisonment made the hope of liberation seem remote. Then those beautiful Mustangs roared overhead, tangible proof of Japan's waning fortunes. The prisoners at Jiangwan included US Marines captured at Wake Island and airmen captured in China and the Pacific.

Howard Allers, Murray Lewis, Paul Webb, and Jim Young—captured after enemy fighters downed their B-25 over Hong Kong in 1942—watched in glee as the camp guards rushed about like chickens with their heads cut off. Soon the frantic soldiers turned their swords and bayonets to prod the prisoners indoors. Lieutenant Allers hobbled into the barracks, slower than most. His left foot had taken a bullet when enemy fighters strafed his wrecked bomber. He received almost no medical treatment during his first six weeks of imprisonment in Guangzhou's city jail. When the Japanese transferred him to Jiangwan, American doctors in the camp did their best for him. They managed to stop the spread of infection and saved his mangled foot from amputation, but the prison's primitive conditions prohibited a full recovery. Allers had only recently been able to walk without the aid of crutches or a cane.

The Marines edged over so the lieutenant could peer out the window. Together they cheered the low-flying fighters attacking the Japanese airfield

The Final Offensive   189

only two miles away. The guards threatened to shoot anyone who emerged before the raid ended and snapped off a few rounds in the direction of those cheering at the windows. The Americans ducked down but quickly sprang back up to look outside again. The guards fired at the planes, too, as they passed low overhead. The panic of the guards and the raw display of American airpower—undeniable proof of Allied progress in the war—made the prisoners' morale soar for the first time since their capture.[2]

The P-51 Mustangs had sortied from Suichuan and Ganzhou. The Japanese drive through central China had left a pocket of territory in Chinese hands, including the two airfields in Jiangxi Province. Fourteenth Air Force had evacuated the bases in June 1944, but Gen Xue Yue's troops kept the Japanese from capturing them. In August, Brig Gen Casey Vincent had sent the 74th Fighter Squadron to Ganzhou and in November sent the 118th Tactical Reconnaissance Squadron to Suichuan.[3] A detachment of B-24 tankers from the 7th Bomb Group had to airlift fuel over the Japanese lines to keep the two units supplied. Completely surrounded by occupied territory, the bases became the ultimate expression of aerial guerrilla warfare and proved to be a thorn in the side of the Japanese. Access to targets unreachable from other airbases in China helped the guerrilla squadrons account for two-thirds of the Fourteenth Air Force's successes between November 1944 and January 1945.

The Shanghai raid represented the climax of guerrilla operations. The seventeen P-51s from the 74th and 118th had staged through Nancheng, 150 miles farther east from Suichuan, and claimed seventy-three Japanese aircraft destroyed for no American losses. Though Japanese sources provide no conclusive number, the 90th Air Regiment alone reported twenty-five of its light bombers destroyed on the ground. Subsequent raids on January 20 and April 2 achieved diminishing returns, and Japanese anti-aircraft fire managed to down a total of six 23rd Fighter Group P-51s. Remarkably, Chinese guerrillas returned all six pilots to American control, even 2nd Lt Harold B. Tollett, who bailed out just one mile east of Longhua; Japanese troops arrived on the scene within minutes, but by then, guerrillas had already spirited him away.[4]

In the wake of Ichi-go and in an effort to stymie continued American air attacks, the Imperial Japanese Army focused on eliminating Allied airbases within range of its new rail corridor. Japanese troops finally captured Suichuan and Ganzhou on January 28 and February 4, respectively.[5] Laohekou fell on March 27.

190   FALLEN TIGERS

In mid-April the Japanese Twentieth Army began a drive to capture the airfield at Zhijiang. The enemy's main body advanced west along the highway from Baoqing while three supporting columns maneuvered to encircle the town. The Chinese and Americans readied the base for demolition, burying bombs in the runway and preparing to evacuate down the Wu River. If the Japanese arrived, they planned to blow the airfield just as they had with the central China bases in 1944. The specter of occupation frightened Gong Kaibing, but he could not afford to evacuate his family. He would have to stay put and tough it out.[6]

However, the Japanese encountered an entirely different situation than they had found a year before during the Ichi-go campaign. General Stilwell's replacement, Lt Gen Albert Wedemeyer, rushed lend-lease weapons and equipment to the embattled Fourth War Area troops and airlifted the New Sixth Army, which had fought with great distinction in north Burma, to Zhijiang as a reserve. Eight American air-ground liaison teams, each consisting of one officer and two enlisted men, went to the front lines with the Chinese troops. Many of them had learned their trade in the fierce fighting on the Salween Front. They used radios and large cloth panels to direct fighters and bombers in close support of friendly ground troops.

Fifty-six P-40s and P-51s from the 5th Fighter Group flew 3,101 sorties in six weeks of operations, expending in excess of two million rounds of .50-caliber ammunition and making liberal use of napalm. "I was assigned one to two missions each day," recalled Huang Xiang-chun, a pilot with the 17th Fighter Squadron. "Our fighters dropped napalm on Japanese-occupied regions and the whole area turned to flames."[7] The enemy fought back determinedly with concentrated surface-to-air fire. "Whenever we were near the target area we had to brave intense anti-aircraft gun, machine gun, and rifle fire," recounted Lu Mao-yin, a pilot with the 27th Fighter Squadron. "It was common for our aircraft to return with several bullet holes." Lu once flew four missions in a single day. "I was so busy that I did not even have lunch," he related. "I didn't have a second of rest until nightfall!"[8] In addition to the fighters, an average of six B-25s from the Chinese-American Composite Wing's 3rd and 4th Bomb Squadrons flew 183 sorties, dropping more than two hundred tons of bombs. Even a detachment of two P-61 night fighters got in on the action, flying fifteen night intruder sorties and dropping almost eight tons of bombs.[9]

The Japanese made repeated advances, but by the beginning of May 1945, their progress had ground to a halt. The mountainous terrain funneled

The Final Offensive 191

their troops along the main highways, leaving them particularly vulnerable to air attack. On the ninth, the Twentieth Army suspended operations.[10] Chinese troops using American equipment, supported by American advisors, and working in concert with joint Chinese-American fighter and bomber squadrons decisively ended the final Japanese offensive of the war.

Meanwhile, at dawn on May 9, almost seven hundred miles to the east, more than a thousand prisoners of war assembled on the baseball field at the Jiangwan camp. The guards conducted a quick headcount and then marched them to the railway station about a mile and a half down the road. Lieutenant Allers limped along with the bedraggled crowd of men. He had expected to remain indefinitely at the camp while the war continued on faraway battlefields. The raids by Fourteenth Air Force P-51s had been his first concrete clue to Japan's waning fortunes. As the empire began to contract, the Imperial Japanese Army decided to disperse Allied prisoners in camps throughout the home islands.

The guards loaded the men into rickety old boxcars with barbed wire nailed over the windows: fifty men per car for the enlisted, thirty-five to forty for the officers. Each car contained a large tin of drinking water, a case of hardtack, and an empty five-gallon can to use as a latrine. Bamboo sleeping mats covered the floors, though the men hardly had enough room to sit down, let alone lie down. An archaic steam engine pulled them from the station and through the countryside at barely more than ten miles per hour, first to Nanjing and then to Beiping, traveling at night to avoid American air attacks.

Four Marines escaped on the night of the tenth; one of them had smuggled aboard a pair of pliers and cut the barbed wire covering one of the windows. AVG pilot Lewis Bishop learned of their plan and followed them, jumping from the moving train into the darkness. The New Fourth Army picked up the runaways and returned them to American control. Allers could not contemplate escape due to his crippled left foot. He remained a prisoner, enduring harsh treatment by the guards and suffering from a lack of food and medical care.[11]

It took five days for the train to reach Beiping. The guards herded the prisoners into warehouses, where they spent the next month living and sleeping on bare concrete floors in stifling heat. Three new inmates joined them there, all Fourteenth Air Force Mustang pilots. Second Lieutenant Samuel Chambliss had bailed out on April 14 after ground fire brought his fighter

192   FALLEN TIGERS

down four miles south of Xiangcheng in Henan Province. He arrived at Beiping on May 20. "Legs badly burned & his emaciated gaunt appearance indicates starvation & bad treatment," noted one of his fellow prisoners.

James Wall and Harold Klota arrived on June 10. First Lieutenant Wall had been strafing a railyard near Shangqiu on December 6, 1944, when ground fire severed one of his oil lines. Members of his flight saw him bail out and run eastward, away from the burning wreckage of his crashed fighter. Japanese troops apprehended him shortly thereafter. First Lieutenant Klota had taken a bullet through his right ankle and bailed out low to the ground when his Mustang went down on April 2, 1945. His captors ended up amputating his injured right leg below the knee.[12]

The purgatory of Beiping ended on June 19. Another rail journey brought the prisoners to the port of Busan (Pusan) on the southern tip of the Korean Peninsula, where they boarded a ship to cross the submarine-infested strait to Honshu at the end of June. The prisoners had finally arrived in what they irreverently dubbed "the land of the flying red asshole."[13] They traveled by train through Tokyo north to Aomori, where the Japanese separated the officers and enlisted men. Most of the enlisted went to camps on Honshu. The officers traveled by ferry to the port of Hakodate on the island of Hokkaido, arriving on July 4. From there, the Japanese distributed them to several different camps. Allers endured another sixteen-hour train ride to Hakodate Branch Camp Number 4, near the mining town of Ashibetsu in the island's hilly interior. Seventeen other airmen joined him there, nearly a quarter of those captured in the China Theater.[14] This included Murray Lewis, his navigator on the Hong Kong raid, and the Mustang pilots Chambliss, Klota, and Wall.

Throughout the war, eighty-two aviators from the AVG, China Air Task Force, and Fourteenth and Twentieth Air Forces had become prisoners of the Japanese in the China Theater. Twenty-five did not survive the experience. Of those who died, the United States never recovered the bodies of sixteen, all of whom remain missing in action. Only three prisoners successfully escaped, all of them from the AVG: Charlie Mott and Black Mac McGarry, with the help of the OSS and Free Thai partisans, and Lewis Bishop after having jumped from the train en route to Beiping. The population at Hakodate Branch Camp Number 4 also included three Britons, forty-five Australians, and twenty-four US Marines. Colonel William Ashurst, a Marine captured in north China at the beginning of the war, represented the Allied captives as senior-ranking officer.

The Final Offensive   193

Every day, the prisoners trudged out of the camp to work ten-hour shifts in the nearby Mitsui coal mine. The backbreaking labor only further diminished their fading strength. Hope of liberation seemed more remote than ever before. Then, B-29s operating from the Mariana Islands dropped two atomic bombs on Hiroshima and Nagasaki on August 6 and 9, respectively. Japan surrendered to the Allies on the fifteenth. Two days later, the managers of the Mitsui mine informed the prisoners of the surrender. In a conciliatory gesture they invited Colonel Ashurst and several other officers to dinner at the company clubhouse on the twentieth; Lieutenant Lewis was the only airman who joined the Marines at the event.

After that, everything changed at the prison camp. The guards departed, leaving the prisoners in charge. They posted their own guards and spelled out "US PW" in big letters on the roof of one of the buildings. In late August, US Navy warplanes noticed the message and dropped barrels full of food, medicine, and clothing. Years of harsh imprisonment under the thumb of a proud and ruthless enemy had finally come to an end. The prisoners' health slowly began to recover; their spirits soared.[15]

On September 2, 1945, General of the Army Douglas MacArthur stood with representatives of nine Allied nations aboard the USS *Missouri* in Tokyo Bay to accept the formal surrender of the Empire of Japan. He would shortly take charge of the occupation as supreme commander for the Allied powers and would make repatriation of Allied prisoners his top priority. In his first general order, issued the same day as the surrender ceremony, MacArthur directed the Japanese government to preserve the well-being and safety of all prisoners of war and civilian internees and to ensure the continued administration and supply of the camps. He also mandated they immediately furnish him a complete accounting of all prisoners and internees in their custody, along with their locations.

The next day, the general issued a message for the Japanese government to dispatch immediately to prisoners held throughout the home islands:

The formal surrender of Japan to the Allied Powers was signed on 2 September 1945. General of the Army Douglas MacArthur has been named Supreme Commander for the Allied Powers. United Nations Forces are proceeding as rapidly as possible with the occupation of the Japanese Home Islands and Korea. The relief and

194 FALLEN TIGERS

recovery of Allied Prisoners of War and Civilian Internees will be accomplished with all possible speed.

Pending the arrival of Allied representatives, the command of this camp and its equipment, stores, records, arms, and ammunition are to be turned over to the Senior Prisoner of War or a designated Civilian Internee, who will thenceforth give instructions to the Camp Commander for maintenance of supply and administrative services and for the amelioration of local conditions. The Camp Commander will be responsible to the Senior Prisoner of War or designated Civilian Internee for maintaining his command intact.

Allied representatives will be sent to this Camp as soon as possible to arrange for your removal and eventual return to your homes.[16]

In the following weeks, tens of thousands of American troops landed unopposed to begin the occupation of Japan. The US Army sent out approximately seventy teams to find and repatriate Allied prisoners. The Eighth Army reached Hokkaido during the second week of September. On the eleventh, its units liberated the camp at Ashibetsu. By the thirteenth, all one hundred of the camp's former inmates had reached Chitose Air Base, near Sapporo, by train. There they boarded Army Air Force C-47s bound for Tokyo to begin processing back to the United States.[17]

On August 21, twelve days after the atomic bombing of Nagasaki, a twin-engine Mitsubishi transport landed at Zhijiang. At a ceremony near the field, Brigadier General Kiyoshi surrendered Japanese military forces in China to Gen He Yingqin, commander in chief of the Nationalist Army. When Gong Kaibing learned of the surrender taking place nearby, he was overjoyed. By February 1946, the War Area Service Corps had disbanded, and he returned home. Just as before, Gong supported his family, including his new wife, by working the family farm.[18] But peace proved illusory. In China one war quickly gave way to another. "Japanese surrender has also paved way for final settlement between Chinese Communists and Central Government or an outbreak of large scale hostilities between them in competition for regions to be given up by Japanese," wrote US Ambassador Patrick Hurley the day before the surrender ceremony. "Recent proclamations by Generalissimo on behalf of Central Government, and General Zhu De as Commander of all Chinese Communist forces, indicate that such hostilities are imminent unless a reconciliation can be effected in immediate future."[19]

The Final Offensive   195

In the wake of the Japanese surrender, Communists and Nationalists raced each other to occupy China's major population centers. For Chiang's regime, the conflict ended either far too early or far too late. At the time of Japan's capitulation, his diminished forces had only just begun moving back into areas lost during the Ichi-go offensive. Mao's domain, meanwhile, had expanded exponentially: In 1937 the Chinese Communists controlled only thirty-five thousand square miles of territory with a population of 1.5 million; by 1945 they boasted 225,000 square miles with sixty-five million people. The generalissimo took advantage of American ships and planes to move his armies to urban and industrial centers like Shanghai, Nanjing, and Shenyang, but a speedy occupation did little to repair his government's diminished legitimacy in the eyes of the people. Frankly, he had not done enough, politically or militarily, to protect them—either from the Japanese invader or from corrupt, abusive warlords and politicians.[20]

In many ways, the Ichi-go offensive proved to be the decisive turning point of both World War II in China and the Chinese Civil War—a political and military disaster from which the Nationalist government and its armies never recovered. The ease with which the Imperial Japanese Army cut through central China showed the Guomindang to be completely impotent. Nationalist troops suffered a staggering 750,000 casualties (killed, injured, and missing). While Allied leaders had previously featured China prominently in their strategies to defeat Japan, Ichi-go caused them to write it off as a lost cause. It seemed they could salvage little from the epic catastrophe that had taken place.[21]

The offensive also demonstrated the limits of American leadership in the theater, laying bare the failings of Stilwell and Chennault. The former's myopic focus on Burma and the latter's provocative air attacks intensified the disaster. Their inability to cooperate made things exponentially worse. Stilwell may have been an able battlefield commander, but he proved to be a terrible choice to lead a coalition. While Gen Dwight D. Eisenhower built alliances in Europe, Stilwell systematically alienated everyone around him and imperiled crucial efforts with his caustic personality. Chiang made a wise decision when he insisted on the general's recall in October 1944; he should have demanded it much sooner. As for Chennault, the airman had a talent for working with the Chinese and certainly demonstrated his abilities as an effective tactical and operational leader of air forces. Yet he failed to foresee the strategic failure brought about by his overly ambitious operational plans.

196   FALLEN TIGERS

To the Imperial Japanese Army, Ichi-go represented a last, desperate gamble in a war increasingly turning against it on every front. The enormous investment of men and material in China took place as the US armed forces drew ever closer to the home islands through the Pacific. Japanese troops succeeded in ejecting American warplanes from their bases in central China and captured a rail corridor across the Asian continent. Incessant air attacks robbed that corridor of much of its utility, however, and anyway it connected Japan to an empire under steady erosion by an unstoppable Allied advance. Ichi-go may have been a stunning operational success, but as a gross misallocation of resources, it proved an utter strategic failure.[22]

Meanwhile, with the conclusion of the war against Japan, the US military began the grim and tedious task of collecting its dead. In China, General Wedemeyer entrusted this task to Col David Barrett. The former Dixie Mission commander's language skills, cultural knowledge, and rapport with both Nationalists and Communists alike made him the ideal man to coordinate such an effort. His teams soon crisscrossed the length and breadth of the country, following up on missing aircrew reports and information passed on by local officials.

Investigators in Jiangxi Province interviewed Lin Zengxun, the mayor of Luxi, about the death of George McMillan. "I was there when the plane crashed," he told them. "Six planes came over and suddenly one of them caught fire and crashed in a rice field. The pilot was killed instantly and was buried by the local people behind the temple." He showed them the grave and the crash site near the town of Linjiafang. The serial number on the wreckage matched Mac's P-38. They recovered his body and moved it to the US military section of the Hongqiao Road Cemetery in Shanghai.[23]

During and after the war, the military collected the remains of at least 555 airmen who had been reported missing in the China Theater. But the process of notifying families and returning those remains to the United States proved to be maddeningly slow. For more than two years after Mac's death, his family remained ignorant as to the disposition of his remains. His loss devastated them: His mother's health declined rapidly and his sister returned home after just one semester away at college. Mac's last letter had been to her, one month before his death. "You'll never know how much your letters mean to me young lady," he had written. "I enjoy them lots and feel quite proud that you write so often."[24]

A group of officers who had known Mac visited his family on January 31, 1945, to present his posthumous awards: the Distinguished Flying Cross, the

Bronze Star, the Air Medal with one Oak Leaf Cluster, and the Purple Heart. Finally, on September 24, 1946, the quartermaster general, Maj Gen T. B. Larkin, wrote advising them of the body's location and that the War Department would comply with their wishes for final interment at the government's expense. The family buried Mac at Arlington National Cemetery on March 12, 1948. His mother could not attend the funeral; her health had deteriorated too much. They extended an invitation to General Chennault, then in Washington, DC, having testified before the House Committee on Foreign Affairs just two days before. He also declined. "I've been to too many of these," he wrote apologetically. His decision not to attend the funeral of a man he once told them "was one of my best squadron commanders" added a layer of bitterness to their sorrow.[25]

The China Zone of the American Graves Registration Service (AGRS) searched Frank McKinney's route of flight up to the China border and coordinated with the India-Burma Zone to determine if they discovered any remains of the reconnaissance pilot in their sector. Neither zone found anything that correlated to McKinney. Due to the lack of information, they declared him "KIA-Body unrecoverable" in May 1948. Sterling Barrow and Art Clark knew nothing of their friend's fate until 2012, when Group Captain Sakpinit Promthep, director of the Royal Thai Air Force Museum in Bangkok, found the Thai police reports detailing McKinney's crash in Mae Kua. Barrow found both relief and sadness in the revelation. "I've enjoyed reminiscing about our experiences in China," he said, "but I'd rather be sitting down with Frank McKinney over a cold one face to face—maybe in another life."[26]

An AGRS team hunted for Henry Minco's wreck in northern Thailand but recommended abandoning the search due to the impenetrable jungle and torrential monsoon rains. A panel of officers subsequently declared his remains unrecovereable. It was not until November 8, 2019—almost seventy-five years to the day after he went down—that Maj Klairoong "Puma" Pattumma led a team from Detachment 1 of the US Defense POW/MIA Accounting Agency (DPAA) to finally discover the crash site in the rugged mountains northeast of Lampang. Sadly, Minco's friend Cliff Long passed away just five months before the discovery.[27]

As civil war and unrest spread across China and Southeast Asia, it became increasingly difficult for US authorities to locate and recover fallen airmen still missing in action. In December 1945, President Harry S. Truman sent former Army chief of staff George Marshall to broker a truce. He proved

198   FALLEN TIGERS

unequal to the task. Stilwell's old friend and stalwart proponent made a good-faith effort not to carry his protégé's prejudices with him to China. A little over a year later, however, he threw up his hands in disgust and left. Marshall epitomized the hubris of the US government in believing it understood the dynamics of China's civil war—or in believing it could impose a solution. Though the West feared the specter of worldwide communist domination, the Chinese saw things much differently: what other credo besides communism so effectively agitated against colonialism? For all its talk of self-determination after the First World War, the United States had failed to join the League of Nations. In its absence the league's mandates became a front for imperialism. Where the West saw the threat of Soviet domination, local revolutionaries saw the promise of real self-determination. In their eyes, the West had failed to produce a suitable alternative.[28]

Late in 1949, the search for as-yet unrecovered airmen in China came to a definitive halt. On October 1, Mao stood atop the Gate of Heavenly Peace and proclaimed the founding of the People's Republic of China. The battered remnants of Chiang's Nationalist regime retreated to Taiwan. In the United States, Republicans and Democrats bickered over who had "lost" the country—as if the United States singlehandedly controlled China's destiny. The charge that leftists in the American government had somehow colluded in the Communist takeover led to red scares and the rise of McCarthyism. The United States maintained no diplomatic ties whatsoever with the new People's Republic. This complete lack of contact led the two nations to military confrontation during the Korean War a few years later. While Truman sought to limit the conflict, General MacArthur and the Republicans continually sounded the mantra, "Unleash Chiang!"—they seemed to believe the only thing holding the Nationalists back from retaking the mainland was a simple decision by the United States. Their refrain discounted the fact that the generalissimo had lost the mainland in the first place and discounted the opposition or ambivalence the Chinese people felt toward him. His fate had already been sealed—both by his own actions and by those of the Japanese.[29]

During World War II, competing narratives explaining China's place in the struggle against Japan emerged from the major personalities involved, principally Stilwell, Chennault, Chiang, and Mao. The toxic postwar political climate solidified these contradictory accounts. The ground-truth perspective of American airmen, as described in their contemporary missing aircrew and evasion reports, demonstrate that each of the competing narratives contain

The Final Offensive   199

both truth and fiction. General Stilwell claimed the Nationalists did not or would not fight. Certainly, he experienced great difficulty convincing them to fight on his terms. Although reports did circulate of some corrupt commanders who negotiated battlefield truces with the enemy, to say the Nationalists did not or would not fight at all ignores the guerrillas who risked much and lost much to bring American airmen out of occupied Hong Kong, for example, or from the corridor between Jiujiang and Nanchang. It also ignores the fact that almost as many Nationalist soldiers died opposing the Ichi-go offensive as the United States lost during the entirety of the war. It ignores the fact that Stilwell's myopic focus on Burma cost the Chinese dearly.[30]

Major General Chennault claimed the Nationalists did fight and would have done so more effectively had Stilwell given him free reign to support them. As he learned in central China, however, airpower could only do so much against an overwhelming enemy ground offensive. When collateral damage increased in the absence of effective intelligence, Chennault risked losing the hearts and minds of the very people he sought to protect. He needed to balance his agitation for airpower with careful intelligence and advocacy for meaningful reform and effective training of the Nationalist Army.[31]

Mao claimed the Communists fought ferociously against the Japanese while the Nationalists focused on wiping out the Communists. Chiang claimed the Communists undermined his leadership while his forces fought the Japanese. As Gregg and Beneda discovered, the Nationalist Sixty-Ninth Army did spend most of its energy facing down the New Fourth Army in Hubei Province rather than the Japanese. And apart from other anti-Japanese activities, scores of American airmen owed their lives to Communist troops fighting fearlessly to bring them out from behind enemy lines. Yet as Al Fisher discovered north of the Yellow River, they also fought against Nationalists when they perceived an opportunity and took full advantage of the power vacuum left in the wake of Japanese conquests to expand their influence throughout China.[32]

All of the competing and seemingly contradictory narratives thus contain some element of truth, and partisans of each have had evidence to back up their claims. As the Cold War ground on and America plunged headlong into Korea and Vietnam, the truth mattered less than political alignment, and opinions became increasingly distorted. This particularly confounded the men who had served in China during the war. Where most Americans saw only these caricatures, the veterans saw complexity. In their contact with individual Chinese, whether Nationalist or Communist, they witnessed

200   FALLEN TIGERS

courage, humanity, and selflessness. The numbers speak for themselves: of those airmen who survived the crash or bailout, over 90 percent returned to American control with the help of friendly Chinese, at least 726 in all.[33] When it came down to it, an airman parachuting from his burning plane over an alien landscape did not care about the political beliefs of his rescuers. Chinese of all persuasions saved US aviators from the Japanese and gave them the best treatment possible on their way back to American control.[34]

Many of the American airmen who fought in China continued to serve in the Cold War–era Air Force. Flying in Korea and Vietnam, they found themselves fighting against their former allies. Brick Holstrom became a brigadier general and commanded a nuclear bomb wing in Strategic Air Command. Casey Vincent became deputy chief of staff for operations at Air Defense Command. He died in his sleep on July 5, 1955; those who knew him best believed he had worked himself to death.[35]

Many Chinese also felt conflicted over the People's Republic's rivalry with the United States. Those who, after years of defeat, had seen American planes finally push back against the invader had experienced new hope. Those who came face to face with young American airmen found inspiration in their idealism, gratitude, and bravery. Those who witnessed acts of selfless sacrifice, like that exhibited by Lt Robert Mooney, felt profound gratitude. Cold War enmity suppressed the history of the United States and China's wartime cooperation in both countries. Veterans on both sides did not know how to process or express their experiences. They did not know what meaning to ascribe to their wartime alliance.

In Xiangyun, the monument to Lieutenant Mooney stood until the Cultural Revolution. Amid the spasmodic violence against all things foreign and traditional, the townspeople disassembled it and buried the pieces. Such proved to be the case across the length and breadth of China, with scores of monuments dedicated to fallen Americans hidden or torn down. Gravestones of those yet-unrecovered airmen suffered the same fate, potentially obscuring their place of rest permanently.[36]

During the 1950s, Gong Kaibing turned his education to increasing crop yields for the county administration. His work for the Nationalist government and the Americans at Zhijiang during the war caught up to him during the Cultural Revolution, when both he and his family suffered greatly. "But that was a national tragedy," he later remarked. "A lot of people suffered."[37]

The Final Offensive   201

Relations between the United States and China began to thaw with the visit of President Richard Nixon to Beijing in 1972. For the first time since its founding, the United States opened a dialogue with Mao's government. Both sides began to reexamine their history. The People's Republic came to realize that resistance to Japan and the wartime alliance with the United States did not belong to the Nationalists, or to the warlords, or to any political group for that matter—it belonged to the Chinese people.

For their part, the people of Xiangyun did not forget about Robert Mooney. His sister, Ena Davis, traveled to the town in October 1991 to see where her brother had died. Her visit inspired residents to rebuild the monument. In May 1993, more than fifty years after the young fighter pilot's death, Davis returned to witness its unveiling.[38]

At least 418 American airmen who disappeared on combat missions in the China Theater remain listed as missing in action. Sixteen are known to have been in Japanese custody when they vanished. As many as 175 may have been lost at sea while transiting overwater or engaged in antishipping sweeps. Eighty-one probably went down in the rugged terrain of mountainous Yunnan Province, while the remaining 146 are scattered across the rest of China. Dozens of them probably lie forgotten in unmarked graves.

Occasionally, one of them turns up. In 2006, the US and Chinese governments collaborated to recover the remains of 2nd Lt Robert Hoyle Upchurch, who went missing in bad weather on his first combat mission in October 1944. His parents carved his name on the family funeral plot in High Falls, North Carolina, but his body lay buried near the village of Guidong for more than sixty years. During the war, residents found the wreckage of his aircraft in the mountainous border area between Hunan and Jiangxi. They recovered his body and carried it back to their village over mountain trails, wrapped him in silk, prayed and sang, and buried him at the foot of a Ming Dynasty pagoda. They marked the grave with a cross that identified him simply as *Meiguo Feiji*, "American Airplane." First Ichi-go, then the civil war, prevented his recovery. The villagers kept up the grave for many years, but after the Cultural Revolution, it attracted little attention until a visiting American noticed it in 2003. He reported it to DPAA. Subsequent DNA analysis confirmed Upchurch's identity. The US Army buried his remains in North Carolina with full military honors and his family changed the gravestone to read "Home at last."[39]

Epilogue

Memory

November 1945
McCook, Nebraska

"Do you know who that is?" Elinor Egle asked her friends excitedly. "That's Glen Beneda!" Elinor liked to frequent the USO hall in McCook. All the big bands played in the large auditorium there when they stopped through town overnight. She and her friends enjoyed dancing with the GIs from the nearby B-29 base. "Should I go up and say 'hi' to him?" she asked, "or should I be coy?" Glen had been back in the United States since September 1944, but Elinor had not seen him since he and her brother Ralph left to join the Army Air Forces in 1942. Ralph never came back from the war, but standing there now was Glen, looking fit, handsome, and serious in his dress uniform, sporting a stack of ribbons and a pair of silver wings over his left breast pocket. She went to the restroom with one of her friends wondering if he had noticed her too—wondering if she should say something. When she came out, she found him waiting for her.

"Hello, Elinor." That was it: the start of a whirlwind romance that saw them married just four months later. The war had ended; their new lives had just begun. Glen left the service and the newlyweds moved to Southern California, where he went to work as a fireman. They had twins, Ed and Henry. Glen never talked about the war. Though curious about what her husband had gone through, Elinor never asked; it remained in the past.

Memory is a funny thing, though. Try as he might to leave the war behind him, Glen could not forget about it. When he moved to California, he decided to track down Lee Gregg and get a copy of his walkout diary. The two had never seen each other after they had made it to Kunming, and Glen did not have a chance to get a copy of the journal as they had agreed. He knew Lee's family lived in the San Marino area, so he went there looking for him. He found his mother instead. "Lee got married," she told him. "He bought a boat and he and his wife are sailing the South Seas." Everyone had their own way of exorcising the war's demons, it seemed. Glen asked if she had the walkout diary. She did and typed up a copy for him.

Glen did not mention this visit to his family. In fact, he barely mentioned the war at all for nearly twenty years; he wanted to wipe it from his mind. Getting shot down had been pretty traumatic. It weighed on him. He had always been good at everything he tried, especially as an athlete. In high school he had played football, basketball, and ping pong—he even shot pool. And he had been good at all of it. On a whim, he even ran track. One day, he had been walking home from school, carrying his books and wearing a button-down shirt and khakis. As he passed the track, some of the boys on the team taunted him. "Hey Beneda!" they yelled, "you can't run! Why don't you go out for track?" They were about to run a 440-yard sprint. Glen put down his books and lined up with the rest of the boys, still wearing his school clothes. He beat them all. "Ok Beneda," the coach told him, "you're on the track team."

He never projected a big ego about his athletic prowess. But it certainly came as a blow to train as a fighter pilot only to fall in combat with the enemy. As far as he was concerned, he had done his job—just like everyone else who had served in the war. They won, and he came home; that about summed it up. He did not feel special. He thought about his time in the service, but he did not want to talk about it. War is an ugly thing, and his memories of it had no place alongside his beautiful family. Then Tex Hill formed a veterans group for everyone who had served in the 23rd Fighter Group. Glen went to the meetings; he and the other members shared stories with each other.

"Hey Glen, remember this?" his old war buddies asked him as they spun their tales. He slowly began to open up to his family. He talked about the good things, the funny things, but he still avoided sharing his trauma.

When Nixon visited China in 1972, Glen received a call from Armit Lewis, the pilot who had followed his same route out from behind enemy lines in the fall of 1944.

"Glen, I want to go back to China," he told him. "Do you want to go with me?"

"No," Glen replied. "I don't think I want to go back."

204 FALLEN TIGERS

Armit tried to go, but the State Department told him "not yet." Unfortunately, he suffered a stroke before he could make the journey. When Glen finally did decide to return in 2001, his son Ed accompanied him instead. The trip proved to be a big disappointment—they went on a lot of guided tours that pushed them into silk factories and furniture shops; he felt like they just wanted his pocketbook. He vowed not to go back.

In 2005, however, a Vietnam-era Marine Corps veteran named Jeff Greene called him. He had formed a nonprofit organization called the Sino-American Aviation Heritage Foundation and wanted to put together a group of veterans to visit China for the sixtieth anniversary of World War II. The men would tour the country and speak about their experiences, with the Chinese government paying their airfare and expenses. So far, the group included AVG veteran Dick Rossi and Jimmy Doolittle's copilot on the Tokyo Raid, Dick Cole. Glen declined. "I've been there," he said. "I don't want to go back."

Both Greene and the Chinese government kept after him, though. They called Glen incessantly, filling up his answering machine. Finally, a government representative gave him a new tidbit of information: "You must come!" he told him. "We found your airplane!"

"I never lost my airplane!" Glen shot back. "I know where it is. I crashed it. It's just a piece of junk! I don't need to see it." He sounded indignant, but his curiosity soon got the better of him; he decided to go. This time his wife, son Ed, and grandson Brian went with him. It proved to be a completely different experience than his trip in 2001. Glen enjoyed reminiscing with the other veterans. He also enjoyed the royal treatment.

During one event, a retired general who had served with the New Fourth Army recounted how his unit had rescued several American pilots during the war. He began to list their names: Armit Lewis, Lee Gregg, Glen Beneda—Greene pointed out Glen sitting across the room. "That's Glen Beneda right there."

The retired general proved to be Xia Kui, a veteran of the 5th Division, New Fourth Army, who had met Glen at the local command post near the scene of his bailout in 1944. Li Xiaolin, vice chairman of the Chinese People's Association for Friendship with Foreign Countries, looked on with great interest. Her father, Li Xiannian, had commanded the 5th Division. After the war he had gone on to a successful career in politics, becoming the third president of the People's Republic of China from 1983 to 1988, before his death in 1992. She invited Glen and his family to her hotel room.

Epilogue 205

"I have arranged for you to go to Jianli to see where they're excavating your airplane out of the lake," she told him.

"I don't want to leave the group," Glen protested.

She leaned close, her nose poking into his face. "Glen," she said sternly, "you *will* go."

On September 9, they loaded into a big SUV and left Changsha with a police escort, setting out over the boggy country north of the Yangzi River. The roads soon turned to mere dirt paths between rice paddies. As they neared the village of Luojia, they began to hear the sound of drums and cymbals, first faintly, then louder. A procession of cheering townspeople soon joined behind the SUV. The residents thronged around Glen when he got out. Some shook his hand, others hugged him. A college student who spoke English thanked him for his service.

"I didn't do anything special!" Glen rebutted.

"Sir," the student replied, "if it weren't for you, I would be speaking Japanese."

"Well, if we helped your people, that's wonderful," he conceded, "but your people helped me too. The real heroes were the farmers and civilians and soldiers who carried me. They saved my life!"

The people loaded Glen into a bamboo chair reminiscent of the stretcher on which their predecessors had carried him in 1944 and took him out to the excavation site for his airplane. He looked across the muddy lake bed silently, thoughtfully. For so long he had buried the traumatic events of that day. Now, more than sixty years after the fact, he felt overwhelmed—remembering everything—experiencing the fear, pain, and relief all over again. The visit changed his life. Never in his wildest dreams did he imagine the respect and admiration the Chinese people had for him. Glen had not understood what his service meant to them. Staring across the rice paddies on that September day in 2005, he had an epiphany. After decades of avoiding the topic of his escape from behind enemy lines—of thinking the memories of an ugly war had no place alongside his beautiful family—he realized that, without the help of these people, in this village, he would not have had a family at all.

"I owe a debt to the Chinese people," he told them. "There's no way I can pay it back. They saved my life."

Glen made two more trips to China, the last, in October 2010, against his doctor's orders. By then he had a pacemaker and nine heart stints. But he had to go back to visit Li Xiannian's presidential library and museum to pay his

206　FALLEN TIGERS

respects to the man whose division brought him to safety. Glen carried with him the Nambu pistol the general had given him in 1944 to donate to the museum's collection. The day after he returned to the United States, Glen Beneda suffered a massive heart attack. Three days later, on October 23, 2010, he died.

In accordance with his wishes, on May 11, 2011, Elinor Beneda and her two sons returned to China with a container of Glen's ashes. Li Xiaolin built a beautiful memorial on the grounds of her father's library, and there they interred his remains. His final wishes made a powerful statement about the relationship between American airmen and the Chinese people who fought alongside them and rescued them when they crashed or bailed out. He made a choice to memorialize and humanize his rescuers. Though nameless and faceless to most Americans, their names and faces had lived in his heart.

Prominently displayed at the memorial is a statue of a shark-mouthed P-40. To most Americans its grinning visage represents vengeance for Pearl Harbor. At Li Xiannian's presidential library, it occupies a place of honor next to Glen Beneda's ashes, alongside his story etched in marble. Visitors can readily see that the symbol means much more to the Chinese people. Robert Mooney's comrades learned this at the unveiling of his monument outside Xiangyun in 1943. Glen realized it looking out over the excavation site of his airplane in 2005. Ultimately, it represents something that transcends governments or politics: it is the symbol of cooperation and fraternity between ordinary Americans and Chinese. Both sides sacrificed—not for anything political or partisan but for the liberation of an oppressed people. This, more than anything, is the lesson we learn from the fate of America's missing airmen in China during World War II: two vastly different peoples came together to fight inhumanity and injustice. They left behind a powerful legacy, now largely unknown, but potent with meaning for both the United States and the People's Republic of China.[1]

Acknowledgments

This project would not have been possible without the service, sacrifice, and stories of dozens of Chinese, American, and Thai veterans and war survivors who shared their memories with me. The help of Dave Hayward, in particular, proved indispensable, as did the encouragement of Sterling Barrow, Arthur Clark, and Paul Crawford. I appreciated the warm welcome and fascinating memories from Mr. Bancha Oodjai, Ms. Fong Inma, Mr. Gong Kaibing, Mr. Hu Yaji, Mr. Li Yuntang, Mr. Pei Haiqing, and Mr. Wu Eyang. Several family members of veterans also willingly shared from sometimes very painful memories, particularly Janet McMillan Alford, Ed and Elinor Beneda, Cindy Cole Chal, Bruce Doyle, Lisa Findley, Will Forbes, Margaret Mills Kincannon, Clifford Long, Clay McCutchan, Arianna Opsvig, Janice Barrow Quinn, and Tony Strotman. In addition, Carl Molesworth, Terry Hunter, Samuel Kleiner, and Rod Szasz helped me track down tidbits of missing information. Samuel Hui and Kun Shi provided an incredible amount of help with Chinese sources, as did Fu Shimin and the Western Yunnan Association for the Study of World War II History. Air Chief Marshal Sakpinit Promthep from the Royal Thai Air Force, along with Mr. Richard "Hak" Hakanson and Ms. Wiyada Kantarod, provided crucial research help from Thailand. Dr. Jeremiah Dancy and Dr. Paul Springer provided valuable feedback and encouragement. I am also indebted to Maj Klairoong "Puma" Pattumma, from Detachment 1 of the US Defense POW/MIA Accounting Agency, who believed in my research and led a team of talented professionals to discover the crash site of 2nd Lt Henry F. Minco, including Vina Chhouk, Jared Elison, Benjamart "Apple" Daramart, and Sunan "Jun" Boonjeam. It was one of the great honors of my life to accompany them. Finally, I would

208 Acknowledgments

like to thank series editor Brian Laslie and the team at the University Press of Kentucky for their outstanding work. There are many others besides who made this project a reality and I regret not being able to name every single one of them. Know that I am profoundly grateful for all the support I received in telling the incredible stories of some remarkable people during a horrific time in human history. Thank you all and God bless.

Appendix A

Timeline

1937

May 31: Claire Chennault arrives in China to begin a three-month evaluation of the Chinese Air Force.

July 7: An incident at the Lugou Bridge (also known as the Marco Polo Bridge) near Beiping ignites open warfare between Japan and China, known as the War of Resistance against Japan, which later merges into World War II.

August 8: The Japanese capture Beiping.

August 14–16: Chinese fighters claim fifty-four bombers shot down with the help of the warning net organized by Chennault around the Nationalist Chinese capital at Nanjing.

August 21: Generalissimo Chiang Kai-shek secures Soviet support in his fight against the Japanese with the signing of the Sino-Soviet Non-Aggression Pact.

November: The first of four "volunteer" squadrons of Soviet fighters and two of bombers join the fight in China.

November 26: Shanghai falls to the Japanese.

December 13: Japanese troops capture Nanjing.

1938

June 5–7: On orders from Chiang, Nationalist forces demolish the Yellow River dams near Zhengzhou. Resulting floods stop the Japanese advance in north China but cost the lives of at least half a million Chinese civilians, with many millions displaced.

210   Appendix A

June 26: Japanese troops capture Jiujiang.
October 27: The Japanese capture Hankou.
December: The Burma Road opens.

1939

May 4: Japan begins terror-bombing attacks against Chongqing.
May 11–September 16: Tension between Japan and the Soviet Union erupt into battle along the border between Japanese-occupied Manchuria and Soviet-allied Mongolia. Despite winning an overwhelming victory, the Soviets begin pulling their airmen out of China following the signing of a cease-fire agreement.
September 1: Nazi Germany invades Poland.
September 3: Britain and France declare war on Germany.
September 17–October 6: The First Battle of Changsha results in a Chinese victory under the leadership of Gen Xue Yue.
December 18–January 11, 1940: Two armored divisions of China's Fifth Army stop the Japanese army's advance into Guangxi Province.

1940

March 30: Former premier of the Nationalist republic Wang Jingwei collaborates with the Japanese to form the Reorganized National Government of China, headquartered at Nanjing.
September 13: The Mitsubishi A6M Type Zero Carrier Fighter scores its first air-to-air victories in a dogfight over Chongqing, downing thirteen Soviet-built fighters of the Chinese Air Force for no losses.
September 22: The Japanese invade French Indochina.
November 14: Chennault arrives in the United States to help lobby for creation of a volunteer fighter group manned by experienced American aviators, eventually securing the verbal approval of President Franklin Roosevelt.

1941

July 24: MS *Bloemfontein* departs San Francisco with twenty-eight pilots and ground crewmen destined for the AVG, including George B. McMillan.

Timeline   211

July 28: The first contingent of AVG volunteers arrive in Rangoon.

September 6–October 8: Second Battle of Changsha results in a Chinese victory under the leadership of General Xue.

September 15: McMillan arrives in Rangoon with the last major group of AVG personnel.

December 7: Japanese carrier aircraft make a surprise attack on the US Pacific Fleet at Pearl Harbor.

December 8: The US Congress declares war on the Empire of Japan. Japanese troops invade Thailand.

December 11: Nazi Germany declares war on the United States. Hours later, Congress responds with a declaration of war against Germany.

December 18: Japanese warplanes resume terror bombing of Kunming. Chennault dispatches thirty-four AVG Hawk 81A2s to defend the city.

December 20: In their first combat of the war, AVG fighters shoot down four of ten Japanese bombers attacking Kunming. None of the American fighters are shot down, though one makes a forced landing after running out of fuel.

December 22–January 14, 1942: President Roosevelt and Prime Minister Winston Churchill convene the Arcadia Conference in Washington, DC. They agree on a strategy to defeat Germany first and announce the formation of the China Theater, with Generalissimo Chiang as its supreme Allied commander.

December 23: The Japanese Army Air Force launches a massive air raid against Rangoon, Burma. Erik Shilling crash-lands sixty miles west of Kunming when the engine of his Curtiss CW-21 fails. His experience inspires the creation of the "Blood Chit."

December 24–January 15, 1942: Third Battle of Changsha results in a Chinese victory under the leadership of General Xue.

December 25: McMillan receives credit for three Japanese bombers destroyed in a massive air battle over Rangoon. He crash-lands after his fighter is hit in the engine but returns to his unit that evening.

1942

January 17: McMillan leads a flight of four Hawk 81A2s to intercept three Japanese bombers over southern Yunnan Province. His flight shoots down all three with no losses.

January 25: Thailand declares war on the United States and Great Britain.

212   Appendix A

February 24: Lieutenant General Joseph W. Stilwell arrives in India to take command of American forces in the China-Burma-India Theater.

March 7: The Allies evacuate Rangoon.

April 9: The US Army Air Forces reactivate Chennault in the temporary grade of colonel.

April 18: Sixteen B-25 bombers under the command of Lt Col James H. "Jimmy" Doolittle take off from the aircraft carrier USS *Hornet* and bomb targets in the Japanese home islands. Insufficient coordination takes place to receive the bombers in China; one diverts to Russia. In China, three airmen are killed and eight are captured. Without warning or preparation, the Chinese rescue the remaining sixty-four.

April 29: The Japanese capture Lashio, the start point of the Burma Road.

May 7–9: Air strikes by the AVG and a counterattack by the Chinese Seventy-First Army stop the Japanese advance at the Salween River in western Yunnan Province.

May 8: Japanese troops capture Myikyina.

May 10: Japanese troops capture Tengchong.

June 3: Only one of six B-25s arrive unscathed at Kunming after flying from India to China as the first US Army reinforcements for the AVG. Three hit a weather-obscured mountain en route, while another becomes lost—its crew bailing out north of Kunming. Enemy fighters shoot up one over Lashio, but it manages to limp the rest of the way to the airfield. Shortly thereafter, Tenth Air Force announces the formation of the CATF under the command of Chennault, now a brigadier general.

July 4: The AVG officially disbands.

August: Colonel Merian C. Cooper becomes chief of staff of the CATF.

October 25: Twelve B-25s and seven P-40s make the CATF's first raid on occupied Hong Kong. One B-25 and one P-40 are shot down. Four airmen are captured, but three others are rescued by friendly Chinese.

November 12: Lieutenant Colonel Clinton D. "Casey" Vincent reports to China as the CATF operations officer.

November 22: Vincent leads an attack on Japanese shipping in the Indochinese port of Hong Gai.

November 28: Cooper relinquishes his position as chief of staff for the CATF after Gen George Marshall demands his recall in response to a provocative letter he wrote criticizing Stilwell.

Timeline 213

December 26: First Lieutenant Robert Mooney is shot down in a dogfight over Xiangyun, Yunnan Province. He bails out too late to save himself in order to keep his fighter from crashing into the town and killing Chinese civilians. Despite the efforts of a local doctor to save him, Mooney dies later that night. Five months later, the people of Xiangyun dedicate a stone monument in his honor.

1943

March 10: The CATF becomes the US Fourteenth Army Air Force under the command of Chennault, now a major general.

May 12–25: The Allies hold the Trident Conference in Washington, DC. Chennault and Stilwell both attend. President Roosevelt decides to pursue an air-centric strategy in China.

July 6: Twenty-five P-38 Lightnings of "Squadron X" (later the 449th Fighter Squadron) depart Constantine, Algeria, to become the first augmentation to Chennault's force of P-40 Warhawks in China. Second Lieutenant Lee Gregg volunteers to join the unit.

July 23: Lieutenant General Moritaka Nakazono's 3rd Air Division begins a campaign to wipe out the Fourteenth Air Force. The first flight of P-38 Lightnings from Squadron X arrives in China.

July 25: Second Lieutenant Glen Beneda claims a Japanese fighter "probably destroyed" during an air battle over Hengyang.

August 20: Ki-44 Shokis from the 85th Air Regiment shoot down two P-40s for no losses over Guilin. The new Japanese fighters have a clear technological advantage over the American fighters.

September 9: Second Lieutenant Billie Beardsley unwittingly kills General Nakazono when he shoots down a Japanese transport southeast of Guangzhou, effectively ending the 3rd Air Division's offensive to destroy the Fourteenth Air Force.

September 27: The 11th Bomb Squadron makes its first counter-shipping sweep over the open sea, losing one B-25 in the Gulf of Tonkin. A Chinese sailing junk saves four of the crewmembers.

October 17: Second Lieutenant Francis Forbes bails out of his P-40 during a raid on a Japanese encampment along the Salween River. He attempts crossing the river after four days of evading capture on the west bank. Pei

214   Appendix A

Haiqing, a deserter from the Nationalist Army, witnesses his crossing and pulls him from the river.

October 29: C Flight of the 21st Photo Reconnaissance Squadron moves to the new airbase at Suichuan, in Jiangxi Province, 250 miles east of Guilin.

October 30: Ki-43 Hayabusas of the 25th Air Regiment ambush two flights of P-38s over Jiujiang, shooting down four Lightnings. Two pilots return to Allied control and one is captured. The squadron commander eventually dies from his wounds.

October 31: First Lieutenant Winfree Sordelett flies a nine-hour reconnaissance mission from the airbase at Suichuan to Sasebo and Nagasaki. He is the first American airman over the Japanese home islands since the Doolittle Raid.

November 9: Lieutenant Colonel McMillan takes command of the 449th Fighter Squadron.

November 25: Colonel David Lee "Tex" Hill leads fourteen B-25s, seven P-51s, and eight P-38s in a surprise attack on the Japanese airfield at Hsinchu, Taiwan. His warplanes claim forty-six Japanese aircraft destroyed for no losses.

December 1: Hill barely survives a dogfight between Ki-44s and his P-51s near Hong Kong. Two members of his flight are shot down but return to Allied control with the help of friendly Chinese.

December 26: Vincent orders a detachment of fifteen P-40s and P-51s from the 76th Fighter Squadron to move to Suichuan.

December 31: Twenty-five B-24s of the 308th Bomb Group attack the railyards at Lampang, Thailand. Six Royal Thai Air Force fighters launch to intercept, but are unable to engage.

1944

January 6: Colonel Vincent orders a detachment of eight P-38s from the 449th Fighter Squadron to move to Suichuan.

February: The Japanese 3rd Air Division becomes the Fifth Air Army.

February 6: Vincent orders the rest of the 449th Fighter Squadron forward to Suichuan.

February 12: Eleven Ki-44s and fourteen Ki-43s attack Suichuan. Fourteen P-38s and ten P-40s and P-51s engage the enemy south of the field,

Timeline   215

resulting in the loss of at least eight Ki-44s for the loss of only two Allied fighters.

February 26: Vincent leads the first flight of Merlin-engine P-51B Mustangs to China.

April 17: Japan's China Expeditionary Army launches phase one of the Ichi-go offensive, with approximately 148,000 soldiers moving south from the Yellow River bend to capture the Beiping–Hankou Railroad.

April 29: Major Rex Barber and 2nd Lt Robert Campbell are shot down in an ambush over Jiujiang. Barber had shot down Adm Isoroku Yamamoto and had knowledge of American code breaking secrets. Fortunately, Chinese guerrillas keep him out of Japanese hands.

May 6: Fifty-four American warplanes attack Hankou in an effort to staunch the Ichi-go offensive. Defending Japanese fighters shoot down three P-38s and one P-51. Lieutenants Gregg and Beneda bail out over occupied China.

May 11: Forty thousand troops of the Chinese Expeditionary Force cross the Salween River to take western Yunnan Province back from the Japanese.

May 27: Eight divisions of the Japanese Eleventh Army march south from Hankou toward Changsha while two divisions of the Twenty-Third Army march north from Guangzhou toward Qujiang in phase two of the Ichi-go offensive.

June: Fourteenth Air Force halts daytime sea sweeps by B-25s in favor of nighttime sweeps by radar-equipped SB-24s. Though American commanders think the SB-24s are more effective against Japanese shipping, postwar reports prove otherwise.

June 1: Vincent visits General Xue in Changsha.

June 15: Seventy-five B-29 Superfortresses of the Twentieth Air Force take off from airfields near Chengdu, Sichuan Province, to attack the Imperial Iron and Steel Works at Yawata in northern Kyushu—the first heavy bomber raid on Japan during the war.

June 16: Vincent orders the airfield at Hengyang evacuated.

June 20: Japanese troops reach the outskirts of Hengyang, beginning a forty-seven-day siege. General Fang Xianjue's Tenth Army holds out bravely, but in vain.

June 22: Lieutenants Gregg and Beneda arrive at Laohekou airbase after forty-eight days behind enemy lines, having been rescued by the Communist New Fourth Army.

216   Appendix A

June 23: Vincent is promoted to brigadier general, becoming the second-youngest general officer in the history of the US Air Force.

June 24: Lieutenant Colonel McMillan dies in a crash after enemy small-arms fire cripples his P-38 near Pingxiang, Jiangxi Province.

July 22: The US Army Observer Group, known as the "Dixie Mission," arrives at the headquarters of the Chinese Communist Party in Yan'an. Included among them is 1st Lt Henry Whittlesey, an officer with the Fourteenth Air Force's AGAS.

July 24: Twenty-one P-40s of the 5th Fighter Group (Provisional), CACW, make a surprise attack on the airfield at Bailuozhen, claiming twenty-six Japanese fighters destroyed on the ground. A repeat of the mission just four days later results in claims for eleven more enemy aircraft destroyed.

August 3: General Stilwell's troops capture Myitkyina.

August 8: Japanese troops capture Hengyang.

September 7: Japanese troops capture Lingling.

September 14: The Chinese Expeditionary Force liberates Tengchong.

September 21: Captain Donald Burch crash-lands his P-40 near Yanshi, Henan Province. A collaborator turns him over to the Japanese, and he spends the rest of the war as a prisoner.

October 18: President Roosevelt recalls Stilwell. Lieutenant General Albert Wedemeyer takes command of American forces in the China Theater.

November 5: First Lieutenant Franklin H. McKinney crashes his Lockheed F-5E reconnaissance plane in a thunderstorm at Mae Kua, Thailand.

November 11: Japanese troops capture Guilin. Chinese puppet troops pick up four members of a B-29 crew who bailed out sixty-five miles northwest of Nanjing. A Japanese patrol insists the Chinese hand over the Americans, reportedly shooting one of the airmen when he resists. The other three become prisoners of war. Sixteen Fourteenth Air Force Lightnings and Mustangs dogfight five Thai fighters over Lampang. The RTAF admits to losing all five of its interceptors, but P-51 pilot 2nd Lt Henry F. Minco is reported missing in action. First Lieutenant Rudolph C. Shaw bails out near Cao Bang, Vietnam. A Viet Minh leader by the name of Ho Chi Minh personally escorts him back to Kunming.

December 18: Eighty-five B-29s join two hundred Fourteenth Air Force fighters and bombers in a massive fire-bombing attack on Hankou. The

Japanese supply base is decisively destroyed, but as many as forty thousand Chinese civilians are killed.

1945

January 17: Seventeen P-51s from the 74th Fighter Squadron and 118th Tactical Reconnaissance Squadron attack Japanese airfields in Shanghai, claiming seventy-three enemy aircraft destroyed for no losses.

January 28: Japanese troops take Suichuan.

February 4: Japanese troops take Ganzhou.

February 6: Captain Robert Kunz evacuates a B-29 crew from a secret airfield near the Shanxi-Henan-Hebei border in an unarmed B-25. AGAS officer Captain Whittlesey had worked with the Communist Eighth Route Army to prepare the field. Unfortunately, Japanese troops executed Whittlesey after capturing him on January 20.

March 3: Kunz returns to the secret airfield to fly out another nine rescued airmen and Whittlesey's body.

March 9: The Japanese take over Indochina in a coup overthrowing the colonial French regime.

March 27: Laohekou falls to the Japanese.

April: The Japanese Twentieth Army begins a drive on Zhijiang, in western Hunan Province.

May 9: The Japanese order a halt to the Zhijiang campaign after Chinese troops and Chinese and American fighters and bombers mount an effective defense. Meanwhile, the Japanese evacuate the Jiangwan prisoner of war camp in Shanghai, first moving the prisoners to Beiping and then to the Japanese home islands.

May 10: AVG pilot Lewis Bishop and four US Marines escape from a Japanese prison train en route to Beiping.

July 14: First Lieutenant Paul Crawford is rescued by the Eighth Route Army after he bails out near Jiexiu, Shanxi Province.

August 6: A lone B-29 drops an atomic bomb on Hiroshima.

August 9: A lone B-29 drops an atomic bomb on Nagasaki. The Soviet Union declares war on the Empire of Japan and invades Manchuria.

August 15: The Empire of Japan announces it will surrender to the Allied powers.

218   Appendix A

August 21: A Japanese delegation surrenders to the Chinese at Zhijiang.

September 2: The formal surrender ceremony takes place aboard the USS *Missouri* in Tokyo Bay. General of the Army Douglas MacArthur makes repatriation of Allied prisoners a top priority. Ho Chi Minh declares Vietnamese independence.

September 11: US Army troops liberate Allied prisoners held at the Hakodate Branch Camp Number 4 at Ashibetsu, Hokkaido, including eighteen airmen captured in China.

December 20: General of the Army George Marshall arrives in China to negotiate peace between the Nationalists and Communists.

1947

January 8: Marshall leaves China. His mission to prevent civil war is a failure.

1949

October 1: Mao Zedong announces the founding of the People's Republic of China. Chiang Kai-shek and his Nationalists retreat to Taiwan.

1972

February 21–28: President Richard Nixon visits the People's Republic of China, ending more than twenty-two years of diplomatic impasse.

1993

May: The people of Xiangyun rebuild the monument to 1st Lt Robert Mooney, destroyed during the Cultural Revolution.

2005

September 9: Glen Beneda returns to Jianli and meets the Chinese who rescued him in 1944.

2010

October 23: Glen Beneda dies.

2011

May 11: Elinor Beneda and her sons travel to China to inter Glen's ashes at the presidential library of Li Xiannian, commander of the 5th Division, New Fourth Army, which rescued him during the war.

2019

November 8: Major Klairoong "Puma" Pattumma leads a team from the Defense POW/MIA Accounting Agency Detachment 1 to discover Lieutenant Minco's crash site in the rugged mountains northeast of Lampang, Thailand.

Appendix B

Chinese Transliteration

PINYIN	WADE GILES/TRADITIONAL	
Anyi		安义
Bailuozhen	Pailiuchi	白螺镇
Beiping (now Beijing)	Peiping	北平 (北京)
Cao Xingren	Tsao Hsing-jen	曹醒仁
Chongqing	Chungking	重庆
Dawushan	Dawu Mountain	大悟山
Dong Qiyuan		董齐元
Gaoxiong	Kaohsiung (Takao)	高雄
Gong Kaibing		龚开炳
Guangzhou	Canton	广州
Guilin	Kweilin	桂林
Guomindang (GMD)	Kuomintang (KMT)	国民党
Jiang Jieshi	Chiang Chieh-shih (Chiang Kai-shek)	蒋介石
Jiayi	Chiayi	嘉义
Jingbao	Ching Pao	警报
Leiyun	Loi Wing	雷允
Li Xiannian		李先念

222 Appendix B

Li Yuntang		李云堂
Liu Zhenghua	Liu Cheng-hua	劉正華
Lu Caiwen		卢彩文
Mao Zedong	Mao Tse-tung	毛泽东
Meiguo	Mey Gwa (America/USA)	美国
Ming Zhongyi	Ming Chung-yee	
Nujiang	Salween River	怒江
Pei Haiqing		裴海清
Shaoyang (Baoqing)	Paoching	邵阳 (宝庆)
Shenyang	Mukden	沈阳
Song Meiling	Soong May-ling (Madame Chiang)	宋美龄
Song Ziwen	Soong Tse-ven (T.V. Soong)	宋子文
Taiwan	Formosa	台湾
Tian Nong		田农
Tong Shiguang		童世光
Wu Eyang		伍鄂阳
Xia Kui		夏夔
Xinzhu	Hsinchu (Shinchiku)	新竹
Xu Hua-jiang	Hsu Hua-chiang	
Xue Yue	Hsueh Yueh	薛岳
Yan Xishan	Yen Hsi-shan	阎锡山
Zhang Gewei	Chang Ko-wei	
Zhijiang	Chihkiang (Chekiang)	芷江

Notes

Author's Note

1. The database includes several aces, though having to crash-land or bail out hardly constituted their best day.

2. Frank J. Olynyk, *AVG & USAAF (China-Burma-India Theater) Credits for the Destruction of Enemy Aircraft in Air-to-Air Combat World War 2* (n.p.: self-published, 1986); Office of Statistical Control, *Army Air Forces Statistical Digest* (Washington, DC: Government Printing Office, 1945), 89.

3. Joseph W. Stilwell, *The Stilwell Papers*, ed. Theodore H. White (1948; repr., Cambridge, MA: Da Capo, 1975), 76–80; Claire Lee Chennault, *Way of a Fighter*, ed. Robert Hotz (New York: G. P. Putnam's Sons, 1949), 223; Jay Taylor, *The Generalissimo: Chiang Kai-shek and the Struggle for Modern China* (Cambridge, MA: Harvard University Press, 2009), 143, 171.

Prologue

1. Until the summer of 1944 the three original squadrons of the 23rd Fighter Group used colors for their radio call signs: the 74th "Red," the 75th "White," and the 76th "Blue." The 449th Fighter Squadron went by the call sign "Black."

2. These "Zeros" were in fact twenty-four Ki-43-II Hayabusas from the veteran 25th Air Regiment.

3. David Lee Hill, *"Tex" Hill: Flying Tiger*, with Reagan Schaupp (2003; repr., San Antonio: Universal Bookbindery, 2004), 239; Glen Beneda, interview by Daniel Jackson, July 22, 2008; US Army Air Forces, "Missing Air Crew Report 4732," 1944, M1380, National Archives and Research Administration, Washington, DC.

4. Beneda interview 2008; US Army Air Forces, "Missing Air Crew Report 11971," 1944, M1380, National Archives and Research Administration, Washington, DC.

5. AGAS-China, "Evader's Narrative Report: Story of Lee O. Gregg," 1944, Air Force Historical Research Agency, Maxwell Air Force Base, AL, Reel A1322, microfilm; MIS-X Section, CPM Branch, "Evasion Report No. 431, Gregg, Lee O.," 1944, Air Force Historical Research Agency, Maxwell Air Force Base, AL.

224   Notes to Pages xiv–5

6. The soldier, Tian Nong, tried to reassure the American he had been rescued by friendly Communists by saying, "Stalin, Mao Zedong, Eighth Route Army, New Fourth Army," but Beneda did not recognize the names in Chinese.

7. AGAS-China, "Evader's Narrative Report: Story of Glen Beneda," 1944, Air Force Historical Research Agency, Maxwell Air Force Base, AL, Reel A1322, microfilm; Beneda interview 2008; Xia Kui, *Saving American Pilots*, trans. Zhang Jusheng (n.p., 2006), 5.

8. AGAS-China, "Story of Lee O. Gregg"; Lee O. Gregg, "Shot Down May 6th, 1944, near Hankow," unpublished diary, 1944.

9. Philip D. Caine, *Aircraft Down! Evading Capture in WWII Europe* (Washington, DC: Brassey's, 1997), 2; unless otherwise noted, all statistics on missing airmen in China are derived from the author's database of missing aircrew and evasion reports.

10. John D. Plating, *The Hump: America's Strategy for Keeping China in World War II* (College Station: Texas A&M University Press, 2011), 1.

1. Aerial Oppression

1. Theodore H. White and Annalee Jacoby, *Thunder out of China* (Cambridge, MA: Da Capo, 1980), 7, 9, 11, 13–15.

2. Military History and Translation Office, "An Interview with Maj. Gen. Xu Hua-jiang" in *The Immortal Flying Tigers: An Oral History of the Chinese-American Composite Wing* (Taipei: Ministry of National Defense, 2009), 112–13.

3. Hakan Gustavsson, *Sino-Japanese Air War, 1937–1945: The Longest Struggle* (Stroud, England: Fonthill Media, 2016), 85.

4. Charles Older, interview by Frank Boring, April 26, 1991, Grand Valley State University Digital Collections, www.digitalcollections.library.gvsu.edu.

5. Claire Lee Chennault, *Way of a Fighter*, ed. Robert Hotz (New York: G. P. Putnam's Sons, 1949), 88–89.

6. Hangkong Weiyuanhui, 航空委员会

7. Gustavsson, *Sino-Japanese Air War*, 85.

8. Daniel Ford, *Flying Tigers: Claire Chennault and his American Volunteers, 1941–1942*, 2nd ed. (New York: Harper Collins, 2014), 10.

9. Chennault, *Way of a Fighter*, 21, 23, 40, 47, 49, 54.

10. Max Chennault, "Flying Tigers Up Sun," in *Up Sun!*, ed. Wallace Little and Charles Goodman (Memphis, TN: Castle Books, 1990), 9.

11. Chennault, *Way of a Fighter*, 58, 73.

12. Gustavsson, *Sino-Japanese Air War*, 76.

13. Rana Mitter, *Forgotten Ally: China's World War II, 1937–1945* (New York: Houghton Mifflin Harcourt, 2013), 106–7; Iris Chang, *The Rape of Nanking: The Forgotten Holocaust of World War II* (New York: Penguin Books, 1997), 4, 6.

14. John M. Kelley, "Claire Lee Chennault: Theorist and Campaign Planner" (master's thesis, School of Advanced Military Studies, 1993), 7.

15. Mitter, *Forgotten Ally*, 160, 190.

16. Gong Kaibing, interview by Kun Shi and Daniel Jackson, August 7, 2017; Tan Guanyue, interview by Kun Shi and Daniel Jackson, August 7, 2017.

17. Chennault, *Way of a Fighter*, 78.

18. Jay Taylor, *The Generalissimo: Chiang Kai-shek and the Struggle for Modern China* (Cambridge, MA: Harvard University Press, 2009), 144.

19. Chennault, *Way of a Fighter,* 42.

20. Ernest Hemingway, "Chinese Build Air Field," in *By-Line: Ernest Hemingway, Selected Articles and Dispatches of Four Decades,* ed. William White (New York: Scribner Classics, 2002), 337–38.

21. Also called the Huangpu Military Academy (Wade Giles: Whampoa).

22. The branch in Kunming opened in 1935 at the site of the old Yunnan Military Academy. Alumni of the old academy included Zhu De, commander in chief of the People's Liberation Army.

23. Liu Zhenghua, interview by Samuel Hui and Pan I-jung, March 2013.

24. "Chinese-American Composite Wing History," 1944, Air Force Historical Research Agency, Maxwell Air Force Base, AL, Reel A8352, microfilm.

25. Charles F. Romanus and Riley Sunderland, *United States Army in World War II, China-Burma-India Theater: Time Runs Out in CBI* (Washington, DC: Government Printing Office, 1959), 369–70.

26. White and Jacoby, *Thunder out of China,* 72, 99, 131.

27. Eugenie Buchan, *A Few Planes for China: The Birth of the Flying Tigers* (Lebanon, NH: University Press of New England, 2017), 51, 188.

2. Hope for China

1. R. T. Smith, interview by Frank Boring, April 23, 1991, Grand Valley State University Digital Collections, www.digital collections.library.gvsu.edu.

2. R. T. Smith, *Tale of a Tiger: The Adventure-Packed Daily Diary of One of the Flying Tigers' Top Aces* (Van Nuys, CA: Tiger Originals, 1986), 39.

3. George McMillan Flight Records, July 1941, George B. McMillan Collection, Winter Garden Heritage Foundation, FL.

4. George McMillan to Malcolm McMillan, September 26, 1941, McMillan Collection.

5. George McMillan to Mrs. Malcolm McMillan, July 26, 1941, McMillan Collection.

6. George McMillan to Gladys Bray Hamilton, July 27, 1941, McMillan Collection.

7. Smith, *Tale of a Tiger,* 41.

8. David Lee Hill, *"Tex" Hill: Flying Tiger,* with Reagan Schaupp (2003; repr., San Antonio: Universal Bookbindery, 2004), 76.

9. Hill, *"Tex" Hill,* 88.

10. Claire Lee Chennault, *Way of a Fighter,* Robert Hotz, ed. (New York: G. P. Putnam's Sons, 1949), 112.

11. Hill, *"Tex" Hill,* 91.

12. Chennault, *Way of a Fighter,* 113.

13. Hill, *"Tex" Hill,* 92.

14. Chennault, *Way of a Fighter,* 113.

15. Hill, *"Tex" Hill,* 93.

16. John R. Alison, interview by Daniel Jackson, May 9, 2007.

17. Thomas D. Harmon, *Pilots Also Pray* (New York: Thomas Y. Crowell, 1944), 124; Hill, *"Tex" Hill,* 88.

226   Notes to Pages 16–24

18. Paul Frillman and Graham Peck, *China: The Remembered Life* (Boston: Houghton Mifflin, 1968), 84–85.

19. George McMillan, diary, December 8, 1941, McMillan Collection.

20. "AVG Diary," December 8, 1942, "Point A," Air Force Historical Research Agency, Maxwell Air Force Base, AL, Reel A8351, microfilm.

21. Robert B. Hotz, *With General Chennault: The Story of the Flying Tigers* (1943; repr., Washington, DC: Zenger Publishing, 1980), 106; Smith, interview by Frank Boring, 1991.

22. Chennault, *Way of a Fighter*, 82.

23. Most Americans assumed *jingbao* meant "air raid," but it actually translates as "alarm" or "warning."

24. Donald S. Lopez, *Into the Teeth of the Tiger* (Washington, DC: Smithsonian Books, 1997), 1.

25. Chennault, *Way of a Fighter*, 128.

26. Chennault, *Way of a Fighter*, 128–29; "AVG Diary," December 20 ("Point X"), 25, 1941.

27. McMillan diary, December 25, 1941.

28. "AVG Diary," 1942; 3rd Pursuit Squadron, "Encounter with Enemy Formation (Bomber) near Mengtsze, Yunnan," January 17, 1942, General Claire Chennault Foundation, Washington, DC; Charles Older, "Combat and Reconnaissance Report," January 17, 1942, General Claire Chennault Foundation, Washington, DC; McMillan diary, January 17, 1942.

29. "AVG Diary," January 17, 1942.

30. McMillan diary, January 17, 1941.

31. George McMillan to Mrs. Malcolm McMillan, February 29, 1942, McMillan Collection.

32. Also known as the Luoluo people.

33. Erik Shilling, *Destiny: A Flying Tiger's Rendezvous with Fate* (Pomona, CA: Ben-Wal Printing, 1993), 118–27; "AVG Diary," December 27, 1941.

34. Author's translation. Lai hua zhu zhan yangren junmin yiti jiuhu, 来华助战洋人军民一体救护 (traditional characters: 來華助戰洋人軍民一體救護). Later versions added "America" (美国; traditional characters: 美國) in parentheses after "foreigner."

35. AGAS-China, "Evasion Story of 1st Lt. Walter Krywy," 1945, Air Force Historical Research Agency, Maxwell Air Force Base, AL, Reel A1322, microfilm.

36. 529th Fighter Squadron, Office of the Intelligence Officer, "Report of Crash Landing and Return of 1st Lt. George F. Snyder," 1945, Air Force Historical Research Agency, Maxwell Air Force Base, AL, Reel A1322, microfilm.

37. Chennault, *Way of a Fighter*, 128–30.

38. Daniel Ford, *Flying Tigers: Claire Chennault and his American Volunteers, 1941–1942*, 2nd ed. (New York: Harper Collins, 2014), 287.

3. Doolittle's Raid

1. Rick Francona, "Japanese Attacks on the Oregon Coast in World War II," *Rotary Club of the State of Jefferson,* https://stateofjeffersonrotary.org/library/programs-1/502 -japanese-attacks-on-oregon-in-world-war-ii.

Notes to Pages 25–35   227

2. US Department of the Air Force, Office of Air Force History, Oral History Interview: Brigadier General Everett W. Holstrom, interview by Dr. James C. Hasdorff, Air University, Maxwell Air Force Base, AL, 1988, 30 [hereafter cited as Holstrom, interview].

3. Charles F. Romanus and Riley Sunderland, *United States Army in World War II, China-Burma-India Theater: Stilwell's Mission to China* (Washington, DC: Government Printing Office, 1953), 62.

4. Joseph W. Stilwell, *The Stilwell Papers*, ed. Theodore H. White (1948; repr., Cambridge, MA: Da Capo, 1975), 49.

5. Joseph W. Stilwell, "Transcript of Diaries, 1900–1946," March 4, 1942, Joseph Warren Stilwell Papers, Hoover Institution Archives, Stanford University, https://digitalcollections.hoover.org/objects/56295.

6. Kang Ri Zhanzheng, 抗日战争.

7. Bruce Ashcroft, *We Wanted Wings: A History of the Aviation Cadet Program* (Randolph Air Force Base, TX: Headquarters, Air Education and Training Command History Office, 2005), 32–33.

8. Ed Beneda and Elinor Beneda, interview by Daniel Jackson, November 29, 2015.

9. Michael D. Roberts, "Fallen Tiger," *Cleveland Magazine*, May 19, 2004.

10. Paul Crawford, interview by Daniel Jackson, October 15, 2016.

11. *Time*, December 29, 1941, 19.

12. Chennault, *Way of a Fighter*, Robert Hotz, ed. (New York: G. P. Putnam's Sons, 1949), 135.

13. R. T. Smith, interview by Frank Boring, April 23, 1991, Grand Valley State University Digital Collections, www.digital collections.library.gvsu.edu; David Lee "Tex" Hill, interview by Frank Boring, February 22, 1991, Grand Valley State University Digital Collections, www.digitalcollections.library.gvsu.edu.

14. T. V. Soong to Claire Chennault, March 14, 1949, Hoover Institution, Stanford, CA.

15. Col. George R. Bailey to SPC Shawn P. Miller, July 13, 1993, AVG Flying Tigers Association.

16. Wang Shuming, interview by Liu Tingyang, June 13, 1991, Grand Valley State University Digital Collections, www.digitalcollections.library.gvsu.edu.

17. George McMillan to mother, February 29, 1942, George B. McMillan Collection, Winter Garden Heritage Foundation, FL.

18. Dennis R. Okerstrom, *Dick Cole's War: Doolittle Raider, Hump Pilot, Air Commando* (Columbia: University of Missouri Press, 2015), 63.

19. Carroll V. Glines, *The Doolittle Raid: America's Daring First Strike against Japan* (Atglen, PA: Schiffer, 2000), 52.

20. Holstrom, interview, 24–27, 30.

21. James M. Scott, *Target Tokyo: Jimmy Doolittle and the Raid That Avenged Pearl Harbor* (New York: W. W. Norton, 2015), 167, 269, 271.

22. Chennault, *Way of a Fighter*, 168, 171.

23. Terry Lautz, *John Birch: A Life* (New York: Oxford University Press, 2016), 74, 77.

24. Holstrom interview, 27–29; James M. Scott, *Target Tokyo: Jimmy Doolittle and the Raid That Avenged Pearl Harbor*, New York: W. W. Norton, 2015, 375, 384–85, 389.

228   Notes to Pages 36–41

4. Enemy Occupation

1. Ethnic Thais living in China.

2. Wu Eyang, interview by Kun Shi, August 18, 2017; Mamie Porritt to James Charlesworth Porritt, December, 4, 1939; October 28, 1940; November 18, 1940, www.warbirdforum.com/porritt1.htm.

3. Paul Frillman and Graham Peck, *China: The Remembered Life* (Boston: Houghton Mifflin, 1968) 116.

4. An air regiment, or *hiko sentai,* was roughly equivalent to an American group.

5. R. T. Smith, *Tale of a Tiger: The Adventure-Packed Daily Diary of One of the Flying Tigers' Top Aces* (Van Nuys, CA: Tiger Originals, 1986), 272.

6. Wu interview 2017.

7. Smith, *Tale of a Tiger,* 271.

8. Christopher Shores, Brian Cull, and Yasuho Izawa, *The Defense of Sumatra to the Fall of Burma,* vol. 2 of *Bloody Shambles: The First Comprehensive Account of Air Operations over South-East Asia, December 1941-May 1942* (London: Grub Street, 1993), 364–65.

9. R. C. Wertz to William D. Pawley, June 18, 1942, https://www.warbirdforum.com/loiwing.htm.

10. Wu interview 2017.

Erik Shilling, *Destiny: A Flying Tiger's Rendezvous with Fate* (Pomona, CA: Ben-Wal Printing, 1993), 161–62.

11. Don Tow, "Heroic and Critical Battles in Yunnan During WWII," http://www.dontow.com/2009/08/heroic-and-critical-battles-in-yunnan-during-wwii (published August 2009).

12. John D. Plating, *The Hump: America's Strategy for Keeping China in World War II* (College Station: Texas A&M University Press, 2011), 94.

13. Joseph W. Stilwell, *The Stilwell Papers,* ed. Theodore H. White (1948; repr., Cambridge, MA: Da Capo, 1975), 108.

14. Pei Haiqing, interview by Kun Shi and Daniel Jackson, August 10, 2017.

15. US Army Air Forces, "Missing Air Crew Report 983," 1943, M1380, National Archives and Research Administration, Washington, DC; US Army Air Forces, "Missing Air Crew Report 984," 1943, M1380, National Archives and Research Administration, Washington, DC.

16. Francis C. Forbes, interview by William Forbes, January 2012; Pei interview 2017.

17. Lu Caiwen, interview by Daniel Jackson, March 2009.

18. Li Yongxiang, "The Ethnic Minorities in Tengchong County and the Anti-Japanese War," *Annual Review of the Institute for Advanced Social Research* 6 (October 2011): 12.

19. Theodore H. White and Annalee Jacoby, *Thunder out of China,* (Cambridge, MA: Da Capo, 1980), 65.

20. David P. Barrett, "Introduction: Occupied China and the Limits of Accommodation," in *Chinese Collaboration with Japan,* ed. David P. Barrett and Larry N. Shyu (Stanford, CA: Stanford University Press, 2001), 8.

Notes to Pages 41–47   229

21. Parks M. Coble, "Japan's New Order and the Shanghai Capitalists: Conflict and Collaboration, 1937–1945," in Barrett and Shuyu, *Chinese Collaboration,* 138; R. Keith Schoppa, "Patterns and Dynamics of Elite Collaboration in Occupied Shaoxing County," in Barrett and Shuyu, *Chinese Collaboration,* 157.

22. Barrett, "Introduction," 3.

23. Schoppa, "Patterns and Dynamics," 164; Barrett, "Introduction," 5.

24. David P. Barrett, "The Wang Jingwei Regime, 1940–1945: Continuities and Disjunctures with Nationalist China," in Barrett and Shuyu, *Chinese Collaboration,* 110.

25. Peter J. Seybolt, "The War within a War: A Case Study of a County on the North China Plain," in Barrett and Shuyu, *Chinese Collaboration,* 208; Rana Mitter, *Forgotten Ally: China's World War II, 1937–1945* (New York: Houghton Mifflin Harcourt, 2013), 218; CCTV, "Journeys in Time: The Chinese Expeditionary Force," CCTV English website, 2012, http://english.cntv.cn/program/journeysintime/20121101/106987.shtml.

26. Barrett, "Introduction," 4, 9–10.

27. Lo Jiu-jung, "Survival as Justification for Collaboration, 1937–1945," in Barrett and Shuyu, *Chinese Collaboration,* loc. 126, 130.

28. Lu interview 2009.

29. Richard Bernstein, *China 1945: Mao's Revolution and America's Fateful Choice* (New York: Alfred A. Knopf, 2014), 295.

30. Thomas Ha, interview by Samuel Hui, September 2014.

31. Li Genzhi, interview by Daniel Jackson and Kun Shi, August 10, 2017.

32. US Forces India Burma Theater MIS-X, "Interrogation of Findley, William S.," 1944, Air Force Historical Research Agency, Maxwell Air Force Base, AL, Reel A1323, microfilm; Lisa Findley, interview by Daniel Jackson, March 4, 2016.

33. XX Bomber Command, Intelligence Section, "Walk-out Report, B-29 Aircraft #237," 1944, Air Force Historical Research Agency, Maxwell Air Force Base, AL, Reel A1322, microfilm.

34. AGAS-China, "Evasion and Walk-Out of the Following Navy Personnel: 1. Albert Basmajian, Lt (J.G.), ASN 264307, USNR, VF 81; 2. George Clark, Ensign, ASN 251438, USNR, VT 22; 3. Donald E. Mize, AMA 3/C, ASN 629–33–11, USNR, VT 22; and 4, Charles George Myers, ARM 3/C, ASN 711–00–06, USNR, VT 22," 1945, Air Force Historical Research Agency, Maxwell Air Force Base, AL, Reel A1322, microfilm; Clark, Mize, and Myers crewed a TBF from VT-22 off the USS *Cowpens.*

35. AGAS-China, "Evasion Story of 1st Lt F. G. McGill, 74th Fighter Squadron," 1945, Air Force Historical Research Agency, Maxwell Air Force Base, AL, Reel A1322, microfilm.

36. US Army Air Forces, "Missing Air Crew Report 8724," 1944, M1380.

37. Li Yuntang, interview by Samuel Hui and Pan I-jung, February 2019.

38. *Army Air Forces Statistical Digest,* 186.

39. Herman Bodson, *Downed Allied Airmen and Evasion of Capture: The Role of Local Resistance Networks in World War II* (London: McFarland, 2005), 10, 20.

40. Though the Nazis garnered some support for their political program in Western Europe, their treatment of Slavs as subhuman generated an effect in parts of Eastern Europe similar to that fostered by Japanese occupation in East Asia.

41. Barrett, "Introduction," 9–10.

230   Notes to Pages 47–57

42. Robert Burris, correspondence with Daniel Jackson, July 2007–August 2009.

43. Arthur W. Clark, *Eyes of the Tiger: China, 1944–1945* (Chapel Hill, NC: self-published, 2015), 96.

44. Malcolm Rosholt, *Rainbow around the Moon: An Autobiography* (Rosholt, WI: Rosholt House, 2004), 150–51.

45. Thomas D. Harmon, *Pilots Also Pray* (New York: Thomas Y. Crowell, 1944), 162.

46. Carl Molesworth, *Sharks over China: The 23rd Fighter Group in World War II* (Washington DC: Brassey's, 1994), 83; Ma Yufu, *Col. C. L. Chennault and Flying Tigers,* ed. Li Xiangping (Beijing: China Intercontinental Press, 2003), 68–69.

47. Diana Lary, "Drowned Earth: The Strategic Breaching of the Yellow River Dyke, 1938," *War in History* 8, no. 2 (April 2001): 206.

48. Ma, *Col. C. L. Chennault and Flying Tigers,* 70; Molesworth, *Sharks over China,* 84.

49. *Army Air Forces Statistical Digest,* 134.

50. Westerners referred to it as Formosa at the time, the name given it by Portuguese explorers.

51. The citizens of Tungjen District, Kweichow, to ranks and files of the USAAF in China, Mailgram, Fourteenth Air Force Historical Office, "China Air Task Force Correspondence," August 15, 1942, Air Force Historical Research Agency, Maxwell Air Force Base, AL, Reel A8351, microfilm.

52. Lu interview 2009.

5. China Air Task Force

1. The five Doolittle veterans were 1st Lt Frank A. Kappeler, Staff Sgt William L. Birch, 1st Lt Eugene F. McGurl, Staff Sgt Omer A. Duquette, and Staff Sgt Melvin J. Gardner.

2. David Lee "Tex" Hill, interview by Frank Boring, February 22, 1991, Grand Valley State University Digital Collections, www.digitalcollections.library.gvsu.edu.

3. First Lieutenant William T. Gross subsequently transferred to the 75th Fighter Squadron. He was killed in action when enemy surface fire brought down his P-40K on February 11, 1943, near the Nan Sang Bridge in Yunnan Province.

4. US Army Air Forces, "Missing Air Crew Report 15936," 1947, M1380, National Archives and Research Administration, Washington, DC; US Department of the Air Force, Office of Air Force History, Oral History Interview: Brigadier General Everett W. Holstrom, interview by Dr. James C. Hasdorff, Air University, Maxwell Air Force Base, AL, 1988, 21, 30, 35; Cindy Cole Chal, email to Daniel Jackson, March 28, 2017; Daniel Ford, "A Pilot of the 2nd AVG," Warbird's Forum, 2010, http://www.warbirdforum.com/klemann .htm; David Hayward, email to Daniel Jackson, October 7, 2015; Robert Klemann, "That Ill-Fated Raid on Lashio," Warbird's Forum, July 2014, http://www.warbirdforum.com /b25s.htm; Arthur Veysey, "The Sky Dragons—Their Exploits over China," *Chicago Tribune,* August 15, 1943, 2; Fourteenth Air Force, 11th Bombardment Squadron, *Squadron History* (Maxwell Air Force Base, AL: Air Force Historical Research Agency, 1945), 36 [hereafter cited as 11th Bombardment Squadron, *History*]; US Department of the Air Force, Office of Air Force History, Oral History Interview: Lieutenant Colonel Horace E. Crouch, interview by Dr. James C. Hasdorff, Air University, Maxwell Air Force Base, AL, 1989, 84–85.

Notes to Pages 57–68   231

5. Claire Lee Chennault, *Way of a Fighter*, ed. Robert Hotz (New York: G. P. Putnam's Sons, 1949), 168.

6. Even the most conservative estimates indicate the AVG downed at least 115 Japanese aircraft, a kill ratio of better than 8:1.

7. William H. Bartsch, *Doomed at the Start: American Pursuit Pilots in the Philippines, 1941–1942* (College Station: Texas A&M University Press, 1995), 153, 428.

8. Carl Molesworth, *Sharks over China: The 23rd Fighter Group in World War II* (Washington DC: Brassey's, 1994), 15–16.

9. R. T. Smith, interview by Frank Boring, April 23, 1991, Grand Valley State University Digital Collections, www.digital collections.library.gvsu.edu; Daniel Ford, *Flying Tigers: Claire Chennault and his American Volunteers, 1941–1942*, 2nd ed. (New York: Harper Collins, 2014), 304, 322.

10. George McMillan to mother, February 29, 1942, George B. McMillan Collection; George McMillan to Mrs. Malcolm McMillan, March 13, 1942, George B. McMillan Collection; George McMillan to his grandmother, May 21, 1942, George B. McMillan Collection.

11. Hugh Crumpler, "How's Your CBI IQ?," *Ex-CBI Roundup*, July 1989, 28.

12. Zbigniew Chichocki, "Merian C. Cooper—Forgotten Hero of Two Nations!" American Polish Cooperation Society, http://www.americanpolishcooperationsociety.com/2017/07/merian-c-cooper-forgotten-hero-of-two-nations; Hugh Crumpler, "How's Your CBI IQ?," *Ex-CBI Roundup*, January 1990, 26–29; Mark Cotta Vaz, *Living Dangerously: The Adventures of Merian C. Cooper, Creator of King Kong* (New York: Villard Books, 2005), 283.

13. Chennault, *Way of a Fighter*, 181–82.

14. *US Army Air Forces in World War II: Combat Chronology, 1941–1945*, comps. Kit C. Carter and Robert Mueller (1973; repr., Washington, DC: Center for Air Force History, 1991).

15. 11th Bombardment Squadron, *History*, 38–40.

16. Chennault, *Way of a Fighter*, 185–86.

17. John M. Kelley, "Claire Lee Chennault: Theorist and Campaign Planner" (master's thesis, School of Advanced Military Studies, 1993), 23.

18. Claire Lee Chennault, "The Role of Defensive Pursuit: The Next Great War," *Coast Artillery Journal* 76, no. 6 (November–December 1933): 413.

19. Tenth Air Force, *History* (Maxwell Air Force Base, AL: Air Force Historical Research Agency, 1945), 115.

20. Chennault, *Way of a Fighter*, 182, 196; Molesworth, *Sharks over China*, 64.

6. Hong Kong

1. These were Ki-43-I Hayabusas of the 24th and 33rd Air Regiments.

2. Wilmer E. McDowell, "The Hong Kong Raid," *Newsletter of the 22nd Bomb Squadron Association* 19, no. 2 (May 2008), 5–6; Fourteenth Air Force, 11th Bombardment Squadron, *Squadron History* (Maxwell Air Force Base, AL: Air Force Historical Research Agency, 1945), 41–42, [hereafter cited as 11th Bombardment Squadron, *History*]; Paul G. Webb, "Shot Down over Hong Kong," *EX-CBI Roundup*, February 1982, 12; Jim Young,

232   Notes to Pages 68–72

Mayday over China: The Diary of Jim Young, WWII POW (self-pub., by Andrew Priddy, 2011) loc. 47, 126, 234 of 974, Kindle; Carl Molesworth, *Sharks over China: The 23rd Fighter Group in World War II* (Washington, DC: Brassey's, 1994), 65–66; Assistant Chief of Air Staff Intelligence Historical Division, *The Tenth Air Force: 1942,* Army Air Forces Historical Studies 12 (Maxwell Air Force Base, AL: Air Force Historical Research Agency, 1944), 115 [hereafter cited as *Tenth Air Force*]; Robert Lee Scott, *God Is My Copilot* (New York: Ballantine Books, 1943), 228; AGAS-China, "Evader's Narrative Report: Lieutenant Cunningham," 1942, Air Force Historical Research Agency, Maxwell Air Force Base, AL, Reel A1322, microfilm.

3. A.R. Wichtrich, MIS-X: Top Secret (Raleigh, NC: Pentland Press, Inc, 1997), 9–10, 20.

4. McDowell, "Hong Kong Raid," 6–7; Molesworth, *Sharks over China,* 67; 11th Bombardment Squadron, *History,* 41–42; *Tenth Air Force,* 116.

5. COGUK to AQUILA writer 1447 A 406, November 19, 1942, Fourteenth Air Force, Historical Office, "China Air Task Force Correspondence."

6. "28 October 1942, WW2 Air Raids over Hong Kong," Gwulo: Old Hong Kong forum, February 2014, https://gwulo.com/node/18944.

7. General Hsieh Mang to Chiang Kai-shek, October 30, 1942, Chiang Kai-shek Papers, doc. 002–090200–00075–333, Academia Historica, Taipei, Taiwan.

8. "28 October 1942, WW2 Air Raids."

9. Molesworth, *Sharks over China,* 163–64, 252.

10. Glenn E. McClure, *Fire and Fall Back: Casey Vincent's Story of Three Years in the China-Burma-India Theater, including the Fighting Withdrawal of the Flying Tigers from Eastern China* (San Antonio: Barnes, 1975), 17–18, 20, 22–23, 44.

11. Frank Dorn, "After the Flag Is Lowered: Autobiography of Frank Dorn," Box 5, Frank Dorn Papers, Hoover Institution Archives, Stanford, CA, 535, 595.

12. US Department of the Air Force, Office of Air Force History, Oral History Interview: Brigadier General Everett W. Holstrom, interview by Dr. James C. Hasdorff, Air University, Maxwell Air Force Base, AL, 1988, 36, [hereafter cited as Holstrom, interview].

13. Brig Gen Francis M. Brady, "Report," December 22, 1942, China Air Task Force Correspondence.

14. C. L. Chennault to Commanding General, Karachi Army Air Base, "Comments on General Brady's Memo to CG, 10th AF, dated December 22, 1942," January 5, 1943, Fourteenth Air Force, Historical Office, "China Air Task Force Correspondence."

15. McClure, *Fire and Fall Back,* 44.

16. Clayton Bissell to Commanding General, CATF, "Special Inspection, CATF" January 15, 1943, in "China Air Task Force Correspondence."

17. "Tables of Organization" C. L. Chennault to Commanding General, Tenth US Air Force, November 15, 1942, in "China Air Task Force Correspondence."

18. Clayton Bissell to Commanding General, CATF, "Tables of Organization," November 25, 1942, in "China Air Task Force Correspondence."

19. Clayton Bissell "Efficiency Report of Chen," May 19, 1943, in "China Air Task Force Correspondence."

Notes to Pages 72–81   233

20. Chennault to Bissell, reply to efficiency report, July 11, 1943, in "China Air Task Force Correspondence."

21. McClure, *Fire and Fall Back,* 48–49, 54.

22. Claire Lee Chennault, *Way of a Fighter,* ed. Robert Hotz (New York: G. P. Putnam's Sons, 1949), 180.

23. McClure, *Fire and Fall Back,* 54–55.

24. Holstrom, interview, 31.

25. McClure, *Fire and Fall Back,* 55.

26. 11th Bombardment Squadron, *History,* 43.

27. McClure, *Fire and Fall Back,* 56, 60.

28. Stilwell, *Papers,* 108.

29. Charles F. Romanus and Riley Sunderland, *United States Army in World War II, China Burma-India Theater: Stilwell's Mission to China* (Washington, DC: Government Printing Office, 1953), 179, 225–26, 241.

30. Joseph W. Stilwell, "Transcript of Diaries," January 8, 1944, http://www.hoover.org/sites/default/files/library/docs/1944_stilwell_diary.pdf.

31. Chennault, *Way of a Fighter,* 212.

32. COGUK to AQUILA writers number 18 1508 A 442, November 28, 1942, Fourteenth Air Force, Historical Office, "China Air Task Force Correspondence."

33. Mark Cotta Vaz, *Living Dangerously: The Adventures of Merian C. Cooper, Creator of King Kong* (New York: Villard Books, 2005) 312–13.

7. Aerial Offensive

1. Clair Lee Chennault, *Way of a Fighter,* ed. Robert Hotz (New York: G. P. Putnam's Sons, 1949), 218; Joseph W. Stilwell, *The Stilwell Papers,* ed. Theodore H. White (1948; repr., Cambridge, MA: Da Capo, 1975), 203.

2. Barbara W. Tuchman, *Stilwell and the American Experience in China, 1911–45* (1970; repr., New York: Grove, 1985), 9–10, 15; Jack Samson, *The Flying Tiger: The True Story of General Claire Chennault and the U. S. 14th Air Force in China* (1987; repr., Guilford, CT: The Lyons Press, 2005), 7; Chennault, *Way of a Fighter,* 218–19.

3. Chennault, *Way of a Fighter,* 216, 221–22, 225–26; Romanus and Sunderland, *United States Army in World War II, China-Burma-India Theater: Stilwell's Mission to China* (Washington, DC: Government Printing Office, 1953), 317, 320–21, 323; Tuchman, *Stilwell and the American Experience,* 367.

4. Joint History Office, *World War II Inter-Allied Conferences* (Washington, DC: Government Printing Office, 2003), 255, 260, 267–68, 270; Romanus and Sunderland, *Stilwell's Mission to China,* 279, 322.

5. Chennault, *Way of a Fighter,* 226.

6. Glenn E. McClure, *Fire and Fall Back: Casey Vincent's Story of Three Years in the China-Burma-India Theater, including the Fighting Withdrawal of the Flying Tigers from Eastern China* (San Antonio: Barnes, 1975), 93.

7. Fourteenth Air Force, 11th Bombardment Squadron, *Squadron History* (Maxwell Air Force Base, AL: Air Force Historical Research Agency, 1945), 47.

234   Notes to Pages 81–88

8. McClure, *Fire and Fall Back*, 66.

9. Headquarters, USAFFE, *Air Operations in the China Area: July 1937 to August 1945*, Japanese Monograph 76 (Washington, DC: Department of the Army, Office of the Chief of Military History, 1956), 75; Romanus and Sunderland, *Stilwell's Mission to China*, 337–38.

10. Fourteenth Air Force, Historical Office, "Backbone of the 14th," 1944, Air Force Historical Research Agency, Maxwell Air Force Base, AL, Reel A8296, microfilm, 3.

11. Orlando Air Base, Adjutant General's Section, Historical Branch, "Fourteenth Air Force Chronology," 1947, Air Force Historical Research Agency, Maxwell Air Force Base, AL, Reel A8303, microfilm, 6; "Backbone of the 14th," 4; Nicholas Millman, email to Daniel Jackson, December 19, 2007.

12. Glen Beneda, interview by Daniel Jackson, July 22, 2008.

13. Christopher Shores, Giovanni Massimello, Russell Guest, Frank Olynyk, Winfried Bock, and Andy Thomas, *Sicily and Italy to the Fall of Rome, 14 May 1943–5 June 1944*, vol. 4 of *A History of the Mediterranean Air War: 1940–1945* (London: Grub Street, 2018), 11–13, 63, 70, 93, 100.

14. Robert Kirtley, email to Daniel Jackson, Oct. 8, 2013.

15. Thomas D. Harmon, *Pilots Also Pray* (New York: Thomas Y. Crowell, 1944), 110.

16. Chennault to Naiden, August 2, 1942, Fourteenth Air Force, Historical Office, "China Air Task Force Correspondence."

17. Office of Statistical Control, *Army Air Forces Statistical Digest* (Washington, DC: Government Printing Office, 1945), 173; Fourteenth Air Force, Historical Office, "China Air Task Force Correspondence."

18. Chennault, *Way of a Fighter*, 252.

19. Carroll V. Glines, *Chennault's Forgotten Warriors: The Saga of the 308th Bomb Group in China* (Atglen, PA: Schiffer, 1995), 71.

20. McClure, *Fire and Fall Back*, 118.

21. Chennault, *Way of a Fighter*, 252.
Hiroshi Ichimura, email to Daniel Jackson, August 19, 2008.

22. Milton Miller, "Still More on General Moritaka Nakazone, [*sic*]" *Jing Bao Journal* (August–September 1984): 16; Richard Maddox, correspondence with Daniel Jackson, 2007.

23. David Lee Hill, *"Tex" Hill: Flying Tiger*, with Reagan Schaupp (2003; repr., San Antonio: Universal Bookbindery, 2004), 233–34, 239.

24. 76th Fighter Squadron, Historian, "Evasion Report of Capt. J. M. Williams," 1943, Air Force Historical Research Agency, Maxwell Air Force Base, AL, Reel A1322, microfilm.

25. Beneda interview 2008; "Backbone of the 14th."

26. Ki-44s may have shot down two P-38s: those of 1st Lt Walter Smith at Guilin on July 24, 1943, and of 1st Lt Art Masterson at Suichuan on February 12, 1944, though it remains unknown whether their assailants were Ki-43s or Ki-44s. Both aircraft went down near friendly airfields, and the pilots walked back without having to evade through occupied territory.

27. Chennault, *Way of a Fighter*, 251.

28. Major General J. A. Ulio to Mrs. Alleen C. Enslen, February 3, 1945.

Notes to Pages 91–101   235

8. Shipping Is the Key

1. Modern Hepu

2. Headquarters Fourteenth US Air Force, Maj F. G. Walsh, Assistant A2, "Evasion Story of Captain Lloyd Murphy," 1943, Air Force Historical Research Agency, Maxwell Air Force Base, AL, Reel A1322, microfilm.

3. Headquarters Fourteenth US Air Force, Maj F. G. Walsh, Assistant A2, "Evasion Story of Captain Lloyd Murphy," 1943, Air Force Historical Research Agency, Maxwell Air Force Base, AL, Reel A1322, microfilm.

4. US Army Air Forces, "Missing Air Crew Report 8018," 1943, M1380, National Archives and Research Administration, Washington, DC.

5. Walsh, "Evasion Story of Captain Lloyd Murphy."

6. Claire Lee Chennault, *Way of a Fighter*, ed. Robert Hotz (New York: G. P. Putnam's Sons, 1949), 222.

7. US Department of the Air Force, Office of Air Force History, *Air Interdiction in China in World War II*, by Joseph Taylor (Maxwell Air Force Base, AL: Air University, 1956), 5.

8. The 22nd Bomb Squadron also lost another five aircraft destroyed or written off on or near friendly airbases for a total of twelve B-25s lost in eleven weeks—out of an authorized strength of just sixteen bombers.

9. Fourteenth Air Force, 22nd Bombardment Squadron, *Squadron History*, Maxwell Air Force Base, AL: Air Force Historical Research Agency, February 1944, microfilm.

10. 22nd Bombardment Squadron, *History*, February–March 1944; US Army Air Forces, "Missing Air Crew Report 3009," 1944, M1380, National Archives and Research Administration, Washington, DC.

11. David K. Hayward, *A Young Man in the Wild Blue Yonder: Thoughts of a B-25 Pilot in World War II* (Huntington Beach, CA: 22nd Bomb Squadron Association, 2013), 171; US Department of the Air Force, Office of Air Force History, Oral History Interview: Brigadier General Everett W. Holstrom, interview by Dr. James C. Hasdorff, Air University, Maxwell Air Force Base, AL, 1988, 37.

12. Taylor, *Air Interdiction in China* 7–8.

13. US Army Air Forces, "Missing Air Crew Report 9612," 1944, M1380, National Archives and Research Administration, Washington, DC; Carroll V. Glines, *Chennault's Forgotten Warriors: The Saga of the 308th Bomb Group in China* (Atglen, PA: Schiffer), 1995, 247, 257–59, 260–62.

14. Taylor, *Air Interdiction in China*, 7–12, 18, 82.

9. Thanksgiving Day

1. 21st Photo Reconnaissance Squadron, *History of Flight C* (Maxwell Air Force Base, AL: Air Force Historical Research Agency, 1944).

2. Fourteenth Air Force, "Chinese-American Composite Wing History," 1944, Air Force Historical Research Agency, Maxwell Air Force Base, AL, Reel A8351, microfilm.

236 Notes to Pages 101–108

3. Carl Molesworth, *Wing to Wing: Air Combat in China, 1943–1945* (New York: Orion Books, 1990), 7, 10.

4. Fourteenth Air Force, "Comparison of Fourteenth Air Force and Chinese American Composite Wing Aircraft Losses," 1945, Air Force Historical Research Agency, Maxwell Air Force Base, AL, Reel A8352, microfilm, 6.

5. Glenn E. McClure, *Fire and Fall Back: Casey Vincent's Story of Three Years in the China-Burma-India Theater, including the Fighting Withdrawal of the Flying Tigers from Eastern China* (San Antonio: Barnes, 1975), 129.

6. George McMillan timeline, n.d., George B. McMillan Collection, Winter Garden Heritage Foundation, FL; Janet McMillan Alford, email to Daniel Jackson, July 15, 2017.

7. McMillan Flight Records, September 1943, McMillan Collection.

8. George McMillan timeline, McMillan Collection.

9. Joseph Cosgrove, "Pursued by Drunks," 1945, memoirs, Winter Garden Heritage Foundation, FL, 31.

10. 449th Fighter Squadron, *Squadron History* (Maxwell Air Force Base, AL: Air Force Historical Research Agency, 1944).

11. Paul Frillman and Graham Peck, *China: The Remembered Life* (Boston: Houghton Mifflin, 1968), 4, 174; Malcom Rosholt, *Rainbow around the Moon: An Autobiography* (Rosholt, WI: Rosholt House, 2004), 73, 114, 117; Terry Lautz, *John Birch: A Life* (New York: Oxford University Press, 2016), 73, 89; Claire Lee Chennault, *Way of a Fighter*, ed. Robert Hotz (New York: G. P. Putnam's Sons, 1949), 258–59.

12. Joseph Cosgrove to Mr. and Mrs. Malcolm McMillan, July 26, 1944, Winter Garden Heritage Foundation, FL; Cosgrove, "Pursued by Drunks," 103.

13. David Lee Hill, *"Tex" Hill: Flying Tiger*, with Reagan Schaupp (2003; repr., San Antonio: Universal Bookbindery, 2004), 227–28.

14. Carl Molesworth, *Sharks over China: The 23rd Fighter Group in World War II* (Washington, DC: Brassey's, 1994), 163.

15. "14th Air Force Strikes at Formosa: Surprise Raid Costs Enemy 46 Planes," *CBI Roundup*, December 3, 1943.

16. Hiroshi Ichimura email to Daniel Jackson, August 19, 2008.

17. McClure, *Fire and Fall Back*, 126, 132, 147.

18. Chennault, *Way of a Fighter*, 265–66.

19. Wesley Frank Craven and James Lea Cate, *Services around the World*, vol. 7 of *The Army Air Force in World War II* (1958; repr., Washington, DC: Government Printing Office, 1983), 128.

20. Molesworth, *Sharks over China*, 178.

21. 21st Photo Reconnaissance Squadron, *History of Flight C*.

22. Molesworth, *Sharks over China*, 103, 186–87.

23. McMillan's flight actually reported encountering twin-engine Ki-45 Type 2 two-seat fighters, codename "Nick," but because the Japanese army air force had no Ki-45s stationed in China at the time, it is far more likely they encountered Ki-48 Lilys, a similar-looking aircraft designed by the same engineer.

24. Keith Mahon, email to Daniel Jackson, May 17, 2014.

25. Ichimura to Jackson, August 19, 2008.

10. Ambush at Jiujiang

1. 76th Fighter Squadron, Office of the Intelligence Officer, "Report of Capt. George," 1944, Air Force Historical Research Agency, Maxwell Air Force Base, AL, Reel A1322, microfilm.

2. 76th Fighter Squadron, Office of the Intelligence Officer, "Evasion Story of 1st Lt. Jack A. Blanco," 1944, Air Force Historical Research Agency, Maxwell Air Force Base, AL, Reel A1322, microfilm.

3. 449th Fighter Squadron, "Report of Second Lieutenant Robert W. Campbell," 1944, Air Force Historical Research Agency, Maxwell Air Force Base, AL, Reel A1322, microfilm.

4. 76th Fighter Squadron, "Report of Capt. George"; 76th Fighter Squadron, Office of the Intelligence Officer, "Evader's Narrative Report: Homer D. Worthington," 1944, Air Force Historical Research Agency, Maxwell Air Force Base, AL, Reel A1322, microfilm.

5. AGAS-China, "Major Rex Barber's Evasion Story from Jap Held Territory," 1944, Air Force Historical Research Agency, Maxwell Air Force Base, AL, Reel A1322, microfilm.

6. 76th Fighter Squadron, "Report of Capt. George."

7. 76th Fighter Squadron, "Evasion Story of 1st Lt. Jack A. Blanco."

8. 449th Fighter Squadron, "Report of Second Lieutenant Robert W. Campbell."

9. AGAS-China, "Major Rex Barber's Evasion Story."

10. "Major Rex Barber's Evasion Story"; 76th Fighter Squadron, "Report of Capt. George."

11. 76th Fighter Squadron, "Evasion Story of 1st Lt. Jack A. Blanco"; AGAS-China, "Major Rex Barber's Evasion Story."

12. Thomas Harmon, "Missing," *Colliers*, June 3, 1944, 40; Robert Schultz to Taylor family, May 15, 1945.

13. AGAS-China, "Major Rex Barber's Evasion Story."

14. 76th Fighter Squadron, Historian, "Evasion Report of Capt. J. M. Williams."

15. AGAS-China, "Evader's Narrative Report: Lieutenant Cunningham."

16. James Reese, interview by Daniel Jackson, September 19, 2015.

17. 76th Fighter Squadron, "Evasion Story of 1st Lt. Jack A. Blanco."

18. US Army Air Forces, "Missing Air Crew Report 1644," 1944, M1380, National Archives and Research Administration, Washington, DC.

19. AGAS-China, "Evasion Story of Lt. Carl E. Kostol, O-749004."

20. 76th Fighter Squadron, "Evasion Story of 1st Lt. Jack A. Blanco."

21. AGAS-China, "Evasion Story of Lt. Carl E. Kostol." "Carl K. Cannon," World War 2 POW Archive, http://www.ww2pow.info;

22. John H. Roush Jr., *World War II Reminiscences* (Bloomington, IN: Xlibris, 2013), 272.

23. Fourteenth Air Force, "1st Lieutenant Eugene McGuire Evasion," 1943, Air Force Historical Research Agency, Maxwell Air Force Base, AL, Reel A1322, microfilm.

11. Operation Ichi-Go

1. Glenn E. McClure, *Fire and Fall Back: Casey Vincent's Story of Three Years in the China-Burma-India Theater, including the Fighting Withdrawal of the Flying Tigers from Eastern China* (San Antonio: Barnes, 1975), 148.

238   Notes to Pages 120–130

2. Glen Beneda, interview by Daniel Jackson, July 22, 2008.

3. AGAS-China, "Major Rex Barber's Evasion Story from Jap Held Territory," 1944, Air Force Historical Research Agency, Maxwell Air Force Base, AL, Reel A1322, microfilm; 76th Fighter Squadron, "Report of Capt. George," 1944, Air Force Historical Research Agency, Maxwell Air Force Base, AL, Reel A1322, microfilm.

4. Terry Lautz, *John Birch: A Life* (New York: Oxford University Press, 2016), 102, 112.

5. Headquarters, USAFFE, *Army Operations in China, January 1944 to August 1945,* Japanese Monograph 72 (Washington, DC: Department of the Army, Office of the Chief of Military History, 1956), 44, 46.

6. McClure, *Fire and Fall Back,* 159.

7. Malcolm Rosholt, *Rainbow around the Moon: An Autobiography* (Rosholt, WI: Rosholt House, 2004), 144; Headquarters, USAFFE, *Army Operations in China,* 13, 18.

8. Ch'i Hsi-sheng, *Nationalist China at War* (Ann Arbor: University of Michigan Press, 1982), 71–72; Headquarters, USAFFE, *Army Operations in China,* 14, 18–19; McClure, *Fire and Fall Back,* 164.

9. Headquarters, USAFFE, *Air Operations in the China Area,* 84–85, 91.

10. David Lee Hill, *"Tex" Hill: Flying Tiger,* with Reagan Schaupp (2003; repr., San Antonio: Universal Bookbindery, 2004), 239.

11. It is possible Morita had been attempting to collapse Jones's parachute and miscalculated, hitting the pilot instead.

12. US Army Air Forces, "Missing Air Crew Report 4732," 1944, M1380, National Archives and Research Administration, Washington, DC.

13. Joseph Cosgrove, "Pursued by Drunks," 1945, memoirs, Winter Garden Heritage Foundation, FL, 84–85.

14. US Army Air Forces, "Missing Air Crew Report 11971," 1944, M1380, National Archives and Research Administration, Washington, DC.

15. McClure, *Fire and Fall Back,* 161.

16. Headquarters, USAFFE, *Air Operations in the China Area,* 89.

17. Hiroshi Ichimura email to Daniel Jackson, Sept. 17, 2008.

18. US Army Chinese Combat Command, "Report on the Salween Campaign," Kunming, China, 1945, Air Force Historical Research Agency, Maxwell Air Force Base, AL.

19. McClure, *Fire and Fall Back,* 160–61, 164; Headquarters, USAFFE, *Army Operations in China,* 19.

20. Malcolm Rosholt, *Dog Sugar 8: A Novel of the 14th Air Force Flying Tigers in China in World War II* (Rosholt, WI: Rosholt House, 1977), 134–35; Rosholt, *Rainbow around the Moon,* 144; Chennault, *Way of a Fighter,* 261.

21. McClure, *Fire and Fall Back,* 165, 168.

22. Rosholt, *Rainbow around the Moon,* 144–46; Claire Lee Chennault, *Way of a Fighter,* ed. Robert Hotz (New York: G. P. Putnam's Sons, 1949), 257, 259, 296; McClure, *Fire and Fall Back,* 164.

23. Rosholt, *Dog Sugar 8,* 26–27.

24. Chennault, *Way of a Fighter,* 256.

25. McClure, *Fire and Fall Back,* 164.

26. Rosholt, *Dog Sugar 8,* 134–36.

27. McClure, *Fire and Fall Back,* 159, 164, 166, 168; Rosholt, *Dog Sugar 8,* 151–52.

Notes to Pages 130–138   239

28. Rana Mitter, *Forgotten Ally: China's World War II, 1937–1945* (New York: Houghton Mifflin Harcourt, 2013), 346.

29. McClure, *Fire and Fall Back,* 165.

30. Charles F. Romanus and Riley Sunderland, *United States Army in World War II, China-Burma-India Theater: Stilwell's Command Problems* (Washington, DC: Government Printing Office, 1956), 369.

12. Collateral Damage

1. Joseph Cosgrove, "Pursued by Drunks," 1945, memoirs, Winter Garden Heritage Foundation, FL, 93–94.

2. Glenn E. McClure, *Fire and Fall Back: Casey Vincent's Story of Three Years in the China-Burma-India Theater, including the Fighting Withdrawal of the Flying Tigers from Eastern China* (San Antonio: Barnes, 1975), 170.

3. Wesley Frank Craven and James Lea Cate, *The Pacific: Matterhorn to Nagasaki, June 1944 to August 1945,* vol. 5 of *The Army Air Force in World War II* (1953, repr., Washington, DC: Government Printing Office, 1983), 222–23.

4. McClure, *Fire and Fall Back,* 157; Malcolm Rosholt, *Dog Sugar 8: A Novel of the 14th Air Force Flying Tigers in China in World War II* (Rosholt, WI: Rosholt House, 1977), 147.

5. McClure, *Fire and Fall Back,* 170.

6. Lou Stoumen, "Chennault and the Fourteenth" *Yank,* October 20, 1944.

7. McClure, *Fire and Fall Back,* 168, 170–71, 177, 202–3, 209.

8. Robert Burris, correspondence with Daniel Jackson, July 2007–August 2009.

9. Burris to Jackson July 2007–August 2009.

10. Jerry Doughty, interview by Daniel Jackson, May 2007.

11. US Army Air Forces, "Missing Air Crew Report 6145," 1944, M1380, National Archives and Research Administration, Washington, DC.

12. Burris to Jackson July 2007–August 2009.

13. US Army Air Forces, "Missing Air Crew Report 6145."

14. Joseph Cosgrove to George McMillan, July 26, 1944, George B. McMillan Collection, Winter Garden Heritage Foundation, FL.

15. Claire Chennault to Malcolm McMillan, June 29, 1944, McMillan Collection.

16. McClure, *Fire and Fall Back,* 171.

17. The Adjutant General to Mr. and Mrs. Malcolm McMillan, October 3, 1946, McMillan Collection.

18. Jim Hyde, interview by Daniel Jackson, May 2007.

19. The 449th lost two P-38s to ground fire in central China during the summer of 1943 and two in Indochina in May and July 1945.

20. Timothy Jung, email to Daniel Jackson, October 6, 2008.

21. The comparison to the P-40 here is key. Fourteenth Air Force lost so many Mustangs in part because beginning in the second half of 1944, they served in such volume, eventually displacing the P-40 as the staple US fighter in China. Warhawks also went toe-to-toe with Japanese soldiers, and yet far fewer fell to surface fire. Of the 237 P-51s reported missing in the China Theater, more than 54 percent fell to surface fire, compared to only 36 percent of the 219 P-40s lost. Not enough P-38s served in China to make a meaningful

240   Notes to Pages 138–148

statistical comparison, though the Lightning clearly fared better in the ground-attack regime. P-47s served in China in such small numbers as to be statistically insignificant.

22. Carl Molesworth, *Sharks over China: The 23rd Fighter Group in World War II* (Washington, DC: Brassey's, 1994), 206–7.

23. AGAS-China, "Story of Harold E. Miller's Evasion," 1945, Air Force Historical Research Agency, Maxwell Air Force Base, AL, Reel A1322, microfilm.

24. AGAS-China, "Notes of Evasion from Enemy Territory by Lt. Edgar W. Headley."

25. Fourteenth Air Force, 25th Fighter Squadron, *Squadron History* (Maxwell Air Force Base, AL: Air Force Historical Research Agency, 1945); Fourteenth Air Force, 528th Fighter Squadron, *Squadron History.*

26. 25th Fighter Squadron, *Squadron History.*

27. US Army Chinese Combat Command, "Report on the Salween Campaign," Air Force Historical Research Agency, Maxwell Air Force Base, AL.

28. Charles F. Romanus and Riley Sunderland, *United States Army in World War II, China-Burma-India Theater: Stilwell's Command Problems* (Washington, DC: Government Printing Office, 1956), 405.

29. 74th Fighter Squadron, "Maj. Cruikshank Evasion Report," 1944, Air Force Historical Research Agency, Maxwell Air Force Base, AL, Reel A1322, microfilm.

30. Though Cruikshank made it back to friendly territory, his injuries necessitated an immediate return to the United States. Between his bailout on June 25, the death of George McMillan on June 24, and the capture of Maj Donald Quigley, commander of the 75th Fighter Squadron, on August 10, Fourteenth Air Force lost three experienced squadron commanders to Ichi-go in just a month and a half.

31. 74th Fighter Squadron, S-2 Officer, "Second Walkout Story of Major Cruikshank, Arthur W.," 1944, Air Force Historical Research Agency.

32. Malcolm Rosholt, *Rainbow around the Moon: An Autobiography* (Rosholt, WI: Rosholt House, 2004), 127.

33. 75th Fighter Squadron, "Return Story of Lieutenant Oswin Elker," 1944, Air Force Historical Research Agency.

34. AGAS-China, "The Story of George W. Denton."

35. AGAS-China, "Statement of Gordon C. Berven."

36. Liu interview 2013, Romanus and Sunderland, *Time Runs Out in CBI,* 147, 161.

37. Peter Harmsen, "The U. S. Firebombing of Wuhan," China in WWII (blog), September 12, 2015 (part 1), www.chinaww2.com/2015/09/12/the-us-firebombing-of -wuhan-part-1; September 16, 2015 (part 2), http://www.chinaww2.com/2015/09/16/the -us-firebombing-of-wuhan-part-2/.

38. Claire Lee Chennault, *Way of a Fighter,* ed. Robert Hotz (New York: G. P. Putnam's Sons, 1949), 328–29.

13. With the Communists

1. Lee O. Gregg, "Shot Down May 6th, 1944, near Hankow." Unpublished diary, 1944. Copy in author's possession; MIS-X Section, CPM Branch, "Evasion Report No. 431, Gregg, Lee O.," 1944, Air Force Historical Research Agency, Maxwell Air Force Base, AL; AGAS-China, "Story of Glen Beneda," 1944, Air Force Historical Research Agency,

Notes to Pages 148–158   241

Maxwell Air Force Base, AL, Reel A1322, microfilm; AGAS-China, "Story of Lee O. Gregg"; Glen Beneda, interview by Daniel Jackson, July 22, 2008.

2. Jay Taylor, *The Generalissimo: Chiang Kai-shek and the Struggle for Modern China* (Cambridge, MA: Harvard University Press, 2009), 175–77; David D. Barrett, *Dixie Mission: The United States Army Observer Group in Yenan, 1944,* China Research Monographs (Berkeley, CA: Center for Chinese Studies, 1970), 20–21.

3. Gregg, "Shot Down"; AGAS-China, "Story of Lee O. Gregg"; Beneda interview 2008; MIS-X Section, "Evasion Report No. 431."

4. Li Xiaolin, dir., *Touching the Tigers: 60-Day Fraternity, 60-Year Friendship* (Beijing: The Chinese People's Association for Friendship with Foreign Countries, 2011), DVD.

5. Ed and Elinor Beneda, interview by Daniel Jackson, November 29, 2015.

6. Claire Lee Chennault, *Way of a Fighter,* ed. Robert Hotz (New York: G. P. Putnam's Sons, 1949), 241, 243–44; Armit W. Lewis, "My Ship Quit on Me," in *Up Sun!,* ed. Wallace Little and Charles Goodman (Memphis, TN: Castle Books, 1990), 118.

14. The Secret Airfield

1. Claire Lee Chennault, *Way of a Fighter,* ed. Robert Hotz (New York: G. P. Putnam's Sons, 1949), 98.

2. Gong Kaibing, interview by Kun Shi and Daniel Jackson, August 7, 2017.

3. US Army Air Forces, "Missing Air Crew Report 5811," 1944, M1380, Record Group 92, Records of the Office of the Quartermaster General, National Archives and Research Administration, Washington, DC.

4. Carl Molesworth, *Wing to Wing: Air Combat in China, 1943–1945* (New York: Orion Books, 1990), 75–76.

5. Fourteenth Air Force, "Chinese-American Composite Wing History," Air Force Historical Research Agency, Maxwell Air Force Base, AL, Reel A8351, microfilm, 23.

6. Glenn E. McClure, *Fire and Fall Back: Casey Vincent's Story of Three Years in the China-Burma-India Theater, including the Fighting Withdrawal of the Flying Tigers from Eastern China* (San Antonio: Barnes, 1975), 180.

7. Donald S. Lopez, *Into the Teeth of the Tiger* (Washington, DC: Smithsonian Books, 1997), 160.

8. Daniel Ford, *Flying Tigers: Claire Chennault and his American Volunteers, 1941–1942,* 2nd ed. (New York: Harper Collins, 2014), 246, 333.

9. Stephen L. McFarland and Wesley Phillips Newton, *To Command the Sky: The Battle for Air Superiority over Germany, 1942–1944* (Washington, DC: Smithsonian Institution Press, 1991), 96, 129–30.

10. John R. Alison, interview by Daniel Jackson, May 9, 2007.

11. René J. Francillon, *Japanese Aircraft of the Pacific War* (London: Putnam, 1979), 214.

12. Office of Statistical Control, *Army Air Forces Statistical Digest* (Washington, DC: Government Printing Office, 1945), 118.

13. Carl Molesworth, *P-40 Warhawk vs Ki-43 Oscar: China 1944–45,* Duel 8 (Oxford: Osprey, 2008), 38, 42; Military Analysis Division, *Japanese Air Power,* US Strategic Bombing Survey 62 (Washington, DC: Government Printing Office, 1946).

242   Notes to Pages 158–171

14. Wesley Frank Craven and James Lea Cate, *Men and Planes,* vol. 6 of *The Army Air Forces in World War II* (1955; repr., Washington, DC: Government Printing Office, 1983), 566, 615.

15. *Army Air Forces Statistical Digest,* 64.

16. Alison interview 2007.

17. David D. Barrett, *Dixie Mission: The United States Army Observer Group in Yenan, 1944.* China Research Monographs (Berkeley, CA: Center for Chinese Studies, 1970), 13; Chennault, *Way of a Fighter,* 326.

18. Barrett, *Dixie Mission,* 13–14, 22, 27–30.

19. Whittlesey arrived in Yan'an as a first lieutenant but received a promotion to captain shortly thereafter.

20. Fourteenth Air Force subsequently called the airfield "Varoff Field," in honor of its first "customer."

21. XX Bomber Command, Escape and Evasion Section, "Walk-Out Report Eleven Crewmembers of B-29 Aircraft Number 42–63363," 1945, Air Force Historical Research Agency, Maxwell Air Force Base, AL, Reel A1323, microfilm.

22. Wade Giles: Chang Ko-wei.

23. Paul Crawford, interview by Daniel Jackson, October 15, 2016.

24. Barrett, *Dixie Mission,* 81–82; XX Bomber Command, "Walk-Out Report Eleven Crewmembers of B-29 Aircraft Number 42–63363"; XX Bomber Command, "Walk-Out Report, B-29 Aircraft #237"; John F. Fuller, *Thor's Legions: Weather Support to the U. S. Air Force and Army, 1937–1987* (Boston: American Meteorological Society, 1991), 113, 118.

25. Francis Morgan, Carl Rieger, Watson Lankford, Dwight Collins, Thomas Carroll, and Harry Changnon, "Richard Vickery's Crew and the Nanking Mission," *Memories* 43 (April 1992): 2–3; XX Bomber Command, "Walk-Out Report, B-29 Aircraft #237."

26. Morgan et al., "Richard Vickery's Crew," 3–4, 8–9; XX Bomber Command, "Walk-Out Report, B-29 Aircraft #237."

27. AGAS-China, "Evasion Story of 1st Lt. Walter Krywy," 1945, Air Force Historical Research Agency, Maxwell Air Force Base, AL, Reel A1322, microfilm.

28. AGAS-China, "Interrogation of Lt. Fisher, Co-pilot of C-46 #779," 1945, Air Force Historical Research Agency, Maxwell Air Force Base, AL, Reel A1323, microfilm; AGAS-China, "Evasion Story of 1st Lt. Walter Krywy."

29. Carolle J. Carter, *Mission to Yenan: American Liaison with the Chinese Communists, 1944–1947* (Lexington: University Press of Kentucky, 1997), 79; AGAS-China, "Interrogation of Lt. Fisher."

30. Morgan et al., "Richard Vickery's Crew," 10; XX Bomber Command, "Walk-Out Report, B-29 Aircraft #237"; AGAS-China, "Evasion Story of 1st Lt. Walter Krywy"; AGAS-China, "Interrogation of Lt. Fisher"; US Army Air Forces, "Missing Air Crew Report 14725," 1945, M1380, National Archives and Records Administration, Washington, DC.

31. Crawford interview 2016; US Army Air Forces, "Missing Air Crew Report 14756," 1945, M1380.

32. US Army Air Forces, "Missing Air Crew Report 14759," 1945, M1380; Crawford interview 2016.

33. Carter, *Mission to Yenan,* 81.

Notes to Pages 172–177 243

15. Thai Fighters

1. Fourteenth Air Force, 25th Fighter Squadron, *Squadron History* (Maxwell Air Force Base, AL: Air Force Historical Research Agency, October 1944).

2. Donald S. Lopez, *Into the Teeth of the Tiger* (Washington, DC: Smithsonian Books, 1997), 167–69.

3. 25th Fighter Squadron, *Squadron History*, November 1944.

4. Michael D. Roberts, "Fallen Tiger," *Cleveland Magazine*, May 19, 2004.

5. Direk Jayanama, *Thailand and World War II*, ed. Jane Keyes (Chiang Mai: Silkworm Books, 2008), 75–77, 153; E. Bruce Reynolds, *Thailand's Secret War: OSS, SOE, and the Free Thai Underground during World War II* (Cambridge: Cambridge University Press, 2005), 8; Edward M. Young, *Aerial Nationalism: A History of Aviation in Thailand* (Washington, DC: Smithsonian Institution Press, 1995), 186; Daniel Ford, *Flying Tigers: Claire Chennault and his American Volunteers, 1941–1942*, 2nd ed. (New York: Harper Collins, 2014), 126.

6. Jayanama, *Thailand and World War II*, 91; Reynolds, *Thailand's Secret War*, xv, 12, 20–21; Young, *Aerial Nationalism*, 183–91.

7. All six hailed from the Tenth Air Force: Capt Albert Abraham, 1st Lt Theodore H. Demezas, Staff Sgt Laurel D. Kinsey, 1st Lt James K. Kintz, 1st Lt Malcolm MacKenzie, and 2nd Lt Dean E. Wimer. A seventh, Maj David N. Kellogg, escaped with the help of the OSS.

8. "6 Army Fliers Welcome Rest in Thai Prison Camp: They Never Worked, Had Plenty to Eat and Read, but Glad to be Free Again," *The Pittsburgh Press*, September 3, 1945; "Yank Internees Recall Courtesy," *India-Burma Theater Roundup* 4, no. 1, September 13, 1945.

9. Bob Bergin, *Tracking the Tigers: Flying Tiger, OSS and Free Thai Operations in World War II Thailand* (Fairfax, VA: Banana Tree Press, 2011) loc. 1042–1082, Kindle.

10. Jayanama, *Thailand and World War II*, 91.

11. Sakpinit Promthep et al., *Ninety Years of Air Power: Royal Thai Air Force* (Bangkok: Royal Thai Air Force, 2003), 56–57.

12. Young, *Aerial Nationalism*, 185, 187, 194, 198, 216.

13. Carroll V. Glines, *Chennault's Forgotten Warriors: The Saga of the 308th Bomb Group in China* (Atglen, PA: Schiffer, 1995), 105, 108–9.

14. Fourteenth Air Force, G Flight, 35th Photo Squadron, *Flight Intelligence Reports* (Maxwell Air Force Base, AL: Air Force Historical Research Agency, 1945).

15. Sterling Barrow, correspondence with Daniel Jackson, 2007, 2011; US Army Air Forces, "Missing Air Crew Report 10057," 1944, M1380, National Archives and Research Administration, Washington, DC.

16. Fong Inma, interview by Daniel Jackson and Richard Hakanson, trans. Wiyada Kantarod, December 8, 2018; Staff Section 2 Field Air Force to Commander in Chief of the Royal Thai Air Force, "Answer to Radiogram 33/6 item 1, 7 November 1944," November 10, 1944, Bangkok, Royal Thai Air Force Museum; Field Police Commander Region 1 to Field Police Commissioner, "Details about Fighter Aircraft," November 20, 1944, Royal Thai Air Force Museum.

17. Sterling Barrow, unpublished diary, 1944; Barrow to Jackson 2011, 2012; Arthur W. Clark, correspondence with Daniel Jackson, 2012.

244   Notes to Pages 181–188

18. Flight Sergeant 3rd Class Chuladit Detkunchorn, "Five vs. Twenty-One," translated by Wiyada Kantarod, Richard Hakanson, and Sakpinit Promthep, *Aviation Magazine* (April 1965); Wing Commander Kamrop Bleangkam, "When I Sent a Mustang to Hell Over Lampang," 1963, Bangkok, Royal Thai Air Force Museum; Boonserm Satrabhaya, *Chiang Mai and the Aerial War* (Bangkok: Saitharn Publication House, 2003), 122–23; Young, *Aerial Nationalism*, 205; 25th Fighter Squadron, *History*, November 1944; 449th Fighter Squadron, *History*, November 1944; US Army Air Forces, "Missing Air Crew Report 10064," 1944, M1380, National Archives and Research Administration, Washington, DC; Joseph N. Fodor, interview by Daniel Jackson, June 21, 2007.

19. 25th Fighter Squadron, *History*, November 1944; 449th Fighter Squadron, *History*, November 1944; Roberts, "Fallen Tiger."

20. 25th Fighter Squadron, *History*, November 1944; Joseph N. Fodor, interview by Daniel Jackson, June 21, 2007.

21. Young, *Aerial Nationalism*, 206, 212, 214.

22. AGAS-China, "Evasion Story of Rudolph C. Shaw, 26th Ftr Sq," 1944, Air Force Historical Research Agency, Maxwell Air Force Base, AL, Reel A1322, microfilm.

23. Dixee R. Bartholomew-Feis, *The OSS and Ho Chi Minh: Unexpected Allies in the War Against Japan* (Lawrence: University Press of Kansas, 2006), 9, 24–25, 27; Young, *Aerial Nationalism*, 176.

24. Bartholomew-Feis, *The OSS and Ho Chi Minh*, 92; Lewis Sherman Bishop and Shiela Bishop Irwin, *Escape from Hell: An AVG Flying Tiger's Journey* (Bloomington, IL: Tiger Eye, 2005), 5, 8–9, 16, 36.

25. Bartholomew-Feis, *The OSS and Ho Chi Minh*, 23–24, 28, 30, 32.

26. AGAS-China, "Evasion Story of Rudolph C. Shaw."

27. Charles Fenn, *At the Dragon's Gate: With the OSS in the Far East* (Annapolis, MD: Naval Institute Press, 2004), 2, 131, 133, 143.

28. US Army Air Forces, "Missing Air Crew Report 12927," 1944, M1380, National Archives and Research Administration, Washington, DC.

29. AGAS-China, "Evasion of Major Edwin J. Witzenberger, 26th Fighter Squadron, from French Indo-China," 1945, Air Force Historical Research Agency, Maxwell Air Force Base, AL, Reel A1322, microfilm.

30. Bartholomew-Feis, *The OSS and Ho Chi Minh*, 119, 124.

31. AGAS-China, "Evasion of Major Edwin J. Witzenberger."

32. Bruce Carnachan, correspondence with Daniel Jackson, 2007; Milton Miller, *Tiger Tales* (Manhattan, KS: Sunflower University Press, 1984), 98–102.

33. Fenn, *At the Dragon's Gate*, 22, 138–39, 143, 152–54; Bartholomew-Feis, *The OSS and Ho Chi Minh*, 153–54, 157, 169, 171.

34. David G. Marr, *Vietnam 1945: The Quest for Power* (Berkley: University of California Press, 1995), 537.

16. The Final Offensive

1. J. G. Ballard, *Miracles of Life: Shanghai to Shepperton, an Autobiography* (New York: Liverlight, 2013), 75, 87, 93; Carl Molesworth, *Sharks over China: The 23rd Fighter Group in World War II* (Washington, DC: Brassey's, 1994), 87–89, 251.

Notes to Pages 189–193   245

2. John F. Kinney, *Wake Island Pilot: A World War II Memoir* (Washington, DC: Potomac Books, 1995), 116, 131–32, 134.

3. Though designated a tactical reconnaissance squadron, the 118th flew P-40s and P-51s as a fighter squadron in the 23rd Fighter Group, though some of its aircraft did have aerial cameras.

4. Molesworth, *Sharks over China*, 163–64, 252, 240; Luther C. Kissick to Daniel Jackson, July 19, 2008; Hakan Gustavsson, *Sino-Japanese Air War, 1937–1945: The Longest Struggle* (Stroud, England: Fonthill Media, 2016), 185; AGAS-China, "Walkout Story of Harold B. Tollett," 1945, Air Force Historical Research Agency, Maxwell Air Force Base, AL, Reel A1323, microfilm.

5. Headquarters, USAFFE, *Army Operations in China, January 1944 to August 1945*, Japanese Monograph 72, Washington, DC: Department of the Army, Officer of the Chief of Military History, 143.

6. Gong Kaibing, interview by Kun Shi and Daniel Jackson, August 7, 2017.

7. Military History and Translation Office, "An Interview with Maj. Gen. Huang Xiang-chun" in *The Immortal Flying Tigers: An Oral History of the Chinese-American Composite Wing* (Taipei: Ministry of National Defense, 2009), 207.

8. Military History and Translation Office, "An Interview with Mr. Lu Mao-yin" in *The Immortal Flying Tigers*, 227.

9. Fourteenth Air Force, Historical Office, "Chihkiang Campaign: 10 April 1945 to 31 May 1945," 1945, Air Force Historical Research Agency, Maxwell Air Force Base, AL, Reel A8302, microfilm.

10. Headquarters, USAFFE, *Army Operations in China*, 168.

11. Lewis Sherman Bishop and Sheila Bishop Irwin, *Escape from Hell: An AVG Flying Tiger's Journey* (Bloomington, IL: Tiger Eye, 2005), 50–51; James D. McBrayer Jr., *Escape! Memoir of a World War II Marine Who Broke Out of a Japanese POW Camp and Linked Up with Chinese Communist Guerrillas* (Jefferson, NC: McFarland, 1995), 10.

12. Gregory J. W. Urwin, *Victory in Defeat: The Wake Island Defenders in Captivity* (Annapolis, MD: Naval Institute Press, 2010), 284.

13. James D. McBrayer, *Escape*, 54; James Taylor, "The Diddled Dozen," in *Up Sun!*, ed. Wallace Little and Charles Goodman (Memphis: Castle Books, 1990), 112.

14. Capt Howard C. Allers, O-397410, 22BS, 341BG; Capt Donald J. Burch, O-667034, 7FS(P), 3FG(P); 2nd Lt Samuel E. Chambliss Jr., O-827385, 529FS, 311FG; 1st Lt Walter A. Ferris, O-702524, 16FS, 51FG; 1st Lt Lauren A. Howard, O-800542, 8FS(P), 3FG(P); 1st Lt Harold J. Klota, O-756616, 28FS(P), 3FG(P); 2nd Lt Murray L. Lewis, O-789254, 22BS, 341BG; 1st Lt Freeland K. Mathews, O-795603, 8FS(P), 3FG(P); 2nd Lt Samuel McMillan Jr., O-815739, 26FS, 51FG; Maj Donald L. Quigley, O-432207, 75FS, 23FG; 1st Lt Richard R. Rouse, O-735669, 11BS, 341BG; 1st Lt Vernon D. Schaefer, O-750858, 770BS, 462BG; 1st Lt Benjamin A. Stahl, O-727572, 25FS, 51FG; 2nd Lt James E. Thomas, O-812174, 118TRS, 23FG; 2nd Lt Alton L. Townsend, O-672253, 11BS, 341BG; 1st Lt James E. Wall, O-422740, 530FS, 311FG; 2nd Lt George T. Walsh, O-741817, 11BS, 341BG; 1st Lt Henry I. Wood, O-789035, 75FS, 23FG.

15. Roger Mansell, "Hakodate POW Camp #4, Ashibetsu," Center for Research: Allied POWs under the Japanese, www.mansell.com/pow_resources/camplists/hokkaido/hakodate_4_main.html; Taylor, "Diddled Dozen," 112; Leo Aime LaBrie, *A Double Dose*

246 Notes to Pages 193–200

of Hard Luck: The Extraordinary True Story of a Two-Time Prisoner of War, Lt. Col. Charles Lee Harrison (New York: Page, 2016); Urwin, *Victory in Defeat,* 302.

16. Supreme Commander for the Allied Powers, *MacArthur in Japan: The Occupation: Military Phase,* vol. 1, supplement, of *Reports of General MacArthur,* ed. Charles A. Willoughby (Washington, DC: Government Printing Office, 1994), 90–92.

17. Urwin, *Victory in Defeat,* 305.

18. Gong interview 2017.

19. "The Ambassador in China (Hurley) to the Secretary of State," August 20, 1945, in *Foreign Relations of the United States: Diplomatic Papers, 1945, the Far East, China,* vol. 7, doc. 392, https://history.state.gov/historicaldocuments/frus1945v07/d392.

20. Tsou Tang, *America's Failure in China, 1941–50* (Chicago: University of Chicago Press, 1963), 51.

21. Rana Mitter, *Forgotten Ally: China's World War II, 1937–1945* (New York: Houghton Mifflin Harcourt, 2013), 346.

22. Claire Lee Chennault, *Way of a Fighter,* ed. Robert Hotz (New York: G. P. Putnam's Sons, 1949), 326; Ch'i Hsi-sheng, *Nationalist China at War* (Ann Arbor: University of Michigan Press, 1982), 80.

23. Edward Witsell to Mr. and Mrs. Malcolm Y. McMillan, October 2, 1946, George B. McMillan Collection. Winter Garden Heritage Foundation, FL.

24. George McMillan to Sarah Elizabeth McMillan, May 24, 1945, McMillan Collection.

25. J. H. Pollock Jr., to Mr. and Mrs. Malcolm Y. McMillan, January 30, 1945, McMillan Collection; T. B. Larkin to Malcolm Y. McMillan, September 24, 1946, McMillan Collection; Chennault to McMillan, June 29, 1944, McMillan Collection.

26. US Army Air Forces, "Missing Air Crew Report 10057" 1944, M1380, National Archives and Research Administration, Washington, DC; Sakpinit Promthep email to Daniel Jackson, May 27, 2012; Sterling Barrow correspondence with Daniel Jackson. 2007–2012.

27. Michael D. Roberts, "Fallen Tiger," *Cleveland Magazine,* May 19, 2004.

28. Mitter, *Forgotten Ally,* 366.

29. Michael D. Pearlman, *Truman and MacArthur: Policy, Politics, and the Hunger for Honor and Renown* (Indianapolis: Indiana University Press, 2008), 258.

30. Joseph W. Stilwell, *The Stilwell Papers,* ed. Theodore H. White (1948; repr., Cambridge, MA: Da Capo, 1975), 76–80; Paul Frillman and Graham Peck, *China: The Remembered Life* (Boston: Houghton Mifflin, 1968), 228; Jay Taylor, *The Generalissimo: Chiang Kai-shek and the Struggle for Modern China* (Cambridge, MA: Harvard University Press, 2009), 297.

31. Chennault, *Way of a Fighter,* 223.

32. AGAS-China, "Interrogation of Lt. Fisher, Co-pilot of C-46 #779," 1945, Air Force Historical Research Agency, Maxwell Air Force Base, AL, Reel A1323, microfilm; Tang, *America's Failure in China,* 51.

33. This does not include the rescues of forty-eight Chinese airmen detailed in American reports, the Doolittle Raiders, naval aviators, or airmen from other numbered air forces not based in China.

34. David D. Barrett, *Dixie Mission: The United States Army Observer Group in Yenan,*

1944. China Research Monographs (Berkeley, CA: Center for Chinese Studies, 1970), 37.

35. Glenn E. McClure, *Fire and Fall Back: Casey Vincent's Story of Three Years in the China-Burma-India Theater, including the Fighting Withdrawal of the Flying Tigers from Eastern China* (San Antonio: Barnes, 1975), 219.

36. Ma Yufu, *Col. C. L. Chennault and Flying Tigers*, ed. Li Xiangping (Beijing: China Intercontinental Press, 2003), 73.

37. Gong interview 2017.

38. Ma, *Col. C. L. Chennault and Flying Tigers*, 73.

39. John Chappell, "Missing WWII Pilot Is Finally Home," thepilot.com.

Epilogue

1. Ed Beneda and Elinor Beneda, interview by Daniel Jackson, November 29, 2015; Glen Beneda, interview by Daniel Jackson, July 22, 2008; Xiaolin Li, *Touching the Tigers: 60-Day Fraternity, 60-Year Friendship* (Beijing: Chinese People's Association for Friendship with Foreign Countries, 2011), DVD.

Bibliography

Interviews and Correspondence

Alford, Janet McMillan. Correspondence with Daniel Jackson. July 15, 2017.

Alison, John R. Interview by Daniel Jackson. May 9, 2007.

Barrow, Sterling. Correspondence with Daniel Jackson. 2007–2011.

Beneda, Ed, and Elinor Beneda. Interview by Daniel Jackson. November 29, 2015.

Beneda, Glen. Interview by Daniel Jackson. July 22, 2008.

Burris, Robert. Correspondence with Daniel Jackson. July 2007–August 2009.

Carnachan, Bruce. Correspondence with Daniel Jackson. 2007.

Chal, Cindy Cole. Correspondence with Daniel Jackson. March 2017.

Clark, Arthur W. Correspondence with Daniel Jackson. 2012.

Crawford, Paul. Interview by Daniel Jackson. October 15, 2016.

Doughty, Jerry. Interview by Daniel Jackson. May 2007.

Findley, Lisa. Interview by Daniel Jackson. March 4, 2016.

Fodor, Joseph N. Interview by Daniel Jackson. June 21, 2007.

Fong Inma. Interview by Daniel Jackson and Richard Hakanson. Translated by Wiyada Kantarod. December 8, 2018.

Forbes, Francis C. Interview by William Forbes. January 2012. Copy in author's possession.

Gong Kaibing. Interview by Kun Shi and Daniel Jackson. August 7, 2017.

Ha, Thomas. Interview by Samuel Hui. September 2014. Copy in author's possession.

Hayward, David. Correspondence with Daniel Jackson. 2015–2020.

Hill, David Lee "Tex." Interview by Frank Boring. February 22, 1991. Grand Valley State University Digital Collections. www.digitalcollections.library.gvsu.edu.

Hyde, Jim. Interview by Daniel Jackson. May 2007.

Kirtley, Robert. Correspondence with Daniel Jackson. October 8, 2013.

Kissick, Luther C. Correspondence with Daniel Jackson. July 19, 2008.

Li Genzhi. Interview by Daniel Jackson and Kun Shi. August 10, 2017.

Li Yuntang. Interview by Samuel Hui and Pan I-jung. February 2019. Copy in author's possession.

Liu Zhenghua. Interview by Samuel Hui and Pan I-jung. March 2013. Copy in author's possession.

250   Bibliography

Lu Caiwen. Interview by Daniel Jackson. March 2009.
Maddox, Richard. Correspondence with Daniel Jackson. 2007.
Mahon, Keith. Correspondence with Daniel Jackson. May 17, 2014.
Older, Charles. Interview by Frank Boring. April 26, 1991. Grand Valley State University Digital Collections. www.digitalcollections.library.gvsu.edu.
Pei Haiqing. Interview by Kun Shi and Daniel Jackson. August 10, 2017.
Reese, James. Interview by Daniel Jackson. September 19, 2015.
Smith, R. T. Interview by Frank Boring. April 23, 1991. Grand Valley State University Digital Collections. www.digital collections.library.gvsu.edu.
Tan Guanyue. Interview by Kun Shi and Daniel Jackson. August 7, 2017.
Wang Shuming. Interview by Liu Tingyang. Jun. 13, 1991. Grand Valley State University Digital Collections. www.digitalcollections.library.gvsu.edu.
Wu Eyang. Interview by Kun Shi. August 18, 2017. Copy in author's possession.

Archival and Unpublished Sources

"The Ambassador in China (Hurley) to the Secretary of State." August 20, 1945. In *Foreign Relations of the United States: Diplomatic Papers, 1945, the Far East, China.* Vol. 7. Document 392. https://history.state.gov/historicaldocuments/frus1945v07/d392.
American Volunteer Group Combat Reports. General Claire Chennault Foundation, Washington, DC.
Chiang Kai-shek Papers. Academia Historica, Taipei, Taiwan.
Dorn, Frank, Papers. Hoover Institution Archives, Stanford, CA.
Evasion Reports. Air Force Historical Research Agency, Maxwell Air Force Base, AL. Reels A1322–3. Microfilm.
Gregg, Lee O. "Shot Down May 6th, 1944, near Hankow." Unpublished diary, 1944. Copy in author's possession.
Japanese Monograph Series. Washington, DC: Department of the Army, Office of the Chief of Military History, 1956.
Kelley, John M. "Claire Lee Chennault: Theorist and Campaign Planner." Master's thesis, School of Advanced Military Studies, 1993.
McMillan, George B., Collection. Winter Garden Heritage Foundation, FL.
Schultz, Robert, to Taylor family, May 15, 1945. Copy in author's possession.
Soong, T. V., Papers. Hoover Institution, Stanford, CA.
Stilwell, Joseph W., Papers. Hoover Institution, Stanford, CA.
Ulio, J. A., to Mrs. Alleen C. Enslen, February 3, 1945. Copy in author's possession.
Unit Histories. Air Force Historical Research Agency, Maxwell Air Force Base, AL. Reels A1322, A8296, A8302–3, A8351–2. Microfilm.
US Army Air Forces. Missing Air Crew Reports, 1943–1947. M1380. Record Group 92. Records of the Office of the Quartermaster General. National Archives and Research Administration, Washington, DC.
US Department of the Air Force. Office of Air Force History. *Air Interdiction in China in World War II,* by Joseph Taylor. Maxwell Air Force Base, AL: Air University, 1956.

Bibliography   251

US Department of the Air Force. Office of Air Force History. *Oral History Interview: Brigadier General Everett W. Holstrom*. Interview by Dr. James C. Hasdorff. Maxwell Air Force Base, AL: Air University, 1988.

US Department of the Air Force. Office of Air Force History. *Oral History Interview: Lieutenant Colonel Horace E. Crouch*. Interview by Dr. James C. Hasdorff. Maxwell Air Force Base, AL: Air University, 1989.

World War II Reports. Royal Thai Air Force Museum, Bangkok.

Published Sources

Ashcroft, Bruce. *We Wanted Wings: A History of the Aviation Cadet Program*. Randolph Air Force Base, TX: Headquarters Air Education and Training Command History Office, 2005.

Ballard, J. G. *Miracles of Life: Shanghai to Shepperton, an Autobiography*. New York: Liveright, 2013.

Barrett, David D. *Dixie Mission: The United States Army Observer Group in Yenan, 1944*. China Research Monographs. Berkeley, CA: Center for Chinese Studies, 1970.

Barrett, David P., and Larry N. Shuyu, eds. *Chinese Collaboration with Japan, 1939–1945: The Limits of Accommodation*. Stanford, CA: Stanford University Press, 2001.

Bartholomew-Feis, Dixee. *The OSS and Ho Chi Minh: Unexpected Allies in the War Against Japan*. Lawrence, KS: University Press of Kansas, 2006.

Bartsch, William H. *Doomed at the Start: American Pursuit Pilots in the Philippines, 1941–1942*. College Station: Texas A&M University Press, 1995.

Bergin, Bob. *Tracking the Tigers: Flying Tiger, OSS and Free Thai Operations in World War II Thailand*. Fairfax, VA: Banana Tree Press, 2011. Kindle.

Bernstein, Richard. *China 1945: Mao's Revolution and America's Fateful Choice*. New York: Alfred A. Knopf, 2014.

Bishop, Lewis Sherman, and Sheila Bishop Irwin. *Escape from Hell: An AVG Flying Tiger's Journey*. Bloomington, IL: Tiger Eye, 2005.

Bodson, Herman. *Downed Allied Airmen and Evasion of Capture: The Role of Local Resistance Networks in World War II*. London: McFarland, 2005.

Boonserm Satrabhaya. *Chiang Mai and the Aerial War*. Bangkok: Saitharn Publication House, 2003.

Buchan, Eugenie. *A Few Planes for China: The Birth of the Flying Tigers*. Lebanon, NH: University Press of New England, 2017.

Caine, Philip D. *Aircraft Down! Evading Capture in WWII Europe*. Washington, DC: Brassey's, 1997.

Carter, Carolle J. *Mission to Yenan: American Liaison with the Chinese Communists, 1944–1947*. Lexington: University Press of Kentucky, 1997.

Carter, Kit C., and Robert Mueller, comps. *U.S. Army Air Forces in World War II: Combat Chronology, 1941–1945*. 1973. Reprint, Washington, DC: Center for Air Force History, 1991.

Chang, Iris. *The Rape of Nanking: The Forgotten Holocaust of World War II*. New York: Penguin Books, 1997.

252 Bibliography

Chennault, Claire Lee. "The Role of Defensive Pursuit: The Next Great War." *Coast Artillery Journal* 76, no. 6 (November–December 1933): 411–17.

———. *Way of a Fighter*. Edited by Robert Hotz. New York: G. P. Putnam's Sons, 1949.

Ch'i Hsi-sheng. *Nationalist China at War*. Ann Arbor: University of Michigan Press, 1982.

Clark, Arthur W. *Eyes of the Tiger: China, 1944–1945*. Chapel Hill, NC: Self-published, 2015.

Craven, Wesley Frank, and James Lea Cate. *Men and Planes*. Vol. 6 of *The Army Air Force in World War II*. 1955. Reprint. Washington, DC: Government Printing Office, 1983.

———. *Services around the World*. Vol. 7 of *The Army Air Force in World War II*. 1958. Reprint. Washington, DC: Government Printing Office, 1983.

———. *The Pacific: Matterhorn to Nagasaki, June 1944 to August 1945*. Vol. 5 of *The Army Air Force in World War II*. 1953. Reprint. Washington, DC: Government Printing Office, 1983.

Fenn, Charles. *At the Dragon's Gate: With the OSS in the Far East*. Annapolis, MD: Naval Institute Press, 2004.

Ford, Daniel. *Flying Tigers: Claire Chennault and His American Volunteers, 1941–1942*. 2nd ed. New York: Harper Collins, 2014.

Francillon, René J. *Japanese Aircraft of the Pacific War*. London: Putnam, 1979.

Frillman, Paul, and Graham Peck. *China: The Remembered Life*. Boston: Houghton Mifflin, 1968.

Fuller, John F. *Thor's Legions: Weather Support to the U.S. Air Force and Army, 1937–1987*. Boston: American Meteorological Society, 1991.

Glines, Carroll V. *Chennault's Forgotten Warriors: The Saga of the 308th Bomb Group in China*. Atglen, PA: Schiffer, 1995.

———. *The Doolittle Raid: America's Daring First Strike against Japan*. Atglen, PA: Schiffer, 2000.

Gustavsson, Hakan. *Sino-Japanese Air War, 1937–1945: The Longest Struggle*. Stroud: Fonthill Media, 2016.

Harmon, Thomas D. *Pilots Also Pray*. New York: Thomas Y. Crowell, 1944.

Hayward, David K. *A Young Man in the Wild Blue Yonder: Thoughts of a B-25 Pilot in World War II*. Huntington Beach, CA: 22nd Bomb Squadron Association, 2013.

Hemingway, Ernest. "Chinese Build Air Field." In *By-Line: Ernest Hemingway, Selected Articles and Dispatches of Four Decades*. Edited by William White. New York: Scribner Classics, 2002.

Hill, David Lee. *"Tex" Hill: Flying Tiger*. With Reagan Schaupp. 2003. Reprint. San Antonio: Universal Bookbindery, 2004.

Hotz, Robert B. *With General Chennault: The Story of the Flying Tigers*. 1943. Reprint. Washington, DC: Zenger Publishing, 1980.

Jayanama, Direk. *Thailand and World War II*. Edited by Jane Keyes. Chiang Mai: Silkworm Books, 2008.

Joint History Office. *World War II Inter-Allied Conferences*. Washington, DC: Government Printing Office, 2003.

Kinney, John F. *Wake Island Pilot: A World War II Memoir*. Washington, DC: Potomac Books, 1995.

LaBrie, Leo Aime. *A Double Dose of Hard Luck: The Extraordinary True Story of a Two-Time Prisoner of War, Lt. Col. Charles Lee Harrison*. New York: Page, 2016.

Bibliography   253

Lary, Diana. "Drowned Earth: The Strategic Breaching of the Yellow River Dyke, 1938." *War in History* 8, no. 2 (April 2001): 191–207.

Lautz, Terry. *John Birch: A Life.* New York: Oxford University Press, 2016.

Li Xiaolin, dir. *Touching the Tigers: 60-Day Fraternity, 60-Year Friendship.* Beijing: Chinese People's Association for Friendship with Foreign Countries, 2011. DVD.

Li Yongxiang. "The Ethnic Minorities in Tengchong County and the Anti-Japanese War." *Annual Review of the Institute for Advanced Social Research* 6 (October 2011): 1–17.

Little, Wallace, and Charles Goodman, eds. *Up Sun!* Memphis: Castle Books, 1990.

Lopez, Donald S. *Into the Teeth of the Tiger.* Washington, DC: Smithsonian Books, 1997.

Ma Yufu. *Col. C. L. Chennault and Flying Tigers.* Edited by Li Xiangping. Beijing: China Intercontinental Press, 2003.

Marr, David G. *Vietnam 1945: The Quest for Power.* Berkley: University of California Press, 1995.

McBrayer, James D. Jr. *Escape! Memoir of a World War II Marine Who Broke Out of a Japanese POW Camp and Linked Up with Chinese Communist Guerrillas.* Jefferson, NC: McFarland, 1995.

McClure, Glenn E. *Fire and Fall Back: Casey Vincent's Story of Three Years in the China-Burma-India Theater, including the Fighting Withdrawal of the Flying Tigers from Eastern China.* San Antonio: Barnes, 1975.

McFarland, Stephen L., and Wesley Phillips Newton. *To Command the Sky: The Battle for Air Superiority over Germany, 1942–1944.* Washington, DC: Smithsonian Institution Press, 1991.

Military Analysis Division. *Japanese Air Power.* US Strategic Bombing Survey 62. Washington, DC: Government Printing Office, 1946.

Military History and Translation Office. *The Immortal Flying Tigers: An Oral History of the Chinese-American Composite Wing.* Taipei: Ministry of National Defense, 2009.

Miller, Milton. *Tiger Tales.* Manhattan, KS: Sunflower University Press, 1984.

Mitter, Rana. *Forgotten Ally: China's World War II, 1937–1945.* New York: Houghton Mifflin Harcourt, 2013.

Molesworth, Carl. *P-40 Warhawk vs Ki-43 Oscar: China 1944–45.* Duel 8. Oxford: Osprey, 2008.

———. *Sharks over China: The 23rd Fighter Group in World War II.* Washington DC: Brassey's, 1994.

———. *Wing to Wing: Air Combat in China, 1943–1945.* New York: Orion Books, 1990.

Office of Statistical Control. *Army Air Forces Statistical Digest.* Washington, DC: Government Printing Office, 1945.

Okerstrom, Dennis R. *Dick Cole's War: Doolittle Raider, Hump Pilot, Air Commando.* Columbia: University of Missouri Press, 2015.

Olynyk, Frank J. *AVG & USAAF (China-Burma-India Theater) Credits for the Destruction of Enemy Aircraft in Air-to-Air Combat World War 2.* N.p.: Self-published, 1986.

Pearlman, Michael D. *Truman and MacArthur: Policy, Politics, and the Hunger for Honor and Renown.* Indianapolis: Indiana University Press, 2008.

Plating, John D. *The Hump: America's Strategy for Keeping China in World War II.* College Station: Texas A&M University Press, 2011.

254 Bibliography

Promthep, Sakpinit et al. *Ninety Years of Air Power: Royal Thai Air Force.* Bangkok: Royal Thai Air Force, 2003.

Reynolds, E. Bruce. *Thailand's Secret War: OSS, SOE, and the Free Thai Underground during World War II.* Cambridge: Cambridge University Press, 2005.

Romanus, Charles F., and Riley Sunderland. *United States Army in World War II, China-Burma-India Theater: Stilwell's Command Problems.* Washington, DC: Government Printing Office, 1956.

———. *United States Army in World War II, China-Burma-India Theater: Stilwell's Mission to China.* Washington, DC: Government Printing Office, 1953.

———. *United States Army in World War II, China-Burma-India Theater: Time Runs out in CBI.* Washington, DC: Government Printing Office, 1959.

Rosholt, Malcolm. *Dog Sugar 8: A Novel of the 14th Air Force Flying Tigers in China in World War II.* Rosholt, WI: Rosholt House, 1977.

———. *Rainbow around the Moon: An Autobiography.* Rosholt, WI: Rosholt House, 2004.

Roush, John H. Jr. *World War II Reminiscences.* Bloomington, IN: Xlibris, 2013.

Samson, Jack. *The Flying Tiger: The True Story of General Claire Chennault and the U.S. 14th Air Force in China.* 1987. Reprint. Guilford, CT: Lyons, 1987.

Scott, James M. *Target Tokyo: Jimmy Doolittle and the Raid That Avenged Pearl Harbor.* New York: W. W. Norton, 2015.

Scott, Robert Lee. *God Is My Copilot.* New York: Ballantine Books, 1943.

Shilling, Erik. *Destiny: A Flying Tiger's Rendezvous with Fate.* Pomona, CA: Ben-Wal Printing, 1993.

Shores, Christopher, Brian Cull, and Yasuho Izawa. *The Defense of Sumatra to the Fall of Burma.* Vol. 2 of *Bloody Shambles: The First Comprehensive Account of Air Operations Over South-East Asia, December 1941–May 1942.* London: Grub Street, 1993.

Shores, Christopher, Giovanni Massimello, Russell Guest, Frank Olynyk, Winfried Bock, and Andy Thomas. *Sicily and Italy to the Fall of Rome, 14 May 1943–5 June 1944.* Vol. 4 of *A History of the Mediterranean Air War, 1940–1945.* London: Grub Street, 2018.

Smith, R. T. *Tale of a Tiger: The Adventure-Packed Daily Diary of One of the Flying Tigers' Top Aces.* Van Nuys, CA: Tiger Originals, 1986.

Stilwell, Joseph W. *The Stilwell Papers.* Edited by Theodore H. White. 1948. Reprint. Cambridge, MA: Da Capo, 1975.

Supreme Commander for the Allied Powers [Douglas A. MacArthur]. *MacArthur in Japan: The Occupation, Military Phase.* Vol. 1, supplement, of *Reports of General MacArthur,* edited by Charles A. Willoughby. Washington, DC: Government Printing Office, 1994.

Tang, Tsou. *America's Failure in China, 1941–50.* Chicago: University of Chicago Press, 1963.

Taylor, Jay. *The Generalissimo: Chiang Kai-shek and the Struggle for Modern China.* Cambridge, MA: Harvard University Press, 2009.

Tuchman, Barbara W. *Stilwell and the American Experience in China, 1911–45.* 1970. Reprint. New York: Grove, 1985.

Urwin, Gregory J. W. *Victory in Defeat: The Wake Island Defenders in Captivity.* Annapolis, MD: Naval Institute Press, 2010.

Bibliography   255

Vaz, Mark Cotta. *Living Dangerously: The Adventures of Merian C. Cooper, Creator of King Kong*. New York: Villard Books, 2005.

White, Theodore H., and Annalee Jacoby. *Thunder out of China*. Cambridge, MA: Da Capo, 1980.

Wichtrich, A.R. *MIS-X: Top Secret*. Raleigh, NC: Pentland Press, Inc, 1997.

Xia Kui. *Saving American Pilots*. Translated by Zhang Jusheng. N.p., 2006.

Young, Edward M. *Aerial Nationalism: A History of Aviation in Thailand*. Washington, DC: Smithsonian Institution Press, 1995.

Young, Jim. *Mayday over China: The Diary of Jim Young, WWII POW*. N.p.: Self-published by Andrew Priddy, 2011. Kindle.

Yu, Maochun. *OSS in China: Prelude to the Cold War*. Annapolis, MD: Naval Institute Press, 1996.

Index

1st Air Brigade, JAAF, 85
1st Fighter Group, USAAF, 83
1st Pursuit Squadron, AVG, 17–18
2nd Bombardment Squadron
  (Provisional), CACW, 101
2nd Pursuit Squadron, AVG, 17–19
2nd Weather Reconnaissance Squadron,
  USAAF, 164
3rd Air Division, JAAF, 81, 84, 86, 121,
  123, 159, 213–14
3rd Bombardment Squadron
  (Provisional), CACW, 190
3rd Pursuit Squadron, AVG, 17–18, 58
Fourth Army, GMD, 127
4th Bombardment Squadron
  (Provisional), CACW, 190
4th Fighter Group, CAF, 2
Fourth War Area, GMD, 190
Fifth Air Army, JAAF, 123–24, 159, 214
5th Air Division, JAAF, 174–75
Fifth Air Force, CAF, 17
Fifth Army, GMD, 5, 39, 210
Fifth Army Air Force, USAAF, 93
5th Fighter Group (Provisional), CACW,
  155–57, 190, 216
5th Division, N4A, 145, 147–50, 154, 204,
  219
7th Bombardment Group, USAAF, 189
7th Fighter Squadron (Provisional),
  CACW, 101
Seventh War Area, GMD, 69

Eighth Army, USA, 194
Eighth Army Air Force, USAAF, 60, 157
Eighth Route Army, CCP, xiv, 160, 162–64,
  166–71, 217, 224
Ninth Army Air Force, USAAF, 60
9th Photo Reconnaissance Squadron,
  USAAF, 99–100
Ninth War Area, GMD, 126, 128
Tenth Army, GMD, 139, 215
Tenth Army Air Force, USAAF, vii, 52, 57,
  59, 68, 71–72, 77, 212, 243
11th Air Regiment, JAAF, 108
Eleventh Army, IJA, 126, 215
11th Bombardment Squadron, USAAF,
  52–53, 57, 71, 92, 100, 120, 213
Twelfth Army Air Force, USAAF, 83
Fourteenth Army Air Force, USAAF, viii,
  xviii, 21, 29, 115, 139, 144, 154, 181,
  189, 191, 213, 216; aircraft, xi, 86, 106,
  177, 216; airmen, 92, 113, 185–86,
  191–2; aircraft/airmen reported
  missing, vii, 93–94, 98, 101, 137–38,
  157, 186; antishipping, 95, 97, 215;
  enemy claimed destroyed, 105, 157,
  159, 189; establishment, 77, 213;
  expansion to Suichuan, 106, 121;
  intelligence, 47, 76, 92, 99, 103, 121,
  127–8
16 Squadron, RTAF, 175–78, 181
17th Bombardment Group, USAAF,
  23–24

258   Index

17th Fighter Squadron (Provisional), CACW, 190

Twentieth Army, IJA, 190–91, 217

Twentieth Army Air Force, USAAF, vii, 130, 154, 160, 192, 215

XXth Army Group, GMD, 139

XX Bomber Command, USAAF, 163, 165–66, 169

21st Photo Reconnaissance Squadron, USAAF, 100, 176, 214

22nd Bombardment Squadron, USAAF, 57, 62, 93–94, 235

Twenty-Third Army, IJA, 126, 215

23rd Fighter Group, USAAF, 57–59, 72, 81, 86, 102, 104, 156, 189, 203, 223, 245

25th Air Regiment, JAAF, 85, 87–88, 109, 115, 124, 126, 214, 223

25th Fighter Squadron, USAAF, 139–40, 172–73, 177, 181

26th Fighter Squadron, USAAF, 138, 183

27th Fighter Squadron (Provisional), CACW, 190

28th Division, GMD, 153

33rd Air Regiment, JAAF, 85, 231

35th Photo Reconnaissance Squadron, USAAF, 176

35th Pursuit Group, USAAF, 70

37th Division, IJA, 121

51st Fighter Group, USAAF, 57

56th Division, IJA, 38

62 Squadron, RTAF, 175

64th Air Regiment, JAAF, 37–38

68th Composite Wing, USAAF, 105, 132, 139

Sixty-Ninth Army, GMD, 150, 153, 199

69th Composite Wing, USAAF, 106, 139

Seventy-First Army, GMD, 38, 212

74th Fighter Squadron, USAAF, 58, 84, 100, 141, 189, 217, 223

75th Fighter Squadron, USAAF, 58, 172, 223, 230, 240

76th Fighter Squadron, USAAF, 58, 82, 101, 106, 214, 223

85th Air Regiment, JAAF, 82, 84, 108, 213

90th Air Regiment, JAAF, 189

118th Flying Training Regiment, JAAF, 109

118th Tactical Reconnaissance Squadron, USAAF, 189, 217, 245

183rd Division, GMD, 114

254th Kokutai, JNAF, 94

308th Bombardment Group, USAAF, 81, 97, 176, 214

311th Fighter Group, USAAF, 160

341st Bombardment Group, USAAF, 176

374th Bombardment Squadron, USAAF, 96

425th Bombardment Squadron, USAAF, 85

449th Fighter Squadron, USAAF, 88, 103, 125, 186, 223; aircraft of, 101, 173, 178, 186, 213, 239; designation, 84, 213; Jiujiang, 101, 109, 116; and McMillan, 102, 106, 108, 132, 134–35, 137, 214; move to Suichuan, 106, 214; North Africa, 83, 104, 213

491st Bombardment Squadron, USAAF, 94

A6M (Mitsubishi) Type Zero Carrier Fighter "Zero," 2, 10, 15, 38, 82, 88, 94, 101, 105, 210

Adair, C. B. "Skip", 14

Aeronautical Affairs Commission, 2–3, 21–22, 224

Afrika Korps, 82

Air Corps Tactical School (ACTS), 3, 14

aircraft carrier, 24–25, 80

Air Defense Command (ADC), 200

airfield construction/repair, 8, 61

Air Force Historical Research Agency (AFHRA), 171

Air-Ground Aid Section (AGAS), viii, 68, 115–16, 162, 184, 216–17

air-ground liaison teams, 190

Air Transport Command (ATC), USAAF, 106, 167–68

Aldworth, Richard T., 13

Algeria, 83, 213

Allers, Howard C., 62–68, 117, 188, 191–92, 245

Index   259

American Graves Registration Service (AGRS), 197
American Volunteer Group (AVG), 4, 10–11, 13–14, 19, 21, 28–29, 33, 52–53, 55, 175, 185; aircraft/airmen reported missing, vii, 20–21, 186, 217; captured airmen, 20, 174, 182, 191–92, 217; combat, 16, 18, 22, 37–38, 48, 50, 57–58, 60, 157, 211–12, 231; commanded by Chennault, viii, xviii, 60, 99; disbandment, 57–58, 101, 212; joining, xviii, 12, 210–11; spirit, 70–71, 73–74, 102; veterans, xix, 100–103, 204
Americus, Georgia, 27
An, Mr., 90–92
Anhui Province, 22, 32, 166
Ankrim, Thomas, 173
Annapolis. *See* United States Naval Academy
Anyi County, 113, 221
Aomori, 192
Arcadia Conference, 25, 211
Arlington National Cemetery, 197
Armstrong, Eric, 170
Armstrong, John D., 16
Army Air Force Proving Ground. *See* Eglin Field
Arnold, Henry H. "Hap," 32–33, 59, 81, 84, 130
Ashibetsu, 192, 194, 218
Ashurst, William, 192–93
Associated Press, 185
Atkinson, Peter W., 16
atomic bomb, 193–94, 217
Australia, 192
Aviation Cadet Qualifying Exam (ACQE), 26

B-10 (Martin) Model 139, 175
B-24 (Consolidated) Liberator, 81, 84–85, 154, 156, 189; antishipping, 92, 95–98, 215; statistics of missing, xviii, 88, 138; Thailand, 176, 214
B-25 (North American) Mitchell, 23, 74, 78, 81, 94, 117, 129, 139–40, 153, 157,

176; antishipping, 89, 92–95, 97–98, 109, 213, 215; arrival in China, 52, 54, 56–57, 212; CACW, 100–101, 104–5, 190; Doolittle Raid (1942), 29–32, 212; Hankou mission (1944), xi, 120, 125–6; Hong Kong raid (1942), 44, 62–63, 65, 68, 188, 212; secret airfield rescue, 164–65, 169, 217; statistics of missing, xviii, 88, 138, 235; Thanksgiving Day raid (1943), 70, 100, 104–5, 214
B-29 (Boeing) Superfortress, 202; atomic bombings, 193, 217; bombing Japan, 81, 121, 129–30, 150–51, 169, 215; crews captured, 44, 216; crews rescued by Communists, 154, 160, 162, 164–67, 217; firebombing Hankou, 130, 144, 169, 216; statistics of missing, xviii, 88, 98, 138
back flag. *See* blood chit
Bailuozhen, 156–57, 216, 221
Baishiyi, 2
Ballard, J. G., 187–88
bandits, 117, 152
Bangkok, 174–75, 181, 197
Baoqing, 142, 190, 222
Baoshan, 38, 143
Barber, Rex T., 86, 107, 109, 111, 115–16, 118–20, 215
Barrett, David D., 161–62, 164, 196
Barrow, Sterling, 176–77, 197, 207
Batavia, Java, 14
Bayse, William W., 57
Beardsley, Billie M., 85–86, 110, 213
Beat, Walter B., 85
Becker, Maxwell, 116
Beihai, 90–91
Beijing, 201, 221. *See also* Beiping
Beiping, 5, 123, 154, 163, 191–92, 209, 217, 221
Beiping-Hankou Railway, 121, 123, 126, 147, 150, 163, 215
Beitun Field, 176
Belgian Resistance, 46
Beneda, Brian, 204

260   Index

Beneda, Edward "Ed," 202, 204, 206–7, 219
Beneda, Elinor, 202, 204, 206–7, 219
Beneda, Glen E., 21, 106; arrival in China, 82, 146, 213; Hankou mission (1944), xii-xvi, 2, 60, 120, 125, 146, 156, 215; joining USAAF, 26–27, 146; post-war, 202–6, 218–19; rescued by Communists, 145–54, 160, 199, 205–6, 218–19
Beneda, Henry, 202, 206, 219
Bertrand, 184
Berven, Gordon C., 143
Betts, Richard, 89
Birch, John M., 34, 103, 121
Bishop, Lewis S., 182, 191–92, 217
Bissell, Clayton L., 57–59, 69–73, 76, 78
Black River, 184
Blanco, Jack A., 110, 112, 115–19
Bloemfontein, MS, 12, 14, 210
blood chit, xiv, 21–22, 44, 90, 110, 167, 211, 226
Bodson, Herman, 46
Breese, Fred, 89–90
Bremerton, Naval Station, Washington, 24
Brisbane, Australia, 14
British Army Aid Group (BAAG), 68–69
Broussard, Frank L., 163
Burch, Donald J., 45, 216, 245
Burge, James, 56
Burma, xx, 36, 40, 44, 174, 179, 197; Tenth Air Force, vii, 57, 173; AVG, 12, 16, 18, 22, 28–29, 37, 211; CATF, 60, 71; Japanese conquest, 26, 32, 37–40, 53, 59, 74–75, 102–3, 173, 175–6; north campaign, 39, 74–75, 77–80, 82, 129–31, 144, 190, 195, 199; reconnaissance, 100, 176
Burma Road, 17, 28, 38, 48, 50, 210, 212
Busan, 192

C-46 (Curtiss) Commando, 165, 168
C-47 (Douglas) Skytrain, xviii, 35, 53, 59, 88, 161, 194

C-87 (Consolidated) Liberator Express, 77–78
Calcutta, 173
Cam Ranh Bay, 78
Cambodia, 25, 182
Campbell, Robert W., 109–16, 119, 215
Cannon, Carl K., 117–18
Cao Bang, 182–83, 216
Caofang, 115
Cao Xingren, 69, 221
Ca River, 93
Carswell, Horace S. Jr., 96–97
Central Aircraft Manufacturing Company (CAMCO), 13–14, 36
Central Military Academy, 9, 43, 126, 143, 225
Chalermkiat Wattanangura, 177–79, 181
Chambliss, Samuel E. Jr., 191–92, 245
Champion, Robert, 161–62
Chan, Charlie, 27
Chan, Joseph, 92
Changde, 128
Changsha, 5, 9, 47, 126–29, 132, 139–40, 205, 210–11, 215
Chen, Mr., 113
Chengdu, 130, 164, 215
Chenggong, 96
Cheng Ku-wan, 92
Chennault, Claire Lee, 51; AGAS, 68–69, 162; air plan, 75–77–81, 195, 213; air support to Nationalist armies, ix, 128, 199; antishipping, 78–80, 92–93, 95, 98; AVG formation, 10, 210; AVG operations, 14–21, 28, 32–33, 52, 57–58, 60, 211; Rex Barber, 107, 118; CAF adviser, 2–4, 209; CATF, 57–61, 68–76, 212; commander of Flying Tigers, viii, xviii-xix; Communists, 150, 153–54, 160, 162; Doolittle Raid reaction, 32–33, 57; firebombing, 93, 144; Fourteenth Air Force established, 77–78, 213; Ho Chi Minh, 183, 185–86; intelligence, 3, 99–100, 128; George McMillan, 88, 101–3, 136–37, 197;

P-38s vs P-51s, 83–88, 213; Stilwell, 25–26, 74–78, 80, 129–31, 133, 195, 198, 213; summer air offensive (1943), 81–82, 84–85, 87, 121; Casey Vincent, 70–74, 81, 84, 87, 104–6, 128, 130, 133, 140; warning net, 3, 17–18, 33, 60, 116, 128, 178, 209
Chennault, Max, 4
Chenxian, 142
Chiang Kai-shek, 8, 28, 42, 127–28, 175, 211, 221; Chennault, 3–4, 32, 77, 130, 154, 160; Communists, ix, 8, 75, 148, 154, 161, 166, 171, 194, 198–99, 218; Nationalist Army, 5, 8–9, 38; New Fourth Army, xv, 148; regime, xii, 9–11, 195, 198; Soviet Union, 4, 209; Stilwell, 25–26, 38, 75, 77, 79, 129–30, 143, 160–61; uniting China, 3, 5, 8; Yellow River, 5, 50, 144
Chiang, Madame. See Song Meiling
Chiang Mai, 175–76, 178
Chiang Rai, 175, 178, 180
Chiarello, Robert, 90
Chiayi, 85, 221
China Air Task Force (CATF), vii–viii, xviii, 29, 57, 60, 68, 71–78, 98, 157, 186, 192, 212–13
China-Burma-India (CBI) Theater, vii–viii, 52, 59, 63, 131, 212
China Expeditionary Army, IJA, 121, 123, 215
China lobby, 27
China National Aviation Corporation (CNAC), 53, 59
China Theater, x; Arcadia conference, 25, 211; statistics of missing aircraft/ airmen, xv, 46, 56, 87, 99–100, 117, 137, 157, 159, 186, 192, 196, 201, 239; Wedemeyer, 143, 216
Chinese Air Force (CAF), 2–4, 10, 51, 100–101, 209–10
Chinese-American Composite Wing (CACW), 100, 105, 120, 124, 155, 157, 190, 216
Chinese army. See Nationalist Army

Chinese Communist Party (CCP): collaborators, 43; expansion, 151, 154, 163, 195; liaising with Americans, 148–49, 154, 161, 171, 196, 216; Nationalists, ix, 5, 8, 10, 42, 75, 127, 148–50, 161–62, 194–95, 199, 218; rescuing American airmen, 149–50, 154, 160, 163, 171, 199
Chinese Expeditionary Force (CEF), 74, 129, 139, 176, 215
Chinese National Military Commission, 69
Chinese People's Association for Friendship with Foreign Countries, 204
Chinese War Ministry, 99
Chitose Air Base, 194
Chongqing, 14, 26, 28, 75, 153, 161–62, 221; air raids, 1, 4, 81, 85, 210; terminus for Doolittle Raid, 30, 34–35, 59
Chuladit Detkunchorn, 178–80
Chung Ho-keng, 92
Churchill, Winston, 25, 79–80, 211
Citadel Military College, 12
Civil War, Chinese, 195, 198, 201, 218
Clague, Douglas, 68
Clark, Arthur, 176–77, 197, 207
Cleveland, Ohio, 27, 139
Cochard, Hubert, 184
Colbert, Robert T., 86–87
Cold War, viii, 199–200
Cole, Richard E. "Dick," 204
collaboration, collaborator, ix, 42–43, 47, 161, 166–68, 210; betraying airmen, 32, 44–46, 66, 112, 216; helping airmen, xx, 44–46, 91; imagined, 88, 116
Columbia, South Carolina, 24–25
Columbia River, 24
Combined Chiefs of Staff (CCS), 77, 82
conscription, 8–10, 39, 41
Conway, Richard "Dick," 179
Cooper, Merian C., 59–61, 70, 73, 75–76, 81, 104, 212
Cosgrove, Joseph, 103, 135–36

262   Index

Crawford, Paul M., 27, 160, 170–71, 207, 217
Cruikshank, Arthur W. Jr., 140–41, 241
Cultural Revolution, 200–201, 218
Cunningham, Joseph W. "Joe," 63–69, 117
Curtiss-Wright Corporation, 158
CW-21 (Curtiss-Wright) Demon, xviii, 20, 211

Dadong, 43
Dai Li, 128
Dai people, 36
Da Nang, 93, 96
Davis, Doreen, 185–86
Davis, Ena, 201
Dawu Mountain, 145, 221
DC-3. See C-47
Decoux, Jean, 182
Defense POW/MIA Accounting Agency (DPAA), 197, 201, 207, 219
Demon Interceptor. See CW-21
Denton, George W., 142
Desper, Dale, 178
Dinjan, 52–54, 56–57
Dixie Mission, 161–62, 164, 166, 168, 170, 196, 216
Dog Sugar Eight (DS8), 47, 127
Do Len, 94
Dong Dang, 182
Dong Qiyuan, 49, 221
Dongting Lake, 124, 156, 159
Don Muang airfield, 175
Donovan, William J. "Wild Bill," 59, 76
Doolittle, James H. "Jimmy," 25, 29–32, 34, 52, 103, 204, 212
Doolittle Raid, 29–31, 59, 100, 106, 212, 214; aftermath, 79; capture, 44, 59; reception, 32–33, 57, 246; veterans, 52, 93, 204, 230
Dutch East Indies, 28, 70, 82
Dothan, Alabama, 160

E14Y (Yokosuka) Navy Type 0 Small Reconnaissance Seaplane "Glen," 24
East China Sea, 31

eastern line of communications (ELOC), 106–7
East River, 68
Egle, Elinor. See Beneda, Elinor
Egle, Ralph W., 26, 154, 202
Eglin Field, Florida, 25, 31, 102
Eisenhower, Dwight D., 26, 195
Elker, Oswin H. "Moose," 142
Ellwood Oil Field, California, 24
Enslen, Lewden M., 84, 88
European Theater of Operations (ETO), xi, xvi, xviii, xx, 26–27, 42, 46–47, 60, 78, 83–84, 195, 229

F-4/5 (Lockheed) Lightning, xviii, 44, 99–100, 176, 216
F-6 (North American) Mustang. See P-51
F4U (Vought) Corsair, 102
F6F (Grumman) Hellcat, 102
Fang Xianjue, 139–40, 215
Feng Pei-chian, 156
Fenn, Charles, 183–86
Findley, William S., 44
Fisher, Albert J., 167–69, 199
Flag. See blood chit
Flomer, Leonard, 178
Flying Tigers, xii, xviii, 28–29, 32, 50–51, 73–74, 81, 185
Fodor, Joseph N., 179–81
Fong Inma, 176–77, 207
Forbes, Francis C., 40, 213
Ford, Daniel, 157
Formosa. See Taiwan
forward echelon, 81, 84–85, 100, 104–5. See also 68th Composite Wing, USAAF
Foshee, Ben, 38
Foss, Palmer, 186
France, 60, 182–85, 210. See also Vichy France
Free China, 4–5, 17, 22, 47–48
Free Thai Movement, 174, 181, 192
French Foreign Legion, 184
French Indochina. See Indochina
French Resistance, 184
Frillmann, Paul, 16, 37, 103

Index   263

Fujian Province, 8
Funk, James, 89

G3M (Mitsubishi) Type 96 Land-based
    Attack Aircraft "Nell," 105
Gan River, 114, 142
Ganzhou, 105, 189, 217
Gaoligong Mountains, 39, 129
Gardner, James H., 94
George, Kenneth E., 110–12, 115, 119, 121
Germany, 25, 59, 157, 210–11
Glenn, Edgar E. "Buzz," 81
Gobi Desert, 160, 170
Gong Kaibing, 5, 155–56, 190, 194, 200,
    207, 221
Gray, Robert M. "Bob," 30–31
Great Depression, 27, 41, 46
Greater East Asia Co-prosperity Sphere,
    41, 118
Great Snow Mountain, 55
Great War. See World War I
Greene, Jeffrey "Jeff," 204
Gregg, Lee O., 108, 202; North Africa,
    82–83, 213; arrival in China, 84;
    Hankou mission (1944), xi-xiii, 2, 60,
    88, 120, 124, 146, 156, 215; rescued by
    Communists, xv-xvi, 145–54, 160, 199,
    204, 215
Griffith, Charles E., 124
Gross, William T. "Bill," 54–57, 230
Guangdong Province, 8, 123
Guangxi Province, 8, 39, 61, 96, 123, 210
Guangzhou, 90, 100, 138, 221; Allied
    raids, 60, 74, 78, 84–85, 213; Ichi-go,
    123, 126, 215; jail, 67, 188; Japanese
    airfields, 61, 108; ratlines, 68
Guernsey, Jean, 58, 102
Guhezhen, 45
Guidong, 201
Guilin, 68, 70, 100, 104–5, 161, 214, 221;
    forward airfield, 61, 74, 78, 81; Hong
    Kong raid (1942), 61, 68–69; Ichi-go,
    120, 126, 128, 132, 137, 140, 142–43,
    216; summer air offensive (1943), 82,
    84, 108, 213, 234

Guiyangzhen, 143
Guizhou Province, 51, 74
Gulf of Tonkin, 78, 89, 92, 94, 97, 213
Guomindang (GMD), xx, 1, 3, 20, 111,
    155, 160, 183, 200–201, 209, 221;
    Chiang's regime, viii, xii, 3, 10–11, 128,
    148–50, 198; collaboration, 42–43, 210;
    Communists, ix, 148, 162, 166, 171,
    194–96, 218; corruption, viii-ix, 10;
    reimbursing rescuers, 21, 115; Stilwell,
    75, 143
Guzhen, 166

Habecker, John, 173, 178–79
Hainan Island, 78, 94, 96, 99
Hai Phong, 60, 74, 90, 98, 182, 186
Haishing, 14
Hakodate Branch Camp Number 4, 192,
    194, 218
Hamilton Field, California, 23
Hammer, Maax C., 16
Hangzhou, 34
Hankou, 4, 9, 75, 100, 103–4, 137, 154,
    156; firebombing (1944), 130, 143–44,
    169, 216–17; Japanese base, xii, 1, 78,
    84–85, 107, 121, 123, 126–27, 215;
    Japanese capture, 5, 107, 210; raid
    (1944), xi-xii, 2, 60, 88, 120 124–26,
    145, 153, 215
Hanoi, 19, 73, 182–84, 186
Han people, 20
Han River, xii
Harding, Hampden, 94
Hata Shunroku, 121, 123–24, 126, 140
Hawaii, 12
Hawk 75 (Curtiss) Special, 4, 175
Hawk 81A2 (Curtiss) Tomahawk. See P-40
    (Curtiss) Warhawk "Shark"
Haynes, Caleb V., 53, 59, 61–63
Haywood, Thomas C., 19
Headley, Edgar W., 138–39
Hebei Province, 162, 168, 217
Helms, Earle E., 107
Henan Province, 45, 121, 162, 168, 192,
    216–17

264 Index

Hengshan, 141
Hengyang, 9, 45, 61, 155; Ichi-go, 120,
125, 127, 132, 139–41, 215–16;
summer air offensive (1943), 81–82,
213
He Yangling, 34
He Yingqin, 194
High Falls, North Carolina, 201
Hill, David Lee "Tex," xix, 13, 28, 55, 58,
86–87, 102, 104–5, 120, 203, 214
Hill, Thomas J. "Tom," 170
Hillier, Walter, 96–97
Himalayas, 38
Hiroshima, 193, 217
Ho Chi Minh, 183, 185–86, 216, 218
Hokkaido, 45, 192, 194, 218
Holstrom, Everett W. "Brick," 23–25,
29–35, 52, 57, 62–63, 70–71, 74, 81,
93, 200
Holtz, William, 90–91
Hong Gai, 73, 92, 212
Hong Kong, 10, 45, 78, 96, 98, 100,
199; first raid (1942), 44, 50, 61–63,
67–69, 73, 81, 104, 188, 192, 212;
Tex Hill dogfight (1943), 86, 116,
214; summer air offensive (1943),
84–85
Hongqiao Road Cemetery, 196
Honolulu, Hawaii, 13–14
Honshu, 192
Hoover, Travis, 30–31
Hoover Institution, 28
Hornet, USS, 29–30, 32, 34, 52, 212
Hsinchu, 99–101, 103, 214, 222
Huang, Mr., 148, 150
Huangmei, 88
Huang Xiang-chun, 190
Hubei Province, 9, 43, 143, 150, 199
Huizhou, 87
Hump: airlift, 17, 38, 53, 59, 61, 74, 78,
80–81, 106–7; transit over, 35, 52–53,
57, 62, 72, 84, 120, 173
Hunan Province, 5, 8, 75, 123, 155, 201,
217
Huo Kuizhang, 139

Hurley, Patrick J., 194
Hurricane (Hawker), 38

I-25, IJN, 24
Ichi-go, 121–23, 140, 144, 190; air
opposition, 130, 142, 157, 159, 189,
215, 240; consequences, 137, 144,
195–96, 199, 201; phase one, 126, 150,
154, 215; Stilwell, 131, 143
Imperial General Headquarters, 121, 123
Imperial Iron and Steel Works, 130, 151,
215
Imperial Japanese Army (IJA), 83, 149,
182, 189, 191; China occupation, viii,
41–42, 44; China subjugation, 1, 4, 50;
Ichi-go, xii, 121, 129, 154, 195–96;
revenge for assisting airmen, xix,
34–35
Imperial Japanese Navy (IJN), 1, 24, 104–5
India, 80, 109, 197; Hump terminus, xx,
35, 38, 52, 120, 212; Stilwell, 38–39, 74,
212; Tenth Air Force operations, vii,
57, 62–63, 70, 93, 99
India Air Task Force (IATF), 59
Indochina, 25, 94, 96, 100, 175, 182–3;
aircraft/airmen reported missing, vii,
181, 186, 239; airmen captured, 20,
182, 186; airmen rescued, 183, 186;
Allied raids, 19, 73, 78, 93, 173, 212;
Japanese base, 18, 60, 90, 182, 210;
Japanese coup, 184, 217; Japanese rail
corridor, 123, 154
Indonesia. See Dutch East Indies
Ingalls, Eleanor, 163
Inner Mongolia, 160
International Red Cross, 118
Iran, 32
Italy, 3, 25, 83

Jagersfontein, MS, 14
Japanese Army Air Force (JAAF), 16, 37,
51, 69, 81, 105, 108, 158, 211
Japanese Navy Air Service (JNAS), 51
Japanese People's Anti-war League,
149–50

Java Pacific Line, 12
Jialing River, 1
Ji'an, 114–15
Jiangsu Province, 154
Jiangwan prisoner of war camp, 67, 166, 182, 188, 191, 217
Jiangxi Province, 20, 34, 107; airmen rescued, 32, 114, 142; airmen killed, 137, 196, 201, 216; Allied airfields, 8, 100, 189, 214; Xue Yue, 127, 189
Jianli, 205, 218
Jieling, 142
Jietou, 44
Jiexiu, 170, 217
Jing'an, 113
Jiujiang, 5, 47, 88, 101, 107, 109–11, 115–19, 199, 210, 214–15
Joint Chiefs of Staff (US), 130
Jones, Robert, 179
Jones, William P., xii, 88, 124, 146, 238

Kaifeng, 121, 168
Kakimoto, Masayoshi, 92
Kamrop Bleangkam, 178–81
Kansas City, Missouri, 49, 137
Kaohsiung, 95, 221
Karachi, 52, 59, 70, 72, 77, 84, 101, 120
Keng Tung, 175
Kennedy, John, 106, 139
Kenney, George C., 93
Khuang Aphaiwong, 181
Khun Tan Range, 178–79
Ki-21(Mitsubishi) Army Type 97 Heavy Bomber "Sally," 175
Ki-27 (Nakajima) Army Type 97 Fighter "Nate"/"Ota," 109, 175–76, 178–81
Ki-30 (Mitsibishi) Army Type 97 Light Bomber "Ann," 175
Ki-43 Hayabusa (Nakajima) Army Type 1 Fighter "Oscar," 157; attacking Allied airfields, 37–38, 48, 84, 108; comparison to other fighters, 81–82, 87–88, 158, 234; identified as "Zero," xii, 2, 38, 63, 85, 125–26, 223, 231; intercepting Allied raids, xii-xiii, 47,

63–64, 85, 87, 109, 115–16, 124–26, 156, 214; strafing airmen, 65, 110, 146
Ki-44 Shoki (Nakajima) Army Type 2 Fighter "Tojo," 81–84, 86–88, 99, 108, 116, 156, 158, 213–15, 234
Ki-48 (Kawasaki) Army Type 99 Light Bomber "Lily," 107–8, 124, 236
King Kong, 59, 61
Kirtley, Robert E., 83
Kiyoshi, 194
Klemann, Robert, 52–57
Klota, Harold J., 192, 245
Kobe, 29, 78
Ko Kha, 175, 180–81
Korea, 78, 123, 192–93
Korean War, 198–200
Kouzes, Peter M., 167
Kowloon, 63, 69
Kroll, Robert, 89
Krywy, Walter, 21, 166–69
Kunlun Pass, 5
Kunming, 20, 47, 61, 74, 203; airfield, 4, 19, 53, 55–57, 72–73, 84, 93–94, 99–100, 212; AVG, 16–19, 28, 48, 50, 211; Central Military Academy, 9, 43, 225; Chennault's headquarters, 4, 21, 25, 81, 128, 133, 153, 183, 185; Ho Chi Minh, 183, 185, 216; Japanese bombing, 4, 16–18, 28, 48, 86, 211
Kunz, Robert C., 164–65, 169–70, 217
Kyushu, 130, 151, 165, 215

L-5 (Stinson) Sentinel, xviii
Lampang, 175–81, 197, 214, 216, 219
Lang Son, 182
Lao Cai, 18–19
Laohekou, 153, 168, 189, 215, 217
Laos, 25, 182
Larkin, T. B., 197
Lashio, 37–38, 53, 55–56, 212
League for the Independence of Vietnam. *See* Viet Minh
League of Nations, 198
Leiyun, 36–38, 221
Leland, Gordon C. "Gordie," 52–55, 57

266 Index

LeMay, Curtis E., 144, 169
Lend-Lease Act, 74, 79, 130, 143, 190
Lewis, Armit W., 154, 203–4
Lewis, Murray L., 63, 65–67, 188, 192–93, 245
Liangshan, 153
Lianshui River, 142
Lianzhou, 91–92
Life magazine, 28
Lingling, 57, 61, 81, 85, 103–4, 120, 132, 140–41, 216
Lingshan, 92
Linjiafang, 137, 196
Lin Zengxun, 196
Liuku, 39
Liu Zhenghua, 9, 43, 143–44, 222
Li Xiannian, 148, 150, 153, 204–6, 219, 221
Li Xiaolin, 204–6
Li Yuntang, 45, 207, 222
Lockheed Corporation, 158
Long Chunwu
Long, Clifford, 173, 181, 197
Longhai Railway, 167
Longhua Airdrome, 187–89
Longling, 42, 129, 140, 173
Long March, 127
Long Shengwu, 40
Long Yun, 8, 40
Longueil, Charles L., xii
Lopez, Donald, 172–73
Louisiana, 3, 14, 77
Love Zebra Five (LZ5), 142
Lu Caiwen, 40–43, 51, 222
Luce, Henry R., 27
Luftwaffe, 83, 157
Lugou Bridge. *See* Marco Polo Bridge
Luke Field, Arizona, 27
Luliang, 168
Lu Mao-yin, 190
Luojia, 205
Luoluo. *See* Yi people
Luoyang, 3
Luxi, 137, 196
Luzon, 187

MacArthur, Douglas, 193, 198, 218
Macau, 66
Mae Kua, 177, 197, 216
Magwe, 37
Mahon, Keith, 107–8
Mahony, Grattan M. "Grant," 82
Malaya, 70, 80, 173
Manbeck, Lee P., 117
Manchuria, 4, 60, 123, 160, 210, 217
Mangleburg, Lacy F., 17
Mangshi, 140
Mao Zedong, ix, xiv, 60, 160, 162, 170–71, 195, 198–99, 201, 218, 222, 224
March Field, California, 23
Marco Polo, 40
Marco Polo Bridge, 209
Mariana Islands, 169, 193
Marich, Nicholas "Nick," 62–69
Marines. *See* United States Marine Corps
Mariposa, USS, 70
Marshall, George C. Jr., 32–33, 76, 79, 130, 197–98, 212, 218
Martin, Robert W. N. "Bob," 57
Masterson, Arthur W., 108, 234
Matterhorn, 129
Maxwell Field, Alabama, 14
McCarthyism, 198
McChord Field, Washington, 23
McCook, Nebraska, 26, 202
McCool, Harry C., 31
McDowell, Wilmer E., 62
McGarry, William "Black Mac," 174–75, 192
McGill, Frederick J., 45
McKinney, Franklin, 176–77, 197, 216
McMillan, Charles, 102
McMillan, George B. "Mac," 449th Fighter Squadron, xix, 101–4, 106–8, 115, 132, 214, 236; AVG, 12–13, 16–20, 29, 48, 58, 101, 210–11; detached service, 109, 120; killed, 134–37, 142, 196–97, 216, 240
McMillan, Malcolm Jr., 58
McMillan, Malcolm Y., 135–36
McMillan, Sarah Elizabeth "Sissy," 58, 136, 196

Index   267

Medal of Honor, 97
Mediterranean Theater of Operations
    (MTO), xi, 80, 83, 108. *See also* North
    Africa
Mengzi, 19, 184
Military Intelligence Service-X (MIS-X),
    68, 163
Miller, Harold E., 138
Miller, Henry L. "Hank," 25
Miller, Otto, 180–81
Minco, Henry F., 27, 139–40, 173, 177,
    179–81, 197, 207, 216, 219
Ming Zhongyi, 141, 222
mining, 98, 193
Minneapolis, Minnesota, 25
missing aircrew report (MACR), vii-viii,
    196, 198
Missouri, USS, 186, 193, 218
Mitsui coal mine, 193
Mohanbari, 173
Mong Cai, 90
Mongolia, 4, 210
Mooney, Robert H., 49–50, 144, 200–201,
    206, 213, 218
Morgan, Francis B., 165–67, 169
Morison Field, Florida
Morita, 124, 146, 238
Mott, Charles, 174, 192
Murphy, Lloyd J., 89–93, 97
Myitkyina, 131, 176, 212, 216

Nagasaki, 78, 100, 193–94, 214, 217
Nagoya, 29, 78
Nakajima Aircraft Company, 158, 175
Nakazono Moritaka, 81–82, 85–86, 159,
    213
Nanchang, 4, 32, 44, 59–60, 107, 110–11,
    115, 199
Nancheng, 70, 189
Nanjing, 3–5, 42–45, 50, 78, 165, 191, 195,
    209–10, 216
Nanning, 92
Nanwan River, 36
Nanxiang, 92
Nanxiong, 105

Napier Field, Alabama, 160
Nationalist Army, 40, 42, 51, 141, 161;
    desertion, 39–40, 214; Ichi-go, 130,
    141, 154, 195, 199; officials, 91–92, 194;
    rebuilt, 74, 130; sorry state, 9, 130
Nationalist Party. *See* Guomindang
    (GMD)
Nazis, xx, 25, 38, 42, 46, 83, 182, 210–11,
    229
Netherlands, 46
New Delhi, 57, 70, 74, 77
New Fourth Army, CCP: Japanese People's
    Anti-War League, 149–50; Nationalist
    hostility, xv, 148–49, 166, 199;
    operating area, 160, 167; other airmen
    rescued, 44, 154, 163, 166–67, 191;
    rescuing Gregg and Beneda, xiv-xv,
    145, 152, 204, 215, 219, 224
New Sixth Army, GMD, 190
New Third Army, GMD, 115, 121
New York, New York, 27, 104
Nguyen Tat Thanh. *See* Ho Chi Minh
Nixon, Richard M., 201, 203, 218
North Africa, xx, 26–27, 38, 77, 82–84, 88,
    107. *See also* Mediterranean Theater of
    Operations (MTO)
North American Aviation, 158
Northern Expedition, 127
Nujiang. *See* Salween River

Office of Strategic Services (OSS), 45, 59,
    76, 170, 174–75, 183, 185–86, 192, 243
Older, Charles H. "Chuck," 19
Omaha, Nebraska, 26
O'Neal, George K., 92
O'Neal, James, 96–97
Operation Ichi-go. *See* Ichi-go
Operation Matterhorn. *See* Matterhorn
Opsvig, John T., xii, 88, 124
Orlando, Florida, 102
Orlando Sentinel, 101
Osaka, 29, 78

P-38 (Lockheed) Lightning, 99, 139, 158,
    186; arrival in China, 83–84, 88, 213;

268　Index

Hankou mission (1944), xi-xii, 120, 124–26, 145–46, 215; Jiujiang ambushes, 47, 88, 109, 116, 214; McMillan's death, 134–35, 137, 196, 216; move to Suichuan, 106, 108, 214; statistics of missing, xviii, 87–88, 137–38, 234, 239–40; summer air offensive (1943), 84–86; Thailand, 173, 177–81, 216; Thanksgiving Day raid (1943), 101–2, 104–5, 214

P-39 (Bell) Airacobra, 102

P-40 (Curtiss) Warhawk "Shark," 4, 27, 45, 57, 72, 74, 94, 102, 110, 140–43, 146, 154, 156, 158, 160, 172, 216, 230, 245; AVG, 14–19, 22, 37–38, 58, 182, 211; CACW, 101, 155–57, 190, 216; Hankou mission (1944), xi, 120, 125–6; Hong Kong raid (1942), 61–62, 64, 68, 212; Robert Mooney, 48, 50; move to Suichuan, 106, 108, 214; Salween Front, 39, 139–40, 213; shark mouth, xi, 17, 22, 48, 206; statistics of missing, xviii, 87–88, 138–39, 239; summer air offensive (1943), 81–83, 85–86, 213

P-47 (Republic) Thunderbolt, xviii, 81, 88, 130, 138, 240

P-51 (North American) Mustang, 21–22, 27, 102, 110, 160, 164–67, 170, 173, 183, 190, 192, 245; arrival in China, 86, 172–3; comparison to other fighters, 83–84, 86–87, 138–39, 158, 239; Hankou mission (1944), xi-xiii, 120, 124–26, 146, 215; move to Suichuan, 106, 108, 214; Shanghai mission (1945), 70, 187–89, 191, 217; statistics of missing, xviii, 87–88, 138; Thailand, 173, 177–81, 216; Thanksgiving Day raid (1943), 101, 104–5, 214

P-61 (Northrop) Black Widow, xviii, 138, 190

Pacific Ocean, 10, 13, 98. See also Pacific Theater of Operations (PTO); South West Pacific Area (SWPA)

Pacific Theater of Operations (PTO), xviii, xx, 11, 196. See also South West Pacific Area (SWPA)

Palmer, Sam L., 83, 104

Pan American Airways (Panam), 10, 12, 53

Pantelleria, 83

Patterson, Elon W., 167

Patterson, Robert, 103

Pattumma, Klairoong "Puma," 197, 207, 219

Pawley, William D. "Bill," 14

PBY (Consolidated) Catalina, 175

Pearl Harbor, Hawaii, 11, 16, 23–26, 29–30, 50, 52, 70, 206, 211

Pearl River, 64, 66, 86

Peck, Alton, 56

Pei Haiqing, 39–40, 207, 213–14, 222

Pendleton, Oregon, 23

Pensacola, Naval Air Station, Florida, 25

People's Militias, 167

People's Republic of China (PRC), ix, 198, 200–201, 204, 206, 218

Perry Field, Florida, 27

Phibun Songkhram, 174–75, 181

Philippines, 14, 28, 58, 70, 82, 187

Pinellas Field, Florida, 160

Pingxiang, 134–35, 142, 216

Ploesti, Romania, 154

pointie-talkie, xiv, 21–22, 44, 90, 110–11, 146, 167

Poland, 59, 210

Polikarpov I-15, 2

Portugal, 66, 230

Potez 25A2, 184

Pound, Alfred Dudley Pickman Rogers, 80

Project 157, 52, 57, 62–63

puppet regimes. See collaboration

Qiongshan, 94

Qiongzhou Strait, 94

Qiyang, 143

Qujiang, 68, 87, 126, 215

Quzhou, 32, 34–35

Rangoon, 14, 17–20, 37–38, 80, 174, 211–12
Rape of Nanjing, 43
Ravenholt, Albert, 185
Re.2001 (Reggiane) Falco II, 83
Rector, Edward F., 13, 58
Red Army, 162, 225
Red Cross. *See* International Red Cross
Red Flower Mountain, 55
Red River, 182, 186
Reed, William Norman "Bill," 13, 101
refugees, 5, 9, 38, 43, 51, 128, 132, 184
Regia Aeronautica, 83
Reorganized National Government of China, 42–43, 210
Rickets, Freeman, 57
Roll, Frederick A. Jr. "Fred," 109
Rolls-Royce (Packard) Merlin, xiii, 120, 172, 215
Rommel, Erwin, 82
Roosevelt, Franklin D., 34, 113; antishipping, 79, 92–93, 106; AVG, 10–11, 210; Arcadia Conference, 25, 211; Stilwell, 25, 79–80, 129, 143, 161, 216; support China by air, xx, 75, 77, 80, 213; Trident Conference, 77–81, 213
Rosholt, Malcolm L., 47, 103, 127–29, 142
Rossi, John R. "Dick," 28, 204
Royal Air Force (RAF), 14, 17–18, 38, 124, 175
Royal Thai Air Force (RTAF), 175, 177–78, 181, 197, 207, 214, 216
Royal Thai Army, 174–75
Ruse, John C. "Johnny," 56, 74

Saigon, 184
Saito Tougo, 108
Sakagawa Toshio, 124, 126
Sakpinit Promthep, 197, 207
Salween Front, 129–30, 139, 143, 173, 176, 190
Salween River, 38–40, 128–29, 212–13, 215, 222
San Antonio, Texas, 104–5

San Diego, California, 11
San Francisco, California, 10, 12, 23, 29
San Marino, California, 203
Santa Barbara, California, 24
Sapporo, 194
Sardinia, 83
Sasebo, 100, 214
Savoie, William F., 154, 163, 166
SB-24. *See* B-24
Schiel, Frank Jr., 58, 100
Schweinfurt, 157
Scott, Robert Lee Jr., "Scotty," 58–59, 72, 76
Scudday, Fred R. Jr., xi, 124–25
sea sweeps. *See* shipping
Seni Pramoj, 174
Shaanxi Province, 8, 22, 160
Shanghai, 36, 49, 78, 95, 98, 100, 103, 115, 154, 165, 195; loss (1937), 5, 14, 50, 127, 209; prison camp, 67, 166, 182, 187–89, 217; raid (1945), 50, 70, 187–89, 217
Shangqiu, 192
Shangrao, 34
Shan States, 174–75
Shanxi Province, 162, 170, 217
Shaw, Rudolph, 181–83, 185, 216
Shenyang, 162, 195, 222
Sher, Morton, 68–69
Shilling, Eriksen E., 17, 19–22, 99, 211
Shinjuku prison camp, 118
Shintoism, 46
shipping (antishipping), 46, 73, 78–80, 89, 92–98, 106, 157, 201, 213, 215
Sichuan Province, 1, 8–9, 39, 130, 153, 215
Sicily, 83
Simao, 179
Singapore, 14
Sino-American Aviation Heritage Foundation, 204
Skeldon, Joseph L., 57
Smith, R. T., 13, 28, 37
Smith, Walter, 84, 234
Snyder, George F., 22
Somerville, James F., 80

270   Index

Song Meiling, 3–4, 28, 222
Son La, 184
Soong, T. V., 10, 28, 222
Sop Prap District, 177
Sordelett, Winfree, 99–100, 103, 214
South China Sea, 78, 93, 96, 106
Southeast Asia, 197
South West Pacific Area (SWPA), 93, 102,
    121. See also Pacific Theater of
    Operations (PTO)
Soviet Union (USSR), 4, 32, 59, 198,
    209–10, 212, 217
Special Operations Executive (SOE), 174
Spitfire (Supermarine), 102
Squadron X. See 449th Fighter Squadron
Stalin, Joseph V., xiv, 224
State Department (US), 174, 204
Stewart, John, 108
Stilwell, Joseph W.: Chennault, 25–26, 33,
    75–78, 128, 130–31, 133, 199, 212; loss
    of Burma, 25–26, 32, 38, 75, 212;
    Nationalists, ix, 75, 160–62, 195,
    198–9; north Burma, 39, 74, 77–80,
    129–31, 176, 195, 199, 213, 216;
    recalled, 143, 190, 216
Stoneham, Wendell, 125
Strategic Air Command (SAC), 200
Stubbee, Grover, 179, 181
submarine, 23–24, 30, 92, 95, 98, 121, 123,
    192
Suichuan, Thanksgiving Day raid (1943),
    70, 100, 104–5; forward base, 105–10,
    112, 115, 121, 125, 214, 234; Ichi-go,
    129, 132, 134, 137, 217; Shanghai
    mission (1945), 70, 189
Sultan of Morocco, 79
Sumatra, 80
Sun Zhengbang, 43

Taber, Morris F., 93
Tacoma, Washington, 23
Tada Biewkhaimuk, 178–80
Taihe, 114
Taiwan, ix, 85, 222, 230; antishipping, 78,
    92, 95; Nationalist retreat, 198, 218;

Strait, 78, 99, 104, 106; Thanksgiving
    Day raid (1943), 50, 70, 99–100, 103–4,
    106, 214
Taiyuan, 164
Tapp, Charles J. "Charlie," 45
Taungoo, 14, 16–17
Taylor, Tommy J., 116
Tengchong, 39–41, 43–44, 129, 139–40,
    143, 212, 216
Terry and the Pirates, 27
Thailand, vii, 16, 20, 25, 100, 173–77,
    181–82, 197, 211, 214, 216, 219
Thammasat University, 174
Thompson, Elmer, 94
Thompson, Robert, 117
Tian He airdrome, 61, 68
Tianmu Mountain, 34
Tian Nong, 222, 224
Tianzhu, 110
Tiger of Changsha. See Xue Yue
Time magazine, 28–29, 41
Tokyo, 11, 22, 29–31, 52, 78, 92, 118, 151,
    186, 192–94, 204, 218
Tollett, Harold B., 189
Tong Shiguang, xiv, 222
Trident conference, 78–79, 82, 213
Truman, Harry S., 197–98
Tunisia, 82

UC-45 (Beechcraft) Expeditor, 14, 170
UC-64 (Noorduyn) Norseman, 129, 142
United Front, 8, 148, 162, 166
United Press, 185
United States Air Force (USAF), 200, 216
United States Army Air Corps (USAAC),
    2–3, 12–14
United States Army Air Forces (USAAF),
    xix, 21, 28, 32, 53, 59, 84, 158, 171, 174,
    194; aircraft/airmen reported missing,
    viii, xv, 46, 58; joining, 26–27, 102, 202,
    212
United States Army Air Service (USAAS),
    59
United States Army Observer Group. See
    Dixie Mission

Index   271

United States Marine Corps (USMC), 188, 191–93, 204, 217
United States Military Academy, 52, 70, 73, 77
United States Naval Academy, 59
United States Navy (USN), 13, 16, 23, 29–30, 45, 102, 121, 193, 246
University of Chicago, 163
University of Minnesota, 163
Upchurch, Robert H., 201
Uttaradit, 176

Vadenais, Roger R., 140, 178–80
Varoff, George D., 162–64, 242
Vavrick, Albert, 117
Vichy France, 94, 182, 217. *See also* France
Vickery, Richard L., 165
Victoria Harbor, 61
Viet Minh, 183, 185–86, 216
Vietnam, 25, 94, 182–86, 216
Vietnam War, 199–200
Vincent, Clinton D. "Casey," 105–6, 157, 189, 200, 214–16; CATF, 70–74, 76, 93, 212; forward echelon, 81, 84–85, 87; Ichi-go, xii, 120–21, 124–30, 132–34, 137, 139–40, 215; Thanksgiving Day raid (1943), 100–101, 103–5
Vinh, 93–94
Vladivostok, 32

Wad Sunthornkomol, 178–79
Waikiki Beach, Hawaii, 13
Waizhou, 68–69
Wakamatsu Yukiyoshi, 82, 108
Wake Island, 28, 188
Wall, James E., 192, 245
Wallace, Henry A., 161
Wang Dagong, 168
Wang Jingwei, 42–43, 210
Wang Shuming, 17–18
Wan Lai Kam, 176
War Area Service Corps (WASC), 155, 194
War Department (US), 72, 107, 118, 197

warlords, ix, xx, 5, 8–10, 41–42, 195, 201
warning net, 33, 82, 99, 125, 128; AVG, 18–19, 21, 37; enemy warning nets, 116, 178; establishment, 3, 17, 60, 209; Ichi-go, 124, 132–33
Washington, DC, 10, 25, 27–28, 76–78, 80, 83, 130, 137, 174, 197, 211, 213
Wavell, Archibald P., 80
Weatherly, Edison, 93–94
Webb, Paul G., 62, 64–67, 188
Wedemeyer, Albert C., 143, 185, 190, 196, 216
Weizhou Island, 89
West Point. *See* United States Military Academy
White, Theodore H., 41
Whittlesey, Henry C., 162–64, 166, 169–70, 216–17, 242
Wichtrich, A.R., 68
Wilder, Rodney R. "Hoss," 24
Williams, James M., 86–87, 116–17
Williams, Jesse, 92
Willkie, Wendell L., 75
Winter Garden, Florida, 101
Witzenburger, Ed, 183–84
World War I, 27, 59, 198
Wright Twin Cyclone, 31, 54
Wuding River, 22
Wu Eyang, 36–38, 207, 222
Wu River, 190
Wuzhou, 68, 87

Xia Kui, 204, 222
Xiamen, 95
Xi'an, 160, 162–65, 169–71
Xiangcheng, 192
Xiang River, 120, 127–29, 142–43
Xiangtan, 128–29, 142
Xiangyun, 48–50, 144, 200–201, 206, 213, 218
Xinjin, 164, 169
X-Ray Force, 74, 176
Xue Yue, 5, 126–29, 132, 142, 189, 210–11, 215, 222
Xu Hua-jiang, 2, 101, 222

272   Index

Yamamoto Isoroku, 86, 107, 215
Yan'an, 160–64, 166, 170–71, 216, 242
Yangjie, 93–94
Yang Yinting, 44
Yangzi River, xii, 1, 4–5, 8, 107, 121, 124, 127, 153, 160, 205; antishipping, 78, 88, 98, 106, 109, 116
Yank magazine, 133
Yanshi, 45, 216
Yan Xishan, 8, 222
Yawata, 130, 151, 215
Yellow River, 5, 50, 121, 123, 144, 160, 168, 199, 209, 215
Yellow Sea, 170
Yen, Mr., 152
Yichang, 85, 153
Yi people, 20, 226
Yiu, Mr., 112, 116
Yoke Force. *See* Chinese Expeditionary Force
Yokohama, 29, 78
York, Edward J. "Ski," 25
Young, James N. "Jim," 62–67, 188
Yuanshui River, 135

Yuelu Mountain, 127, 129
Yunnan Province, 4, 8, 42, 48, 51, 68, 213, 230; aircraft/airmen reported missing, 46, 201; AVG, 17, 22, 28, 36, 60, 211–12; Central Military Academy, 9, 143; Salween Front, 74, 215; summer air offensive (1943), 81, 84–85
Yunnanyi, 47–48, 140, 172–73, 176–78, 181
Yu River, 92

Zeuske, Wilmer, 56
Zhang Gewei, 163–64, 169, 222, 242
Zhanghuang, 92
Zhangshu, 114
Zhejiang Province, 32, 34
Zhengzhou, 5, 121, 209
Zhijiang, 5, 142, 155–57, 172, 190, 194, 200, 217–18, 222
Zhou Enlai, 162
Zhu De, 162, 194, 225
Zhuzhou, 129, 140

A Mitchell Institute Book
Aviation and Air Power
Series Editor: Brian D. Laslie

In his work *Winged Defense,* Brigadier General William "Billy" Mitchell stated, "Air power may be defined as the ability to do something in the air." Since Mitchell made this statement, the definition of air power has been contested and argued about by those on the ground, those in the air, academics, industrialists, and politicians.

Each volume of the Aviation and Air Power series seeks to expand our understanding of Mitchell's broad definition by bringing together leading historians, fliers, and scholars in the fields of military history, aviation, air power history, and other disciplines in the hope of providing a fuller picture of just what air power accomplishes.

This series offers an expansive look at tactical aerial combat, operational air warfare, and strategic air theory. It explores campaigns from the First World War through modern air operations, along with the heritage, technology, culture, and human element particular to the air arm. In addition, this series considers the perspectives of leaders in the US Army, Navy, Marine Corps, and Air Force, as well as their counterparts in other nations and their approaches to the history and study of doing something in the air.

THE MATERIAL CULTURE OF TABLEWARE